DT 30.5 .A356 1985

3730

African independence

| | DATE DUE | | |
|---|---|---|---|
| 2 libr | | | |
| 2 Vouts to 11/07 | | | |
| | | | |
| | | | |
| | | | |
| | | | |
| | | | |
| | | | |
| | | | |
| | | | |
| | | | |

# AFRICAN INDEPENDENCE

## The First Twenty-Five Years

EDITED BY

Gwendolen M. Carter and Patrick O'Meara

INDIANA UNIVERSITY PRESS
*Bloomington*

First Midland Book Edition 1986

© 1985 by Indiana University Press

Manufactured in the United States of America

**Library of Congress Cataloging in Publication Data**
Main entry under title:

African independence:

  Bibliography: p.
  Includes index.
  1. Africa—Politics and government—1960–  —
Addresses, essays, lectures. 2. Africa—Economic
conditions—1960–  —Addresses, essays, lectures.
3. Africa—Social conditions—1960–  —Addresses,
essays, lectures. I. Carter, Gwendolen Margaret,
1906–  . II. O'Meara, Patrick.
DT30.5.A356  1985      960'.32      84-48457
ISBN 0-253-30255-2
ISBN 0-253-20348-1 (pbk.)
2   3   4   5  89  88   87   86

This volume and its accompanying seminar and conference on the first twenty-five years of African independence are the culmination of Gwendolen M. Carter's ten years of teaching at Indiana University. Over the past twenty-five years changes, leaders, and new directions on the African continent have been her primary area of scholarly concern. With boundless energy she has lectured, taught, and written about the needs, issues, and aspirations of Africans, and her many books and articles have provided insights for generations of students, scholars, and decision makers.

PATRICK O'MEARA

# Contents

# PREFACE

Over twenty-five years have elapsed since the Gold Coast became the first sub-Saharan state to gain independence. This anniversary was marked by differing assessments of the political and economic performances of the African states that had become independent since 1957. The prevalence of excessive and unrealistic criticism led us to seek more informed and balanced judgments. We therefore invited a number of the most outstanding scholars in the United States to weigh the achievements, limitations, and promise of the past twenty-five years of African independence.

To prepare for the book we organized a weekly lecture series at Indiana University, open to the public as well as to the whole student body, during the Fall Semester, 1983–84. Each Wednesday night individual participants presented a public lecture, which was followed by a graduate seminar composed of outstanding American and African students. Participants in the public lecture and the seminar contributed notably to the volume through pertinent questions and comments, which led on occasions to vigorous and enlightening debate. We were able to bring virtually all the contributors to the volume to the Wingspread Conference Center, Racine, Wisconsin, through a generous grant from the Carnegie Corporation of New York. The warm hospitality provided through the Johnson Foundation and its staff made a perfect setting for a full and productive discussion based on the prior availability of the manuscripts, not only to the contributors themselves, but also to a number of outside critics who contributed to the discussion. We wish to acknowledge publicly the contributions made at the time by Mabel M. Smythe, C. R. D. Halisi, John N. Paden, Mark Tessler, Ed Brown, E. Philip Morgan, Richard E. Stryker, Sheldon Geller, and Fred Hayward, who participated in the Conference as discussants or chairpersons.

We also wish to acknowledge the encouragement and support received from the Cummins Engine Foundation, the Dean of International Programs at Indiana University, the African Studies Program at Indiana University, and the Ford Foundation.

We very much appreciate the assistance given this entire project by the staff of the African Studies Program, in particular, Judith Wilkinson, who coordinated the entire project; N. Brian Winchester; and Sue Ann Hanson, who typed and prepared the manuscript for publication.

G. M. C.
P. O'M.

INTRODUCTION

# African Independence:
# The First Twenty-Five Years

*Gwendolen M. Carter and Patrick O'Meara*

The last of the continents to be gripped by the drive for independence, Africa is still engaged in exploring the parameters of self-determination. This search for viable independence is carried on in different ways internally, within Africa's many and varied states, and externally in their relations with the international powers of Western Europe and North America, and with the Soviet Union and China.

These studies of the first twenty-five years of African independence analyze the character and dimensions of one of the world's great and most recent experiments in self-government. Africa has suffered the rape of its people through the slave trade that carried so many of them to different parts of the world and the exploitation of its natural resources. Above all Africa has been marked by colonialism and the carving up of its land by the dominant European powers, particularly in the period beginning in 1884–85 with the Congress of Berlin. These powers responded to their own interests with little or no regard for the ethnic, linguistic, economic, or geographic features of the territories they acquired.

The colonial era and its concrete and dominating presence have passed although it would be imprudent to underestimate the imprint of colonial "habits of mind" on postcolonial rulers, structures, and actions. New and different challenges face these states now. *African Independence: The First Twenty-Five Years* considers the forces that have affected the African states that achieved independence in the late 1950s and 1960s and evaluates their continuing impact and relevance.

The strength and effectiveness of independent Africa's democratic, military, and one-party states have been conditioned by varied traditions, ethnic loyalties, religious tensions, environmental characteristics, and external links. Many analysts agree that despite their diversity African states have more in

common with each other than they have with other parts of the world and that
their desire for association has been reflected in their efforts to establish and to
maintain a continent-wide organization—The Organization of African Unity.
The major crises that the OAU has confronted reflect inevitable strains resulting from ideological differences, boundary disputes, and power rivalries; but
its very existence has never been questioned. It is noteworthy that most countries on the African continent have refrained from major interstate conflicts
and have attempted, with varying degrees of success, to develop cooperative
regional organizations.

The world into which African states at first moved as accepted independent entities was one characterized by faith in progress, and captivated by scientific and technological advances. Post–World War II generations in both the
East and the West had lost their sense of proportion, and as Goran Hyden
points out, African leaders shared this sense of Prometheus unbound. Today
growing technical and economic problems continue to beset the African
states, hampering their development and reinforcing their dependence on external aid.

Despite vast amounts in aid between 1962 and 1978, the African continent
was in a worsening economic situation as the 1980s began. The 1981 *World
Development Report of the World Bank* (NY: Oxford University Press, 1981)
foresaw no growth in per capita income for Africa during the next decade and
the 1983 Report was no more encouraging. Population growth continues to
outpace food production, partly due to persistent drought and a languishing
rural economy. Foreign exchange reserves continue to diminish while debts
continue to rise. As some African states approach virtual bankruptcy, the International Monetary Fund makes much-needed loans dependent on states accepting internal fiscal and economic changes. Donor agencies in some countries now wait to see whether the IMF's terms are met before extending their
aid; but some African leaders, like President Julius Nyerere of Tanzania,
maintain that such practices are neocolonialist.

It is worth noting that the economic assistance extended to African countries by the United States is consistently less than is generally believed. Taking
into account its contributions to the multilateral development banks, American aid amounts to less than 10 percent of all external development assistance.
Although the Carter administration sought substantial increases in aid to Africa, it was no greater in real terms in 1979–80 than in 1969–70. The Reagan
administration shifted the proportion of its direct aid toward military rather
than economic assistance and decreased its proportion of the funds for international donor agencies, thereby noticeably reducing their total resources.

Major questions of ideological discourse are never far below the surface of
Africa's everyday life. Today, Africa has a high incidence of unemployment

and increasing poverty while a tiny proportion of the population accumulates great wealth, derived in large measure from patronage and manipulation of political authority. As Ali Mazrui points out, Africa has a favorable climate for socialism; but he also believes that it has an inhospitable soil for it. The favorable climate, he maintains, is intellectual and normative but the infertile soil is political and economic.

African leaders need a more creative partnership with their people and with external powers and donors. Ultimately political stability depends on economic progress. Whether this can be achieved in the next twenty-five years remains uncertain.

Twenty-five years after independence, African states face common challenges and dilemmas. They need to evaluate both the benefits and the limits of independence. Is it true the lives of most Africans have only marginally improved? Is it the fault of the Africans themselves that some African economies have collapsed, or has this been the result of forces beyond their control?

The careful analyses in this volume indicate that while some of Africa's problems are inherited from the colonial past, others have been created by African leaders themselves. Hostile environmental factors and world-wide economic problems have also played a role in creating Africa's present dilemma. What is occurring on the African continent is a dynamic ongoing process, constantly subject to changing national and international pressures, which in turn create opportunities for the evolution of new political institutions and choices.

The contributors to this volume have long been major analysts of African politics and economics, many of them since before independence. Their insights provide a wealth of knowledge and understanding of the most crucial issues that have faced independent African states during their first formative quarter century of independence. Their perceptions of the past and present will be of value as Africa confronts the challenges and opportunities of the next quarter century and will provide valuable signposts both to the African states and to those concerned with Africa's future.

# AFRICAN
# INDEPENDENCE

CHAPTER 1

# The Colonial Imprint on
# African Political Thought

*Richard L. Sklar*

Europeans have ruled in Africa continuously since the conquest of
Ceuta, on the Moroccan coast, by Portugal in 1415.[1] Until the mid-nineteenth
century, European rulers, commercial companies, and brigands were frequently associated with the transoceanic trade in slaves. Only when it "was
being rendered obsolete by the rapid technological advance of industrial production"[2] did the traffic in humans subside as it was displaced by commercial
interests in the animal, vegetable, and mineral products of Africa. During the
1870s, rival European powers accomplished a "gigantic haul" of African territory. Jurisdictional disputes between them were adjusted at the 1885 Conference of Berlin, which recognized and reconciled the territorial claims of Britain, France, Germany, Italy, Portugal, Spain, and the King of the Belgians.
With varying degrees of foresight and responsiveness to the views of their
subjects, these powers, their successors, and European settlers effectively set
the agendas of political debate in Africa until the very foundations of colonial
rule itself were shattered during World War II.

At no time, however, were the colonial, or precolonial, European agendas
for Africa passively accepted by African leaders without protest, counter-
proposals, or initiatives intended to enhance the autonomy, power, or security
of indigenous African people. These political encounters between Africa and
Europe are reflected in a demonstrably rich history of ideas, centuries old and
copiously augmented during the post–World War II era of nationalist assertion
and decolonization.[3] As yet, however, African political ideas have not been
examined systematically and with reference to the categories and traditional
concerns of political theory. Such analyses would surely clarify both the contributions of colonialism to African political thought and the constraints
which have inhibited or distorted its development. Neither the magnitude nor
the intensity of these impacts will occasion surprise, but their persistence as

**1**

postcolonial impediments to original thought, clothed in anticolonial disguise, may escape detection.

## Anticipation: Blyden's Dilemma

The history of political thought is punctuated by the works of individuals who appear to sum up the aspirations of specific nations or groups of people with ideas that have universal relevance. Jean-Jacques Rousseau, the inspirational genius of the French Revolution, became the patron saint of revolutionary democrats everywhere. G. W. F. Hegel elevated the spirit of German nationalism to the plane of a philosophy of history with far-reaching implications for diverse national and other social movements. Similarly, Edward Wilmot Blyden (1832–1912) promoted African cultural nationalism by appealing in principle to the values of racial pride and exclusivity.

Born of African descent on the Danish (now American) West Indian island of St. Thomas, young Blyden emigrated in 1850 to Liberia, where he became a Presbyterian minister and a professor of classics at Liberia College. A powerful writer and gifted linguist, Blyden mastered Latin, Greek, Arabic, Hebrew, and Spanish in addition to his first language, English. Educator and statesman, he served Liberia as Secretary of State (1865–66) and as Ambassador to Britain and Minister Plenipotentiary to Britain and France at various times between 1877 and 1905. From time to time, he held official positions relating to the education of Muslim communities in the British colonies of Lagos and Sierra Leone. He also traveled regularly to the United States, where he expounded the moral ties which bind Americans of African descent to their ancestral homeland.[4]

In a lifetime of intellectual and literary endeavors, manifest in essays, books, pamphlets, newspaper columns, letters, and speeches,[5] Blyden ceaselessly espoused the controversial and now discredited doctrine of innate racial capacities; in his view, every racial group was endowed by Providence with a special creative potential. "Each race," he wrote, "was equal but distinct; it was a question of difference of endowment and difference of destiny."[6] Africans, he held, were gifted with superior aptitudes in matters of spirituality and religion; their crowning achievements, he believed, would be recorded in those fields. Indeed, he declared, "Africa may yet prove to be the spiritual conservatory of the world."[7] But Africa would not be able to follow its destiny under the yoke of alien domination. Africans should seek freedom by learning to rely upon their own cultural resources and innate capacities for cultural advancement.

Blyden's biographer, Hollis R. Lynch, has observed that his thought may have been influenced by "the writings of such European philosophers and na-

tionalists as Herder, Fichte, Hegel and Mazzini, who advocated racial and national unity and averred that every people had its special mission to fulfil."[8]
Herder's influence appears to have been paramount; his nationalism, like that
of Blyden, summoned people to serve their nation without seeking to dominate other nations or peoples. Unlike his European counterparts, however,
Blyden affirmed the dignity and integrity of a racial group that was about to
lose whatever remained of its historic, precolonial independence. Hence his
dilemma. His demand for racial autonomy was contemporaneous with the
partition of Africa by the colonial powers.

Yet Blyden was not attracted to lost causes; nor was he disposed to utter
lamentations. He understood that no force on earth could prevent the colonial
occupation of Africa and did not regret the tide of history. On the contrary, he
viewed political imperialism with favor as a necessary stage of historical development which could, if wisely conducted, have highly beneficial effects for
the people of Africa. In that regard, he shared the pro-imperialist sentiments
of most progressive and worldly intellectuals of his time, including Marx, Engels, and the younger Lenin.[9]

Nonetheless, Blyden was not about to clamber aboard any European band-
wagon. The unfailing mark of serious thought is an ability to perceive the divergent implications of related ideas that resemble one another in important
respects. Blyden knew and warned that colonial domination would be justified on the despicable ground that African cultural values were inherently inferior to those of Europe. In defense of African values, he constructed a
shield of cultural nationalism to repulse the assault of European cultural imperialism. By word and example, he stood for intimate political collaboration
with the imperial overlord without ever conceding a cultural strongpoint.

"All thinking Africans," he told a British audience in 1901, "gladly cooperate" with Britain and France to the degree that their respective systems
of rule "accord with native ideas and native customs and traditions."[10] He
praised the French for their better appreciation of the Islamic authorities and
communities, which secured communal order, pious direction, and dignity for
millions of people in the African hinterland. Despite his personal commitment
to Christianity "as the ultimate and final religion of humanity," he reached the
objective conclusion that Islam, propagated by missionaries who were co-
racial and co-cultural, was better suited than Western Christianity to impart a
progressive impulse to slumbering Africa. "Mohammedanism," he declared,
"is the form of Christianity best adapted to the negro race."[11] Blyden's conception of Christianity was essentially Hegelian: that it is a world-historical
religion of universal significance. This, however, does not impose an obligation upon Africans of Christian persuasion to accept European renditions of
the basic message and doctrines. To the contrary, he taught, Africans should

innovate indigenous expressions of Christianity and dispense with churches "conceived on Roman, Teutonic or Anglo-Saxon lines."[12] Blyden's vision of African equality in a world of complementary cultures justifies an extravagant encomium, penned by his great disciple, the West African nationalist Joseph E. Casely Hayford: "The work of Edward W. Blyden is universal, covering the entire race and the entire race problem."[13]

Unconventional, disturbingly prophetic, invariably controversial, Blyden's views were not, however, idiosyncratic or distant from the perceptions of avant-garde African and Afro-American thinkers. Although he did not attend the Pan-African Conference of 1900, held in London, its principal literary product, an appeal "To the Nations of the World," conformed with his point of view. Written mainly by W. E. B. DuBois (with whom he had virtually no personal contact),[14] the appeal contained this famous, Blydenite declaration: "The problem of the twentieth century is the problem of the color line."[15] Its measured prose admonished the imperial powers to discharge their trusts responsibly and with regard to the ideal of human equality.

> If now the world of culture bends itself towards giving Negroes and other dark men the largest and broadest opportunity for education and self-development, then this contact and influence is bound to have a beneficial effect upon the world and hasten human progress. But if, by reason of carelessness, prejudice, greed and injustice, the black world is to be exploited and ravished and degraded, the results must be deplorable, if not fatal—not simply to them, but to the high ideals of justice, freedom and culture which a thousand years of Christian civilization have held before Europe.[16]

## Toward "Colonial Freedom"[17]

The forms of colonial rule were established by imperial governments and their proconsuls with very little, if any, thought spared for the creation of bridging mechanisms which might foster the development of complementary institutions in the neighboring territories of different European empires. Hence the abiding preoccupation of Pan-Africanist scholars, from Blyden to Thomas Hodgkin,[18] with the varieties of colonial governance in Africa. In this terrain of administrative and conceptual complexity, the clearest divide appears to lie between autochthony and diffusion. Autochthonous institutions are home-grown or indigenous; they spring from the soil.[19] By contrast, diffusion signifies the export or transference of forms and practices from the metropole to the colony. These two types do not encompass all forms of colonial rule in Africa. A third type, despotism, should be designated for colonial orders which deny the principle of autochthony while they regiment their subjects in a manner that cannot be justified with reference to the legal system of the metropolitan country itself.

Autochthony was the principle championed by Blyden and his disciples[20] with intense fervor. Yet Blyden was mistaken in his opinion that African institutions would be accepted more readily by French overlords than British. Ultimately, France, in keeping with its centralizing political tradition, adopted an incorporative colonial system, one which undermined autochthonous institutions and defined freedom as the attainment of French citizenship. In the long term, British policy proved to be the more flexible and pragmatic. With agnostic objectivity, Hodgkin observed that Britain's vaunted "empirical" or "piecemeal" method of colonial management was self-servingly opportunistic and shrewdly adapted to the varied political situations of eastern, central, and southern, as well as western, Africa.[21]

Colonial systems in Africa were often differentiated on the basis of three crucial variables: the relative enjoyment or denial of political rights; the existence of a relatively free or controlled market for both land and labor; and the reciprocal or invidious valuation of Africal culture, i.e., cultural equality or inferiority as a premise of public policies. Judged by these criteria, the great majority of West Africans in both British and French dependencies were relatively free and fortunate by comparison with Algerian Muslims and black Kenyans, Rhodesians, or South Africans, whose countries were controlled by European settlers. Although the principle of autochthony was embodied in the administrative systems of all British dependencies, it was of far greater significance in those dependencies, such as Ghana, Nigeria, Sierra Leone, The Gambia, and, in southern and eastern Africa, Basutoland, Bechuanaland, Swaziland, Uganda, and Zanzibar, where the absence or insignificance of a white settler element meant that indigenous political institutions could, if nurtured, become effective centers of power.

AUTOCHTHONY IN BRITISH AFRICA: THE CASE OF NIGERIA

In British colonial Africa, the principle of autochthony underpinned a widely practiced policy known as "indirect rule," which connotes the exercise of political power through the medium of indigenous authorities. Margery Perham, whose expositions of this policy in Africa are primary sources for scholars, wrote of its acceptance by colonial officials thus: "During the thirties almost everywhere in British Africa I found 'indirect rule' was the gospel."[22] The strengths and weaknesses of this method of colonial rule were grandly displayed in Nigeria, Africa's most populous country, where it had been devised by Lord Lugard and implemented by that towering figure in colonial history and his followers during the early decades of the twentieth century.[23] In a celebrated treatise on "colonial policy and practice," based mainly on Asian examples, J. S. Furnival[24] has elucidated the economic basis of indirect rule: it affords the cheapest and most efficient way for a colonial power to extract tropical produce. By contrast, settler communities and colonies valued chiefly as markets, where transactions have to be regulated according to uniform standards, require direct rule involving the introduction of imported legal institutions.

To be sure, the ubiquitous resort to indirect rule by Britain in Africa was motivated by the dictates of expedience and parsimony: in 1925, Britain governed 20 million Nigerians with a mere 200 administrative officers.[25] A Governor of Nigeria commended indirect rule as "the best means for securing peace, prosperity and contentment of the people at a price which *they* can afford to pay (italics mine).[26] Yet it was also justified by colonial officials and theorists on moral and political grounds as well. Lord Lugard, the principal architect of this so-called system of Native Authority, defined its purpose loftily as "the regeneration of Nigeria . . . through its own governing class and its own indigenous institutions."[27] His successor, Sir Hugh Clifford, reiterated this conception in a famous address to the Nigerian Council, affirming, in addition, the separate national destiny of each of the various indigenous states included within the boundaries of Nigeria. "Assuming," he ventured to say,

> that the impossible were feasible—that this collection of self-contained and mutually independent Native States, separated from one another, as many of them are, by great distances, by differences of history and traditions, and by ethnological, racial, tribal, political, social and religious barriers, were indeed capable of being welded into a single homogenous nation—a deadly blow would thereby be struck at the very root of national self-government in Nigeria, which secures to each separate people the right to maintain its identity, its individuality and its nationality, its own chosen form of government; and the peculiar political and social institutions which have been evolved for it by the wisdom and by the accumulated experience of generations of its forebearers.[28]

Clifford's extreme position on the potential autonomy of the historic "native state" was, in fact, a heresy of British colonial thought. It was discarded by succeeding administrators and colonial theorists for the more convenient idea that the proper role of the indigenous authority system was adaptation to the purposes of local government. Nonetheless, responsible officials continued to link the native authority system to their proposals for reorganization of the Nigerian central government. Thus, in 1939, Sir Bernard Bourdillon, the wartime Governor of Nigeria, who was later described by Lord Hailey[29] as "the real author" of the first postwar constitution, wrote:

> I see no reason why the native authorities and the elected parliament should not be complementary parts of one harmonious system, nor why the eventual representative Government should not be representative of and function through acknowledged Native Authority.[30]

Accordingly, in the 1945 constitutional proposals of his successor, Sir Arthur Richards, local native authorities, dominated by traditional elements, were designated as the primary units of representation from which members were sent to the newly created regional Houses of Assembly. The latter, in turn, were empowered to select representatives to the central Legislative Council. It was said, in defense of these proposals, that the creation of regional Houses of Assembly would promote the unity of Nigeria by enlarging the "unit of political consciousness" from local to regional dimensions. The official position, summarized by Sir Arthur in the Nigerian Legislative Council, was based on the dogma of indigenous institutions and its corollary, the presumed absence of Nigerian national unity.

> I claim for this constitution that it is firmly based on African institutions. . . . I do not think that Nigeria is yet a sufficiently coherent whole, whether in the political, social or economic sphere, to be capable of immediate and full self-government.[31]

If these contentions were persuasive, it would have followed, as asserted by officialdom, that the dissenting nationalists, who were active mainly in a few urban centers, represented sectarian interests rather than the general interests of the dependency at large. Now the broad outline of colonial political thought has taken shape: African freedom is consistent with representation "in accordance with custom"; that alone is *real* representation, since African societies are culturally unadapted to Western types of representation. This observation implies cultural difference rather than inferiority, although the language of racial inferiority would sometimes slip in. Thus did the colonizer turn Blyden's thought upside down in order to concoct a perverse sort of cultural nationalism, suited to the needs of Empire. Since "real representation" is functional, the educated and nationalist minority should sit at the feet of recognized traditional authority.

Among Nigerian nationalists, the most influential critic of colonial thought and practice was Nnamdi Azikiwe, a journalist and magnetic leader of a pan-Nigerian national council. During the 1930s, in both scholarly and popular contexts, Azikiwe, like Blyden before him, argued that Africans under colonial rule have been "mis-educated" to acquiesce in their own subjugation. "Their training," he wrote, "has so alienated them from their own background that they do not understand their own vital capacities."[32] In the postwar debate over Nigeria's constitutional evolution, Azikiwe disputed the premises of orthodox colonial theory. "Nigeria," he declared, addressing the Legislative Council in 1948,

> can no longer be regarded as a mere geographical expression. It is also an historical expression. The various communities inhabiting this country have great traditions

and a rich heritage of culture which, if pooled together, can make Nigeria great and enable her to take her rightful place among the family of nations.[33]

Inevitably, nationalistic thought, in quest of a basis for Nigerian unity, embraced the democratic principle of popular sovereignty. When British officials questioned the authority of Azikiwe and his associates to speak in the name of Nigeria, they responded by demanding democratic elections based on universal suffrage to organize "the collective will of the electorate" and bring forth legitimate representatives of the people. In Nigeria, as in other emergent nations, democratic elections were valued by nationalists not only or primarily to secure individual liberty but also and with greater urgency to promote national solidarity, a prerequisite to the transfer of power.

At bottom, the doctrine of popular sovereignty could not be reconciled with the colonial theory of indirect representation based upon the system of native authority. It is important to appreciate that indirect rule was not merely concerned with its most obvious aspect, the investiture and recognition of chiefs, but with the development of each tribal community as an organic whole.[34] Official planners, influenced by the ideology of the native authority system, believed that African communities should be represented in the emergent state structure by their traditional authorities and by representatives chosen "in accordance with custom." Under the first postwar constitution, a specified number of chiefs were chosen to sit in the various legislatures in addition to representatives nominated by Native Authorities. Azikiwe and his colleagues objected to their inclusion in the embryonic legislative assemblies on the ground that in law they were part of the machinery of administration, subject to removal by the Governor, and not responsible to their constituents. In his celebrated *Political Blueprint of Nigeria*, Azikiwe, anticipating the eventual disappearance of chieftaincy from political life, advocated a policy of restricting chiefs to "constitutional" or presidential roles in the local government councils of rural areas.[35] In 1950, he summed up "the trend of general opinion, particularly in the Southern Provinces . . . that Chiefs should be encouraged to perform their traditional, that is, ceremonial and religious roles; and that when they exercise power it should not be based on privilege but should be democratically exercised."[36] Many of his associates believed that separate Houses of Chiefs would be appropriate as upper chambers at the regional or state level of government. Such "second chambers" were intended to objectify the dignity of indigenous institutions rather than to detract from the principle of democratic representation. Thus, in an election manifesto of 1951, the National Council of Nigeria and the Cameroons declared:

We will retain and respect our institution of Natural Rulers. Where a legislative assembly is established for them, its function should be purely advisory and consultative. In establishing our new government we must keep or revise those institutions that make Africa Africa. We are proud of them and we shall cherish them.[37]

In effect, the nationalists had made a significant distinction. They agreed with officialdom that tribal communities were, in a sense, organic and that traditional authorities were national assets, consecrated by custom to perform ceremonial, religious, and circumscribed political roles mainly internal to their corporate communities. But in demanding representation based on universal suffrage, the nationalists rejected the prescribed organic relationship between local Native Authorities and the general legislative assemblies. They insisted that the political functions of "natural rulers" and other traditional authorities should not include the right to represent their communities in the decisional organs of the modern state. For the purpose of political representation, the traditional community was conceived, not as a corporate entity, but as a collectivity of individuals, each of whom is entitled to representation according to the democratic and egalitarian rule of one person, one vote, one value.

On the plane of political theory, the struggle between colonialism and nationalism reenacted a great conflict in the history of ideas. The colonial dogma of indigenous institutions revived the conservative European doctrine of "historic rights," meaning, in the words of historian Carl L. Becker, "that every people has . . . at any given time, the social order which nature has given it, the order which is on the whole best suited to its peculiar genius and circumstance, the order which is accordingly the embodiment of that freedom which it has achieved and the starting point for such further freedom as it may hope to attain."[38] Against that conservative doctrine, Nigerian nationalists invoked the principle of popular sovereignty to vindicate the radical doctrine of "natural rights." Whereas the colonial theory assumed the functional rationality of the social order, the logic of the nationalist theory postulated the rationality of the individual. Whereas the colonial theory accepted the premise that in African society men and women were functional parts of social organisms, the nationalists believed that every person was an end in him- or herself. Whereas colonial theory valued the preservation of a hierarchical order, the nationalists adopted the doctrine of progress and looked ahead with optimism to an egalitarian new order in which communal values would survive, but not at the expense of individual rights.

Among Nigerian political thinkers, the foremost exponent of communal rights is Obafemi Awolowo, a lawyer, leader in the movement for independence, statesman, and redoubtable politician. In southwestern Nigeria, the region of Awolowo's birth and ascendancy, numerous *obas* or kings preside over the affairs of traditional segments of the Yoruba-speaking people. In the precolonial era, their powers were strictly limited by custom and by their councils of chiefs, who represented the constituent kin-groups of society. In effect, the indigenous political tradition was constitutional as well as monarchical. But this was, at first, misunderstood and, subsequently, ignored by British administrators, who converted the *obas* into autocratic instruments of indirect rule. Consequently, nationalist protest against colonial rule was fueled by a desire to restore the traditional balance between kings, chiefs, and people.[39]

During the crucial era of nationalist assertion after World War II, Awolowo argued that the various cultural-linguistic entities in Nigeria have indigenous constitutions which have been distorted and abused under alien rule. By rights, he maintained, the constitution of every cultural group should be its own "domestic concern," and every such group should be allowed to develop its own political institutions within the framework of a Nigerian federation.[40] In Awolowo's thought, as in the colonial situation itself, individual rights and dignities are inseparable from group rights and dignities. As Isaiah Berlin has explained, the colonial subject feels personally degraded because of the degradation of his/her group or people, and the crux of the struggle for colonial freedom inheres in "the search for status."[41]

Awolowo's conception of self-determination for each cultural-linguistic entity within a multicultural federation conserves the symbolic significance of traditional reference groups which no longer exercise coercive authority. By fusing liberal individualism with cultural pluralism, the theoreticians of emergent Nigeria (here represented by the two most influential nationalists) established a connection between their cultural traditions and democracy which had been disputed by the theoreticians of indirect rule. In practice, the system of indirect rule did (and could) not impart a sense of racial dignity to the common man. As Blyden's heirs, the nationalists entered a compelling claim of their own to the principle of autochthony.

### POLITICAL DIFFUSION IN FRENCH AFRICA

In French Africa, the economic impulse toward indirect rule was superseded by a more powerful ideological inclination to incorporate overseas territories within a unitary empire controlled by Paris. With few exceptions, indigenous authorities were shorn of their autonomy and converted into subservient administrative functionaries. Until 1946, all but a few Africans (e.g., inhabitants of the historic "four communes" of Senegal) were legally designated "subjects" rather than "citizens"; they were deprived of fundamental liberties and were liable to punishment without trial, dispossession of land, and compulsory labor.[42] In keeping with the postwar spirit of respect for human rights, the architects of the Fourth Republic embraced the ideal of "emancipation" for "France Overseas." But they defined emancipation unequivocally as a personal rather than a national objective. French citizenship was conferred upon all subjects with the proviso that the rights to vote and hold office were contingent upon a wide variety of alternative personal achievements—educational, occupational, economic, military, or domestic, e.g., mothers of two children "living or dead in the service of France."[43] By 1956, the electorate—those entitled to vote for deputies in the National Assembly—in French Black Africa "equalled about one-third of the metropolitan electorate."[44] However, the ratio of African citizens to deputies was raised so as to severely limit African representation, lest France become the legislative "colony of her colonies."[45]

Evidently, the ideal of "emancipation" for Africans would not be realized within the French Republic. From the African standpoint, there was no honorable alternative to sovereign independence; the great issue of French African politics at that stage was interterritorial unity (embodied in the two federations of Equatorial and West Africa) versus "balkanization" or territorial separation. When, in 1956, the French government opted for territorial autonomy in order to extinguish the dreams of interterritorial nationalists,[46] the die was cast for fourteen francophone republics to emerge in western Africa.

In British dependencies, African nationalists used the idea of natural rights to combat the conservative colonial doctrine of historic rights. By contrast, in France Overseas, the overlord granted citizenship status and, by degrees, individual rights in order to strengthen the bonds of empire. While the latter policy was contradictory and ultimately futile, it did blur the moral issue for nationalists. Thus did Léopold Sédar Senghor, in his role as a postwar deputy from Senegal in the French National Assembly, champion the cause of equal citizenship for Africans within the French Republic and, without hesitation, defend the military policies of successive French governments in Indochina, Tunisia, and Algeria.[47]

Yet Senghor and other proponents of "emancipation" within the empire could not escape the reality of its main cultural implication, to wit, African acceptance of European cultural leadership. Like Blyden but half a century later, at the close rather than the beginning of the colonial era, Senghor advocated a cultural exchange relationship between Europe and Africa for their mutual benefit, whereby African humanism would enrich Europe while European technology would modernize Africa. The outcome, he acknowledged, would be "a new civilization whose center will be in Paris."[48]

Having accepted the theory of a united empire (subsequently refined in thought and expression as a "Franco-African Community"), with Paris as its central city, Senghor and like-minded Africans were all the more determined to affirm the unique humanistic qualities of African culture. To that end, they embraced the francophone philosophy of *négritude*, formulated by black poets in Paris—primarily Aimé Césaire, Léon Demas, and Senghor him-self—during the 1930s.[49] Its premise of "counter-acculturation"[50] appeared to resolve the contradiction between political identification with a European em-pire and cultural differentiation. In the end, however, African cultural free-dom could not be reconciled with European imperial control.

DESPOTISM AND DEFIANCE

Despotic forms of government were imposed upon Africans in the Bel-gian Congo, Portuguese Africa, and the white settler states of Kenya, Rho-desia, and South Africa. Among them, the Belgian system was unique in its purity and simplicity. A "colonial trinity," which consisted of an absolutist administration, a conservative Catholic Church, and the great enterprises formed to extract minerals and tropical produce, controlled the means of ac-culturation and livelihood from cradle to grave. "Not only," as Crawford Young has observed,

> was this triple alliance a virtually seamless web but each component, in its area of activity, was without peer in tropical Africa in the magnitude of its impact.[51]

From time to time, the colonial order was defied by protest movements of a kind that are born of cultural despair induced by the systematic destruction of indigenous institutions. Such movements have frequently involved a form of ideology which has been called "the catastrophic myth,"[52] derived in part from Judeo-Christian eschatology and in part from indigenous cultural val-ues. A core belief is the certainty of providential intervention, directly or through a messianic agent, in connection with an apocalyptic catastrophe for the hated conqueror. In the Lower Congo, a "prophet," Simon Kimbangu, rallied villagers in 1921; his message combined puritanical discipline with anti-European protest in anticipation of supernatural intervention against the oppressor. When, in the latter 1950s, participative politics and elections were introduced, abruptly and virtually without any previous experience, the radi-cal Kimbanguist tradition melded with various partisan causes; a political poster "showed Peter giving the keys of the kingdom to [Joseph] Kasavubu [a nationalist leader], on the instructions of Kimbangu."[53] This was poetically just, since messianic nationalism in Africa, like négritude, was an expression of racial dignity against the stigma of a colonial master's contempt.

One Congolese thinker, Patrice Lumumba, burned from love to hatred of the colonizer during his meteoric appearance in world history. Within the short span of a few years, he switched from ardent advocacy of a "common patrimony" for Belgians and Congolese to vehement rejection of colonial norms and precepts.[54] After his violent death at the hands of rivals who were amenable to Western tutelage, Lumumba's heirs, notably Pierre Mulele,[55] were associated with syncretic blends of Marxist-Leninist-Maoist revolutionary thought and messianic supernaturalism.[56] With effects that were not less tragic than bizarre, a nonindigenous theory was adduced to justify the non-scientific practice of utopian revolutionaries. It would be difficult to imagine a more poignant legacy of colonial despotism.

In the Portuguese Empire, despotic institutions were common to the metropole and its dependencies since the establishment, in 1928, of a durable dictatorship by Antonio de Oliveira Salazar. However, the citizens of metropolitan Portugal were entitled to juridical rights which were enjoyed by no more than a tiny minority of persons in the African territories, namely, Europeans, persons of mixed racial descent, and *assimilados*—Africans who had qualified for citizenship by satisfying a number of cultural requirements, including literacy in Portuguese and the maintenance of a European-type lifestyle. So long as this system of legal statuses remained in effect, fewer than 2 percent of the indigenous African population managed to qualify as citizens. All the rest were governed by administrative regulations, involving forced labor, beatings, and other summary punishments without recourse to any court. When, in 1961, full Portuguese citizenship was extended to Africans in law and theory, the dual status system was still retained in practice. Compulsory labor, underpinned by pervasive rural indebtedness, lingered in Angola and Mozambique until its enforcement was rendered impractical by the spread of warfare and resort to counterinsurgency measures during the latter 1960s.[57]

Liberationist ideology in the Portuguese sphere was profoundly affected by the culture bar, which determined the social status of every person. The preeminent nationalist leaders of Angola, Mozambique, and Guinea—Agostinho Neto, Eduardo Mondlane (until his assassination in 1969), and Amilcar Cabral (assassinated in 1973)—had impeccable acculturative credentials. Like Lumumba, all three were, at first, willing to seek freedom for Africans in association with the metropolitan sovereign until they were disabused of that illusion by appalling experiences. However, the turn to revolutionary politics by an ever-growing number of African intellectuals did not diminish the significance of the culture bar in nationalist political thought. As John Marcum has observed, with respect to Angola, revolutionary *assimilados* and persons of mixed descent, influenced by Portuguese Marxists, rejected the idea of "racial struggle" against the Portuguese and asserted the primacy of both class analysis and class conflict for revolutionaries.

The result was a tonal dichotomy: *urban/acculturated-intellectual/multiracial versus rural/ethnopopulist/uniracial.*[58]

This intellectual cleavage continues to rend the fabric of lusophonic Africa, surfacing with the coup of 1980 in Guinea-Bissau and reappearing tragically in Angola, where it has been exploited by South Africa and the rival superpowers.

In the despotic realms of Belgian and Portuguese Africa, colonialism was never the proverbial "school for democracy"[59] that offered a basic education in public affairs, labor relations, and professional endeavor in the manner of British and, to a lesser extent, French colonial Africa. Nor was any such training in anticipation of self-government provided for the indigenous people of white settler states within the British African Empire. In Kenya, Rhodesia, and South Africa, black Africans were systematically excluded from the best farmlands, compelled by mixtures of taxation and coercion to labor for Europeans for minimal wages, subjected to various forms of administrative despotism, stigmatized by settlers as cultural inferiors, deprived of educational opportunity, and excluded from the professions, while the white settlers in their midst prospered and ruled over them with arrogant disdain for their trampled rights. In colonial South Africa, the ideology of the catastrophic myth grew to classic proportions during the nineteenth century, as indigenous societies of the Eastern Cape were disrupted and driven to the point of despair by expansionist Europeans. In 1857, beleaguered Xhosa

> expected two suns to rise, the skies to fall on the whites, the dead to rise to war on the whites, and the earth to be covered with wheat and cattle. They killed and consumed all their cattle in anticipation of the day, and the tribes were broken by starvation.[60]

It is, as yet, too early to judge the long-term political effects of racial oligarchy as it was practiced in British Africa. The patently racist combination of despotism for blacks and liberal democracy for whites would probably bode ill for the future of liberal government were it not for the fact that Africans have aspired to the very political freedoms that have brightened the lives of their oppressors. When the despotic governments of colonial Africa are compared, the liberal legacies of British rule loom large in striking contrast to the wholly illiberal traditions of Belgian and Portuguese colonialism. Already a principled inclination toward limited government is evident in Kenya, Tanzania, and Zambia—one-party states all—and Zimbabwe, where a one-party future is probable. To varying degrees, these postcolonial states of British provenance give scope to judicial independence and other mechanisms of divided power. Tanzania, Zambia, and Zimbabwe have instituted ombudsman-like commissions to receive complaints from citizens and investigate alleged abuses of authority. Nor have the labor movements in these countries abandoned their traditions of autonomy; indeed, the struggle for trade union autonomy against an imperious government could be identified, plausibly, as the core issue of Zambian politics for the past two decades. Nowhere in Africa is the tradition of British liberalism more firmly rooted than in South Africa, where it has always been subordinated to the forces of white supremacy and racial despotism. Can its survival in a future nonracial order be seriously doubted?

REFLECTIONS

In 1958, an eminent Protestant layman and educator reflected on the British policy of adaptation to local circumstance in his native Nigeria thus:

> In the North, the British officials identified themselves with the people in one way only—they spoke the language fluently. Of course, people feel a bond with those who speak their language. The British did not need interpreters. But in every other way they were white supremacists. When a British man came by on foot the African got off his horse and grovelled; and the Englishman expected it. In the South, the British administrators studied the language of the people but never mastered it. They always used interpreters. But here they shared their religion [Christianity], and they imparted democratic government.

Reading this statement from an interview file twenty-six years after it was recorded, I am reminded of a fierce cultural pride intermixed with some prejudice toward the Islamic civilizations of Northern Nigeria; of personal autonomy derived from a powerful sense of rectitude, yet tethered by psychological dependence upon the European source of that rectitude.

> In tragic life, God wot,
> No villain need be! Passions spin the plot:
> We are betrayed by what is false within.[61]

More recently, a Namibian clergyman replied with disdain to my question about the prospect for competitive politics in a liberated Namibia: "But that is a Western idea!" he objected. Silently, I wondered about Christianity; was it, too, not a Western import? Had I pressed the question, I might have heard a Blydenite or Senghorist answer.

Arguably, the spiritual foundation of individualism, attributable to Christian teachings, gave rise in colonial Africa to an individualist philosophy of natural rights. Undoubtedly, Africa's own spiritual heritage has produced a tradition of communitarian solidarity; it has also nurtured the philosophy of *négritude* and other forms of the "dignitarian"[62] persuasion in African social thought. In quest of enlarged secular freedom, political reformers of Islamic conviction have invoked the Koran and Islamic principles of justice in their opposition to arbitrary rule.[63] From the depths of their despair, a succession of brave souls have uplifted the hearts of their compatriots with myths of deliverance. From their encounters with philosophy and science, intellectuals in all colonial empires have derived basic elements for their theories of liberation. The abundance and diversity of these freedom-seeking ideas in the struggle against colonial rule is an immense resource for postcolonial thinkers who must grapple with the awesome problems of social reconstruction.

### Toward Postcolonial Freedom

Postcolonial Africa is a congeries of some fifty or more sovereign states. Only once have any two of them merged their sovereignties to form a durable union, namely the United Republic of Tanzania, established in 1964; otherwise Africa's political map is a colonial legacy. Many flags fly over a common domain of intractable problems, including deficient food production, distorted industrialization (Africa's main industrial products are for export and not for home use), harmful trading relations with the industrial countries, and governmental institutions that are ineffective and lacking in popular support.

Confronting these problems, the first generation of African intellectuals might have repaired for guidance to the temple of social science—that informal collegium of academic prophets and priests whose collective endeavors, stretching from classic sources in Smith, Marx, and Weber to the neo-Parsonian study of "new nations," had produced the hallowed theory of "modernization."[64] Were they truly disciples of the European and American "masters" of social science, African social theorists would have acknowledged the authority of Apter's observation[65] that Western society, having pioneered the processes of industrialization, was "a model (or at least a standard) for the comparison of countries elsewhere." Given the paradigmatic eminence of modernization theory, and its vigorous promotion by an academic elite in concert with the global expansion of American economic and cultural interests,[66] its failure to take Africa by storm is remarkable. Although African intellectual resistance to Western orthodoxy in the social sciences has not been examined comprehensively, a recent survey of Africa's encounter with American political science discloses the guarded awareness of African scholars to a potential "tyranny of received paradigms."[67] Citing an earlier survey of African historical studies (with special reference to intellectual history),[68] Coleman and Halisi perceive African critiques of American political science to be "part of the general movement toward cultural decolonization of the Western overlay, the assertion of intellectual independence, and the search for authenticity."[69] Claude Ake's scholarly polemic against "Western social science scholarship on developing countries" as a form of "imperialism in the guise of scientific knowledge"[70] is a mainstream rather than a deviant work in the milieu of academic discourse in Africa. Concerning Western analyses of "political development," with particular reference to studies sponsored by the influential Committee on Comparative Politics of the Social Science Research Council (U.S.A.), and "with the exception of [works in] the Marxist tradition," Ake warns,

> Western social science scholarship on developing countries is imperialism in the sense that (a) it foists, or at any rate attempts to foist on the developing countries, capitalist values, capitalist institutions, and capitalist development; (b) it focuses social science analysis on the question of how to make the developing countries more like the West; and (c) it propagates mystifications, and modes of thought and action which serve the interests of capitalism and imperialism.[71]

And,

> It is becoming increasingly clear that we cannot overcome our underdevelopment and dependence unless we try to understand the imperialist character of Western social science and to exorcise the attitudes of mind which it inculcates.[72]

While these strictures are, on several counts, highly debatable (e.g., the separability of modernization, including capitalist modernization, from the Marxist tradition would be a preliminary issue),[73] it would be difficult to deny that the leading theories of political development, as they have been formulated by Western scholars of functionalist or pluralist persuasion, do not probe deeply into the problems of social and imperial domination. During the 1960s, a specifically anti-imperialist intellectual tendency, known as "underdevelopment theory,"[74] emerged in conjunction with revolutionary struggles and resistance to American hegemony in various parts of the world. In Latin American studies it is called *dependencismo*;[75] in African studies, it is known as the theory of "neocolonialism."[76]

### CLINGING TO THE COLONIAL IMAGE
In 1961 Edward Shils set forth a model of society based upon the conception of center-periphery relationships.[77] "Society," he asserted, "has a center." This was not meant to be a spatial conception, but an idea about the values, beliefs, and institutions that give order to society. In the social "hinterland" or periphery, he wrote, "attachment to the central value system becomes attenuated." For example, in "pre-modern and non-Western societies," most lives are remote from the central value system; in a symbolic sense they are "*outside* society." However, the elites of such societies crave access to the center and act to reproduce the institutions of the central zone in the periphery.[78]

Center (or core)-periphery images have been used to explicate both preindustrial imperial relationships[79] and modern-era relationships between industrial and nonindustrial countries.[80] The presence of that imagery in African studies has grown with the popularity of underdevelopment theory itself.[81] Various versions of the core-periphery image of world order project a world system of interacting parts all of which are subject to control by a defined center; since control is systemwide, the idea of peripheral autonomy is excluded from the image as a logical contradiction. In underdevelopment theory, the proverbial core is depicted as an exploitative and culturally hegemonic center, encompassing the capitalist heartlands of North America, Western Europe, and Japan. In most versions, the main mechanism of capitalist imperialism is identified as unequal exchange,[82] which is to say that the prices of primary products produced and exported by the nonindustrial countries fail to keep pace with the prices of manufactured goods which they import. Hence a deterioration in the terms of trade for the nonindustrial countries, resulting in the never-ending and ever-growing exploitation of "peripheral" populations.

As a social construct, the core-periphery image is reminiscent of the French and Portuguese images of empire; each projected the vision of a unified civilization, centered respectively in Paris and Lisbon. Invariably, as we learn from the philosophy of Senghor and the sociology of Shils, the content of this construct is cultural; its implicit message is the subservience of peripheral to central or metropolitan culture. Its basic presuppositions coincide with the European world view during colonial times. Intellectuals who peripheralize themselves by embracing this image of reality are unlikely to escape the abyss of cultural despair from which desperate flights of imagination— myths of deliverance—repeatedly take wing. A few thinkers, by themselves, could de-peripheralize many others by posing nonconformist questions: What *if* society does *not* have "a center"? What *if* core-periphery relationships are secondary rather than primary principles of social coordination?

Core-periphery images of international relationships are powerfully fortified by the influence of yet another Eurocentric doctrine, namely, the Marxist theory of class determination. Classical and standard Marxist doctrines teach that classes in society form and consolidate as a result of the prevailing mode of economic or material production. Class consciousness is understood to be the manifest awareness of common interests on the part of people who occupy similar positions in the *economic* structure of society. This viewpoint may obscure more than it reveals about the nature of class formation in Africa and other newly industrializing regions, where "relations of power, not production"[83] appear to be the basic determinants of a society's class structure. Absent that conception, orthodox Marxist thinkers have been unable to comprehend the existence of credibly self-motivated and self-directed dominant classes in the "periphery." Thus Samir Amin, a leading proponent of the core-periphery idea in Marxist thought, asserts that peripheral society is "mutilated"; its structure is "truncated" and "dominated by the 'great absentee' of colonial society: the dominant metropolitan bourgeoisie."[84] The idea of an autonomous and developmental bourgeoisie, based on political and social foundations, would be alien to his thought.

In newly developing countries, the great issues of ideological discourse are never far beneath the raw surface of everyday life. Where millions subsist in conditions of material squalor, why should a tiny percentage of the population accumulate immense wealth derived, in large measure, from patronage and more dubious manipulations of political authority? And why should public policies be rooted in theories of society which evade or de-emphasize questions of inequality and exploitation? The appeals of Marxism to social scientists who grapple with the dilemmas of development radiate from the illumination that Marxist theories shed upon the limitations of more conventional doctrines. However, the undeniable merit of Marxism as a critical theory does not mean that Marxist analyses and prescriptions for change are, themselves, reliable guides for the salvation of human life in Africa or elsewhere. Yet the critical virtues of Marxism are often assumed to have miraculously constructive practical applications as a matter of faith.[85] In their Leninist forms, Marxist doctrines countenance the formation and assumption of power by "vanguard" parties, which are presumed to know and correctly interpret the real or true interests of the working class or people. From the practical standpoint of those whose interests are presumed to be known by a chosen few, and from the intellectual perspective of elite theory, vanguard elitism for the postcolonial era may be reminiscent of developmental elitism during the colonial era in its twilight.

The elitist philosophy of colonial administration in French Africa, its proclaimed *mission civilisatrice*, involving reliance upon carefully chosen, acculturated *évolués*, is familiar to students of colonial Africa.[86] However, the comparably deliberate and systematic cultivation of an elite culture with developmental values in British Africa is far less well known because that process was obscured by the policies of autochthony, administrative devolution, and phased self-government. In a penetrating analysis of British colonial philosophy from 1939 to 1964, J. M. Lee has explained the pivotal idea of "good government" thus:

> The developmental philosophy which inspired the movement for colonial development after 1940 turned the trusteeship tradition in a more positive direction. It wished to transform colonial society by social reform. The official classes in each colony were asked to devote themselves to welfare schemes, and at the same time

to maintain the same standards of efficiency in administering law and order which were associated with the pre-war system. Good government meant that the official classes accepted full responsibility for development schemes, neither more nor less. It was expected that local politicians and local civil servants would eventually arise to take over full responsibility, and therefore reconstitute the official classes. This process was often described as creating 'a political class', which meant envisaging the creation of a native elite capable of running the machinery required to join the society of states in the international order. Whenever the local elite set the same standards of good government as British officials, the transfer of power had been completed.[87]

In this philosophy, the value of democratic participation was marginalized by comparison with the cultivation of "a responsible political class." Lee has revealed the broad basis of agreement among British Tories, Socialists, and colonial officials on the essentials of acculturated elitism.

The chief connexion between the assumptions of the official classes and the policy for colonial development lay in the conviction that power could only be transferred legitimately if it were given to an experienced ruling class. A great deal of metropolitan discussion about the colonies obscured this essential fact. The tendency to interpret conflict over colonial policy in terms of the different pressure groups involved—from the Movement for Colonial Freedom at one extreme to the 'Katanga lobby' on the other—disguised the degree to which they shared common beliefs. Arguments between them were often about whether or not a particular group of nationalist politicians constituted a responsible political class, rather than about the manner in which power should be transferred. They might disagree on the identity of the *elite* which were to become the successors of colonial authority, particularly in multiracial societies, but they all accepted the procedure of free elections whereby the *elite* could establish its right to rule. Those who argued for the limitation of the franchise in elections usually lacked confidence in the *elite* which claimed the right to exercise political power. Any interpretation of events which divides metropolitan opinion into two opposing camps—'economics first' versus 'politics first', 'christian imperialists' versus 'economic imperialists', or 'native rights lobby' against 'the City'—runs the danger of ignoring part of the broad consensus in British life. British policy makers were determined to leave behind in each country indigenous 'official classes' which had a faith in good government. The unexpected quickening in the speed of Britain's withdrawal from colonial responsibility in the late 1950s upset their plans to effect this operation, but not their intentions.[88]

To illustrate the importance attached to elite acculturation, Lee cites Oliver Lyttelton's vain attempt, as Colonial Secretary, to persuade Edward Frederick Mutesa II, the Kabaka of Buganda, to accept British conceptions of the proper relationship between his traditional domain and the Protectorate of

Uganda. Lyttelton presumed that his appeal to Mutesa, as "a fellow Grenadier," would be irresistible. Lee remarks, matter-of-factly,

> Until this date [1953], confidence in Britain's policy for colonial development owed its origin to a belief which could hardly be stated in explicit terms, that colonial experience had induced British habits of mind among the leaders of the indigenous peoples.[89]

It would be imprudent to underestimate the imprint of colonial "habits of mind" on the postcolonial rulers regardless of their forensic ideologies. In a path-breaking contribution to the theory of class domination in Africa, Arrighi and Saul[90] discerned a pattern of elitist management and personal enrichment in the practices of avowedly socialist regimes in Africa. From the statements of Sékou Touré, they adduced "an overt sanction of the norm of *enrichessez-vous* for the bureaucratic groups (of party and state)";[91] from Nkrumahist sources, an unmistakable partiality for managerial elitism rather than egalitarian socialism.[92] The proximity of Touré's era, and Nkrumah's, to the era of paternalistic planning for African colonies by French and British overlords should quicken our perception of the colonial imprint on all forms of postcolonial vanguard elitism.

The veil of radicalism enchants, mystifies, and ultimately deceives the unwary beholder. At this juncture in the development of African political thought, it hides the awful evidence of colonial descent. Three features behind the veil bear surprising resemblance to prominent characteristics of colonial thought; these probable legacies of the colonial era may be identified thus: the core-periphery image of world order; a theory of social class that is derived from the experience and study of early capitalist development in Europe; vanguard elitism, be it left and Leninist or right and corporatist. The image of colonialism is easily embraced, but it offers little prospect of a liberating conception.

BREAKING AWAY

Everywhere in the Third World, where necessitous and oppressed peoples seek freedom from want and fear, revolutionary theories are enormously influential. Among them, Marxism-Leninism, reared upon foundations that are substantially scientific and endowed with immense prestige by the examples of successful revolutionary warfare under Marxist-Leninist auspices in China and Vietnam, is clearly the most widely accepted and respected theory of social revolution. However, in countries governed by communist (Marxist-Leninist) regimes, Marxism, as an intellectual persuasion, is burdened with the yoke of its presumed political authority and the implied onus of responsibility for conditions that breed social discontent. In those circumstances, lib-

eralism is more revolutionary than Marxism; indeed the revolutionary potential of Marxism in the communist world trails behind that of populism, utopian
socialism, and religious fundamentalism. Nor have the several regimes of
avowed Marxist-Leninist orientation in Africa set examples of achievement
that commend emulation.[93] As a strategy of economic development, the time-
honored (and tarnished) Bolshevik theory of "primitive socialist accumulation" is manifestly unsuited to conditions in agrarian Africa for several reasons, including exponential population growth, the extremely high cost of
critical imports, endemic problems of statist economic management, and the
probability of intense rural resistance to collectivization.

Dissatisfaction with Marxism-Leninism as a theory of social revolution
and reconstruction for the agrarian and newly developing countries is evident
in the current development of African political thought. However, skeptics are
not at all inclined to disregard the critical insights of Marxist theory, e.g., the
dehumanization of labor when it becomes a commodity for exchange. To the
contrary, they place a high value on Marxist contributions to creative social
thought. But their awareness of unprecedented problems—demographic, economic, and social—and the exigent need for new ideas limit their patience for
dogmatic theorizing, involving the importation of sterile "new orthodox-
ies"[94] or the "tyranny of borrowed paradigms."[95]

Yet a negative injunction against dogmatism does not respond to the need
for original social thought. Blyden's thought was original because it anticipated the comprehensive impact of colonial domination and charted a course
of resistance to cultural imperialism together with a tentative program for
principled interaction with colonial institutions. His heirs in Africa pursued
the goals of racial emancipation, cultural development, and political independence to the end of the colonial era. Now the historic framework of colonial
and anticolonial theorizing has become an impediment that exerts negative
pressure on the process of creative thought. It is largely irrelevant to the issues
and problems of the postcolonial world and restricts the scope of moral and
scientific inquiry. For a conceptual breakthrough it has become necessary to
break away from the colonial/neocolonial fixation.

Hence the importance of a remarkable statement by Peter P. Ekeh,[96] in the
form of an "inaugural lecture," as professor and head of the department of
political science at the University of Ibadan in 1980. Despite the emotive impact of colonial imagery in Africa, the study of colonialism, which has been
zealously pursued by African historians, has been neglected by political scientists and sociologists. Ekeh observes that conceptualizations of colonialism
have scarcely advanced beyond Georges Balandier's explication of "the colonial situation" in 1951. Balandier's approach was "fruitful" because it cor-
rected a "false" and misleading separation of European initiatives and Af-

rican reactions in previous studies of colonial situations. However, Ekeh contends, Balandier's conception

> does not make sufficient allowance for the supra-individual consequences that flow from the colonial situation and that transcend the space-and-time specifications of colonization and reactions to colonization. Now that we have lived beyond colonial rule itself we must update our sociological conceptualization of colonialism over and above the colonial situation. We must search for the totality of colonialism as a reality *sui generis*, as a phenomenon in its own right.[97]

Thus far, Ekeh avers, social scientists have failed to identify and properly classify the various "social formations" that have emerged from the "confrontations, contradictions, and incompatibilities" of colonial situations. With some courage, given his immediate audience, Ekeh attributes this shortcoming, in part, to the immense influence of the "Ibadan school of history," which is, he respectfully acknowledges, "the most illustrious and consolidated body of knowledge in this land."[98] The Ibadan (and, we should add, associated) historians inspired Afro-centric scholarship by establishing the field of precolonial and autonomous African history. But, he insists, "the massive impact of the Ibadan School of History was to lead to the conscious and deliberate running down of the significance of colonialism in Africa." To illustrate the dominant historical theory, he cites Jacob Ajayi's evocative characterization of colonialism as "one episode in the continuous flow of African history."[99]

For the colonial impact on Africa to be absorbed and transformed into a source of intellectual strength, its significance must be grasped firmly and not minimized. Warning against the seductive influence of Ajayi's attractive episodic metaphor, Ekeh proposes an alternative metaphor: colonialism, he declares,

> constitutes an epochal era in Africa. It represents a congeries of events and consequences which can be equated in significance to an epoch, in its Toynbean fullness. Indeed, I believe it will help our intellectual mastery of colonialism if we denote the attributes of epochs which colonialism shares with such dominant world epochs as the Industrial Revolution and the French Revolution.[100]

From this standpoint, he envisages "an undiscovered territory in the realm of social formations which social historians and social scientists can explore in the study of colonialism."[101] As a starting point, he proposes an original classification of "social formations in colonialism," which indicate new analytical perspectives on the institutions of postcolonial Africa. His approach (which need not be further elaborated here) marks a significant breakthrough toward postcolonial freedom in political thought and analysis because it acknowledges that colonialism produced "enduring social formations."[102] Those who follow Ekeh's lead and help to enlarge his breakthrough may be inclined to see dismissive attitudes toward colonialism as evidence of a well-known psychological defense mechanism, namely, denial. Until the centrality of colonialism, its "epochal" nature, and transformative influences have been deeply and objectively investigated by African scholars, the demon of colonialism—the psychology of dependence—cannot be exorcised from African political thought.

By coming to terms with colonialism, by acknowledging and fully crediting the "epochal" roles of heretofore underappreciated African builders of durable institutions under colonialism, social scientists and theorists would refocus the study of Africa on Africa itself, on African initiatives and responsibilities, achievements and failures, rather than African responses to external initiatives or African grievances against olden or neocolonialism. An Afrocentric political science would be neither anticolonial nor, reflexively and as a matter of intellectual convention, anti-imperialist, regardless of the relevance or irrelevance of that posture to the problems of African development. Greater realism in scholarship would be conducive to a similar temper in policy with the probable result of heightened effectiveness in the management of public affairs.

For example, the necessity of productive and market relationships between newly developing countries and transnational enterprise is now beyond serious question. All African states, regardless of their ideological preferences, need to import capital and technology from abroad. The most, if not the only, reliable sources of these necessities are the transnational business enterprises. Hence African political leaders, socialist and nonsocialist alike, seek to collaborate with foreign firms, often by means of host state participation in transnational business partnerships. In a thoughtful and original contribution to discourse on this vital subject, Sayre P. Schatz[103] has discerned a "process of convergence" in the attitudes and policies of Third World governments toward transnational investors. He gives the name "assertive pragmatism" to this realistic and satisfying posture which is manifestly superseding the earlier reflexive attitudes of supine receptivity and, at the other extreme, passionate rejection of the inevitable. A political theory of transnational corporate enterprise, which would weigh its potential effects from a developmental perspective, but without doctrinal prejudice, would be relevant to the uncharted and perilous passage of rich country–poor country relationships in the postcolonial age.[104]

Realistic policies founded upon empirical analyses and conducted from an Afro-centric standpoint would indicate alternatives to the philosophies of militarism, religious fundamentalism, and sterile statism which threaten to engulf large parts of Africa. Such archaic, yet presently dangerous, creeds germinate in deep feelings of rage and resentment against existing imbalances of wealth and power in the world. Morality aside, it is now evident that neither formulistic dogmatism nor utopian idealism will suffice to break the chain of postcolonial disasters in Africa. In the struggle against poverty and injustice, victories will be earned by those who are able to interact effectively with the originative and productive institutions of their time, and not by those who lament their plight and declaim against the order of existence.

In Africa, as elsewhere in the modern world, political thought needs political science to light the way toward feasible reforms of existing economic, political, and social organizations. A relatively small number of exemplary contributions by political scientists are both Afro-centric in design and notable for their unconventional analyses which suggest new ideas about political authority and change, e.g., Whitaker[105] on parliamentary and local government, Ekeh[106] on citizenship, and Chazan[107] on political participation. As Eme O. Awa[108] has written, "The task before us [as political scientists in Africa] is to forge tools of analysis and social engineering that will enable us to liberate our people." However, in the first postcolonial generation of African political thinkers, subliminal, reactive, and disorienting preoccupations with colonialism and neocolonialism have interfered with the vocation of "problem-solving" political science. The colonial imprint is indelible, but it need not be pervasive and should be allowed to fade without misguided enhancement. When its depressant effect has been reduced by realism, the colonial imprint on Africa will become negligible by comparison with Africa's own imprint on world culture and politics.

## NOTES

1. Robert W. July, *A History of the African People*. Third Edition. New York: Scribner's, 1880, p. 186.
2. K. Onwuka Dike, *Trade and Politics in the Niger Delta, 1830–1885*. Oxford: The Clarendon Press, 1956, p. 11.
3. Robert W. July, *The Origins of Modern African Thought*. New York: Praeger, 1967. See also Claude Wauthier, *The Literature and Thought of Modern Africa*. Trans. Shirley Kay. London: Pall Mall, 1966, and Onigu Otite (ed.), *Themes in African Social and Political Thought*. Enugu, Nigeria: Fourth Dimension Publishers, 1978.
4. Hollis R. Lynch, *Edward Wilmot Blyden: Pan Negro Patriot, 1832–1912*. London: Oxford University Press, 1967, and Hollis R. Lynch, *Black Spokesman: Selected Published Writings of Edward Wilmot Blyden*. New York: Humanities Press, 1971; also Robert W. July, *Origins of Modern African Thought*.

5. Lynch, *Black Spokesman: Writings of Edward Wilmot Blyden*.

6. Lynch, *Edward Wilmot Blyden, 1832–1912*, p. 60.

7. Edward W. Blyden, *Christianity, Islam and the Negro Race*. Second Edition. London: W. B. Whittingham, 1888, p. 143.

8. Lynch, *Edward Wilmot Blyden, 1832–1912*, p. 60.

9. Shlomo Avineri, *Karl Marx on Colonialism and Modernization*. New York: Doubleday, Anchor Books, 1969. See also Bill Warren, *Imperialism: Pioneer of Capitalism*. London: NLB and Verso Editions, 1980, pp. 11–47.

10. Lynch, *Black Spokesman: Writings of Edward Wilmot Blyden*, p. 324.

11. July, *Origins of Modern African Thought*, p. 227.

12. Kola Adelaja, "Nineteenth Century Social Thought: Blyden's Ideas on Religion," in Onigu Otite (ed.), *Themes in African Social and Political Thought*. Enugu, Nigeria: Fourth Dimension Publishers, 1978, p. 193.

13. Lynch, *Edward Wilmot Blyden, 1832–1912*, p. 241.

14. Lynch, *Black Spokesman: Writings of Edward Wilmot Blyden*, p. xxxiii.

15. Imanuel Geiss. *The Pan-African Movement*. Trans. Ann Keep. London: Methuen, 1974, p. 190.

16. Ibid., p. 191.

17. Kwame Nkrumah, *Towards Colonial Freedom*. London: Heinemann, 1962. This subtitle is adapted from the title of a pamphlet written by Kwame Nkrumah in 1942 and published twenty years later.

18. Thomas Hodgkin, *Nationalism in Colonial Africa*. London: Frederick Muller, 1956.

19. Kenneth C. Wheare, *The Constitutional Structure of the Commonwealth*. Oxford: Clarendon Press, 1960, p. 89. See also Kenneth Robinson, "Constitutional Autochthony in Ghana." *Journal of Commonwealth Political Studies* 1, no. 1, November 1961, pp. 41–55.

20. July, *Origins of Modern African Thought*, p. 464.

21. Hodgkin, *Nationalism in Colonial Africa*, pp. 40–45.

22. Margery Perham, *The Colonial Reckoning*. New York: Knopf, 1962, p. 68.

23. Margery Perham, *Native Administration in Nigeria*. London: Oxford University Press, 1937. See also Ntieyong U. Akpan, *Epitaph to Indirect Rule*. London: Cassell, 1956.

24. J. S. Furnival, *Colonial Policy and Practice*. Cambridge, England: Cambridge University Press, 1948, pp. 277 and 284.

25. Michael Crowder, *West Africa under Colonial Rule*. Evanston, Ill.: Northwestern University Press, 1968, p. 198.

26. Sir Bernard Bourdillon, *Memorandum on the Future Political Development of Nigeria*. Lagos: Government Printer, 1939, p. 2.

27. Margery Perham, *Lugard: The Years of Authority, 1898–1945*. London: Collins, 1960, p. 470.

28. Quoted in James S. Coleman, *Nigeria: Background to Nationalism*. Berkeley and Los Angeles: University of California Press, 1958, p. 194.

29. Lord Hailey, "Introduction to 'Nigeria's New Constitution' by Sir Bernard Bourdillon," *United Empire* 37, no. 2, March–April 1946, p. 76.

30. Bourdillon, *Memorandum on Future Political Development of Nigeria*, p. 5.

31. Quoted in Joan Wheare, *The Nigerian Legislative Council*. London: Faber, 1950, pp. 248–252.

32. Nnamdi Azikiwe, *Liberia in World Politics*, 2 vols. London: Stockwell, 1934, p. 396.

33. Nnamdi Azikiwe, *Zik: A Selection from the Speeches of Nnamdi Azikiwe*, ed. Phillip Harris. Cambridge, England: Cambridge University Press, 1961, p. 102.

34. L. P. Mair, *Native Policies in Africa*. London: Routledge, 1936. See also Perham, *Native Administration in Nigeria*, p. 346.

35. Nnamdi Azikiwe, *Political Blueprint of Nigeria*. Lagos: African Book Company, 1943, pp. 19–22.

36. Azikiwe, *Zik: Selection from Speeches of Nnamdi Azikiwe*, p. 77.

37. Manifesto of the N.C.N.C. Lagos: n.d.

38. Carl Becker, *The Declaration of Independence*. New York: Knopf, 1953, pp. 265–266.

39. Richard L. Sklar, "Nigerian Politics: The Ordeal of Chief Awolowo, 1960–1965," in Gwendolen M. Carter (ed.), *Politics in Africa: 7 Cases*. New York: Harcourt, Brace & World, 1966, p. 122.

40. Obafemi Awolowo, *Path to Nigerian Freedom*. London: Faber, 1947, pp. 53–54.

41. Isaiah Berlin, *Two Concepts of Liberty*. Oxford, England: Clarendon Press, 1958, pp. 39–47.

42. Hodgkin, *Nationalism in Colonial Africa*, p. 35.

43. Ruth Schachter Morganthau, *Political Parties in French-Speaking West Africa*. Oxford: Clarendon Press, 1964, p. 56.

44. Robert L. Delavignette, "French Colonial Policy in Black Africa, 1945 to 1960," in L. H. Gann and Peter Duignan (eds.), *Colonialism in Africa, 1870–1960*, Vol. 2. Cambridge, England: Cambridge University Press, 1970, p. 261.

45. Morganthau, *Political Parties in French-Speaking West Africa*, p. 56.

46. Ibid., p. 72.

47. Irving Leonard Markovitz, *Léopold Sédar Senghor and the Politics of Négritude*. New York: Atheneum, 1969, pp. 80–94.

48. Ibid., p. 89.

49. Abiola Irele, "Négritude or Black Cultural Nationalism." *The Journal of Modern African Studies* 3, no. 3, October 1965, pp. 321–348. See also Walter A. E. Skurnik, "Léopold Sédar Senghor and African Socialism," *The Journal of Modern African Studies* 3, no. 3, October 1965, pp. 349–369, and Markovitz, *Léopold Sédar Senghor and the Politics of Négritude*, pp. 40–58.

50. Irele, "Négritude or Black Cultural Nationalism," p. 348.

51. Crawford Young, *Politics in the Congo*. Princeton, N.J.: Princeton University Press, 1965, p. 10.

52. Francis D. Wormuth, "A Typology of Revolution and Ideology." In *Essays in Law and Politics* by Francis Dunham Wormuth, eds., Dalmas H. Nelson and Richard L. Sklar. Port Washington, N.Y.: Kennikat Press, 1978, pp. 196–197.

53. Young, *Politics in the Congo*, p. 391.

54. Rene Lemarchand, "Patrice Lumumba," in W. A. E. Skurnik (ed.), *African Political Thought: Lumumba, Nkrumah, and Touré*. Denver, Colorado: University of Denver. Monograph Series in World Affairs, 1967–1968, pp. 32–33.

55. Herbert Weiss, "Pierre Mulele," in Charles-André Julien (ed.), *Les Africains*. Paris: Editions J. A., 1977, pp. 159–189.

56. Crawford Young, "Rebellion and the Congo," in Robert I. Rotberg and Ali A. Mazrui (eds.), *Protest and Power in Black Africa*. New York: Oxford University Press, 1970, pp. 987–1000.

57. Gerald J. Bender, *Angola under the Portuguese: The Myth and the Reality*. Berkeley and Los Angeles: University of California Press, 1978, pp. 135–196. See also Thomas H. Henriksen, *Mozambique: A History*. London: Rex Collings, 1978, pp. 115–224.

58. John A. Marcum, "The Anguish of Angola: On Becoming Independent in the Last Quarter of the Twentieth Century." *Issue* 5, no. 4, (Winter), 1975, p. 6.

59. Rupert Emerson, *From Empire to Nation*. Cambridge, Mass.: Harvard University Press, 1960, p. 227.

60. Wormuth, "Typology of Revolution and Ideology," p. 197.

61. George Meredith, *Modern Love*. First pub. 1862; rev. 1892. London: Rupert Hart-Davis, 1948, p. 43.

62. Ali A. Mazrui, *Towards a Pax Africana*. London: Weidenfield and Nicolson, 1967, p. 57.

63. John N. Paden, *Religion and Political Culture in Kano*. Berkeley: University of California Press, 1973, pp. 273–305.

64. Dean C. Tipps. "Modernization Theory and the Comparative Study of Societies: A Critical Perspective." *Comparative Studies in Society and History* 15, no. 2, March 1973, pp. 199–226.

65. David E. Apter, *The Politics of Modernization*. Chicago: The University of Chicago Press, 1965, p. vii.

66. Robert A. Packenham, *Liberal America and the Third World*. Princeton, N.J.: Princeton University Press, 1973.

67. James S. Coleman and C. R. D. Halisi, "American Political Science and Middle Africa: Universalism vs. Relativity." *The African Studies Review* 26, nos. 3 and 4, 1983, p. 49. See also S. Egite Oyovbaire, "The Tyranny of Borrowed Paradigms and the Responsibility of Political Science: The Nigerian Experience." In Yolamu Barongo (ed.), *Political Science in Africa: A Critical Review*. London: Zed Press, 1983, pp. 239–254.

68. Leo Spitzer, "Interpreting African Intellectual History: A Critical Review of the Past Decade, 1960–1970." *African Studies Review* 15, no. 1, April 1972, pp. 113–118.

69. Coleman and Halisi, "American Political Science and Middle Africa," p. 49.

70. Claude Ake, *Social Science as Imperialism*. Ibadan, Nigeria: Ibadan University Press, 1979, p. vi.

71. Ibid., p. vi.

72. Ibid., p. vii.

73. David E. Apter, "Political Studies and the Search for a Framework." In Christopher Allen and R. W. Johnson (eds.), *African Perspectives: Papers in the History, Politics and Economics of Africa presented to Thomas Hodgkin*. Cambridge, England: Cambridge University Press, 1970. See also Warren, *Imperialism: Pioneer of Capitalism*.

74. Colin Leys, *Underdevelopment in Kenya*. Berkeley: University of California Press, 1974, pp. 1–27.

75. David G. Becker, *The New Bourgeoisie and the Limits of Dependency: Mining, Class, and Power in 'Revolutionary' Peru*. Princeton, N.J.: Princeton University Press, 1983, p. 3.

76. Michael Barratt Brown, *The Economics of Imperialism*. Harmondsworth, England: Penguin Books, 1974, pp. 256–284. See also Yolamu Barongo, *Neocolonialism and African Politics*. New York: Vantage Press, 1980.

77. Edward Shils, "Centre and Periphery." In *The Logic of Personal Knowledge: Essays Presented to Michael Polanyi*. London: Routledge and Kegan Paul, 1961, pp. 117–130. See also Edward Shils, *The Constitution of Society*. Chicago: The University of Chicago Press, 1982, pp. 93–109 and xv–xvii for the germination of this idea.

78. In this essay, Shils is primarily concerned to outline the trend of center-periphery relations in modern Western states. My brief summary highlights a subsidiary theme that Shils has further developed in various other publications. I have previously published it in Sklar, "La Domination de Classe sur le Continent Africain," *Esprit*, no. 21, September 1978, p. 5.

79. Shmuel N. Eisenstadt, *The Political Systems of Empires*. New York: The Free Press, 1969. See also Immanuel Wallerstein, *The Modern World-System*, Vols. I and II. New York: Academic Press, 1974 and 1980.

80. Immanuel Wallerstein, "Dependence in an Interdependent World: The Limited Possibilities of Transformation within the Capitalist World Economy." *African Studies Review* 17, no. 1, April 1974, pp. 1–26, and Immanuel Wallerstein, "The Rise and Future Demise of the World Capitalist System: Concepts for Comparative Analysis." *Comparative Studies in Society and History* 16, no. 4, September 1974, pp. 387–415. See also Samir Amin, *Unequal Development*. Translated by Brian Pearce. New York: Monthly Review Press, 1976.

81. Bruce J. Berman, "Clientism and Neocolonialism: Center-Periphery Relations and Political Development in African States." *Studies in Comparative International Development* 9, no. 2, Summer 1974, pp. 3–25. See also Timothy M. Shaw, "Dependence as an Approach to Understanding Continuing Inequalities in Africa." In V. Y. Mudimbe (ed.), *La Dépendance de L'Afrique et les Moyens d'Y Rémedier: Africa's Dependence and the Remedies*. Paris: Berger-Levrault, 1980.

82. Arghiri Emmanuel, *Unequal Exchange*. Trans. Brian Pearce. Monthly Review Press, 1972.

83. Richard L. Sklar, "The Nature of Class Domination in Africa." *The Journal of Modern African Studies* 17, no. 4, December 1979, p. 537.

84. Samir Amin, *Accumulation on a World Scale*. 2 vols. Translated by Brian Pearce. New York: Monthly Review Press, 1974, p. 387. See also Amin, *Unequal Development*, p. 294.

85. Claude Ake, *Revolutionary Pressures in Africa*. London: Zed Press, 1978. See also Nzongola-Ntalaja, *Class Struggles and National Liberation in Africa*. Roxbury, Mass.: Omenana, 1982.

86. Morganthau, *Political Parties in French-Speaking West Africa*, pp. 10–16.

87. J. M. Lee, *Colonial Development and Good Government*. Oxford: Clarendon Press, 1967, pp. 13–14.

88. Ibid., p. 195.

89. Ibid., p. 198.

90. Giovanni Arrighi and John Saul, "Socialism and Economic Development in Tropical Africa." *The Journal of Modern African Studies* 6, no. 2, August 1968, pp. 153–165.

91. Ibid., p. 155.

92. Ibid., p. 157.

93. Crawford Young, *Ideology and Development in Africa*. New Haven: Yale University Press, 1982.

94. Olatunde J. B. Ojo, "Towards a Development Oriented Political Science Curriculum." In Yolamu Barongo (ed.), *Political Science in Africa: A Critical Review*. London: Zed Press, 1983, pp. 56–69.

95. These contributions appear in a symposium that includes doctrinaire as well as skeptical essays (Barongo, *Political Science in Africa: A Critical View*). Their balanced juxtaposition is no less significant than the indisputable centrality of orientation with respect to Marxism as the leading intellectual issue in this symposium. See Oyovbaire, "The Tyranny of Borrowed Paradigms and the Responsibility of Political Science: The Nigerian Experience," in ibid, pp. 239–254.

96. Peter P. Ekeh, *Colonialism and Social Structure*. Ibadan: University of Ibadan. An Inaugural Lecture delivered at the University of Ibadan 5 June 1980, 1983.

97. Ibid., pp. 4–5.

98. Ibid., p. 9.

99. Ibid., p. 10, quoting J. F. Ade Ajayi, "The Continuity of African Institutions under Colonialism," in T. O. Ranger (ed.), *Emerging Themes in African History*. Nairobi: East African Publishing House, 1968, p. 194.

100. Ekeh, "Colonialism and Social Structure," pp. 6–7.

101. Ibid., p. 11.

102. Ibid., p. 7.

103. Sayre P. Schatz, "Assertive Pragmatism and the Multinational Enterprise." *World Development* 9, no. 1, January 1981, pp. 93–105.

104. Richard L. Sklar, "Postimperialism: A Class Analysis of Multinational Corporate Expansion." *Comparative Politics* 9, no. 1, October 1976, pp. 75–92. See also David G. Becker, "Development, Democracy, and Dependency in Latin America." *Third World Quarterly*, 6, no. 2, April 1984, pp. 411–431.

105. C. S. Whitaker, *The Politics of Tradition: Continuity and Change in Northern Nigeria, 1946–1966*. Princeton, N.J.: Princeton University Press, 1970.

106. Peter P. Ekeh, "Colonialism and the Two Publics in Africa: A Theoretical Statement." *Comparative Studies in Society and History* 17, no. 1, January 1975, pp. 91–112.

107. Naomi Chazan, "The New Politics of Participation in Tropical Africa." *Comparative Politics* 14, no. 2, January 1982, pp. 169–189.

108. Eme O. Awa, "Teaching Political Science in African Universities: A Problem-Solving Approach." In Barongo (ed.), *Political Science in Africa: A Critical Review*, p. 32.

CHAPTER 2

# The United Nations:
# Its Role in Decolonization

*Donald F. McHenry*

Twenty-five years of African independence falls significantly short of the thirty-nine-year history of the United Nations. Yet one cannot review African independence without noting the crucial role played by the United Nations in bringing independence to fruition. Nor can one review the past or future of the United Nations without taking into account the signal role which the African independence movement and independent African states have had and will have on the United Nations. Indeed the future of the United Nations may depend heavily upon how its new offspring learn to use the United Nations in resolving the complex problems which face them in their further development and which face the community of nations as it learns to work together to resolve those conflicts which still too often lead to armed conflict.

For colonial Africa and for colonial peoples around the world, the promise of the United Nations outshone that of its predecessor, the League of Nations. Much of the rhetoric—of the United States at least—during the war portended a world of people responsible for their own government. Indeed, one could hardly conduct the war in pursuit of the "four freedoms" without contemplating extensive changes. Yet we know that the postwar world envisioned by the United States differed markedly from the postwar world seen by America's allies. At Casablanca, at Dumbarton Oaks, and later at San Francisco and at the sites of other high-level meetings of World War II, these differences came to the fore and the philosophical frameworks which resulted from these talks were to reflect extensive compromises.

The League of Nations was the first to introduce the concept that the international community had some oversight responsibility for the manner in which colonial peoples were treated by the country which claimed sovereignty over them. Indeed the League of Nations structure was a marked departure from the concept that to the victor belongs the spoils. Such a concept was consistent with the views of the idealistic Woodrow Wilson who had held that the "well being and development of such peoples form a sacred trust of civilization." The "spoils" of the losing side in World War I were placed under international oversight, the mandate system, of the League of Nations. Australia, Belgium, France, Japan, New Zealand, South Africa, and the United Kingdom were given the responsibility for administering former German territories under the oversight of the League. And, indeed, whatever else may be said of the League, it seems to have taken seriously its responsibility to look after its new wards—at least under the norms which existed in the twenties and thirties.

But the vision of the League with regard to its new wards was limited. The mandates were divided into three classes: Class A, formerly part of the Turkish Empire, consisted of Palestine, Iraq, Syria, Transjordan, and Lebanon; Class B, former German territories, consisted of Cameroons, Ruanda-Urundi, Tanganyika, and Togoland; and Class C consisted of South West Africa and small territories scattered in the South Pacific. The Class A mandates were provisionally recognized as independent, needing only advice until they were able to stand alone. Class B needed to be fully administered by the responsible country. On the other hand, sparseness of population, remoteness from the centers of civilization, geographic contiguity to the administered country, and other factors justified administration of Class C mandates as if they were an integral part of the administering country. In reality, few in the League ever envisaged an independent status for C mandates.

Although there had been considerable discussion of the future of colonial territories prior to the San Francisco Conference, that subject was one of the few which did not have a draft provision for conference consideration.

We know that feelings regarding the disposition of colonial territories after the war ran strong. Roosevelt was appalled by what he saw in British-ruled Gambia when he stopped briefly on his way to Casablanca. Much to de Gaulle's dismay, FDR also reacted negatively to the idea of returning Indochina to French rule once the area was liberated. De Gaulle and Winston Churchill, of course, had other ideas. Churchill put it bluntly: He did not become the King's first minister to preside over the liquidation of the British Empire. Later, after Roosevelt's death, the United States was to cool its advocacy of self-determination, particularly as regards the Pacific Islands.

The compromises which produced the trusteeship system were closely tied to the fate of other colonial territories and, ironically, were a precursor of the debates which were to dominate early United Nations discussion of colonialism. At San Francisco, China argued that the goal of the United Nations for colonial territories should be "independence or self-government" instead of simply "self-government." The United Kingdom argued that self-government did not exclude independence but that independence alone would set a goal which might be inappropriate for some territories. The final compromise called for self-government or independence for those territories placed under trusteeship and simply "self-government" for those colonial territories—now called non-self-governing territories—which were not placed under trusteeship. In either event, whether under trusteeship or not, the United Nations and its member nations assumed an unprecedented responsibility for those peoples who were not independent.

United Nations oversight was more extensive for Trust Territories. A principal organ of the United Nations, the Trusteeship Council, looked after their welfare. The Council met regularly, required detailed annual reports, dispatched visiting missions, and supervised plebiscites to determine what political status inhabitants might wish. On the other hand, those colonial territories whose administrators chose not to place them under the Trusteeship System had less stringent oversight but, in an advance over the League, general obligations were enumerated. Chapter XI of the Charter, the Declaration Regarding Non-Self-Governing Territories, required colonial powers to, among other things, promote self-government and to transmit regularly to the United Nations Secretary General information on the economic, social, and educational conditions in the territories. Significantly, no information on political conditions was required.

In Africa, only Egypt, Ethiopia, and Liberia were independent and original members of the United Nations. It was eleven more years before other African countries (Morocco, Sudan, Tunisia) were added and these were North African and heavily Arab. However, it was not a period of inactivity in the United Nations. The Trusteeship Council regularly and systematically considered countries in the system which included seven African countries (Ruanda-Urundi under Belgium; Cameroons and Togoland under France; and Cameroons, Tanganyika, and Togoland under the United Kingdom). Slowly but surely the principal issues and procedures involving the process of self-determination began to emerge. The Trusteeship Council examined reports submitted by the administering authority; received petitions orally and in writing directly from the inhabitants or from persons appearing on their behalf; regularly dispatched visiting missions to the territories; made recommendations; and sent its reports and recommendations to the General Assembly. It was a Trusteeship Council visiting mission which sent a special mission to British Togoland and ultimately recommended the holding of a plebiscite under United Nations supervision to ascertain whether the people wished to remain under trusteeship or join in union with neighboring and soon to be independent Gold Coast. General elections under United Nations supervision resulted in a government favoring independence rather than autonomy within the French Union, the outcome of a French-conducted plebiscite. The United

Nations was also involved in the complicated series of plebiscites to determine what would happen to the people of Kamerun, a former German colony administered by the United Kingdom as if it were a part of Nigeria. In the final analysis, a majority of the Northern Cameroon decided to join the new independent Federation of Nigeria while the inhabitants of the southern part of Cameroon decided to join with the French Cameroon, also under trusteeship and soon to be independent. The United Nations also played important roles in the independence of the remaining African trust territories.

Although the responsibility of the United Nations regarding trust territories was more specific than with regard to non-self-governing territories, procedures with regard to the latter began to be hammered out shortly after the formation of the United Nations. In fact, despite the great attention paid to the African-championed Declaration on the Granting of Independence to Colonial Countries and Peoples, passed in 1960 and better known as the Colonialism Declaration, most of the important procedures were passed in the fifteen years prior to the admission of the first large group of African states. In 1946, the General Assembly reminded members of their obligations to submit information on dependent territories under their administration and prepared a list of dependent territories on the basis of the list. The kind of information to be included was spelled out. Political information was optional; but as early as 1947 the United Nations had taken the position that since the goal of dependent territories was self-government, it was necessary for the United Nations to receive information on political developments in the territories. An ad hoc committee consisting of both administering and nonadministering members was established. Finally, the Assembly decided to determine when members were obligated to submit information and when that obligation ceased.

Positions taken early on these procedures were to be the substance of United Nations debate both before and after the great influx of African countries in 1960.

South Africa, in 1946, sought to incorporate South West Africa. It was rebuffed by the General Assembly, which advised South Africa to place the mandated territory under the new Trusteeship System. South Africa refused and stopped submitting information on the territory. Thus began the dispute between the United Nations and South Africa which has lasted throughout the organization's history.

Spain and Portugal were not original members of the United Nations. Thus their colonies did not appear on the original list of territories for which information had to be submitted to the United Nations. Both countries were admitted in 1955. Spain's colonies were listed in 1960 voluntarily. However, the Assembly itself declared the Portuguese territories to be non-self-governing despite the Portuguese position that the territories were Overseas Provinces and therefore an integral part of the Portuguese nation.

Positions taken were to affect the United Nations greatly not only on questions of colonialism but on matters across the United Nations agenda. The Charter of the United Nations contained the same mixture of idealism, centrism, pragmatism, and compromise found in the Constitution of the United States. The ideas of international oversight and, indeed, decolonization were a part of the new system. However, there was also the traditional concept of sovereignty which was also to be respected. Almost from the outset a kind of working compromise was reached: Criteria were set under which the United Nations could fulfill its oversight responsibilities but actual observance was a voluntary action of the colonial power. Thus, at the outset, states were not obligated to submit information on the political development of their colonies but were expected to do so in order for the United Nations to monitor development toward self-government.

For most of the original members of the United Nations this pragmatic approach, which respected sovereignty but accomplished international oversight, was acceptable. However, it would prove unacceptable to the territories wanting independence and to newly independent members anxious to champion the cause for those still in colonial status. The new countries looked upon these gentlemanly procedures as unacceptable. They came to reject the idea that one country could be sovereign over another. They saw the procedures followed as legal niceties, used by some to delay self-determination and by some, such as Portugal, as procedures to avoid self-determination entirely.

Two of the earliest cases involving self-determination to come before the United Nations concerned Morocco and Tunisia. Both questions were taken up as early as 1951 at the initiative of six Arab countries. But initially there was great resistance to putting either question on the agenda of the United Nations. Even when it did so, the United Nations did so gingerly. Faced with French objections that discussion was an invasion of domestic jurisdiction, the United Nations avoided the issue of self-determination by discussing maintenance of peace and security. United Nations consideration of Algeria followed a similar course. Slowly the General Assembly took up the question of self-determination, moving decisively once a large number of newly independent countries had been admitted to the United Nations in 1960.

The question of the apartheid policy of South Africa was not on the agenda of the United Nations until 1952. South Africa was an original member of the United Nations. As such it undertook a general obligation under Articles 55 and 56 of the Charter to promote the human rights of its citizens without regard to race, sex, language, or religion. However, sovereignty, as interpreted at the time, prevented discussion of apartheid unless it was a dispute between states or a situation likely to lead to a threat to international peace and security. Thus, the initial discussion of the situation in South Africa involved persons in South Africa of Indo-Pakistan origin. The item remained on the agenda from 1946 until it was combined with the general question of apartheid in 1962, almost seventeen sessions later.

The year 1957 saw the granting of independence to the first colony in black Africa (Liberia and Ethiopia were never colonies and were original members of the United Nations). The British colony of the Gold Coast became independent as Ghana and was admitted to United Nations membership. Guinea followed in 1958 when France broke its ties with the country following the decision of Guinea not to move into a new status but remain a dependent of France. Nineteen-sixty, however, was the decisive year. In a speech before the South African parliament, British Prime Minister Harold Macmillan warned South Africa that the "wind of change" was blowing through the African continent. He warned that national consciousness was a political fact which must be taken into account in national policy. Macmillan's message went unheeded in South Africa, but its accuracy can be seen in the fact that seventeen countries attained their independence and were admitted to the United Nations in 1960. An additional ten countries, including two from the Caribbean, were to be independent by the end of 1962.

Just as India and Pakistan had initiated the consideration of South Africa and the Arab countries had advocated the consideration of Morocco and Tunisia, the newly independent countries became leading advocates within the United Nations for independence for the remaining dependent areas. The major step in this direction took place at the 1960 meeting of the United Nations, the same session in which a large number of former colonies were admitted to membership. The Assembly passed the Declaration on the Granting of Independence to Colonial Countries and Peoples. Resolution 1514, the Colonialism Declaration as it was to be called, declared that the subjection of peoples to alien domination and exploitation constituted a denial of fundamental human rights. Contrary to the principle of both the Charter and the Covenant of the League that dependent areas should be prepared for self-determination, the Colonialism Declaration held that inadequacy of political, economic, social, or educational preparedness should never serve as a pretext for delaying independence. It called for immediate steps to transfer all powers to territories without regard to distinctions of race, creed, or color. Finally, the Declaration expressed a distinct preference for independence as the outcome of an act of self-determination by using the two terms interchangeably.

The Colonialism Declaration was not supported by the principal colonial powers nor by the United States (they abstained), accustomed to the earlier compromise between idealism and pragmatism. Not only was tutelage rejected, but the Assembly seemed to be asserting powers which belonged to sovereign countries. And the principle of self-determination seemed to be tainted by predetermining the choice of political status which could be chosen. Later in its session, the Assembly passed a resolution (1541) which sought to spell out the choices which may be part of an act of self-determination; but it was clear from the time of the passage of the Colonialism Declaration that independence was to be favored.

The question of decolonization had become intensely involved in the East-West conflict before the passage of the Colonialism Declaration. African delegates, new to United Nations politics, rejected versions of the Declaration put forward by the Soviet Union. Nevertheless, the Colonialism Declaration was a ready instrument for political conflict. In 1961, the Soviet Union proposed an agenda item. The Soviet Union noted that the year-old declaration had not been implemented and proposed that the Assembly elaborate practical measures for implementing the Declaration, set target dates for implementation, and provide for measures for supervision and control of acts of self-determination by the United Nations. The General Assembly passed a resolution, sponsored by thirty-eight African and Asian states, noting that the Declaration had not been implemented but referring mostly to the Portuguese territories, territories that had been subjected to increasing ruthlessness. The Assembly decided to establish a seventeen-country committee to keep implementation under review. The Committee, later expanded to twenty-four and called the Committee of Twenty-Four, was to play a major role in decolonization. It was largely controlled by African and Asian members who could count on the support of Eastern European members. The Committee traveled widely, heard petitioners, and issued recommendations to the Assembly. Priority was given to the larger African territories. Little of the genteel pragmatism of earlier years remained. In addition, the Committee advocated measures thought by some members to be the responsibility of the Security Council.

While it can be argued that some of the dogmatic principles might conceivably be applicable to larger territories, there was and is a question of their application to smaller areas in Africa, such as the Gambia, or to insular areas. However, the movement for independence as an outcome of self-determination was such that the arguably more practical arrangements such as had been followed in the trusteeships were given little serious consideration.

Despite the enormous change which was to take place as a result of decolonization, the process took place relatively peacefully and with little controversy. However, Southern Rhodesia, the Portuguese territories, and South West Africa proved difficult and led to bloodshed and calls for coercive action.

Most of the political discussion took place in the United Nations in the Committee of Twenty-Four, the General Assembly, or the Security Council. Usually it was a case of a recommendation by the Committee of Twenty-Four to the General Assembly that the Security Council institute some kind of sanction because continuation of the situation constituted a threat to international peace and security. Here, too, the United Nations found itself in a debate about its own procedures. Most European members questioned whether the Committee of Twenty-Four had the authority to find a threat to international peace and security, holding that that competence belonged only to the Security Council. Moreover, they questioned whether a threat existed and opposed the application of economic sanctions as illegal, inappropriate, and likely to be ineffective. For African and Asian members these were again legalisms, calling into question the commitment of the Western countries to decolonization. The fact that each of the controversial areas involved continued domination by white settlers also introduced charges of racism.

It was clear, however, that there was a special case in Southern Africa. Portugal wished to hang on to its empire; South Africa continued to desire legal title to South West Africa, later to be called Namibia; and the whites in Southern Rhodesia wished to take legal title to independence without taking into account the wishes of the majority African population. These areas, along with South Africa itself, came to be known as the White Redoubt, an area whose governments actively cooperated with one another even though, arguably, their attitudes toward race differed. The entire United Nations system, including the specialized agencies, became consumed with consideration of self-determination for the Redoubt.

Independence was to come to the Portuguese territories and to Southern Rhodesia but not until after frequent consideration by various United Nations bodies and an exacerbation of the differences between the newly independent countries and some of the countries which had colonies or were thought to be able to influence the situation. Fighting was carried on along a broad front in the Portuguese territories, putting considerable strain on poverty-stricken Portugal. United Nations resolutions were increasingly sharp in their denunciation first of Portugal and later of influential countries such as members of NATO, particularly the United States. Calls for assistance to those fighting Portugal appeared in resolutions. Sanctions were demanded and passed in the Committee of Twenty-Four and the General Assembly, only to be voted down, usually by veto, in the Security Council. Again the argument was sharply focused between those who thought almost any measure should be used to end Portuguese colonialism and those who believed that, however much they disliked Portuguese policy, the Charter of the United Nations and practicality placed sharp restrictions on what the United Nations could do.

In the end, independence for the Portuguese territories came with stunning swiftness. The Portuguese government was overthrown by its own military. The continuation of political restrictions in Portugal itself, the demands of the fighting on the scarce resources of poverty-stricken Portugal, the casualties in a far-off war, and the political opprobrium proved too great. The new government immediately announced its intention to grant independence. Unfortunately, the unity which had not been too well concealed in the fight of the liberation groups against Portugal now came clearly to the surface—with the assistance of South Africa. Conflict among contending groups was to delay the admission of Angola to the United Nations, for the Soviet Union and Cuba had come to the aid of one group (which today governs and is recognized by most major countries except the United States) and the United States supported the opposition. Angola was admitted to the United Nations in 1977, but the fighting continues. Angola still appears frequently on the agenda of the Security Council but in connection with Namibia and the use of that territory by South Africa to attack Angola, to support Angolan factions, and to retain Namibia.

Independence in Angola and Mozambique had a profound effect on the situations in Southern Rhodesia and Namibia. The White Redoubt had been greatly reduced in size. The protection previously provided by sympathetic Portuguese administration was pierced.

Southern Rhodesia had been under discussion since 1962 when the General Assembly requested the Colonialism Committee to consider whether that territory was self-governing and therefore exempt from the requirement that information be submitted to the United Nations. The United Kingdom objected on the grounds that the territory, though under British sovereignty, had been self-governing since 1923. The Committee and later the General Assembly declared the territories non-self-governing and began periodical consideration of what it said was the failure of the United Kingdom to comply with the Colonialism Declaration. In the meantime, developments within Southern Rhodesia moved in the direction of increasing racial discrimination and conflict. Southern Rhodesia sought independence from the United Kingdom without meeting the democratic requirements which the British thought essential. The result was a unilateral declaration of independence by Southern Rhodesia leading the British to seek the assistance of the United Nations in bringing its rebellious colony back into line.

For the first time in its history the United Nations crossed the legal lines which had been so strongly resisted by the United Kingdom and other Western countries. First voluntary, then selective mandatory, and finally comprehensive mandatory sanctions were placed on Southern Rhodesia. But Southern Rhodesia was not to attain independence as Zimbabwe until 1980. In the meantime, the economic and political pressures placed on Southern Rhodesia were reinforced by large-scale military action undertaken by black Rhodesian groups. Independent Mozambique not only served as a staging area for military operations but helped to tighten the economic pinch on Southern Rhodesia by cutting off transit of supplies and freeing Zambia to take economic measures.

It can be argued that the rebellion in Southern Rhodesia would have been bloodier or even more prolonged without sanctions and that the international community, faced with the Rhodesian decision, could not afford to do nothing. However, the institution of sanctions may have lasting effects on the ability of the United Nations to enforce its decisions. Sanctions were widely violated, and actions by the United Nations to stop violations were ineffective. Indeed, the United Nations refrained from taking actions against Portugal and South Africa despite their open violations of sanctions. The feeling is widespread that sanctions cannot work. In reality, the United Nations never instituted sanctions in the way in which its own studies suggested they must be used, in large measure because of resistance from some of its members who feared that the effect on them would be too great.

As indicated earlier, Namibia has been a concern of the United Nations from the outset. Even when the membership from Africa, besides South Africa, was limited to Egypt, Ethiopia, and Liberia, the organization refused to agree to South African requests to annex the territory. The United Nations insisted on placement of the territory under the trusteeship system so that it could monitor development. South Africa's refusal to do so, its introduction of apartheid into the territory, and its refusal to submit information to the United Nations led to a long series of challenges in the World Court, which repeatedly affirmed the authority of the United Nations to exercise responsibility over the territory even as the Court affirmed that South Africa was not obligated to place the territory under trusteeship. When, in 1966, the World Court refused to decide that South Africa had violated its Mandate (on the grounds that the parties bringing the case did not have standing to receive a judgment), the General Assembly, in a decision later upheld by the Court, decided to revoke South Africa's Mandate and to assume direct responsibility for the territory. It was a decision which remains unenforced: South Africa refuses to abide by the Assembly's action, and numerous meetings of the Security Council have failed to reach agreement on a course of action to force South African compliance.

Repeatedly frustrated in their efforts, African delegations, supported by other non-Western delegations, began to follow the path they followed on Southern Rhodesia. Resolutions supporting armed struggle received approval, usually over the reservations or opposition of some Western delegations. Moreover, the General Assembly "recognized" the South-West Africa People's

Organization as the sole legitimate representative of the Namibian people. Efforts to resolve the Namibian question without further violence continued, notably through the work of the so-called Contact Group, consisting of the representatives of five Western countries. Agreement on a framework for a settlement was reached in 1978 after long and arduous negotiations and incorporated in Resolution 435 of the Security Council. However, South Africa refused to go ahead with implementation. Numerous excuses have been given, including the charge that the United Nations is biased. However, that same bias must have been present, if indeed it is present, when South Africa agreed to the settlement. Later, South Africa, now with the support of the Reagan Administration in the United States, conditioned implementation on the withdrawal of Cuban forces from Angola. No mention of Cuban forces was made at the time of South Africa's agreement.

It is obvious that South Africa has not yet decided that it will relinquish its control over Namibia except under conditions favorable to it. Moreover, barring an unforeseen catastrophe, the United Nations is unwilling, indeed unable, to dislodge South Africa. It is equally clear that the United Nations, which championed the cause of Namibia long before its inhabitants were able to do so, and which did so before being pressed by newly independent countries, will continue to press for Namibian independence under conditions which guarantee freedom of choice.

It is the question of apartheid in South Africa which has probably consumed more time and generated more emotions than any topic discussed in the United Nations with the possible exception of the Middle East. As noted earlier, the question of apartheid presented the United Nations with political if not legal problems from the outset. But given the repressive policies implemented by the Nationalist Party when it took power in South Africa in 1948 and the admission of African countries to the United Nations, it was inevitable that sharp differences would occur. At every session of the General Assembly, South Africa's policies have been on the agenda. Over the years various special commissions or committees of individuals, experts, or countries have met to consider the question.

The United Nations Security Council became involved in 1960 after South African police fired upon unarmed demonstrators peacefully protesting pass laws. The Security Council meeting after Sharpville led to the first of several visits by Secretaries General to South Africa to discuss either apartheid or Namibia. No progress was made on the fundamental premises of apartheid. Indeed, the South African government moved ahead to implement its plans and repressed all opposition. Inevitably, African and Asian members of the United Nations began to call for measures designed to isolate South Africa and force it to abandon apartheid and abide by United Nations resolutions.

Resolutions were introduced to that effect in the General Assembly and actually passed. The Assembly, however, could only make recommendation and attempts to have the Security Council pass similar resolutions failed, failed that is until August 1963 when the Security Council decided to impose a voluntary embargo on the sale of arms and ammunition to South Africa in order to avoid contributing to a situation which might threaten international peace and security.

Consideration of apartheid in the United Nations led to African frustration. Again, the Western countries were accused of hiding behind legalisms, of racism, and of placing commercial interests in South Africa above human rights. African frustrations were exploited by the Soviet Union in its criticism of the West and later by Arab countries which deliberately phrased their own resolutions on the Middle East in a manner to take advantage of African sensitivities on apartheid. The fact that South Africa and Israel cooperated on arms and that Africans were sympathetic to the desire of Palestinians for self-determination did little to help keep the issues separate or to keep the debate rational. Both the African and the Arab states adopted a practice of bringing up their concerns on a broad range of agenda items in almost every part of the United Nations and the United Nations system.

Despite constant consideration of apartheid, including a special committee which concentrates solely on the issue, and a widespread information campaign to spread word about the evils of apartheid, the United Nations has not taken additional coercive action against South Africa except in the arms embargo area. Reacting to the torture death of Steve Biko while in police custody, the Security Council decided in 1977 to make the arms embargo mandatory. South Africa was cut off from those states such as France and Israel which had loosely observed the voluntary arms embargo. The other action which ought to be noted here concerns South African representation in the United Nations General Assembly and the Specialized Agencies. The Algerian President of the Assembly in 1974 ruled South African credentials were not in order, thus preventing South Africa from taking a seat. The ruling remains in effect. Similar action was taken, albeit by votes, in the International Labor Organization.

Again it may be questioned whether the United Nations has had any effect in ameliorating conditions in South Africa. Apartheid remains, but in some respects it has been changed substantially. One can argue that South African desire to avoid political, cultural, and economic isolation has led to a rounding of the edges of apartheid and that this might not have occurred without United Nations pressure. It can be argued that South Africa has developed its own arms industry and become less dependent on others. Here, too, the cost to South Africa has been high. One can speculate that perhaps the costs (using that word in a broad sense) might reach the point where, when combined with the violence which was inevitable, they might lead South Africa to make structural changes in apartheid.

This brief review of Africa and the United Nations during the first twenty-five years of African independence would not be complete without some reference to the Congo, now Zaire. The Congo was abruptly granted independence by Belgium on 30 June 1960. Unlike France and the United Kingdom, Belgium had done little to prepare its colonies for independence. Education was woefully inadequate; participation in government was nonexistent. When, within a week of independence, the army mutinied, Belgian administrators and settlers left hurriedly, Belgian troops intervened, and the Katanga province sought to break away, the United Nations was asked by the new "government" to dispatch military assistance. The Security Council agreed and on 12 July 1960 authorized the Secretary General, Dag Hammarskjold, to establish a United Nations force which eventually numbered 20,000 men. It was a fateful decision. Before the United Nations forces withdrew in 1964, the Soviet Union had ceased cooperation with the Secretary General and refused to pay its share of the costs of the operation; the United Nations forces were engaged in fighting aimed at preventing civil war; and Dag Hammarskjold was killed in an airplane crash while en route to the area. The effect on the United Nations was long lasting. A financial and constitutional crisis grew out of the Soviet failure to pay its bills, and the authority of the Secretary General was set back for some time.

While there were far-reaching consequences for the United Nations, some good may have come out of the Congo fiasco. United Nations civil personnel worked alongside the troops to provide training and human infrastructure for the Congo government; the first of what might have been a series of secession actions throughout Africa was prevented; and the big-power rivalry was kept out of Africa—at least temporarily.

In the first twenty-five years of African independence, the Untied Nations has played the role of mid-wife, doctor, educator, and policeman. It has provided a platform where African concerns could be taken beyond the regional reach of the Organization of African Unity or even the political limitations of the Commonwealth of Nations. Indeed, both of these organizations were used to add force to proposals in the United Nations. Particularly in the early years, the United Nations was a training ground for African statesmen, even on occasion a respectable exile for political foes. Many early African diplomats became well known beyond their country (and mourned when disfavor led to their imprisonment or death). The United Nations has also played a role in African economic and social development, especially through the Economic

Commission for Africa, the World Bank, and the International Monetary Fund. World Health Organization programs have been instrumental in eradicating diseases such as smallpox, and the Food and Agricultural Organization has provided both food and technical assistance. These substantial United Nations programs are given too little attention and, indeed, are passed over too briefly here. Undeniably, however, the first twenty-five years of African independence were concentrated on political questions involving decolonization and, to a lesser extent, consolidation of statehood. The next twenty-five years must concentrate on economic development, free of the abortive rhetorical efforts surrounding the so-called new international economic order.

It is not clear what role the United Nations will play in helping Africa with its economic development and in helping with the inevitable pushes and pulls of further political development. The United Nations itself has not fared particularly well in the wake of its enormous success in bringing about a revolution, largely peacefully. The breakdown of the delicate compromise between idealism and sovereignty led to inevitable strains, frequently made more difficult by the East-West conflict. The African approach to decolonization shook the status quo, and neither existing states nor institutions fare very well under rapid change. The time has come to tone down the rhetoric, to decrease the frequency of resolutions, and to work cooperatively and sensitively with other nations. In the final analysis, African states are weak and impoverished; and it is the weak and impoverished who need the United Nations the most, both as a platform and to protect their sovereignty and to promote their development.

CHAPTER 3

# The Marginality of African States

*Robert H. Jackson and Carl G. Rosberg*

## The Independence Gap

"Independence" is a shorthand expression for a revolutionary change in twentieth-century politics. It signifies the right of indigenous peoples to govern the territorial jurisdictions formed under colonial rule. The universal extension of this human right of self-determination was the moral and political achievement of the anticolonial revolution. Africans agitated and in some cases fought for independence, but it was also a consequence of important changes outside Africa. The most important was a transformation of the prevailing norms of international legitimacy following World War II.[1] European colonialism became illegitimate, and the unqualified right of all colonial peoples to self-government became a basic norm of the international community. The role of the United Nations was particularly instrumental in bringing about Third World independence.[2] But it was also an expression of the democratic revolution of the twentieth century, which is Kantian more than Marxian by inspiration, and as a result of which people everywhere and not merely those in the more developed countries are considered to possess a *categorical human right* to sovereign statehood.

The transfer of sovereignty from colonial overlords to African nationalists was a clear acknowledgment of Africans' human rights but not necessarily of their preparation for self-government. To be sure, some colonies had achieved significant political and socioeconomic development by the time of independence: Ghana, Nigeria, and Senegal exhibited noteworthy constitutional progress; Guinea, Ivory Coast, Malawi, Mali, and Tanzania displayed substantial internal unity; Ghana, Zaire, Zambia, Kenya, and Nigeria had good economic potential. But other empirical foundations of some of these countries were far from solid, as Guinea, Ghana, Zaire, and Nigeria have demonstrated by their severe problems since independence.

In fact, many emergent African states were not very soundly constituted at

**45**

the time of independence and some offered little promise of achieving empirical viability afterwards. The boundaries of many countries, particularly
but by no means exclusively in French-speaking Africa, were arbitrarily
drawn by the colonial powers and were not encouraging frameworks of unified, legitimate, and capable states: for example, Mauritania, Benin, Togo,
Upper Volta, Niger, Chad, Central African Republic, and Congo-Brazzaville.
The French referred to Mauritania, with much accuracy, as "the vacuum."
But with the single exception of Guinea, which seized independence in 1958,
all the units of the French empire in West and Equatorial Africa, regardless of
their stage of development of the colonies, were given independence within
the same year—1960. The Belgian Congo (Zaire) became sovereign with very
little preparation in the same year. The Portuguese opposed African nationalism by military force, and their colonies collapsed into independence largely
as a result of anticolonial warfare. Even the British—whose philosophy of
decolonization (which Hodgkin characterized as "empiricism" as contrasted
to the rationalism of the Belgians and the French) acknowledged the different
stages of development of their individual African colonies—were unable or
unwilling to make independence conditional on their internal development.[3]
In African decolonization, empiricism was subordinated to rationalism more
often than not.

An *African* state was a juridical reality in international law but it was not
necessarily an empirical reality in national fact at the time of independence.
In most cases the empirical reality as a functioning government was still primarily the presence, knowledge, experience, skills, routines, and resourcefulness of *European* officials who had embodied the colonial state. Independence therefore opened a gap between the international legitimacy and the
internal marginality of many emergent African countries. The gap often presented a real political dilemma to the new African rulers: they usually could
retain European officials only by compromising their national independence
and could dispense with them only at the risk of undermining governmental
performance.

A striking and perhaps an extreme illustration of the marginality of African states at independence is Zaire. The colonial political entity known as
the Belgian Congo was in theory, practice, and content almost entirely Belgian. When an African mutiny in the armed forces immediately following independence at the end of June 1960 led at once to a mass exodus of the
Belgians, the empirical state disintegrated and only the juridical shell remained. In the following several years a major rescue operation mounted by
the United Nations was required to restore some of the conditions of empirical
statehood. But the resultant structure has not proved to be very successful not
least because the international community has very limited authority, re-

sources, and capacities to bolster the internal empirical conditions of any of its member states. At the present time some twenty-five years after independence, significant empirical problems of statehood persist in Zaire and there is little likelihood that they will soon be resolved.

Since independence the emperical conditions of many sub-Saharan states have not developed substantially and have deteriorated in some cases. The human suffering authored by politics has been extensive: Africa contains the world's largest number of refugees. Genocide has occurred in at least one country—Burundi—and ethnic massacres have shaken Rwanda and Uganda; serious and sometimes violent ethnic strife has erupted in many countries and political discrimination based on ethnicity has been widespread.[4] By 1983 there had been at least fifty successful coups; in addition, there had been numerous unsuccessful coup attempts and major plots. Civil wars have been waged in Angola, Chad, Ethiopia, Nigeria, Sudan, and Zaire; and serious internal conflicts just short of war have shadowed the political life of many other countries. Dictatorship has not been uncommon, and in at least two cases— Uganda and Equatorial Guinea—vast numbers of people suffered political abuse and often physical deprivation before the dictators—Idi Amin and Francisco Macias—were overthrown. Less abusive forms of personal rule have been widespread.[5]

The economic performance of sub-Saharan governments has generally been poor, and the socioeconomic conditions of some countries have been adversely affected—for example, Ghana, Uganda, and Tanzania. Corruption has become part of the structure of African politics, and in some countries— for example, Ghana, Liberia, Nigeria, and Zaire—it is virtually a way of life. Some of the decay of African states—particularly of economic conditions— has undoubtedly been owing significantly to forces beyond the control of Africans, such as the rapid increase in world oil prices in the 1970s, the great inflation that followed, the fluctuation and frequent decline of world prices for Africa's primary agricultural and mineral exports, the global recession of the early 1980s, and drought.[6] But some decay—particularly but not exclusively of civil and political conditions—is undoubtedly the result of actions by African governments, especially rulers (as we argue later).

The institutional problem of African states reminds us that states do not exist empirically apart from the people involved in them. They are human institutions that are formed, enlarged, strengthened, united, divided, weakened, undermined, discarded, and occasionally even destroyed by the actions of people. States are what people make of them. Of course, a viable state also requires material resources, but these are not usually determining factors. Viable states existed in Europe long before the industrial revolution provided governments with a vastly increased resource base. Indeed, the ancient Egyptians, Greeks, Romans, Chinese, and Persians were successful state-builders, as were the preindustrial Japanese, Turks, English, French, Spaniards, Swiss, and Scandinavians. Successful state-building in any particular case appears to be much more the result of the desires, efforts, skills, dispositions, values, and fortunes of the people involved, particularly rulers, than of material resources. In Zaire after independence the resource base of the country had remained the same, but many people and most leading politicians were acting contrary to Zaire's requirements and in accordance with ethnic obligations or personal interests.

One might conclude from the contemporary adversities of African states that the survival of many is in doubt; however, this is not the case. Their continued existence is not conditional on their empirical viability. Instead, it depends upon the international community which upholds the independence of African states regardless of either their internal conditions or the conduct of their rulers. External sovereignty rather than internal legitimacy and capability is the lifeline of sub-Saharan states: the international community and its doctrine of self-determination gave them life in the first place and it has sustained their political independence ever since (as we argue elsewhere).[7] Under current international norms a sovereign government's incivility or incapacity is not a legitimate ground for withdrawing sovereignty or condoning external intervention to attempt to establish more tolerable internal conditions. Intervention on these grounds would amount to international paternalism and would be difficult to distinguish from colonialism. Paradoxically, self-determination has been reduced to what it was in Europe prior to the democratic age: a sovereign right of princes and not of peoples; the exclusive prerogative of rulers to enjoy an internationally guaranteed freedom from unsolicited foreign intervention. The only apparent condition placed on this right, apart from the requirement that rulers refrain from acts of foreign intervention and subversion—which are among the basic prohibitions of the Organization of African Unity and the United Nations—is that they be indigenous.[8]

The underdevelopment of sub-Saharan countries and their socioeconomic adversities in particular are widely acknowledged and have been studied from a variety of theoretical perspectives. But the relationship between external sovereignty and internal underdevelopment has largely gone unnoticed. Perhaps this is because most social scientists, non-Marxists and Marxists alike, have emphasized material conditions at the expense of legal and moral factors in their studies of underdevelopment. Perhaps it is because self-determination has been regarded by almost everyone as an unqualified political good. However, self-determination, like any other institution, has concrete repercussions which result in a mix of costs and benefits. The costs are greater in countries where governments are unable or unwilling to use their independence to provide the people with political goods.[9] Unfortunately, there are many such governments in sub-Saharan Africa today.

### A Concept of the State

Our introduction has intimated a concept of the state and the states system which may be unfamiliar and require some explication. For Max Weber, whose concept is very influential among social scientists, the state essentially consists of an apparatus of governance with a monopoly of force over its territorial jurisdiction and population. Weber's classical nineteenth-century concept can explain "empirical statehood."[10] But it cannot account adequately for a novel, late twentieth-century phenomenon: the international right of many new Third World states to exist without demonstrating much internal capacity to do so; it cannot explain "juridical statehood."

Many sub-Saharan countries cannot be considered to be "states" by Weber's definition: they came into existence without possessing the means of force required to compel the colonial power to withdraw and they have remained in existence regardless of their empirical inadequacies. As we indicated, independence was usually a moral victory over colonial powers who decided not to defy critical world opinion and clamorous and articulate demands for decolonization by anticolonial groups both at home and in their colonies. Moreover, since independence there have been African governments which have for extended periods been unable to hold an effective monopoly of force throughout their territorial jurisdictions. Angola, Chad, Ethiopia, Sudan, Uganda, and Zaire are prime examples. The international right of self-determination of all colonies regardless of their empirical statehood has been vital in enabling these marginal states and others to persist.[11]

The presence of these novel political entities calls for a revised concept of the state. One such concept is the following: by "state" we mean a defined territory occupied by a permanent population, with a national government that is recognized as sovereign by most other states and by the international community. This is international or juridical statehood, and it is the essence of the state in international law.[12] In addition, the national governments of states usually have the following empirical properties in varying degrees: (1) internal legitimacy, either of their institutions or ideologies or of their rulers personally, and (2) an apparatus of power—consisting of personnel, finances, techniques, facilities, equipment, materiel, and other organizational resources and capacities—that is capable of enforcing national sovereignty and carrying out public policy. This is internal or empirical statehood, and it is the essence

of the state in political theory.[13] Most social science studies of the state, including Weberian and Marxian approaches, are confined to this empirical
facet of statehood.

Juridical statehood is a necessary property of contemporary states, but
empirical statehood is not. The Transkei, Bophuthatswana, Venda, and Cis-
kei—"homelands" in South Africa—do not possess statehood because they
lack external sovereignty even though they are about as substantial empirically
as Lesotho and Swaziland, which do possess it because they are sovereign internationally. Only South Africa recognizes the homelands, but Pretoria's recognition alone is utterly inadequate for juridical statehood. During the Nigerian civil war (1967–70), Biafra proved initially to be almost as powerful
militarily as Nigeria, but this did not suffice to make Biafra a state. Juridical
statehood was denied to Biafra by the international community (with the exception of four African countries which recognized its rebel government).
Had Biafra succeeded in securing international legitimacy, separatist and irre-
dentist movements in other African countries would have been emboldened to
seek statehood, with seriously disruptive consequences to the regional states
system. Such a possibility undoubtedly deterred most African states from recognizing Biafra, and Biafra's failure to achieve juridical statehood established a significant precedent.[14]

The preservation of juridical statehood against the claims of internal rebels is not a problem of African rulers today—even if rulers are not in control
of the territories in dispute. The turbulent case of Chad suggests that rebels
can deprive statesmen of sovereignty only by seizing it from them: that is, by
capturing Ndjamena. Sovereignty appears to derive from the occupation of a
capital city and its environs only and not from the control of an entire country.
Perhaps this reality is also a reason why the coup is such a winning stratagem
in African politics: in a disorganized state it requires modest organization and
skill to seize the presidential palace in a capital city; moreover, a successful
coup is rewarded with international legitimacy.

Our alternative concept also helps to clarify the problem of state-building.
Today in sub-Saharan Africa (and perhaps in some other parts of the Third
World as well) state-building is a novel problem of developing the empirical
conditions of statehood in circumstances where the juridical conditions already exist. In general, this is a reversal of the historical experience of state-
building in Europe, where external sovereignty was achieved by governments
whose empirical statehood could not be denied.[15] Moreover, in Europe and
elsewhere before the unqualified right of self-determination became a basic
norm of international society, the necessity of maintaining effective control of
a country in order to retain sovereignty was a powerful incentive for rulers to
pursue national development. "The states of Europe . . . were surrounded by

actual or potential competitors. If the government of one were lax, it impaired its own prestige and military security. . . . The states system was an insurance against economic and technological stagnation." [16] In sub-Saharan Africa and some other parts of the Third World today juridical statehood is a disincentive rather than a goad to state-building. Rulers do not have to be apprehensive of losing their sovereignty to internal rebels who control alienated regions because the latter have no prospect of securing international legitimacy over their opposition. Rulers also do not have to worry about losing their sovereignty to more capable foreign rivals. The new international system with its built-in mechanism of ruler protection does not induce rulers to build the internal legitimacy and capability of their governments. Weberian and Marxian concepts of the state, which are strongly influenced by the experience of European statehood and focus primarily on the state as an agency of power and on the states system as a balance of power, obscure these contemporary political realities.

### The Internal Legitimacy of African States

While every African state possesses international legitimacy, not every one can credibly claim to possess internal legitimacy. African nationalists did not usually acquire international legitimacy by first acquiring internal legitimacy; they usually secured it, as we have noted, by convincing the international community that colonial control was no longer legitimate. But colonial illegitimacy and African legitimacy are not the same. Seldom did African nationalism result in the creation of a new national identity as a basis for the internal legitimacy of the new state. To the contrary, nationalism had the paradoxical effect of raising ethnic consciousness and conflict at the same time that it promoted independence. For most Africans subnational ethnicity is a moral good and an important object of social as well as political identity. Competitive politicians are therefore strongly tempted to politicize ethnicity if given the opportunity and if it is to their advantage. Thus independence frequently fostered national disunity and discord which undermined the internal legitimacy of many African governments without affecting their external legitimacy.

Attempts were usually made in the later colonial period to establish an institutional basis for the emergent African state prior to the transfer of sovereignty. This was most earnestly undertaken in some British territories; no serious undertakings of this kind occurred in Portuguese territories. However, the formal constitutions which were adopted seldom constituted an empirical foundation of national legitimacy. They were alien imports which acquired little indigenous value. Even in Ghana and Nigeria, where some African poli-

ticians endeavored to make them work, they were not successfully institutionalized. Since independence most constitutions have been honored in the
breach—either by civilian rulers attempting to retain power or by soldiers attempting to seize power by unconstitutional means. Moreover, some constitutions have been arbitrarily amended by autocrats seeking to give an aura of
legality to their personal absolutism. It cannot be said that constitutional government has fallen to the wayside in African politics, for it was rarely adopted
successfully in the first place. Because most formal constitutions of African
states have not shaped political behavior, they are of limited interest to political scientists.

Like constitutions, the political and civil institutions and offices embodied
by them have had little influence on political behavior. The institutions and
even the bureaucratic structures of many African countries are unreliable:
their rules and requirements are not usually reflected in the behavior of the
people who are subject to them. Public officers cannot be counted on to perform their official duties. While they are instrumentally attached to the offices
they occupy and derive great personal and political advantages from them,
they are likely to be legally and morally detached from them and therefore
from the public interest and from the state. Their moral conduct may well
be shaped by the indigenous communities to which they belong—kinship,
clan, sectarian, patron-client, or ethnoregional groups—which are still firmly
rooted in most countries. When most Africans think of their obligations, they
are likely to think first of their communal obligations and only belatedly, if at
all, of their civic duties.[17]

The national realm of open, public politics that usually existed for a brief
and somewhat artificial period before and immediately after independence
has withered and been supplanted by personal power, influence, and intrigue
in most sub-Saharan countries. Those with power have restricted the political
process to "palace politics,"[18] an elite activity of jockeying for power and
place among big men and their collaborators who are usually concerned only
with their own narrow interests. The palace is rarely occupied by politicians
who have been placed there by the people in a competitive election and who
therefore see themselves and act as popular representatives. Little public politics or even political activity takes place outside the palace, unless we consider the public posturing of rulers or the private machinations of subjects
who desire to keep peace with the regime and its agents to be "politics." The
only political activity that ordinarily is possible is conspiracy and the threat or
use of force to resist a regime or to displace it, and such an activity can be
engaged in only by those who are prepared and equipped to take serious risks.
But even when a ruler and his regime are replaced, it rarely results in anything

more than a change of personnel; a new clique occupies the palace, but palace politics remains.

Personal rule and palace politics in sub-Saharan Africa have been significantly different from their counterparts in historical Europe or in contemporary Latin America. In predemocratic Europe rulers were empirical statebuilders who established dynastic states over territories and subjects they had acquired in competition with other statesmen or internal opponents.[19] The palace eventually became the seat of a dynasty which acquired international legitimacy from the emergent states system—which was literally a "society of princes"—by exhibiting empirical statehood.[20] In Latin America also most new states were originally the handiwork of political and military adventurers—*caudillos*—who established their de facto control of territories and peoples after a period of instability which followed the disintegration of the Spanish empire.[21] Only colonial Brazil remained whole, at first under the direct rule of the Portuguese crown and later as a republic. The personally established Spanish-speaking states eventually developed their own international community in Latin America, independent of that of Europe, but along similar institutional lines.[22] In Europe the palace has virtually disappeared as the seat of government—even in Portugal and Spain. In Latin America it still exists, but it is usually open to solicitation and consultation from the major organized interests in the country which cannot be ignored: the military, the church, industrial and commercial business corporations, trade unions, the professions, and other corporate entities. Governance in most Latin American countries is the art of forming and maintaining a stable coalition of corporate supporters without usually going so far as to institute representative democracy.[23]

There is, as yet, little substantial solicitation or consultation in African politics, not least because the corporate sectors are still more nominal than real and consequently are not strong enough to demand consultation. "Trade unions," "universities," "professions," and such exist in most countries, but their corporate significance and power are usually negligible and often undermined by members' communal attachments or private desires. Even where trade unions are significant, as in Zambia, they are under the control of a largely personal government.[24] If the palace is linked to anything of political importance in society, it is usually to noncorporate ethnic groups by means of patron-client ties. The palace in African politics is therefore rarely a creature of a social class interest—save, perhaps, for the state "bureaucracy" and "military," which themselves are often nominal more than real and are prone to internal factionalism, personalism, and breakdowns in discipline. Consequently, regime and society in sub-Saharan African countries are usually marked more by separatism and indifference than by integration, transaction, or antagonism. The relative ease with which some African countries have repeatedly been taken over by political amateurs—usually soldiers—is more than a casual indicator of the discontinuity between palace and people.

Not every sub-Saharan country has had to endure the revolving doors of palace politics with the accompanying instability. Many have experienced more enduring systems of personal rule—within the lifespan of the ruler. Admittedly, some long-lasting personal regimes rest almost exclusively on the power, guile, and ruthlessness of dictators—Mobutu's Zaire and Touré's Guinea are two well-known examples. But some personal regimes have endured by virtue of the ruling elite's desire and effort to provide political goods. Where government has secured a considerable measure of legitimacy—as for example, Ivory Coast, Kenya, Senegal, Tanzania, and Zambia—it has been owing substantially to the skill and forbearance of personal rulers. However, unlike institutional government, personal rule is the artifact of talented and public-spirited politicians who cannot live forever, and it is for that reason temporary and uncertain.

In modern states political legitimacy that is independent of personal rulers and can therefore be said to belong to the state must usually be generated by measures to expand representation and participation. One reason for the political success of Kenyatta's Kenya was the ruler's willingness to encourage genuine political access to most of the leadership positions in his regime—excluding his own—based on competitive elections within the ruling Kenya African National Union (KANU) party. Kenyatta thereby gave Kenyan politics a public dimension. It is noteworthy that his successor, Daniel arap Moi, has not interfered with Kenya's one-party democracy; indeed, he has used it to his own political advantage by holding elections and appointing newly elected politicians to leadership posts in his regime. Following the constitutional succession of Moi to the presidency established by Kenyatta, Kenya may now possess a degree of institutional legitimacy that is entirely independent of the ruler's personal authority. It is perhaps also noteworthy that the Kenyan model of one-party democracy has recently been adopted by Ivory Coast. At the time of writing some degree of popular choice in the selection of political leaders was also provided within the framework of a single ruling party in Gabon, Malawi, Sierra Leone, Tanzania, and Zambia.

These experiments with one-party democracy, although unequal in their historical significance and some of them with practically no history at all, are among the attempts registered in African politics to get beyond personal rule and to establish an institutional foundation of internal legitimacy. They may also be the most practical method of democratic institition-building in contemporary African circumstances of sharp ethnic division and limited democratic experience. But they are not the only noteworthy democratic experiments. More pluralistic democracy has been practiced since independence in Gambia and Botswana, although these countries are more politically benign and lack the ethnic divisiveness of most others. Zimbabwe's 1980 independent constitution provided for a multiparty system for ten years, but the ruling Zimbabwe African National Union hopes to achieve a one-party state earlier. In Senegal one-party rule was abandoned in 1976, and several parties now compete openly for public office. In Nigeria an ambitious attempt to reconstitute a federal democracy with a multiparty system was completed in 1979, following more than a decade of military government. Two national elections were successfully held (1979 and 1983), but on the eve of 1984 a fifth military coup ended the Nigerian democratic experiment. Constitutional democracies were briefly set up in Ghana on two separate occasions (1969 and 1979) and in Upper Volta on one occasion (1978), but each one was destroyed by military intervention not long afterwards.

These African experiments with democracy strongly suggest that political institutionalization involves time, patience, skill, dedication, and perseverance on the part of those who desire it. Unfortunately, not enough politicians and soldiers may desire it, or the most ambitious and capable may not. But the experiments also suggest, beyond doubt, that democratic institutionalization is possible in contemporary sub-Saharan Africa if leaders do desire it.

## The Capability of African States

Most sub-Saharan states are also marginal in organizational terms. The government apparatus of power usually has very limited capability and reliability. This deficiency is the result of widespread empirical conditions such as the following: low levels of education, inadequate practical training, lack of experience of public officials; cultural attitudes that impair administrative work and routine and therefore hinder law enforcement and policy implementation; shortages of talented manpower; inadequate or unavailable facilities, equipment, and materiel; and limited finances. These conditions are specific expressions of general levels of socioeconomic development in the sub-Saharan region, which are among the lowest in the world. Moreover, the arbitrary ex-colonial size, shape, and location of a number of African countries hold out limited promise of national development. In some cases development planning would have to begin with the fundamental question as to whether the inherited territorial jurisdiction was a suitable framework for development. But the immediate and profound self-interest of ruling elites in the perpetuation of their own power makes it unlikely, to say the least, that such a question will be asked, let alone seriously considered or acted upon.

Government deficiencies are often exacerbated by ambitious statist policies which are based on the uncritical assumption that governmental capabilities exist to assume the major burden of socioeconomic development. In sub-
Saharan Africa this assumption is not usually valid. Not only are economies
underdeveloped, but governments are still a long way from being rational and
cost-effective instruments of socioeconomic progress.[25] Moreover, the mere
presence of sizable government staffs, budgets, facilities, and other material
resources is not the eqiuvalent of capability. "Government" may be merely
another layer of consumers. Assigning major national development goals directly to government agencies and increasing the size of government for this
purpose may only increase the consumption of scarce national resources. The
rationalist-planning state model of government has been found wanting in
many parts of the world besides Africa, but African governments are less
likely than almost any others to be reliable instruments of socioeconomic
progress.

The general incapability of African governments must be seen in historical context. Colonial governments were usually statist. But such governments were limited in their substantive aims: they were concerned with the
pursuit of metropolitan interests, and an apparatus of power necessary for a
colonial dependency was usually all that was established. A colony does not
have the same range of governmental functions and responsibilities as an independent state. Local colonial governments did not have to be very large because part of the burden of government was borne by colonial bureaucracies
located in the metropole. Local colonial bureaucracies usually were significantly smaller, in relation to national population and wealth, than those of
their African successors, whose staffs and budgets were rapidly enlarged following independence.

The performance of many postindependence governments was adversely
affected by policies of rapid Africanization which were connected to their internal legitimacy problem: to demonstrate that an African state existed in fact
as well as in name and to garner popular legitimacy, it was usually necessary
for governments to rapidly Africanize their administrative staffs, almost always at a cost in performance. To be sure, some countries were somewhat
better equipped with trained African personnel at independence: Cameroon,
Ghana, Kenya, Nigeria, Senegal, Uganda. When Zimbabwe became independent in 1980, there was a large pool of overseas university-trained personnel to
draw upon. In contrast, in 1960 there were more than 4,600 Europeans in
senior civil service ranks in Zaire but only 3 Africans.[26] While some of this
discrepancy undoubtedly reflected racial discimination, some of it also reflected an extreme shortage of qualified Africans. The rapid reversal of this
ratio after independence was a significant factor in the initial disintegration of

the empirical state in Zaire. Ivory Coast and Malawi, each with a strong personal ruler at the helm, were able to resist popular demands for rapid restaffing with inexperienced African personnel. But most other governments were unable or unwilling to do this. Therefore, independence usually markedly reduced government capability at the very moment when far more was being demanded of it.

The general incapability of African governments must also be seen in socioeconomic context. Sub-Saharan countries rank among the world's least developed by most important measures: Gross National Product (GNP) per capita, level of industrialization, size of wage employment, degree of literacy, extent of education. Only Nigeria, with a population approaching 100 million and about 44 percent of the region's total economic output, presently exceeds the GNP of the small territory of Hong Kong. About two-thirds of the world's poorest countries are African, according to both the United Nations Conference on Trade and Development and the World Bank.[27] Moreover, the average annual growth rates of all sub-Saharan countries are very low, which means that the region is getting poorer in relation to other major regions. This is all the more disquieting since poorer regions usually grow more rapidly than wealthier regions. Although the overwhelming majority of Africans still live in rural areas and are engaged in agriculture, of which subsistence farming makes up at least half of the total agricultural output, the region is nevertheless becoming increasingly dependent on food imports. In 1950 there was self-sufficiency in food, but by 1978 some 12 million tons of cereals had to be imported; by 1990, if present trends continue, food imports will rise to 45 million tons. There is a serious prospect of mass starvation. The region's rapid growth in population contributes to both slow growth rates and the food crisis.

Most African countries and consequently their governments are highly dependent on international economic resources and capacities over which they exercise little control, such as foreign trade and aid, external investment, foreign technology and foreign skills, and world prices for their primary commodity exports. Dependency was intensified in the 1970s by a fivefold increase in the price of oil imports, which created severe foreign exchange and inflation difficulties for many countries. It was also aggravated by a deterioration in the terms of trade for most African mineral exports and by slow growth, and often stagnation, in nonfuel exports. The food crisis has added to the external dependency of many countries. Moreover, the small size and low productivity of domestic economies place limits on the taxes and other revenues that can be mobilized by national governments. Many that cannot or will not accept constraints are driven to borrow heavily from international bankers and run up the national debt. External indebtedness grew from $6 billion in 1970 to $32 billion in 1979.[28] And it continues to increase rapidly.

These travails have occurred at the same time that the size of sub-Saharan governments, as well as their involvement in national economies, have markedly increased. Although the governing apparatus of most colonies had increased substantially in size and functions since the end of World War II, it was still of modest scale at independence in most countries. During the past twenty-five years African states have become directly and deeply involved in commercial and productive activities which before independence were largely confined to the private sector: marketing, banking, transport, mining, manufacturing, in some cases even agriculture.

A 1981 World Bank study reported that public employment had reached the astonishing level of between 40 and 74 percent of total recorded paid employment in seven African countries for which data were available; it had increased far more rapidly than private employment since independence.[29] Spending on public administration, defense, and education had increased far in excess of economic growth. For twenty-one countries, expenditure on public administration and the military grew at almost twice the annual rate of economic growth. In four countries (Liberia, Mauritania, Sierra Leone, and Tanzania) government grew still more rapidly, and in three others (Chad, Uganda, and Upper Volta) government continued to expand at a high rate while the economy actually registered a negative rate of growth. If a government is intrinsically inefficient, then a mere increase of its size without an increase of its capability can result only in economic decline because resources are effectively wasted. Unfortunately, this is the situation of a number of sub-Saharan countries.

Some African rulers have complained publicly about the laxity, indifference, and even the incompetence of government officials. In Sudan, after seizing power in 1969, General Nimeiri is reported to have complained that "about 75 percent of [Sudanese] officials did not work."[30] In Cameroon, President Ahidjo commented in the late 1960s:

> A marked laxity among all civil servants is becoming more and more apparent. . . . In the majority of the administrative offices, even up to central services . . . there reigns such carelessness and such anarchy that even the least informed and least aware are . . . sorely troubled over the future of our civil service.[31]

In a 1977 report on Tanzania's troubled socialist journey, President Nyerere candidly denounced government (and parastatal) officials for incompetence, corruption, and failure to carry out duties with public spiritedness and ideological commitment: "Slackness at work, and failure to give a hard day's effort in return for wages paid, is a form of exploitation; it is an exploitation of other members of the society."[32]

Such evidence of government debility suggests that "government" in many sub-Saharan countries is often more nominal than real: Bureaucracies are likely to be private places where public resources and authority are commandeered by people who work not so much for as in the government. Such "officials" are likely to impair the capability of government, and in extreme cases they might very well destroy it. In Zaire and Ghana government has been appropriated by "free enterprising" officials who are preoccupied with gratifying their own or their supporters' private desires for power and wealth.[33] Zaire is the unusual case of a state that operates to a marked degree by "corruption"—which is probably a misnomer since corrupt conduct is the rule rather than the exception. In effect, government is the property not of the public but of those who control it, with President Mobutu and his ruling elite taking the lion's share.

Ghana at independence in 1957 had good prospects for a continuation of the economic and political development that had occurred during the colonial era. However, since independence Ghana has deteriorated under a succession of different governments—civilian and military, socialist and capitalist—who have spirited away public resources to such an extent that the economy has suffered a major long-term decline. Today Ghana is one of the more marginal states in West Africa—a textbook case of civil and socioeconomic decay. When gross government incompetence and misconduct and corresponding public cynicism and mistrust become settled features of political life, as they have in Zaire and Ghana, they are probably extremely difficult to reverse without foreign intervention. But if foreign personnel were brought in to restore the minimal conditions of empirical statehood, it would make a mockery of a country's political independence.

The decay of empirical statehood in sub-Saharan Africa is by no means an inevitable or irreversible process. On the contrary, it is very significantly the result of government conduct. Some countries have exhibited respectable administrative capability and corresponding socioeconomic development. Ivory Coast and Kenya are well-known examples—although they have experienced some difficulties since the late 1970s.[34] Ivory Coast, with a physical, socioeconomic, and cultural environment very similar to neighboring Ghana and a less promising posture at independence in 1960, has achieved sustained economic growth. The government of Ivory Coast has been profoundly different from the governments of Ghana; the primary difference has been the economic enlightenment and political acumen of the ruler. Houphouët-Boigny has recognized that socioeconomic progress depends on a government service staffed by skilled, experienced, dedicated, and honest officials who know how to manage the local economy. The presence of a large number of competent and reliable French nationals in the Ivorian public service and parastatals is

not coincidental to the Ivorian achievement. The Ivorian ruler's economic enlightenment consists in his utilization of these officials; his political acumen
consists in his ability to get away with it. Under his stewardship, and by the
agency of a reliable managerial state which has been Africanized belatedly
and gradually without adverse effects on its performance, the Ivory Coast has
become a prosperous country in sub-Saharan terms.

Kenya also has exhibited substantial and prolonged socioeconomic development since independence in 1963. It embarked upon independence with an
administrative capacity inherited from the colonial rulers, to provide not only
the conditions of law and order, but also a proven system of agricultural management and extension services which had been built originally to serve
Kenya's highly productive European settler agricultural economy. Kenyatta
surprised many observers by his prudent acceptance of this inheritance, which
was also an acceptance of the basic political-economy assumptions behind
it—namely, that the socioeconomic role of government was primarily to supervise and serve a private economy. Major political efforts went into the cautious Africanization of the government administration, with general administrative rosters coming first and technical positions last. Similar efforts went
into the Africanization of the agricultural exporting economy, which had been
developed largely by Europeans during the colonial period. Consequently,
government and economy continued to perform well following independence.
Many ordinary Kenyans benefited from the socioeconomic goods of a reliable
government, particularly an effective agricultural management policy. Moreover, Kenya's one-party democracy regularly has enabled voters to dismiss
politicians who do not contribute sufficiently to the welfare of their districts.
The prudent and patriarchal rule of Kenyatta undoubtedly contributed to the
country's performance.

Nkrumah once said that socialism was necessary in sub-Saharan Africa
because capitalism was too complicated. The socioeconomic ills of Nkrumah's
Ghana and Nyerere's Tanzania, among other African experiments with socialism, make it extremely difficult not to conclude that the first part of this
statement is mistaken if by "socialism" is meant extensive statism in socioeconomic affairs. But the socioeconomic goods of Houphouët-Boigny's Ivory
Coast and Kenyatta's Kenya do not support the opposite conclusion that capitalism is necessary. Instead, they suggest that Africans must establish reliable
governments of reasonable size and responsibility if they are to enjoy increased socioeconomic goods. Our examples indicate that government reliability entails at least the following: prudent and knowledgeable rulers; able
and responsible administrative and technical staffs; incremental policies. Ambitious projects to bring about a major socioeconomic transformation of society and economy by unreliable and heavily staffed governments are likely

not only to fail, but also to result in increased socioeconomic hardship. In short, the building of a reliable government is not a revolutionary enterprise; it is a prudent project of gradually building upon what already exists and works.

## Sovereignty and State-Building

As we have discussed, sub-Saharan jurisdictions are maintained not by African governments individually or by a balance of power but by the norms of the states system—that is, by the recognition of other states; by the rules of the Organization of African Unity (OAU) which are concerned primarily with the preservation of inherited colonial boundaries; by other international organizations, particularly the United Nations; and by general international law. Angola has been invaded and temporarily occupied in the south by a hostile state—South Africa—and its government also has lost control of substantial territory in the southeast to an internal opponent—Jonas Savimbi's National Union for the Total Independence of Angola (UNITA), which has received material assistance from Pretoria. But South Africa could not annex occupied Angolan territory and expect to have such a fait accompli recognized by the international community, and UNITA could not expect to acquire external sovereignty over the Angolan territories it controls. Angola's international legitimacy has prevented both developments. External sovereignty is a concrete international lifetime that both permits marginal African states to survive and upholds the privileges of rulers. In sub-Saharan Africa sovereignty is an international right not of peoples but of rulers—their "negative freedom" from external intervention.[35]

The fundamental motivation in African politics is to acquire and to retain sovereignty, which is bestowed more or less automatically upon those who are for the time being in control of a national government. The methods of acquiring such control and of exercising it, and the territorial extent of it, are considerations of little or no practical importance in determining the right in any particular case. Coups d'etat, abusive and incompetent governance, and incomplete territorial control have been as sufficient in determining it as democratic elections, constitutional and developmental government, and effective central regulation of an entire territory. At the time of writing (1983) the problematical government of Flight Lieutenant Rawlings in badly decayed Ghana was as sovereign as the well-founded government of President Houphouët-Boigny in Ivory Coast. In contemporary Africa sovereignty and empirical statehood are utterly separate phenomena. Indeed, the emergence of many marginal states—not only in Africa, but also in Oceania and other parts of the Third World—has necessitated virtually the abandonment of any empirical requirements of statehood. Otherwise, international trusteeships would have to be established over marginal states, and it is very unlikely that either developed or underdeveloped governments would be willing to enter such relationships.

The international community cannot intervene in the internal affairs of a sovereign member to prevent its empirical deterioration, even if a government seriously undermines the civil and socioeconomic conditions of its jurisdiction—as the politically abusive and economically incompetent governments of Presidents Mobutu in Zaire, Amin in Uganda, and Macias in Equatorial Guinea have done. The empirical grounds that once were embodied in international law to justify the withdrawal of sovereignty—such as the absence of an "effective government"[36]—are no longer acceptable in international practice for the intensely practical reason that if they were, sovereignty would probably have to be withdrawn from a fairly large number of Third World countries and some alternative international authority established to take its place.

Even the massive violation of human rights is insufficient to justify international action. When President Nyerere's army invaded Uganda and overthrew the tyrannical government of Idi Amin in 1979, the action was roundly condemned by African leaders, including the chairman of the OAU.[37] They were preoccupied with the singular fact that one African state had invaded another and overthrown its ruler, and they were anxious that this action not establish a dangerous precedent in African international relations. The episode disclosed in no uncertain terms that the right to external sovereignty is considered by Africa's rulers to be absolute. In addition, the leaders have emphasized the importance not only of "human rights" but of "peoples' rights" and have resolved to prepare an "African Charter of Human and Peoples' Rights."[38] Evidently, "peoples' rights" are collective rights that can be claimed only by sovereign governments. We should not expect either national populations as a whole or the numerous traditional nationalities into which they are divided—ethnic communities—to acquire effective rights against sovereign governments under such a charter. Nor should we expect the rights of individuals to balance those of sovereigns.

Under current international norms the international community can confer juridical statehood, but it cannot confer empirical statehood because this is an internal condition of a government's domestic legitimacy and effectiveness. The most that the international community can contribute to empirical statehood is foreign aid and favorable external conditions that might assist an independent government in its efforts at state-building. Moreover, if African governments engage in state-building but are handicapped by a shortage of human and material resources or "positive freedom" to act[39]—as sub-Saharan state-builders are—they cannot usually depend upon the international community to provide sufficient aid to overcome their incapacity; nor can they expect their appeals to the conscience or self-interest of rich countries to meet with an adequate response.[40] At present there is no mandatory system of international aid, and the amount of material foreign assistance is a tiny fraction of global resources. The international community does not exist primarily to promote state-building, nor has it ever existed for that purpose. It remains largely what it has always been: a conservative system for maintaining international order rather than a developmental system for building up weaker and less fortunate members.

Owing to the region's underdeveloped material conditions, it might be concluded that indigenous civil development is not realizable in African countries. On the contrary: it is fully realizable because it is contingent not on material resources but on civic morals and political practices which are within the reach of everyone. Political institutionalization, the practice whereby politicians and other powerful actors in a country subscribe to impersonal and impartial rules, depends on the understanding, desire, willingness, and ability of African leaders. The fact that such countries as Botswana, Kenya, and Senegal have managed to institute workable and acceptable practices in their political life demonstrates both that civil development is not precluded by underdeveloped socioeconomic conditions and that it is contingent mainly on rulers and other national leaders.

The development of a poor country's governmental apparatus—organizational development—involves other factors, however. This facet of statebuilding always involves material resources at least in part; thus it is usually open to influence and sometimes even to control by external agencies whose resources are sought and sometimes depended upon. A resource donor can exercise external leverage over a domestic economy and therefore indirect leverage over government organizational development; direct external leverage is also possible. Dependency theorists rest their interpretations of African underdevelopment on this possibility. They usually argue that foreign resources are employed by external powers—public as well as private—to manipulate African socioeconomic development in a way that favors those powers' material interests and denies substantive development to the dependent country. African ruling elites are sometimes seen as implicated in this manipulation.[41]

The dependency analysis assumes both the desire and the capacity of African governments to serve foreign interests effectively. It might be safer to assume that external agencies with material interests in African countries have a strong desire to exercise leverage over African governments to ensure that their grants, loans, and investments will not be wasted or mismanaged and that African rulers know this. External leverage over an underdeveloped

African government may be limited by its very underdevelopment; government disorganization and corruption may even thwart it, as seems to be the case in Zaire. In such circumstances external agencies may be powerless. They may be able to bribe government officials or seek their individual cooperation by other means, but they may nonetheless not be able to get the government to perform effectively in the direction they desire.

A significant new form of external leverage over the economic policies and practices of African governments (and other Third World governments which have become major international debtors) is loan conditions set by the International Monetary Fund (IMF). The virtual bankruptcy of some countries, including several in Africa, has recently transformed the IMF's primary mission into that of financially disciplining such countries by making much needed loans contingent upon internal reforms. (Of course, for the major debtors such as Mexico, Brazil, and Argentina a reverse leverage exists in the threat of default, which would seriously disrupt the international economy.) The much smaller and weaker sub-Saharan debtors do not hold such a threat. In Zaire the IMF installed its own personnel in central state agencies as a condition of making additional loans, but without noteworthy success in reducing the corruption, financial chaos, and indiscipline of the Mobutu regime.[42]

Such loan conditions arrangements have been condemned by Third World governments as a form of neocolonialism. Some African rulers have complained that the IMF is undermining their independence (which it is), and one finance minister is reported as saying: "My country is now a colony of the IMF. I am not making a judgement, merely stating a fact."[43] This is an important development in international relations which restricts the freedom of the regimes which have been affected by it. But it is too early to determine whether or not it is a permanent encroachment on the freedom of rulers who have badly mismanaged their political economies. If it proves to be permanent, it will indeed be a partial reversion to a regime of international paternalism by countries which are wealthy and capable over those which are not.

Sub-Saharan governments remain far more dependent on their own resourcefulness than on external resources, however. As we indicated, the development of government capability and of the economy is possible and has occurred in some countries, and it has been contingent upon the enlightenment of the rulers and the practical knowledge and reliability of public officials. The governments of Ivory Coast and Kenya give the appearance of avoiding economic ideology, either capitalist or socialist, and of pursuing economic practices and policies that are carefully adjusted to the real conditions of their national economies. By contrast, at least until recently the government of Tanzania has given the impression of believing that economic policy can be guided by statist ideology to produce development. But the lack of substantial Tanzanian development, the high costs where it has occasionally occurred, and the evident deterioration in parts of the economy throw a shadow on this belief. In short, it is not solely the quantity of resources available that appears to be crucial to organizational development in sub-Saharan Africa; it is the quality of governments.

In enlightened autocracies, such as Ivory Coast, there appears to be an understanding on the part of government as to what constitutes a successful dynastic state; long ago it was summarized by Francois Quesnay, "*Pauvre payson, pauvre royaume; pauvre royaume, pauvre roi*" (Poor peasant, poor king; poor king, poor kingdom).[44] Largely as a result of the Ivorian government's prudent and realistic economic statecraft, the Ivorian peasantry enjoys one of the highest standards of living of any African peasantry, and Ivory Coast has one of the best records of economic growth in the sub-Saharan region.[45] But enlightened governments have been the exception rather than the rule in sub-Saharan Africa since independence. This is not the place to attempt to explain why, but we are convinced that at least the intimation of an explanation is contained in the logic of personal rule. In the conditions of contemporary Africa, enlightened government is an independent variable; as we have noted, the survival of a personal regime does not depend upon organized governmental capability and the consequent capacity to foster socioeconomic goods. Indeed, a logic of personal rule—get what you can while you can—encourages the opposite: the personal appropriation and consumption of resources by those with power, usually in the form of nepotism, corruption, and patronage. This is what most Africans have come to expect of their rulers. Lacking the political opportunities to organize themselves, the people are in no position to deter rulers from engaging in such behavior. Those who are in a position to deter, such as the military, are themselves usually more interested in consumption than in development. And foreign agencies can provide only limited deterrence. Only African rulers can independently set a government on a course of organizational development.

The crucial problem of state-building in most sub-Saharan countries at the present time is the profoundly political necessity of changing the behavior of powerful people—political and military leaders in particular—so that the state is supported rather than undermined by their actions and is thereby able to provide the citizen with political goods. While this is a difficult task, it is not impossible to achieve. The ability of anyone to provide support ultimately is not a question of resources; it is a question of will.

## Summary and Conclusion

State marginality is a pervasive condition in sub-Saharan Africa that was brought about by a revolutionary change in the international system in which self-determination was extended to arbitrary political units and unproven governments. Juridicial statehood was usually acquired before a solid foundation of empirical statehood had been established: the internal legitimacy and capability of most sub-Saharan countries was not substantial at the time of independence. Only a minority of African governments have realized noteworthy civil and socioeconomic development since then by reasonable, prudent, and fortunate decisions. The majority of countries have experienced some of the following typical adversities: some rulers squandered national resources, or engaged in abusive misgovernment, or pursued ill-advised ideologies; some governments foundered amid turbulent and uncontrollable natural or social forces, or presided over jurisdictions which offer very limited opportunities for development. Marginality is not an abstract quality of states; on the contrary, it is a concrete condition of people who experience deprivations of human rights and socioeconomic welfare authored by their own governments.

The underdevelopment of sub-Saharan countries is generally acknowledged. But underdevelopment is usually understood in materialist terms and attributed to adverse socioeconomic conditions in these countries and their global circumstancs; it is not usually considered to be also in part an adverse civil condition that is manifested in the current rules and practices of the international community. Indeed, to notice a relationship between underdevelopment and self-determination is to question a silent assumption of the international community, namely, that self-determination is an absolute right of sovereign governments and is free of any substantial costs. At present, the costs of self-determination is a taboo subject.

The international community and the United Nations in particular cannot be expected to raise a question that would provoke a storm of protest from many Third World governments and their supporters, whose voice is a majority in the General Assembly. For the present, the question can only be addressed indirectly, unofficially, and pragmatically. The recent role of the IMF is an acknowledgment of the problem that is suggestive of the new kind of international relations and responsibilities that are necessary. However, it is not a formal change in the international system whereby some responsibility for the provision of socioeconomic goods is vested in international bodies and it is vociferously opposed by many Third World leaders. As regards the abusive practices of some independent regimes, at the present time all that seems possible are activities of private, voluntary organizations such as Amnesty International which investigate and publicize the human rights violations of sovereign governments. Major practical barriers presently stand in the way of international changes that might address the root problems of marginal statehood, and we are under no illusions that the international community can or will adjust its rules and practices on this issue in the foreseeable future.

Our immediate concern is with the theoretical barriers to such change.

Conventional development policy originally considered self-determination to be a necessary condition of Third World development. According to General Principle xiv of the U.N. Conference on Trade and Development held in 1964 "Complete decolonization . . . is a necessary condition for economic development and the exercise of sovereign rights over natural resources."[46] However, the existence of sub-Saharan countries which have been independent for several decades but have experienced little development casts doubt on the proposition.

More recently the relationship has been ignored, probably because decolonization has run its course. The 1969 Report of the Commission on International Development (Pearson Commission) reviewed numerous socio-economic issues of Third World development but gave scant attention to the economic problems of small-scale jurisdictions and ignored obstacles to economic integration presented by sovereign governments and ruling elites in particular.[47] The 1980 Report of the Independent Commission on International Development Issues (Brandt Commission) glossed over these questions and appealed to the sense of social justice and the self-interest of the North for a greater transfer of resources to the South.[48] Both commissions recognize the resource scarcities and material needs of the South, but fail to draw some crucial distinctions as to the location of need and responsibility within and among southern countries. "The South" is a statistical abstraction; in fact, there are many southern regions and countries at different levels of civil and socio-economic development. Moreover, the inequalities in most southern countries are very large with rulers and other government officals, among others, enjoying enormous privileges usually at the expense of ordinary citizens. The question why substantial resources should be transferred to governments that may be corrupt or incompetent or negligent or abusive has not been addressed by these and similar reports. Of course, it would be an entirely different question if the transfer of resources could be made directly to needy southern citizens.

Why development theory has largely ignored the relationship between self-determination and underdevelopment is a question that we can only touch upon. Theorists may also be unwilling to raise taboo subjects; however, it seems more likely that their concepts obscure the relationship. Marxian development theory conceptually excludes the independent reality and effects of juridical statehood by its views of morals, law, and the state as superstructure. For example, dependency theory focuses on global economic relationships in accounting for Third World underdevelopment and ignores international law. Non-Marxian development theory considers the juridical sphere to be "normative" and therefore insubstantial and insignificant. For example, Weberian theory conceptualizes international relations as primarily power relations; the juridical sphere is seen as a facade with no independent consequences on the behavior of governments or the development of states. The consequences of international law and morality, and the costs and benefits of self-determination in particular, cannot be investigated if the important distinction between juridical and empirical statehood is not drawn or if the juridical is not considered to be a significant *independent* variable.[49]

## NOTES

1. We follow Wight's definition: "By international legitimacy I mean the collective judgment of international society about rightful membership of [sic] the family of nations." Martin Wight, *Systems of States*, ed. Hedley Bull (London: Leicester University Press in Association with the London School of Economics and Political Science, 1977), p. 153.

2. *Everyman's United Nations: A Complete Handbood of the Activities and Evolution of the United Nations During Its First Twenty Years, 1945–1965* (New York: United Nations, 1968), pp. 370–371, 396–399. The 1960 United Nations General Assembly Declaration on the Granting of Independence to Colonial Countries and Peoples stated: "All peoples have the right to self-determination"; "Inadequacy of political, economic, social, or educational preparedness should never serve as a pretext for delaying independence."

3. Thomas Hodgkin, *Nationalism in Colonial Africa* (London: Frederick Muller, 1956), Part I.

4. Leo Kuper, *Genocide* (Harmondsworth: Penguin Books, 1981).

5. Robert H. Jackson and Carl G. Rosberg, *Personal Rule in Black Africa: Prince, Autocrat, Prophet, Tyrant* (Berkeley: University of California Press, 1982).

6. See *Accelerated Development in Sub-Saharan Africa: An Agenda for Action* (Washington, D.C.: World Bank, 1981).

7. Robert H. Jackson and Carl G. Rosberg, "Why Africa's Weak States Persist: The Empirical and the Juridical in Statehood," *World Politics* 35, 1 (October 1982): 1–24.

8. Wight, pp. 168–172.

9. The term "political goods" refers to desirable social conditions and individual rights and protections provided by the state, such as civil and political rights, social welfare, and economic opportunities. The term originated with J. Roland Pennock, "Political Development, Political Systems, and Political Goods," *World Politics* 18, 3 (April 1966): 420–427. We are not referring to what economists term "public goods" or "collective goods," although there are some similarities.

10. Max Weber, *The Theory of Social and Economic Organization*, ed. Talcott Parsons (New York: Free Press, 1964), p. 156. See also Youssef Cohen, Brian R. Brown, and A. F. K. Organski, "The Paradoxical Nature of State Making: The Violent Creation of Order," *American Political Science Review* 75, 4 (December 1981): 901–910.

11. Robert H. Jackson and Carl G. Rosberg, "Why Africa's Weak States Persist"; and by the same authors, "Pax Africana and its Problems," *Africa in the Post-Colonial Era*, eds. Richard E. Bissell and Michael Radu (Rutgers, N.J.: Transaction Press, 1984), pp. 157–182.

12. Ian Brownlie, *Principles of Public International Law*, 3rd ed. (Oxford: Clarendon Press, 1979), ch. 4, and "Why Africa's Weak States Persist," p. 3.

13. Michael Oakeshott, "The Vocabulary of a Modern European State," *Political Studies* 23 (June and September 1977): 319–341, 409–414.

14. See John J. Stremlau, *The International Politics of the Nigerian Civil War 1967–1970* (Princeton: Princeton University Press, 1977).

15. As J. Crawford points out, "Sovereignty, in its origin merely the location of supreme power within a particular territorial unit, necessarily came from within and therefore did not require the recognition of other states or princes." ("The Criteria for Statehood in International Law," *British Year Book of International Law*, 1976–1977, p. 96).

16. E. L. Jones, *The European Miracle: Environments, Economies, and Geopolitics in the History of Europe and Asia* (Cambridge, England: Cambridge University Press, 1981), pp. 118–119.

17. Robert Jackson, *Plural Societies and New States: A Conceptual Analysis*, Research Series No. 30 (Berkeley: Institution of International Studies, 1977), pp. 20–26.

18. Bernard Crick, *In Defense of Politics* (Harmondsworth: Penguin Books, 1964), pp. 20–24.

19. Jones; also see the classical study by Jacob Burckhart, *The Civilization of the Renaissance in Italy*, vol. 1 (New York: Harper Colophon Books, 1958), part 1. For a specific example of European state-building, see Gerhard Ritter, *Frederick the Great* (Berkeley, Los Angeles, London: University of California Press, 1968).

20. Wight, ch. 3.

21. Jacques Lambert, *Latin America: Social Structure and Political Institutions*, trans. Helen Katel (Berkeley, Los Angeles, London: University of California Press, 1967), ch. 8.

22. Peter Lyon, "New States and International Order," in *The Basis of International Order*, ed. Alan James (London: Oxford University Press, 1973, pp. 31–34).

23. Charles Anderson, *Politics and Economic Change in Latin America* (Princeton, N.J.: Van Nostrand Co., 1967), ch. 4.

24. See Cherry Gertzel, "Labour and the State: The Case of Zambia's Mineworkers Union—A Review Article," *Journal of Commonwealth and Comparative Politics* 13, 3 (November 1975): 290–304.

25. Jon R. Morris, "The Transferability of Western Management Concepts and Programs: An East African Perspective," in *Education and Training for Public Sector Management in Developing Countries*, ed. Lawrence D. Stifel, James S. Coleman, and Joseph E. Black (Special Report from the Rockefeller Foundation, March 1977), pp. 77–83.

26. Crawford Young, *Politics in the Congo* (Princeton: Princeton University Press, 1965), p. 402.

27. See *Accelerated Development in Sub-Saharan Africa*, p. 3.

28. *Accelerated Development in Sub-Saharan Africa*, pp. 17–23.

29. Ibid., pp. 40–41.

30. Peter Kilner, "The Sudan: A Year of Revolution," *African Affairs* 60 (October 1970), p. 375.

31. Quoted in Victor T. LeVine, *The Cameroon Federal Republic* (Ithaca and London: Cornell University Press, 1971), p. 142.

32. Julius Nyerere, *The Arusha Declaration Ten Years After* (Dar es Salaam: Government Printer, 1977), pp. 27–48.

33. On Zaire, see Colin Legum, ed., *Africa Contemporary Record: Annual Survey and Documents 1976–1977* (New York and London: Africana Publishing, 1978), p. B 528. On Ghana, see Richard Jeffries, "Rawlings and the Political Economy of Underdevelopment in Ghana," *African Affairs* 81, 234 (July 1982): 307–317, and Dennis Austin, "Ghana and the Return to Civilian Rule: 1," *West Africa* 2851 (4 February 1972): 115.

34. Colin Legum, ed., *Africa Contemporary Record: Annual Survey and Documents 1981–82* (New York and London: Africana Publishing, 1981, B 449–452, B 203–208.

35. On the concept of "negative freedom," see Isaiah Berlin, *Four Essays on Liberty* (London, Oxford, New York: Oxford University Press, 1969), ch. 3.

36. See Brownlie, pp. 74–82.

37. Colin Legum, ed., *Africa Contemporary Record: Annual Survey and Documents 1979–80* (New York: Africana Publishing, 1981), pp. A 61–2.

38. Ibid., p. C 21.

39. On the concept of "positive freedom," see Berlin.

40. The self-interest and conscience of the North are premises for altering North-South relations adopted by the Brandt Commission. See *North-South: A Program for Survival* (Report of the Independent Commission on International Development Issues [Cambridge, Mass.: MIT Press, 1980]).

41. The literature on African dependency is vast, but see especially Colin Leys, *Underdevelopment in Kenya: The Political Economy of Neo-Colonialism* (Berkeley and Los Angeles: University of California Press, 1974) and by the same author "African Economic Development in Theory and Practice," *Black Africa: A Generation After Independence, Daedalus* 111, 2 (Spring 1982): 99–124.

42. See "Blumenthal Report: Mobutu's Financial Secrets Exposed," *New African* 184 (January 1983): 11–14.

43. Quoted in Richard Hall, "The Paymasters Who Are Africa's New Colonialists," *The Observer* (31 July 1983).

44. Quoted in Ludwig von Mises, *Nation, State and Economy: Contributions to the Politics and History of Our Time*, trans. Leland B. Yeager (New York and London: New York University Press, 1983), p. 31.

45. *Accelerated Development in Sub-Saharan Africa*, p. 36.

46. Quoted in P. T. Bauer, *Equality, the Third World, and Economic Delusion* (Cambridge: Harvard University Press, 1981), p. 164.

47. *Partners in Development: Report of the Commission on International Development* (New York, Washington, London: Praeger Publishers, 1969).

48. In particular, see the introductory essay by Willy Brandt, *North-South*, pp. 7–29, and ch. 1.

49. In John Lonsdale's long and comprehensive survey of the literature on African states the topic of external sovereignty is explicitly discussed only as a very brief aside in a footnote. See his "States and Social Processes in Africa: A Historiographical Survey," *The African Studies Review* XXIV, 2/3 (June/September 1981): 139, 207.

CHAPTER 4

# State-Ethnic Relations
# in Middle Africa

*Donald Rothchild*

Students of state-ethnic relations in Africa have tended to make use of two rather straightforward models of analysis. A "control" model focuses attention on efforts of the state to repress, isolate, or dissipate ethnic and other interest demands through political, administrative, or military coercion. The "consociational" model, recently put forward by some analysts as a realizable alternative for multiethnic societies, presupposes, by contrast, a more or less open organization of social divisions along party lines, leaving the management of ethnic and other demands to conciliation among elites of the various groups. But while the latter model supposes a degree of cooperation among elites, internal cohesion within groups, and public acquiescence in formal compromise that is scarcely apparent in Africa today, the former one presupposes effective administrative power most African states are far from possessing.

Neither the control nor the consociational model describes African realities adequately; nevertheless, as we shall see, elements of both are present in Africa. African states run the gamut from largely coercive, control-oriented states like South Africa to pluralistic systems such as Nigeria under the federal constitution of 1979. And all along the continuum the state employs a variety of mechanisms to manage ethnic relations. Thus public policies which abolished chieftaincy (Guinea) denied the right to organize ethnic-based associations (Kenya, Zaire) and political parties (Ghana), or promoted single-party or no-party systems are common control mechanisms designed to overcome what are perceived to be adverse effects of ethnic political action. At the same time, implicit principles of proportional representation and allocation of

I wish to express my appreciation to the editors and to Michael Foley, Arend Lijphart, Percy Hintzen, Maure Goldschmidt, Mark Tessler, and Edmond Keller for helpful comments on the first draft of the manuscript.

71

resources, co-optation of ethnic elites and factions, and informal bargaining between the state center and representatives of the ethnic (or ethnoregional) "periphery" are widespread consociational-type practices. Politics is not normally the zero-sum relationship described by June Kronholz: "Tribal loyalties run deep in Africa . . . the government owns the land, the crops, the industry . . . and the winner takes it all. There isn't any second place in African politics."[1]

In order to understand state-ethnic relations, then, a more complex model is needed, one which explicitly recognizes the unique aspects of the middle-African situation (a region including those African-led countries between the Sahara and South Africa which are horizontally stratified societies, i.e., societies which are segmented but which accept the moral equality of their various identity groups). Historically, middle-African states such as Zambia, Uganda, and the Cameroun moved quickly from the formal, regularized process of political exchanges hammered out with the departing colonial powers on largely Eurocentric lines, to forms of indirect and informal exchanges within the parameters of one-party or no-party states. Postcolonial middle-African regimes, anxious to consolidate their hold over the bureaucratic apparatus as well as the society at large, shunned classical, European formulas of statecraft and sought to restructure conflict along controlled yet cooperative lines. Legal oppositions, constitutional guarantees, and the autonomous competing centers of power established by the independence constitutions were rejected in favor of systems of control dominated by the executive and administrative branches of government.

Yet the reduced scope for antagonistic conflict resulting from these measures hardly brought an end to ethnoregional rivalries, and African leaders moved quickly to accommodate ethnic (as well as other interest group) demands through informal and quiet bargaining among elites. Thus, even in Guinea, where Sékou Touré's *Parti Démocratique de Guinée* abolished the institution of chieftaincy and the ethnic-based party committees, party officials had to take special care, in the early years at least, to blunt the force of local particularism by means of ethnic balancing.[2] Hence, in contrast to the classical models of hegemonic ("control") and consociational conflict management, the middle-African situation often subtly reconciles the realities of political exchange among disparate groups with the central state elites' insistence upon enhanced control. Such practices allow, even encourage, agreement on political exchange outcomes while containing, and often avoiding, the zero-sum antagonisms which might otherwise undermine the frail political order.

The model which characterizes this situation will be described here as "hegemonial exchange." It is not a pure case of centrally determined coordination ("control") because the middle-African state is "soft"[3] and lacks the capacity to impose unilaterally its decisions on ethnoregional groups; it is also not a pure case of direct negotiations among ethnoregional spokesmen combined in a freely elected coalition of elites ("consociationalism") because open, partisan competition in elections has been shunned. Rather, as an ideal type, hegemonial exchange is a form of state-facilitated coordination in which a somewhat autonomous central state and a number of considerably less autonomous ethnoregional (and other) interests engage in a process of mutual accommodation on the basis of commonly accepted procedural norms, rules, or understandings.[4]

Like any control system, hegemonial exchange is a means to the end of political stability. The state, whether led by a particular ethnic elite or not, may seek to channel conflict along constructive lines by adopting expedient courses of political action that will ensure the participation of elite spokesmen in the decision-making process and promote measures of reciprocity in the distribution of tangible public goods. In effect, the dominant political elite, conscious of the state's limited capacity in middle Africa, exchanges participation and distributable resources for local support and compliance with its regulations. It seeks to foster coordination within a framework of control.

In a hegemonial exchange type arrangement, the process features continuous informal exchanges at the political center between key state actors and spokesmen for ethnoregional and other group interests [within the context of a single- or no-party system]. Ethnoregional intermediaries, themselves members of the dominant political class[5] as well as spokesmen for subnational interests, must engage in simultaneous negotiations in two political arenas—with diverse ethnoregional factions at the periphery and with the central leadership in the cabinet or party national council—and also in face-to-face relations with members of the executive and bureaucracy. Further interchanges with the spokesmen for other ethnic interests may take place when the elite cartel assembles or at sessions of the national legislature.[6]

In terms of the regularity of these exchanges, the styles and preferences of the state leader or leaders and of the ethnoregional intermediaries are critical to the persistence—and hence the enduring nature—of these relationships. Where the state leadership makes effective use of its elite cartel or its two-way exchanges with ethnic interests to facilitate mutual accommodations, and where ethnoregional spokesmen also are prepared to act in accordance with the state's prevailing norms and values and to direct group demands along recognized lines, constructive conflict may materialize. The partially autonomous state and the subregional actors will then be encountering one another in conformity with state guidelines.[7]

Such a conflict-resolving outcome seems most likely to occur when both core and periphery actors shape their political behavior so as to advance the mutual interests of the dominant political class of which both are a part. This identification with dominant class interests, however, may weaken the exchange process if it undermines the subregional intermediary's perceived ties to his local constituency base, causing a burgeoning of candidates with claims to local legitimacy. As Nelson Kasfir notes, the central government could then find itself in a situation where it "is actively looking for local leaders with whom to bargain but cannot find anyone likely to be effective because the local groups are too fragmented." Although such a situation gives central authorities great leverage, it has the disadvantage, as Kasfir points out, that bargains struck could come unstruck.[8] Hence, a process of hegemonially controlled reciprocity can only be expected to settle conflict amicably on a long-term basis where both state and ethnoregional actors interact in accordance with the state's organizing principles, while maintaining minimal legitimacy among their diverse publics. And the transfer of state resources in the process of hegemonial exchange must be seen to benefit ethnoregional clients as well as patrons if the political relationship is to gain broad acceptance over time.

This rough sketch will be filled out in the following pages by showing that hegemonial exchange, rather than current Western models of conflict management, conforms to practices at work in much of middle Africa during the past twenty-five years. In doing this, the chapter also seeks to indicate that, contrary to the impression conveyed in the popular press, state-ethnic relations are not normally adversarial encounters; on the contrary, soft state conditions incline the dominant political class to strengthen its ability to govern by reconciling exchange and control. Finally, in the concluding section, the chapter will touch briefly on the possible costs of a hegemonial exchange approach in terms of economic efficiency and effective political leadership.

### Evidence of Hegemonial Exchange

The evidence on hegemonial exchange practices in middle Africa is highly fragmentary and varied, running from ad hoc transactions between state and ethnic representatives at the top of the hierarchy to a more broadly encompassing network of exchanges within an informal grand coalition of elites. The practices of political exchange are so various, in military and civilian-led regimes alike, that the critical question is less the reality of interchanges than the legitimacy accorded them by the state.

For instance, the military governor or commissioner of a subregion may differ little from his civilian counterpart either in his operational mode or in his closeness to his constituents' demands.[9] This was brought home in a forceful manner to this author in an April 1976 interview in Tamale with the regional commissioner of the northern region of Ghana. In the commissioner's description of efforts to negotiate directly on behalf of his region with the Minister of Finance and appropriate ministry officials in Accra there was little to distinguish it from what might have been expected of a civilian broker for ethnoregional interests. Nigeria's military governors, the sole official points of contact with the Supreme Military Council and the Federal Executive Council during the Ironsi regime in 1966, were careful to recognize the higher authority of the head of the National Military Government and the Supreme Commander of the Armed Forces and to adopt a national perspective, so far as possible, on policy matters; nevertheless, they did not remain long in office before coming to advocate subregional interests at the center. Robin Luckham notes: "Although none of the Military Governors had entirely abandoned the anti-political image . . . , they began to conceive of themselves as administrators and leaders concerned with the interests of their regions as a whole, in much the same way that they had previously identified with the national interest."[10]

In postrevolutionary Ethiopia, provincial commissioners appointed by the Dergue, more often than not originally hailing from the area over which they now exercise authority, act as ethnoregional buffers, making demands upon the center for public goods.[11] And in neighboring Sudan, the man who served as president of the High Executive Council for the southern region during part of the 1981–82 period, Major-General Gasmallah Rassas, behaved in a manner similar to that of his civilian predecessors and successor. He traveled to Khartoum, sometimes accompanied by the regional minister of finance, education, or health, to negotiate with President Gaafar Nimeiri or the appropriate ministers for increased public allocations on behalf of his constituents.[12] In brief, then, hegemonial exchange practices, often unrecognized and lacking in legitimacy, are by no means restricted to regimes led by civilians or, for that matter, to regimes which are non-Marxist in orientation.

Although civilian-led regimes, which exhibit various forms of two-party or coalitional "bonds between individuals of unequal power and socioeconomic status,"[13] differ considerably as to the legitimacy they accord these political relationships, the reality of these linkages is apparent. The four civilian presidents or acting presidents of the High Executive Council of the Sudan's southern region from the time of the signing of the Addis Ababa agreement in 1972 to the redivision of the south in 1983 (Abel Alier, 1972–78; Joseph Lagu, 1978–80; Peter Gatkouth, 1980–81; and Joseph Tombura, 1982–83) all performed a similar function of representing ethnoregional interests at the center. This process of interest articulation at the center was facilitated for Alier by his also serving as Sudan's vice-president, a post also held by Lagu, the former Anya-Nya leader, during Tombura's tenure in office at the subregional level. Thus, the Nimeiri-led state has come to play a critical role of

mediating among group interests. "Without the extravagant use of patronage
and coordination of parochial interests by Nimeiri through his network of
portégés and informers in the national sphere and supporters in the foreign
sphere," observes Dunstan Wai, "the Nimeiri regime would probably have
collapsed by now."[14]

Political linkages between state leaders and ethnoregional buffers were
also evident in Uganda in the 1960s and in Zambia in the 1960s and 1970s,
but without in either case the president's imprimatur. In Uganda, the decentralized nature of political parties and the continued strong influence of
ethnic and religious politics in the voting process encouraged subregional
politicians and administrators as well as members of parliament to look to
their district power bases for political survival.[15] As a result, they tended to
emerge as the champions of communal interests in their relations with the
center. Acholi politicians, for example, "rarely operated in isolation from the
central government"; rather they forged close links with central government
ministries, seeking financial backing for projects in their area.[16] "Not a few
representatives to Uganda's National Assembly," states Fred Burke, "are inclined to regard themselves (and, just as important, are regarded by their fellow tribesmen) as district-tribal ambassadors."[17]

As ethnoregional brokers, these subregional intermediaries at the center
were expected to engage in reciprocal relations with government officials,
trading compliance and support for public goods to be distributed by the state.
The primary measure of their success as brokers was their ability to extract
resources from the state, a task made easier for those fortunate enough to gain
entry to the inner sanctums of government itself. Those opposition MPs who
appeared to be isolated from the main dispensers of patronage often found
themselves subjected to pressure by visiting delegations of local notables;
these local personalities were intent upon getting their representative to cross
the aisle, and thereby to become linked with the party controlling the public
purse strings.

The trend to single-party rule made little difference in the perceived rules
of this game. A. Milton Obote, the master negotiator (in his early career at
least), compensated for the softness of the Uganda state by entering into political exchanges with ethnoregional spokesmen—either MPs or district sec-
retaries-general—as well as all important and politically strategic interest
groups. As far as the ethnoregional exchanges were concerned, the outcomes
were varied: the Acholi received fiscal allocations, the Sebei movement was
granted a separate district, the Buganda-based Kabaka Yekka movement was,
for a time, included as a coalition partner with the Uganda Peoples Congress,
and so forth.[18] Yet Obote eventually came to distrust this process of state-
ethnoregional exchange. As he outlined his proposal for a multiethnic elec-

toral procedure in 1970, he spoke frankly about the dynamics of political exchange that had dominated Uganda politics in the 1960s: "To reduce it to its crudest form," he declared, "the pull of the tribal force does not accept Uganda as one country . . . does not accept the National Assembly as a national institution but as an assembly of peace conference delegates and tribal diplomatic and legislative functionaries, and looks at the Government of Uganda as a body of umpires or referees in some curious game of 'Tribal Development Monopoly.'"[19] In brief, Obote now deemed a system of ongoing exchange relationships to be threatening to the political stability and developmental requirements of the country. Quite probably, he would have continued to engage in quiet quid pro quos with ethnoregional spokesmen even after his reforms had been enacted, but an open system of reciprocal relations was regarded as offensive in the new, more radical politics he envisaged for the 1970s.

In Zambia, two-directional state-ethnoregional linkages were also apparent in postindependence times, but, as in the case of Obote's Uganda, they again failed to secure official presidential blessing. Kenneth Kaunda has engaged in hegemonial exchange practices in both party and governmental affairs from the time of independence to the present. The national council of the United National Independence Party had regional members "who in actual fact, represent[ed] their respective districts."[20] And, in governmental affairs, the cabinet, as described by Richard Hall, was "always . . . delicately balanced between the tribal poles of the Bemba in the north and the Barotse (Lozi) in the south." Hall elaborates: "President Kaunda had found it expedient to maintain four Bemba and four Lozi in the Cabinet, however the portfolios were distributed. When two ministers, Mundia and Nalilungwe, were told to resign in January 1966 for acquiring shares in companies receiving government loans, they both happened to be Lozi. They were both replaced by Lozi. The balance was maintained."[21]

Interesting, in terms of our concern here with political exchange, is the fact that the Zambian move in 1972 toward a legally established one-party state did not imply an end to the use of the proportional principle in making cabinet appointments in the subsequent 1973–1977 period. Thus, despite the defection of some Bemba MPs in 1971, the allocation of cabinet posts to Bemba-speakers remained steady in the years that followed.[22] It is also pertinent that the political decline and death in 1980 of the Bemba's acknowledged political spokesman, former Vice-President Simon Kapwepwe, did not leave this people without a spokesman for communal interests. Not long after Kapwepwe's death, a new northern "strongman" emerged and gained widespread acceptance—Frederick Chiluba, the head of the Zambian Confederation of Trades Unions.[23]

Nevertheless, as was also the case in the Uganda experience discussed earlier, Kaunda, while recognizing the reality of communal politics in Zambia, refused to accord any legitimacy to the political role of the ethnoregional intermediary. In party affairs, Kaunda rejected the Chuula Commission's recommendation that the UNIP Central Committee be composed of sixteen members, two elected from each province.[24] On the question of representation in the cabinet, he was emphatic in rejecting any link to patronage ties. "From now on," Kaunda declared in 1972, "there is no such thing as a tribal leader with a provincial political base in my Government who claims to be the champion of his province or be its spokesman in Cabinet or outside."[25] Finally, in a speech to a district governors' workshop in Lusaka, the president, decrying the fact that some governors had been drawn into tribal and sectional politics, told his audience that "instead of leading, you were misleading; instead of providing effective administrative machinery, you spent your time disorganising the efforts for unity and development; instead of implementing the Government policy and programmes, you became obstacles."[26] In brief, the ethnoregional patron was stigmatized as a "destructive" reality in the Zambian scene; this person would have to be weeded out for the sake of national unity, stability, and development. Thus the expedience of proportional behavior existed side by side with the rhetorical rejection of existing exchange practices.

So far state-ethnoregional exchanges have been described as a logical outgrowth of two factors: governmental control of scarce resources and electoral systems organized along ethnoregional lines which perpetuate patron-client ties. While this interchange led to ambivalent behavior in Zambia and in Uganda under Obote, it has led to a somewhat more publicly countenanced process of political exchange among elites in countries more explicitly pragmatic in their political cultures. Over time such acceptance has brought a widening of exchange practices, most notably in the case of Jomo Kenyatta's Kenya, to a point where an informal grand coalition—even a rudimentary elite cartel along "consociational" lines—may be said to have temporarily emerged. In such coalitional relationships, where certain rules of the game for the handling of the authoritative actions of the state are understood and acquiesced in, a system of continuous interactions can be said to have developed among top members of the state-ethnoregional elite.

Thus—despite the evident constraints of external dependency, of economic scarcity, and of social pluralism—what Lijphart calls the "politics of accommodation" can be seen to exist in specific hegemonially organized African states. In these situations, flows of exchanges are processed by an elite political class which regulates issue-areas in accordance with the norms, rules, and procedures agreed to by key state and ethnoregional actors. To be sure, the effects of these interchanges may prove highly uneven for different actors; yet this does not in itself preclude stable political relationships—so long as all major parties perceive themselves to be benefiting at least minimally from the ongoing negotiations.

Where a grand coalition operates and regulates state-sectional exchanges, an acceptance, even a kind of legitimacy, is accorded to ethnoregional participants in the political process. Though social differences are "encapsulated" in a one-party system (rather than expressed in multiple parties), a true coalition emerges as state leaders make a conscious adjustment to the reality of ethnoregional identities, stressing the need to include all interests in the decision-making process. Their effort to bring ethnic-based factions into the ruling coalition is an attempt to maintain the political system by means of cooptation. The expedient nature of this recognition is apparent in the secrecy that generally surrounds the state's relationship with ethnoregional intermediaries; yet, in contrast to the disapproval of the broker's role expressed by Obote and Kaunda, state leaders are careful in a hegemonial coalition situation to co-opt and neutralize their potential challengers, not to deny their legitimacy in public.

Two variations of the hegemonial coalition will suffice to illustrate the point. In the Ivory Coast, especially in the 1960s and early 1970s, where the rules of the game involve an "acknowledge[ment]," but not a public display, of ethnic politics, President Félix Houphouët-Boigny has "tried to achieve some ethnic balance in his cabinets in order to mollify the resentment of Baoule dominance."[27] Although the supremacy of the *Parti Démocratique de Côte d'Ivoire* remains evident, Houphouët-Boigny is careful to demobilize potential ethnoregional challengers by co-opting these local intermediaries into the ruling grand coalition at the center.[28] It is apparent that members of the National Assembly continue to draw from constituencies organized in a number of cases along ethnoregional lines.

Aristide Zolberg describes the already familiar pattern of ethnoregional intermediation, as found in the Ivory Coast, as follows: "Viewing themselves as ambassadors of their region and of their ethnic group to the center, or as the spokesmen for the organization to which they belong, the *députés* are concerned mainly with gaining access to the ministers in order to secure tangible benefits for their constituents. Regardless of his specific duties as a member of the executive, each minister is also a kind of superrepresentative who keeps in touch with the country through his clientele of deputies."[29]

Rather than challenging the validity of these ethnoregional appeals, Houphouët-Boigny has prudently provided for their incorporation in what Zolberg calls "a one-party coalition, a heterogeneous monolith."[30] All major ethnic groups are represented in the cabinet, and on a basis roughly proportional to their position in the National Assembly. Playing a key role by dominating and if necessary mediating between the different factions making up the cabinet coalition, Houphouët-Boigny has been able to build a political structure which ensures his political survival at least for the time being. However, given his advanced age (he turned seventy-nine in October 1984), the current political arrangement obviously will not endure; this creates the prospect of new political tensions during the transition period. In this period, as Richard Stryker stresses, "the potential for conflict in the Ivory Coast is certainly very great, particularly along ethnic and generational [and one might add class] lines."[31] An indication of the seriousness of these tensions emerged following the 1980 National Assembly elections, when Houphouët-Boigny felt it necessary to call a meeting of PDCI officials to reconcile the bitter differences that had surfaced between successful and unsuccessful candidates. Hence the Ivory Coast's hegemonial exchange system, which combines central governmental-party control with some proportionality in the distribution of political positions and fiscal resources, is about to undergo a critical test. Unless the various party interests can reach agreement on a "consensus candidate" who is prepared to inject new vigor into the hegemonial grand coalition, the political stability which has long been a hallmark of this ethnically heterogeneous society may be threatened.[32]

Finally, in Kenya a one-party grand coalition of ethnoregional notables gained considerable regime acceptance during the Kenyatta years. A process of state-facilitated political exchange became customary practice, resulting, to the extent that all main actors were included, in relatively stable rules of interaction. On the hegemonic side, President Kenyatta exercised broad administrative control, ruling through the bureaucracy rather than the party; in the rural areas, the president's direct point of contact was via the agency of the provincial administration, whose personnel in the field were directly accountable to his office.[33] In addition, with the major exception of the militant populist interlude associated with Oginga Odinga's Kenya People's Union from 1966 to 1969, Kenya was a de facto one-party state after 1964, when the ruling Kenya African National Union (KANU) absorbed its smaller and more conservative postindependence rival, the Kenya African Democratic Union.

KANU proved, however, to be anything but a tightly organized and centrally disciplined party throughout the Kenyatta period.[34] With the central party organization exercising only loose control over affairs at the branch level, ethnoregional party notables were able to build strong bases of power in their constituencies and then, as in the case of such prominent ethnoregional champions as Ronald Ngala and Paul Ngei, to negotiate over the nature of their participation in the ruling cabinet coalition at the center. KANU, described by Carl Rosberg as resting upon "a coalition of key ethnic groups,"[35] thus united the single-party principle with elements of political exchange and mediation from the top of the hierarchy. "The political system," states Robert

Jackson, "is basically characterized by competition and bargaining between a number of ethnic groups and more modern interest associations on the one hand, and government on the other. . . . Government itself is highly plural, with bargaining and competition occurring among Cabinet members acting on behalf of supporting groups and between the ministries themselves." [36]

But if Kenyatta pragmatically engaged in an ongoing process of exchange relationships with the champions of ethnoregional interests (though notable exceptions here were Odinga and his compatriots, non-Luo as well as Luo, following Kenya People's Union's formation), his successor, President Daniel arap Moi, a Tugan from western Kenya, appears less inclined to expend his political resources in this manner. The consequence has been damage to the networks of interpersonal linkages built up by Mzee (the Old Wise Man) Kenyatta over the years. In the initial period following his accession to power in 1978, Moi moved cautiously, maintaining the Kenyatta constitution and cabinet intact. But by 1982, it had become apparent that Moi had in fact distanced himself somewhat from the hegemonial exchange practices of his predecessor—and with highly destabilizing consequences.

Pointing to the reduced center-periphery linkages as an underlying explanation for the rising tensions in Kenya political life in 1982, one correspondent notes: "Within two years President Moi had demonstrated that he intended to control Kenya through his own proteges rather than by alliances with the acknowledged popular leaders of the various key areas so Oginga Odinga, still preeminent in Luoland in Western Kenya, was prevented from standing in the 1979 election. Others such as Masinde Muliro and Jean Marie Seroney in the Rift Valley and Paul Ngei in Kambaland were soon acknowledged in Kenya's highly politicised society to be on the outside of the ruling group. Even the Vice-President, Mwai Kibaki, the current Kikuyu leader, was increasingly distanced from power." [37] Thus Moi's preference for working closely with political associates drawn from the party but without a solid ethnoregional base of support weakened the linkages between center and periphery, thereby cracking the glue which had held the political system together during the Kenyatta reign. The result was political brittleness at a time of economic stagnation and rising political tensions: public restlessness, governmental repression, and, most unsettling, an attempted coup by a large section of the air force with the sympathy, if not the support, of other interests in the society.

The following year was to see further consolidation of power in Moi's hands. With the isolation and ousting of the former Constitutional Affairs Minister, Charles Njonjo, from KANU, Moi called a new general election. Although the voter turnout was low, all but five cabinet ministers were reelected, and Moi appointed all but three of these to the new cabinet. Significantly, the formerly overrepresented Kikuyus were cut back in a somewhat smaller cabi-

net, but only to a roughly proportional 19 percent. The first impression of the
new cabinet, remarked a correspondent in the *Weekly Review*, was that of a
"well balanced" body—"one that takes care of the political interests of various geographic areas and at the same time appears to be chosen with an eye to
dealing with the kinds of pressures the government in particular, and the country in general, are likely to face."[38] If the structure of understandings and
working relationships so carefully put together by Kenyatta no longer had full
legitimacy in official eyes, Moi, in his efforts to consolidate power, was nonetheless careful to take account of the need for ethnic proportionality and a
broadened inclusiveness.

### African Pragmatists and Exchange Markets

In previous sections, hegemonial exchange was described as offering a
framework for coordinating and facilitating political exchange under conditions of frail institutions, heady expectations, and severe economic scarcity.
Hegemonial exchange channels conflicts along negotiable lines, making amicable agreement over conflicting issues more likely. In so doing, the hegemonial exchange process primarily follows informal but known rules, in particular the principle of proportionality, that is, the allocation of public goods
in accordance with the relative numbers making up the communal groups in a
society. Jürg Steiner notes the central role played by the proportionality principle when he comments that "the more weight the prevalent norm-system
lays on amicable agreement, the more a political system tends to regulate conflicts on proportional principles."[39] The benefits accruing from this exchange
may well go to some groups disproportionately, but if all partners gain some
share, they may come to view continued participation in the process as serving their interests.

Provided the potential bargaining partners are motivated to enter into exchange relationships, and that they make pragmatic or reciprocative apprais-
als of their rivals' intentions, the stage may be set for decisions to be made
according to hegemonial exchange principles. Do regime practices, despite
rhetoric-tinged ideologies and single- or no-party systems in many countries,
indicate a preparedness to operate also according to the proportionality principle? Despite space limitations some sense can be given of middle Africa's
wide range of experiences with hegemonial exchange through an analysis of
the four main issue-areas of African political exchange: political coalition,
elite recruitment, resource allocation, and group rights and protections.

1. *Political coalition.* Where a single ethnic group (and its allies) appear
to have captured control of state institutions (for example, "the ruling
Amhara nation" in Ethiopia[40]), the costs in terms of intense interethnic con-

flict have proved high. Other ethnic peoples feel excluded from the decision-making process and conclude, rightly or wrongly, that public policies are biased in favor of the dominant political group. Their feelings of powerlessness and comparative disadvantage contribute to a decline in the legitimacy of the state itself, provoking ill feeling, negative group memories, and even military coups and attempts at ethnoregional secession.

An alternative to the dominance of a single group is some form of ethnic-based political coalition. Where all major ethnic groups are assured of at least minimal participation in the governing process—whether by formal political rules (for example, the provisions in Nigeria's 1979 Constitution on the "federal character" of decision-making bodies)[41] or by informal rules (in hegemonic Zambia, Kenya, Ivory Coast, Cameroun, Benin, Nigeria [postcoup 1983])—collaboration replaces group competition. Hegemonic exchange, by operating according to widely understood but informal rules on minimal representation of major groups according to the principle of proportionality, has had the effect of encouraging political and state legitimacy. These informal rules differ from situation to situation, but certain ones appear with some regularity:

1. the inclusion of major ethnoregional strongmen in the cabinet and/or party national executive committee
2. the decision not to drop a minister who has been reelected to parliament
3. the maintenance of an ethnic balance by replacing retiring ministers and high party officials with others from the same subregion
4. the preservation, when succession occurs, of a geographical balance in appointments to the president and prime minister as well as within the cabinet and party
5. special measures to include minority ethnic interests in the decision-making process
6. an understanding not to discuss highly emotional, ethnic-related issues outside the political coalition

Efforts to include all major interests have also involved a number of policy initiatives and rules of a special nature. Thus in Zambia (1969) and Kenya (1979) the cabinet was enlarged at least in part to give the president an opportunity to improve ethnoregional balance by including additional spokesmen from underrepresented subregions in the central decision-making process.[42] And in Mauritius provision has been made for multimember constituencies and the reservation of eight seats for the most successful losing candidates in the different communities, with the effect of strengthening a political coalition in which all ethnic interests are represented. In brief, the political coalition acknowledges ethnic diversity and seeks, by including all key groups in the decision-making process, to reduce anxiety and hostility. It co-opts to induce collaboration and exchange. Such a strategy facilitates negotiated settlement, but not without a cost in terms of decisive leadership in developmental or foreign policy matters.

2. *Elite recruitment.* In contrast to the political sphere, where legislatures are elected on a constituency basis and heads of state frequently make conscious efforts to emphasize inclusiveness when forming their central cabinets, recruitment of personnel into the civil service, army, and police has been less proportional. Much of the explanation for skewed recruitment practices lies with colonial policies. Not only did colonial governments discriminate in the way they selected personnel for the higher-level positions in the public service (hiring a disproportional number of Europeans as well as Indian, Lebanese, and Colored auxiliaries) but their practice of appointing European officers and enlisting so-called indigenous "martial races" into the ranks of the military and police also distorted the ethnic balance in these services.[43]

However, it was the colonial regimes' selectivity in developing educational systems (in Kenya's Nyanza and Central provinces, for example, though less so in the others) that has had the most lasting postindependence effects in terms of subregional disparities. Thus the overrepresentation of the Kikuyu and the Baganda in the Kenyan and Ugandan civil services is largely a reflection of those ethnic peoples' close contact with the West, and most especially with the educational systems brought in conjunction with colonialism.[44]

This imbalance in subregional educational opportunities and in the resulting elite recruitment patterns has not gone unnoticed by the leaders of the less-advantaged ethnoregional units. In Ghana, for example, several members of parliament from the less-advantaged north were sufficiently offended by continuing disparities in education and other services to present a motion in the National Assembly in 1970 requesting approval of a special accelerated development program to bring about "a rapid bridging of the gaps."[45] Not only did these ethnoregional spokesmen feel their kinsmen were excluded from their rightful share of public goods, but they viewed increased subregional participation in the various public services as necessary for protection of ethnoregional interests in the central allocative process.[46]

On the whole, progress toward achieving a racial balance in the composition of the civil service did occur over time in the independent middle-African states. However, because the process of modernization gave rise to ethnoregional imbalances among professionally trained applicants for public-service positions, the postindependence state bureaucracy all too often appeared to be captured by a politically powerful and well-placed ethnic group. The Kikuyu in Kenya, the Creoles in Sierra Leone, the Amhara in Ethiopia, the Baganda in Uganda, the Tutsi Hima in Rwanda and Burundi, the Malinké in Guinea,

the Woloff in Gambia, the Bemba in Zambia, and others gained disproportional influence in the affairs of state bureaucracies. And in Nigeria, according to a 1980 calculation, the five states controlled by Obafemi Awolowo's
Western-based Unity Party of Nigeria—Ogun, Ondo, Oyo, Lagos, and Ben-
del—have 67 percent of federal civil service posts above grade 14 salary
scale.[47] In such instances, state power is not autonomous and separate from
the interests of a particular ethnic group, although this does not in itself preclude expediential moves to facilitate reciprocity among ethnic identity groups.

The impact of a marked lack of representation is to kindle suspicions
among the less advantaged that central state institutions are biased in the way
they allocate scarce public goods among competing sectional interests. In response, state-party elites have advocated a variety of policy mechanisms to
allay these suspicions. Some policies, such as those of the Kenya government
placing a higher priority on administrative efficiency than on ethnoregional
proportionality, have emphasized a strict application of the merit principle in
all civil service appointments.[48] To adopt such a position, however, is to entrench existing disparities.

State-party officials elsewhere have introduced other policies and practices which are calculated to be more sensitive to the feelings of people in
the relatively disadvantaged subregions. Informal understandings on proportional recruitment into the public service have surfaced in Malawi, where the
hegemonial leader, President Hastings Banda, has applied an unofficial 1/3-
1/3-1/3 principle and kept secondary school and university selections as well
as civil service appointments roughly in balance by subregion. Civil service
promotions are also scrutinized in terms of candidates' district backgrounds
in order to maintain the procedural understanding on ethnoregional equality.
The effect of this policy of coercive reciprocity administered from above is to
allay the most pronounced fears of people in the educationally disadvantaged
south and center, but at a cost of frustration for a number of educated
northerners.[49]

Proportionality in civil service recruitment has also remained the standard
operating procedure in Ghana over an extended period of time. A breakdown
of the ethnic composition in 1972 of the central government senior staff done
by this author showed a remarkably close parallel between ethnic proportions
in the civil service and the society at large, although some distortions did
emerge. In relation to the total population, the Fanti and the Ga-Adangbe were
found to be overrepresented by 14.9 percent and 12.8 percent respectively,
while the northerners were underrepresented by 16 percent. Nonetheless a
number of groups—the Ashanti, Boron, Akim-Akwapim, Nzima, Ewe, and
others—showed no statistically significant variance from proportionality.[50]

A decade later, under the populist regime of Jerry Rawlings's Provisional

National Defence Council, the government has continued to show great sensitivity to ethnic feelings in Ghana. Various indications of "ethnic arithmetic" in initial appointments appeared soon after the PNDC took control. Not only were two northerners included in the seven-member PNDC (an effort in part to compensate the north, the home base of deposed President Hilla Limann), but the Ewe-led PNDC administration made certain that it appointed as regional secretaries only persons who hailed from the subregion to which they were accredited. "One can conclude from this," one Ghanaian wrote me in October 1982, "that considerations of ethnic arithmetic might have featured prominently in the calculations of a 'radical revolutionary military government,' and that the appointments represented a compromise between ethnic balance and radical political idealism."

Another example of informal rules on ethnic proportionality in a hegemonially structured polity was Sékou Touré's Guinea. Ladipo Adamolekun has drawn attention to Touré's practice of ethnic arithmetic, which the president himself admitted to from time to time, in the distribution of key political and administrative posts in the 1958 to 1967 period. If, according to these data, Touré's own Malinkés were slightly overrepresented and the Forest People underrepresented, the thrust of public policy was definitely in the direction of proportionality. Thus even though Touré ruled out any formal stipulation of proportional representation or a quota system, he was nonetheless careful to invoke elements of reciprocity from the top downward in his unofficial practices.[51]

Less circumspectly, Nigerians have publicly recognized the reality of ethnic attachments and have experimented with proportionality in formal as well as informal recruitment procedures. The Nigerian military government during the 1970–79 period acted on the basis of what Richard Joseph describes as an " 'unofficial' ethnic balance," adopting informal rules on proportionality in its ministerial and parastatal appointments.[52] The constitutionally elected government which succeeded it went further in entrenching proportionality, both through provisions in the 1979 Constitution on the "federal character" of the civil service at the federal level, of quotas for admissions to federal universities, and of the allocation of postgraduate scholarships at institutions of higher learning.

In a recognition of the Nigerian peoples' desire to "give every citizen of Nigeria a sense of belonging to the nation" (Section 277[1]), the 1979 Constitution provided that, in regard to recruitment into federal political and administrative positions, "the composition of the Government of the Federation or any of its agencies and the conduct of its affairs shall be carried out in such manner as to reflect the federal character of Nigeria and the need to promote national unity" (Sect. 14[3]). The difficulty of operationalizing this guideline becomes apparent, however, when one examines the opposition of entrenched interests on the grounds of "efficiency" as well as the doubts of constitutional experts on whether this is appropriately an issue for the courts.[53]

Nigerian practices in setting quotas for university admissions and post-graduate scholarships appear to go some distance toward carrying out the constitutional guidelines on representativeness. Nigeria has had a long experience with quotas in military recruitment, having selected officers for the Nigerian Military Training College on the basis of subregional quotas (50 percent north and 25 percent east and west) as early as 1961.[54] In recent years, however, it is the issue of fixed percentages for admissions and scholarships at institutions of higher learning which was highlighted by northern student demonstrations.

In fact, the north has lagged behind the rest of the country in university admissions, largely a reflection of long-standing subregional disparities in education. In the period 1970–75, students from the eleven states identified by the Federal Military Government as educationally disadvantaged areas (nine northern and two southern) had an average of only 22.4 percent of the university places.[55]

Recognizing the need to equalize subregional opportunities in education, the Federal Military Government initiated a number of measures to promote greater proportionality. It established schools of basic studies affiliated with the older universities in the disadvantaged states, as well as remedial programs at the seven new universities, to help candidates, many drawn from the less advantaged areas, whose qualifications were not quite up to standard. In addition, the Joint Admissions and Matriculation Board (JAMB) was set up to select candidates for admission to the universities.

Some slight improvement in overcoming subregional disparities has occurred since JAMB took on its supervisory role. Thus in 1978–79, 33.3 percent of the candidates for university admission came from the eleven disadvantaged states, up significantly from the 1970–75 figure of 22.4 percent. These figures become more meaningful when one realizes that only 19.8 percent of total applications came from the disadvantaged states.[56] And governmental pressure for increased equity among subregions has not let up with these measures. In July 1980, the Federal Ministry of Education announced a new formula for admission to federal colleges and polytechnics. Henceforth entry would be based upon the following quotas: 20 percent national merit, irrespective of a candidate's state of origin; 50 percent on equal state quotas; and 30 percent on an environmental basis.[57]

Political leaders in other African countries have also advocated or experimented with the use of quotas to restore ethnoregional balance in elite recruitment. Burundi, for example, has halved the number of Tutsi children normally permitted to enter high school on the basis of merit, and Kenya has experimented with formulas to adjust the intake of students to teacher-training colleges to benefit such districts as Kakamega, Busia, Kisii, and Bungoma, which had high proportions of untrained teachers.[58] And in post-Amin Uganda, where the Langi and Acholi have tended to hold a disproportionately heavy percentage of posts in the armed forces, proposals have reportedly been put forward, to the chagrin of the army high command, to move toward district quotas in order to ensure ethnoregional balance.[59] Thus the state, by informal or formal means, has at times acted to promote interethnic reciprocity in Africa. When such state-induced exchange does take place, it reflects the pragmatists' recognition of the strength of ethnic attachments and a willingness to negotiate on specific points of conflict to encourage a sense of common "national" purpose.

3. *Resource allocation.* Subregional resource allocations, mainly reflecting population size rather than subregional need or relative disadvantage, are quite commonplace in middle Africa. Dov Ronen noted that under Dahomey's (now Benin's) Presidential Council in the early 1970s, power, benefits, and goods were distributed among the subregions on a proportional basis "to maintain the delicate political balance."[60] After an extensive period of skewed allocations in the Sudan, de facto proportionality became evident in the 1979–80 and 1980–81 budgets, where the relatively disadvantaged southern region, with 17.8 percent of the population, was allotted 21.1 percent and 20.2 percent of the total allocations respectively.[61]

In Zambia, where President Kenneth Kaunda has been described as pursuing "a strategy of striving for rapid and balanced growth, regardless of the political record of the various ethno-regional groups," developmental expenditures tended in fact to favor relatively disadvantaged north-western, western, and Luapula provinces and not the line-of-rail provinces which had benefited by longer contact with Western capital.[62] Unlike an explicit policy of redistribution, allocations shaped according to the proportionality principle (i.e., on the basis of the numbers of populations) represent an easily administered and low-cost approach to distribution. If, however, it reflects an implicit political exchange of sorts, it nonetheless does little to overcome the configurations of wealth and opportunity inherited from the past.

Despite the constraints of the environment and class and ethnoregional resistance, some middle-African regimes have gone beyond proportionality to implement their promises of equalizing subregional disparities. Yet evidence of redistributional outcomes is spotty. For example, for all the mismanagement and corruption that marked his regime, General I. K. Acheampong in Ghana did seek to extend his support base northward through budgetary poli-

cies which aimed at redressing subregional inequities with respect to per capita capital fund expenditures for secondary schools in 1975–76; however, in
other areas, such as current fund expenditures on primary and middle education, the record was mixed.[63]

In the case of Tanzania, Alan Amey and David Leonard concluded, on the
basis of a statistical breakdown of estimated government and parastatal expenditures by subregion during the 1969–70 to 1974–75 period, that "the
evidence demonstrates that Tanzania is moving toward greater spatial equality
in its government expenditures." Even though absolute inequalities in governmental expenditures remained generally constant, relative inequalities declined by 30 percent—from a relative deviation of 1.31 in 1969 on per capita
distributions of development funds to the subregions to 0.91 in 1974.[64]

In the Cameroun during the 1960s, the largely eastern-led federal government made extensive use of its grants-in-aid program to lay the basis for
increasing interdependence between English-speaking, relatively disadvantaged West Cameroun and the French-speaking, relatively advantaged East
Cameroun. Thus in the 1968–69 fiscal year, federal subsidies to the West
amounted to 1.6 billion CFA francs out of a total of 2.82 billion CFA francs, or
57 percent of the entire subregional budget.[65]

Finally, with the publication of the Okigbo commission report on revenue
allocation in 1982 and the subsequent passage of the 1982 Revenue Allocation
Act, Nigeria turned more decisively toward some measures that were equalizing in their impact. Under the previous operating formula, great disparities
had emerged in per capita allocations: for example, in the 1977–78 fiscal
year, Kano state received an allocation of ₦ 21.670 while that for Rivers, the
main oil-producing subregion, was ₦ 200.289.[66] The revised revenue allocation arrangement provides 35 percent to the states and 10 percent to the local
councils, with the formula for distribution among these state and local governments heavily weighted toward such equity criteria as the size of population and the social development factor as represented by primary school en-
rollments. In brief, as these and other cases suggest, African elites, despite
worsening economic conditions in much of the postindependence period,
have at times adopted aspects of a redistributional approach, in part at least to
encourage collaborative behavior in the periphery.

4. *Group rights and protections*. If the state makes adjustments to protect
minority group political, cultural, economic, and social interests, these calculated moves can be viewed as representing an element of reciprocity initiated
by the dominant elite to promote national cohesion. In the middle-African situation, the state may decide to concede a degree of autonomy to ethnic sections in society, while at the same time retaining dominant political power in

its own hands. Yet the state's act of making such concessions seems likely to give rise to reciprocal obligations, and these will cause ethnic leaders to make counterconcessions which may prove integrative in their consequences.

Middle Africa's experiences with these calculated adjustments is sufficiently wide that a few examples will suffice. In the Cameroun, bilingualism has remained official policy despite the move to a unitary form of government in 1972. The use of the English language in West Cameroun has been respected by government authorities, although French does in fact predominate in the administrative services, army, and institutions of higher learning.[67] In this instance, then, a calculated adjustment has been undertaken which avoids undue hardship for those accustomed to speaking in English. This concession has not stood, however, in the way of a tendency to make increasing use of the French language as the medium of communication in both public and private activities. In other countries (Kenya, Zimbabwe, and so forth), the state has been careful to respect the autonomous social and cultural rights of minority ethnic and racial groups, allowing them considerable freedom as individuals and groups in exchange for compliance and support.

At another level, the state has also presided over the division of its powers to allow ethnoregional units a limited decisional authority in their own right. Thus both Nigeria and the Sudan have divided and redivided their subregions, seeking to strike a balance between the needs of central competence and control and the appeals of subregional self-determination. Nimeiri's 1983 decision to establish eight subregional governments and administrations (including three in the former South) in the Sudan has enhanced the center's ability to concentrate upon critical issues of state while devolving important matters of local concern upon the various subregional authorities, whose autonomous powers should not be underestimated. As one writer commented, "The governors of the regions have become, constitutionally and de facto, the most powerful men in the country after Nimeiri."[68] Nonetheless, the central government's broad list of exclusive powers combined with the president's control over appointments and allocations makes it likely that the political exchange relationship will prove asymmetrical. Within these parameters, however, the possibility for a significant subregional role is not precluded.

To gain central leverage Nigerians have redivided their Federation on three occasions (the last two under the aegis of hegemonial military rulers) while allowing smaller ethnoregional units a limited decisional authority over matters on which both the federal and state governments can legislate. The 1979 Constitution carefully delineated central and subregional powers, setting up two legislative lists. The effect was a noticeable tilt in the direction of central predominance in most critical areas. Even so, the Nigerian subregions worked aggressively within the new constitutional rules to expand their sphere of autonomy. This struggle took place on a variety of fronts: the enlargement of their share of fiscal resources under the new revenue allocation formula, increased administrative competency in such fields as television stations and institutions of higher education, and resistance to the authority of the federally appointed presidential liaison officers. "The demands for state autonomy which have escalated in recent times," write two Nigerian political scientists, "could be seen as attempts to avoid state identities being 'swamped' by the political party in control of the federal government."[69]

In sum, and contrary to much conventional wisdom, political elites in middle-African societies have largely tended toward pragmatic rather than essentialist perspectives on interethnic relations. They have utilized political cultures which emphasize informal rules of exchange on specific conflict issues. Such exchange normally takes place within hegemonial settings, enabling the state to play a crucial role in setting the terms for reciprocity.

### Policy Implications

What are the policy implications of this hegemonial exchange process, which represents a widely practiced and realistic strategy in the middle-African context? In an environment which often lacks open partisan competition, effective state regulation, and an adequate human and material resource base, the classical models for managing ethnic conflict seem somewhat artificial and inadequate. Hence it seems useful to build upon past analyses and to create an alternative model, one which reconciles the features of exchange and control evident in these societies. The hegemonial exchange model, then, is a hybrid. It does not deny the presence of formal institutions of bureaucratic control or of state-ethnic negotiations; rather, it seeks to combine them in ways that reflect the ongoing dynamic of relations prevailing in modern Africa.

As described in this chapter, the practice of African leaders (as distinct from their rhetoric) is to engage pragmatically in a variety of two-party and, in some cases, coalitional exchanges within the context of a hegemonic political system. The state, as a consequence of its dominant political and economic role in these societies, comes to play a key role, setting the terms and costs of these informal and formal exchanges. In many instances, it initiates and presides over the exchange process—forming political coalitions, allocating resources, recruiting elites, recognizing the legitimate boundaries of subregional autonomy, and specifying and enforcing the social and cultural rights of groups. Naturally such a process of hegemonially administered exchange has not always brought minimally acceptable outcomes. The consequences then are political instability and the emergence of threatening perceptions of future relationships. Yet, perhaps surprisingly in the light of the prevailing environmental constraints, these well-publicized, worst-case situations are not the rule. Instead, a number of middle-African societies have come to expect some regularity in their flows of state-ethnic exchanges within the authoritarian one- or no-party context. The effect of this expectation of minimal reciprocity has been to reduce the intensity of conflict, opening the way to what Ali Mazrui describes as an "awareness of reciprocal dependence."[70] Interethnic conflict is kept within bounds when a hegemonially structured exchange relationship is seen to prevail, because all major political actors come to feel minimally included in and rewarded by the decision process.

By bounding conflict, hegemonial exchange facilitates a limited and controlled reciprocity. As such, it may be regarded as a politically expedient approach to the management of ethnic relations under conditions of scarcity. In terms of outcomes, its informal and less regularized practices of amicable exchange may quite possibly prove to be more significant and constructive than the classical alternatives of control or consociationalism. Certainly a liberally oriented consociational system with competing parties is unlikely to be imposed with any success in contemporary Africa; such arrangements must develop over time and be based upon the mutual desire of bargaining partners to collaborate for mutual gain. Hence what seems critical at this juncture is not so much a fully developed system of exchange linkages, but a long-term process of social learning that will move steadily in the direction of regularizing the flows of exchanges. In the middle-African context past experience indicates that hegemonial exchange is at least as likely to produce these predictable exchange relations as any other form of decision process.

As this discussion might suggest, the political advantages of a hegemonial exchange approach are not without their own policy costs. Some possible disadvantages include the following: a system based largely on informal linkages necessarily remains precarious and can disintegrate, especially under severe strain; the limits which are placed on public participation in the political process can lead to widespread frustration and a resulting loss in system legitimacy; a backscratching system entails constraints on political reform and change; the economic scarcity currently prevailing in middle Africa leaves the dominant political elite at the center with little to distribute; and the application of the proportional principle in recruitment and allocation policies may achieve political ends at a high cost in terms of merit and aggregate productivity. If short-term political management emphasizing reciprocity and exchange promotes values of inclusiveness and political stability, the long-term trade-offs may still prove unacceptable to some elites who place a higher value on efficiency or full and active public participation. But these timeless trade-offs can no more be avoided by decision makers in Africa than anywhere else in the world.

NOTES

1. June Kronholz, "Dashed Dreams: Africa's Political Map," *Wall Street Journal*, 31 October 1983, p. 1.
2. Ladipo Adamolekun, *Sékou Touré's Guinea* (London: Methuen, 1976), pp. 128–132. Claude Riviere comments, however, as follows: "The comparative balance in tribal representation that was reached among the cadres tends now to be upset by Malinké predominance and Peul underrepresentation in the policymaking decisions." *Guinea: The Mobilization of a People* (Ithaca, N.Y.: Cornell University Press, 1977), p. 217.
3. On the soft state, see Gunnar Myrdal, *Asian Drama—An Inquiry into the Poverty of Nations*, vol. 2 (New York: Pantheon, 1968), pp. 895–900; and Goran Hyden, "Problems and Prospects of State Coherence," in Donald Rothchild and Victor A. Olorunsola (eds.), *State Versus Ethnic Claims: African Policy Dilemmas* (Boulder, Colo.: Westview Press, 1983), pp. 73–74.
4. On the general types of coordination processes, see Charles E. Lindblom, *The Intelligence of Democracy* (New York: Free Press, 1965), ch. 2.
5. Richard Sklar, "The Nature of Class Domination in Africa," *Journal of Modern African Studies* 18, 4 (1979): 531–532; and Donald Rothchild, "Collective Demands for Improved Distributions," in Rothchild and Olorunsola, *State Versus Ethnic Claims*, pp. 189–192.
6. On the public's perception of legislators as "agents of the periphery at the center," see Joel D. Barkan, "Legislators, Elections, and Political Linkage," in Joel D. Barkan with John J. Okumu (eds.), *Politics and Public Policy in Kenya and Tanzania* (New York: Praeger, 1979), p. 67f.
7. This distinction between the state as partially autonomous actor and as an organizing set of principles is discussed in my "Social Incoherence and the Mediatory Role of the State," in Bruce E. Arlinghaus (ed.), *African Security Issues* (Boulder, Colo.: Westview Press, 1984), ch. 6.
8. Nelson Kasfir, *The Shrinking Political Arena* (Berkeley: University of California Press, 1976), p. 163.
9. As Billy Dudley observes, the military "share the same cultural idiom with the people. . . ." *An Introduction to Nigerian Government and Politics* (Bloomington: Indiana University Press, 1982), p. 123.
10. Robin Luckham, *The Nigerian Military* (Cambridge: Cambridge University Press, 1971), p. 296.
11. Interview, Professor Negussay Ayele, Berkeley, 1 June 1983.
12. Significantly, upon taking up his appointment as President for the High Executive Council for the southern region, Major-General Gasmallah Rassas issued a statement through Radio Juba assuring southerners that he hailed from Bahr el Ghazal procince. "I am a Southerner," he told a *Sudanow* interviewer. "I was born in Bussere (11 miles south of Wau) and my brother and sister are still living there at our home. . . ." *Sudanow* 6, 11 (November 1981): 15. The importance of a regional identifica-

tion is underscored by the experience in Darfur region, where the people rioted over Nimeiry's first choice as governor in 1981 on the grounds that he was not a native of Darfur and secured his replacement. See Colin Legum (ed.), *Africa Contemporary Record 1980–81*, 13 (New York: Africana Publishing Co., 1981): B102.

13. René Lemarchand, "Comparative Political Clientelism: Structure, Process and Optic," in S. N. Eisenstadt and René Lemarchand (eds.), *Political Clientelism, Patronage and Development* (Beverly Hills: Sage, 1981), p. 15.

14. Dunstan M. Wai, "The Sudan: Crisis in North-South Relations," *Africa Report* 27, 2 (March–April 1982): 26; also see his comments in "Geoethnicity and the Margin of Autonomy in the Sudan," in Rothchild and Olorunsola, *State Versus Ethnic Claims*, p. 326.

15. Donald Rothchild and Michael Rogin, "Uganda," in Gwendolen M. Carter (ed.), *National Unity and Regionalism in Eight African States* (Ithaca, N.Y.: Cornell University Press, 1966), pp. 378–379, 384, 394.

16. Colin Leys, *Politicians and Policies* (Nairobi: East African Publishing House, 1967), pp. 32, 44.

17. Fred G. Burke, *Local Government and Politics in Uganda* (Syracuse, N.Y.: Syracuse University Press, 1964), p. 229.

18. Kasfir, *The Shrinking Political Arena*, pp. 167–168.

19. A. Milton Obote, *Proposals for New Methods of Election of Representatives of the People to Parliament* (Kampala: Milton Obote Foundation, 1970), pp. 6–7.

20. Letter from J. M. Mutti to *Times of Zambia* (Ndola), 24 October 1970, p. 6. Mr. Mutti was a member of the controversial Chuula UNIP constitutional commission which called for equal provincial representation on the party's Central Committee.

21. Richard Hall, *The High Price of Principles* (New York: Africana Publishing Corporation, 1969), p. 195.

22. See the data in William Tordoff, "Introduction," in William Tordoff (ed.), *Administration in Zambia* (Manchester: Manchester University Press, 1980), pp. 14–15.

23. Jean-Pierre Langellier, "Zambia's Costly Mistakes," *Manchester Guardian Weekly* 128, 18 (1 May 1983): 14.

24. *Zambia Daily Mail* (Lusaka), 7 October 1970, p. 1.

25. *Sunday Times of Zambia* (Ndola), 9 July 1972, p. 1.

26. *Zambia Daily Mail*, 3 June 1971, p. 1.

27. Robert A. Mortimer, "Ivory Coast: Succession and Recession," *Africa Report* 28, 1 (January–February, 1983): 5, 7.

28. Aristide R. Zolberg, "Politics in the Ivory Coast: 1," *West Africa*, 30 July 1960, p. 847.

29. Aristide R. Zolberg, *One-Party Government in the Ivory Coast* (Princeton, N.J.: Princeton University Press, 1964), p. 283.

30. Zolberg, "Politics in the Ivory Coast: 2," *West Africa*, 6 August 1960, p. 883.

31. Richard E. Stryker, "A Local Perspective on Developmental Strategy in the Ivory Coast," in Michael F. Lofchie (ed.), *The State of the Nations* (Berkeley: University of California Press, 1971), p. 134.

32. Colin Legum (ed.), *Africa Contemporary Record 1981–82* (New York: Africana Publishing Co., 1981), pp. B444–445.

33. See Robert H. Jackson and Carl G. Rosberg, *Personal Rule in Black Africa* (Berkeley: University of California Press, 1982), p. 102.

34. Goran Hyden and Colin Leys, "Elections and Politics in Single-Party Systems: The Case of Kenya and Tanzania," *British Journal of Political Science* 2, 4 (October

1972): 393; Cherry Gertzel, *The Politics of Independent Kenya 1963–8* (Nairobi: East African Publishing House, 1970), pp. 137–138; and Henry Bienen, *Kenya: The Politics of Participation and Control* (Princeton, N.J.: Princeton University Press, 1974), pp. 81–82.

35. Carl G. Rosberg, "National Identity in African States," *African Review* (Dar es Salaam) 1, 1 (March 1971): 86.

36. Robert H. Jackson, "Planning, Politics, and Administration," in Goran Hyden, Robert Jackson, and John Okumu (eds.), *Development Administration: The Kenyan Experience* (Nairobi: Oxford University Press, 1970), pp. 177–178.

37. Victoria Brittain, "Five Months That Took Kenya to the Brink," *Manchester Guardian Weekly* 127, 6 (8 April 1982): 7.

38. *Weekly Review* (Nairobi), 7 October 1983, p. 4.

39. Jürg Steiner, "The Principles of Majority and Proportionality," *British Journal of Political Science* 1, 1 (January 1971): 67.

40. See Bereket Habte Selassie, *Conflict and Intervention in the Horn of Africa* (New York: Monthly Review Press, 1980), p. 27. In corroboration, one correspondent estimated in July 1979 that fifteen out of sixteen members of the Standing Committee, nine of eleven members of the Dergue's Central Committee, thirty-one of thirty-seven ministers and permanent secretaries, and thirteen of fourteen regional administrators are Amharas. *West Africa*, 16 July 1979, p. 1257.

41. For example, the constitution provides that in appointing federal ministers, the President "shall appoint at least one Minister from each State, who shall be an indigene of such State." Federal Republic of Nigeria. *The Constitution of the Federal Republic of Nigeria 1979* (Lagos: Federal Ministry of Information, 1979), Section 135(3).

42. Tordoff, *Administration in Zambia*, pp. 14–15; and Vincent Khapoya, "Kenya Under Moi: Continuity or Change?" *Africa Today* 27, 1 (1980): 21.

43. See Cynthia Enloe, *Police, Military and Ethnicity* (New Brunswick, N.J.: Transaction Books, 1980), ch. 3.

44. For an excellent discussion of this, see V. Subramaniam, "Professional Middle Classes and Post-Colonial Societies," a paper presented to the East African Universities Social Science Conference, Makerere University, December 1971.

45. Republic of Ghana. *Parliamentary Debates*, Official Report, 2nd Series, Vol. 3 (8 June 1970): 520, 534.

46. Arthur A. Nwankwo, "The Ojukwu Factor in Nigerian Politics," *West Africa*, 11 October 1982, p. 2650.

47. *West Africa*, 28 January 1980, p. 140.

48. For example, see *East African Standard* (Nairobi), 28 October 1970, p. 4, and 29 July 1971, p. 4; and *Daily Nation* (Nairobi), 23 June 1973, p. 5, 30 November 1974, p. 3, and 22 February 1975, p. 4.

49. Interview, October 1982; T. David Williams, *Malawi: The Politics of Despair* (Ithaca, N.Y.: Cornell University Press, 1978), pp. 287–288.

50. *Ministry Area Telephone Directory*, Central Government Offices, Accra (December 1972); B. Gil, A. F. Aryee, D. C. Ghansan, *1960 Population Census of Ghana, Special Report 'E', Tribes in Ghana* (Accra: Census Office, 1964), pp. xxxiii–xxxiv; *1970 Population Census of Ghana*, 11 (Accra: Census Office, 1972), p. xxiii.

51. Adamolekun, *Sékou Touré's Guinea*, pp. 130–131.

52. Richard A. Joseph, "Ethnicity and Prebendal Politics in Nigeria: A Theoretical

Outline," a paper presented at the American Political Science Association, Denver, 2–5 September 1982, p. 9.

53. John A. A. Ayoade, "Constitutional Containment of Ethnicity: The Nigerian Case," paper presented at the International Political Science Association, Rio de Janeiro, 9–14 August 1982, pp. 17–18. On UPN opposition to a Senate motion on the implementation of the constitutional provision on the federal character in the civil service and armed forces, see *Daily Times* (Lagos), 9 July 1980, pp. 5, 11.

54. Luckham, *The Nigerian Military*, p. 244; and Okey Onyejekwe, *The Role of the Military in Economic and Social Development* (Washington, D.C.: University Press of America, 1981), pp. 238–240.

55. *Daily Times*, 9 March 1979, p. 2.

56. *West Africa*, 19 March 1972, p. 472; and *Daily Times*, 9 March 1979, p. 2, and 18 March 1972, pp. 1, 3.

57. *Daily Times*, 23 July 1980, p. 5.

58. *West Africa*, 18 January 1982, p. 155; and *Weekly Review*, 27 June 1980, p. 15.

59. Interview, Nairobi, February 1980; also see *Weekly Review*, 25 January 1980, pp. 8–9.

60. Dov Ronen, *Dahomey: Between Tradition and Modernity* (Ithaca, N.Y.: Cornell University Press, 1975), p. 222.

61. *People's Executive Councils' Budgets for FY 80/81* (Khartoum: Ministry of Finance and National Economy, n.d.), mimeo.

62. Dennis L. Dresang, "Ethnic Politics, Representative Bureaucracy and Development Administration: The Zambian Case," *American Political Science Review* 68, 4 (December 1974): 1612–1613; and Donald Rothchild, "Rural-Urban Inequities and Resource Allocation in Zambia," *Journal of Commonwealth Political Studies* 10, 3 (November 1972): 234–238.

63. See Donald Rothchild, "Military Regime Performance: An Appraisal of the Ghana Experience, 1972–78," *Comparative Politics* 12, 4 (July 1980): 475–476.

64. Alan B. Amey and David K. Leonard, "Public Policy, Class and Inequality in Kenya and Tanzania," *Africa Today* 26, 4 (1979): 37–38.

65. Jacques Benjamin, "The Impact of Federal Institutions on West Cameroon's Economic Activity," in Ndiva Kofele-Kale (ed.), *An African Experiment in Nation-Building* (Boulder: Westview Press, 1980), p. 199.

66. Federal Republic of Nigeria, *Report of the Presidential Commission on Revenue Allocation* III (Apapa: Federal Government Press, 1980): 349.

67. Kofele-Kale, *An African Experiment . . .*, p. 165.

68. *Africa Confidential* 24, 13 (22 June 1983): 6; also see, *The Regional Government Act, 1980*, Sects. 6–8.

69. J. Isawa Elaigwu and Victor A. Olorunsola, "Federalism and the Politics of Compromise," in Rothchild and Olorunsola, *State Versus Ethnic Claims*, p. 289.

70. Ali A. Mazrui, *Cultural Engineering and Nation-Building in East Africa* (Evanston, Ill.: Northwestern University Press, 1972), p. 285.

CHAPTER 5

# The Impact of Region on Contemporary African Politics

*Kenneth W. Grundy*

To what extent are West African political experiences different from those of Southern Africa? Have East African politicians developed markedly different institutions and practices than politicians from Central Africa? Can we discern ideological variances or greater levels of regional cooperation or more effective economic performance in one region or another? These sorts of questions force scholars to grapple with a concept, region, that for years they have taken for granted. This paper seeks to begin a preliminary exploration of the impact of region on African politics.

## I. Region as an Analytic Concept

To discuss the regional differences and similarities that have developed in African political systems over the last twenty-five years is not easy. The more we study the problem the more we realize that region is an elusive concept. It poses problems of conceptualization, definition, and operationalization. We assume that region is important, but we are not sure exactly how or why. Indeed, we do not agree even on what it is. On the one hand region is a geographical or spatial construct, capable of being located or delimited on maps and demarcated on the ground. On the other hand region is a shorthand for a congeries of shared social phenomena and properties that correspond in a general way with spatial realities. In still other instances, however, such properties transcend those spatial designations. Here we are referring to questions of race, religion, language, culture, social organization, and economic system. Simply put, people do not subdivide for the convenience of the social scientist or the politician. Analytically, there is overlap and confusion. This does not mean that the concept is useless. It may be superior to other concepts and hence deserve systematic discussion.

Section I examines the analytical problems posed by the concept region. That will be followed by a discussion of how apparent regional differences and similarities are reflected in selected political issues. This discussion focuses on observable regional differences with respect to five major features of political and economic life in independent Africa. These features, treated here as dependent variables, were chosen because they stand out as the most frequently analyzed elements of African politics. First are the struggles for independence and self-government, and the varying levels of violence accompanying those struggles. Second are the organizational and ideological differences associated with patterns of rule. Third is the matter of regime performance according to a variety of developmental indicators. The fourth deals with the roles of the armed forces in politics, especially the question of military intervention into domestic politics. The fifth considers the patterns of establishment and the evolution of regional cooperative functional organizations and provides data on differences among regions. This wide-ranging discussion touches just a few of the many ways that region has contributed to political concerns in Africa. It is intended to be suggestive, not exhaustive.

Part II is followed by a speculative exploration of why ostensibly regional differences exist. It features three dimensions of analysis: the geographical, the temporal, and the cultural. Through this indirect process the tentative conclusion is reached that region indeed matters, but that it is virtually impossible to determine precisely how much. Regional political differences in Africa are seen to be a function of situational variables not normally associated with region in the strict geographical sense. As they have evolved, such variables give the appearance of being regional in nature because their occurrence seems to cluster in spatial patterns that coincide, to some degree, with groupings of physically proximate states. Matters of pace and timing have been critical. Elements such as climate, endemic disease, resources, accessability, and varying colonial and independence policies that emanated therefrom also enter into the analysis. Other distinctions based upon political variables imposed (if not given) have some geographical efficacy, but are less obviously regional or spatial. The settler dimension also deserves coverage, as do other cultural factors that make for diversity as well as uniformity in Africa.

The question of perspective and the focus are matters of the levels and units of analysis.[1] Should black Africa as a whole be emphasized? Many regard black Africa as a discernible unit. Most African polities share more in common with one another than they share with Asian, Middle Eastern, or European regimes.[2] The commonalities of history, culture, economy, social organization, philosophy, and religion must never be overlooked. There are things and ways African that all black peoples share south of the Sahara.[3] A series of cultural traits, diffused throughout Africa south of the Sahara and based on similar modes of adaptation to the natural and historical environment, come to mind. Among them are shared modes of acquisition and production evolving from a land largely unfavorable to agriculture. Related are subsistance patterns resulting from constant efforts at low-yield enterprises. African peoples, as well, have expanded their existential experience and borrowed from and diffused traits through extensive migration, communication, and mass movement far afield. Africa exported valuable products and human beings and was penetrated by and eventually drawn into a global economic structure injurious to African ways and peoples. Thus Africa has been penetrated, ruled, exploited, and proselytized. Above all, Africans have resisted. That much Africans have in common. Granted there are marked differences between individual regimes and peoples, as the country specialist emphasizes, but to stress narrow differences would do violence to the comparative nature of this enterprise, and the fundamental responsibility of the social scientist to look for patterns of behavior and to fashion generalizations about shared properties.

Africanists and publicists refer to regional groupings in Africa such as West Africa, Southern Africa, Equatorial Africa, East Africa, the Horn, and Central Africa as if by some self-evident revelation such rubrics have analytical precision and utility. There is a tendency for peoples physically near one another to share many social traits—language, culture, economic patterns, social organizational forms—that might bring them closer together and encourage them to give greater structure to their shared characteristics and aspirations. But it has also been demonstrated that peoples near to one another are more likely than those far apart to have conflicting interests and even to engage in violent disputes. Shared space, in short, can lead to conflict as well as cooperation.

Assuming that Africa can conveniently be grouped into regions, with only a few controversial exceptions the component parts of each region conform to what might be regarded as traditional divisions of the continent.[4] West Africa includes all of francophone West Africa plus Nigeria, Sierra Leone, Ghana, Guinea-Bissau, and Liberia. Equatorial Africa consists of the states of the former French Equatorial Africa plus Cameroon, Equatorial Guinea, Zaire, Burundi, and Rwanda. In the Horn are Somali, Ethiopia, the Territory of Afars and Issas (Djibouti), and the Sudan. East Africa comprises the three states of Kenya, Tanzania, and Uganda. All states south of Tanzania and Zaire are included in Southern Africa.[5] These groupings can be justified for diverse general and sometimes ideosyncratic reasons, among them culture in the broadest sense, history, geography, convenience, and tradition. Arbitrary—but neat.[6]

## II.  Apparent Regional Differences on Selected Political Issues

Despite differential metropolitan responses to nationalist demands there is a clear-cut pattern to the independence struggle in black Africa. Except for Liberia and Ethiopia, which had maintained their nominal independence throughout the imperial era, and the continuing war in and over Namibia and South Africa, all black African states have gained their juridical independence in the past twenty-five years. The West African states began the process with Ghana in 1957 and ended with Guinea-Bissau in 1974. With but two exceptions (Gambia and Guinea-Bissau) all achieved independence in the five years between 1957 and 1961. Equatorial Africa was not far behind, beginning in 1960 and ending in 1968 with Equatorial Guinea. Except for the latter, all gained independence between 1960 and 1962. Independence for the states of the Horn was strung out from 1956 (Sudan) to 1977 (Afars and Issas). East Africans, with only a single colonial power to deal with, secured their independent status from 1961 to 1963. In Southern Africa independence seems a more disjointed enterprise. South Africa achieved this juridical status in 1910. But for the black-governed states, Malawi and Zambia began the modern process in 1964 to be followed quickly by the former High Commission Territories. Since then the struggle in Angola, Mozambique, and Zimbabwe has been most difficult. Namibia has yet to gain independence and South Africa is still far from majority rule.

The shifting frontiers for the independence struggle have not been ignored by Western policymakers and by African peoples. Nationalist politicians were influenced by colleagues from other territories. If neighbors achieved a timetable leading to independence, then surely one's own state was no less deserving. There is a powerful symbolism associated with black independence, which has been especially encouraging to the black peoples of Zimbabwe, Namibia, and South Africa—just as the independence of India inspired black leaders in West and East Africa before them.

Although it would be difficult to document and demonstrate without qualification, the pattern of nationalist activity has contributed substantially to other aspects of regional similarity and difference. This will be considered later along with the discussion of the causes or possible explanations for regional patterns.

There have been higher levels of violence associated with the independence process in Southern Africa than elsewhere in black Africa. This can be attributed in part to Portuguese and British colonial policies that failed to acknowledge and establish the political and social paramountcy of the indigenous inhabitants. Most of the violence, however, stemmed from the recalcitrance of the more numerous colonial settlers in this region. Data on politically oriented injuries and deaths per thousand people might be revealing.

The duration of the wars for independence can be compared from region to region. The 158 months of armed struggle in Angola, 115 in Mozambique, 152 in Zimbabwe, over 220 so far in Namibia (which has spilled over into Angola), and the continuing violence in South Africa gives Southern Africa the lead by far. Not that the violence associated with the transition to independence elsewhere was insignificant. Data for the Mau Mau emergency indicate an intense war lasting around 50 months and involving officially 13,547 war-related deaths. Virtually every independent African country has suffered a number of politically related deaths and demonstrations and strikes that turned violent, but their scope and scale was limited compared to Southern Africa.

Accompanying the violence in Southern Africa have been much higher levels of regime repression. Data on political prisoners and detentions would confirm this pattern to the struggle. In the Mau Mau emergency the British incarcerated as many as 90,000 Kikuyu, Meru, and Embu in prisons and concentration camps before they were able to contain the insurgency. Likewise, in most other countries high levels of political unrest led to regime repression. But political prisons, rustication, banning, and house arrest became and remain a way of life for Southern Africans associated with nationalist and independence movements.

As for post-independence violence, major civil wars or interethnic violence have smouldered and flared in Nigeria, Chad, Rwanda, Zaire, Uganda, Sudan, Ethiopia, and Angola. Some of this violence has been promoted if not instigated by foreign powers, both African and extra-African. There have also been international conflicts throughout the continent. No region has been spared. Heaviest and most endemic has been the Ethiopia-Somali dispute over the Ogaden in the Horn, the periodic incursions involving Angola and Zaire, the war between Uganda and Tanzania, the struggle for the Western Sahara, and various Chadian factions that have invited in French, Libyan, and other forces. South Africa has sought to destabilize various governments on its borders. Civil disputes have been internationalized. But considering that there are forty-seven black African states and territories, and considering the relative newness of their regimes, the overall levels of postindependence violence have not been extraordinary, especially when compared to the Middle East, the Indian subcontinent, or Southeast Asia.

A second matter of regional differentiation is the question of organizational and ideological styles of rule. Among the generation who piloted their countries to independence in the 1950s and 1960s, few leaders established in their states political/economic institutions radically at odds with the predominant mixed capitalist model. The sorts of enterprises they did foster enhanced the authority of the state in a more interventionist attitude toward the economy. Most, furthermore, paid lip-service to the ideals of a parliamentary model of government. Some regimes evolved into single party systems based on centralized executive rule and bureaucratic dictation. Some experimented with socialist and other participatory techniques. The common denominators were the leaders' determination to stay in power and their dependence upon collaborative bureaucrats, many of whom saw public service as a vehicle for private gain. Thus the states of West Africa, Equatorial Africa, East Africa, and the Horn began their independent existences with relatively cautious and moderate regimes.

Very generally speaking, regional distinctions can be discerned in the organizational and ideological preferences of African regimes. A sort of demonstration effect is at work. This, too, is related to timing. As African nationalism moved southward, the world's tolerance for, and the African leaders' awareness of and familiarity with, more radical systems of government and economy were reflected by the sorts of choices made by African state leaders. There are, of course, many and significant exceptions—Nkrumah's Ghana, Touré's Guinea, and Keita's Mali are examples of West African governments that took rhetorical and policy courses out of step with the accepted accommodationist patterns in the late 1950s and early 1960s, so out of step, one might say, that two were overthrown by military coups and one has modified its stance markedly in the 1970s and 1980s.[7]

Are these regional patterns? Perhaps. Pressure to conform and the behavior of one's neighbors and peers contribute to the situational referents within which politicians must function. A relatively peaceful transition to independence (and again there were exceptions) and colonial powers that sought alternative ways of retaining influence and power in the face of a global commitment to ending formal colonial rule led to a first generation of African leaders who were chiefly reformist. The colonial powers were generally responsible for easing this element into power.

Western governments, of course, were hostile to Marxist-Leninist leaders. In contrast, the socialist world was lavish in expressions of support for particular independence movements. Radical parties were suppressed. In turn, such life experiences—not just for Marxist-Leninists but for many nonideological nationalist leaders—contributed to an inclination toward internal coercion and conformity once these leaders gained power. Stress was on control and suppression of political dissent, internal mobilization, and conformity, tendencies the socialist powers and some Western regimes willingly encouraged and abetted.

Gaps often emerge between rhetoric and practice in African socialist and in scientific socialist regimes. Such gaps are due in part to resource constraints, but they also grow out of the international distribution of forces and domestic environments that make a populist ideology imperative and an individualistic one anathema. This is, in Jowitt's words, an "easy-choice environment."[8]

This first generation of leaders, then, used socialism as a camouflage but practiced, if not capitalism, then some pragmatic version of the mixed economy. Pragmatism, however, was based not on whether a policy "worked" in terms of productivity, efficiency, or equity. Rather, pragmatism marked a path of least political resistance and personal political expediency and material gain. Such an economic system included state capitalism, foreign economic penetration, and bureaucratic entrepreneurship for private gain. The common denominator seemed to be a nationalist commitment to wrest control of political and economic life from foreign forces. Although socialism dominated ideological discourse in the 1960s, it lacked programmatic content. Modified versions of the liberal market economy with considerable state direction and regulation were commonplace amid a chorus of socialist advocacy. By the late 1960s such professions of flaccid and semiotic socialism were in retreat, subject to intense criticism and discredited in practice. This plowed the ground for military takeovers and for a new generation of scientific socialists, especially in yet-to-be independent countries.

In the political field, the first generation built regimes that they hoped would assure for themselves an indefinite tenure in power. Invariably this meant a public posture of populist concern and a private coalition of forces profiting from the new order and determined to defend it. Claude Ake has called the former "defensive radicalism," a sham in which the real intent is to solidify the popularity of the bourgeoisie in power. The long-range effect is to heighten mass consciousness and to highlight the social contradictions in such regimes.[9] The constellation of forces defending the status quo usually transcended national boundaries and often involved the former metropole and other global interests. Eventually for some, their coalitions collapsed. Some were replaced by military rulers or their surrogates, and others led to self-proclaimed scientific socialist regimes. In other instances, the international backing lost interest or became overtly hostile.

Ideological choice involves a political act that may serve domestic as well as international purposes. It can be seen as a device for distancing one's regime from political forces regarded as liabilities. It may also be seen as a symbol and an act of relationship, identifying with politically valuable allies, a form of political differentiation not unlike what consumer economists call brand identity. And it may represent a genuine search for viable guidelines for future policy. Weak elites and weak states must find allies willing and able to help them counter direct military and political threats, neighboring antagonists, or larger global forces that they perceive to be working against their interests.

Ideological choice for much of Africa is not usually a question of making decisions based on a full panoply of alternatives, especially in the economic realm. What alternatives are there to the West when it comes to trade and investment capital? And what alternatives are there to arms supplies from the socialist camp for revolutionary movements? In some respects to offset such constraints, but more importantly to try to legitimize and solidify their claims to rule and to stifle opposition, some leaders openly opt for a Leninist political approach. Marxism-Leninism and scientific socialism are in some respects regarded as the only choices available for revolutionary elites in Mozambique, Angola, Ethiopia, Benin, and the Congo Peoples Republic. Survival and autonomy for elites faced with the threat of political extinction by powerful enemies, especially in Southern Africa, leave little range for negotiation and optimizing. For them, the choice set has never been complete. Had it been complete they still might well have taken the options that they did.

Once the radical elites had realized that their hopes for extensive Soviet economic assistance would be less than they had anticipated, the political survival instincts of the elites led them to respond to the situation by developing "tactical concessions" and ideological compromises. In this context, ideological choice is a function of, inter alia, the situation, not in a sociology of knowledge sense, but in the sense that ideology is largely instrumental to the immediate political needs of the elites vying for power.

Having voiced the scientific socialist option, not only do sources of fraternal aid sharpen, but opposition from the West also solidifies. Western firms are reticent to invest. Even if they were so inclined, United States governmental hostility and the withholding of diplomatic recognition would make doing business difficult. An emphasis on distributive justice rather than production and "growth" likewise flies in the face of Western preconceptions about "development." Ideology in this milieu becomes less a matter of ideal choice and more a function of a composite of conditions, situations, and self-defined expectations.

The first generation of African leaders were the products of a relatively modulated transitional process to independence. Many achieved power with the assistance and blessing of the colonial authorites. It was important for them to demonstrate their nationalist credentials and their independence from the ancien regimes. Rhetoric and ideology served such a purpose. The ideas of African socialism, anti-imperialism, anti-neocolonialism, nonalignment, and negritude (or the African personality) provided such a vehicle for political differentiation. But many of these concepts were ill-defined, confusing, contradictory sets of principles and symbols. They were incoherent pronouncements not based on serious class analysis. The economic models that evolved were flabby mixed economies consisting of thinly disguised state capitalist institutions interacting with foreign private enterprise, a rapidly growing bureaucratic structure, and an economically weak but politically insistent local private sector.

There are, furthermore, the important distinctions between rhetoric (statements of preference and intention), decisions (outputs of the political system), and consequences (policy outcomes or results). One might look for regional differences with regard to economic performance. Unfortunately, the results have been inconclusive. There is a slight tendency for states further into Southern Africa to opt for the political rhetoric of scientific socialism. Yet the regional lines are blurred by similar predilections of states elsewhere on the continent (Benin, Congo Peoples Republic, and Ethiopia, e.g.). Nonetheless, economic performance does not seem to be linked in clear fashion to any regional or ideological model. Success stories (in terms of growth rates) appear in West Africa (Nigeria and Ivory Coast), in East Africa (Kenya), in Equatorial Africa (Gabon), and in Southern Africa (Botswana and Zimbabwe). Failures according to growth criteria likewise are geographically dispersed. No region has a corner on economic growth performance or on lack of performance, and quite idiosyncratic and country-specific historical variables can shape the consequences of state policy.

Crawford Young, in his careful study of the ideology-performance nexus, includes (in addition to GNP growth factors) five other evaluation criteria for judging developmental performance.[10] They are equality of distribution, autonomy and self-reliance, the preservation of human dignity, participation, and the expansion of societal capacity. Despite methodological problems associated with each of these criteria, he is able to arrive at qualified and speculative conclusions.

With regard to income distribution, it would appear that scientific socialist regimes have demonstrated a policy priority to this end, whereas the actual effects of such priorities remain to be demonstrated. Capitalist states permit very high returns to a narrow segment of the elite (political, bureaucratic, business, and expatriate), and socialist states seem more likely to inhibit large concentrations of personal wealth. But for ordinary citizens the differences in net return are marginal. African states that opt for a predominantly capitalist model, however, seem particularly susceptible to large-scale corruption. Perhaps socialist state bureaucrats in Africa have not had sufficient time to entrench and possibly enrich themselves. At least they profess a public ethic that seeks to restrain the privatization of public resources. Likewise, with regard to the delivery of basic state services, there is little if any correlation between ideology and performance.

Autonomy and self-reliance are even more difficult to evaluate. Although Young concludes that there is no "close correlation" between the degree of autonomy and ideology, it would also appear that the Marxist-Leninist states seem to exercise in policy terms a wider range of relationships with outside forces. Note, for examples, Angola's links with Gulf Oil and Benin's membership in the CFA zone, as well as their close ties with Cuba and the USSR.

Young's human dignity criterion refers to degrees of repression and the presence of large refugee populations from the states in question. Regional variations seem to be marginal. Patterns of refugee flow largely grew out of the wars for self-government and internal unrest. Refugees seem to flow most heavily out of Angola, Mozambique, Zimbabwe, Rwanda, Uganda, and Zaire. By and large, the degree of political repression is a function of insecure political elites—region does not seem to figure into the equation except insofar as proximity to zones of violence contributes to refugee flows.

Southern African states with a scientific socialist bent appear determined to engage the populace in political life. Partly this grows out of their achievement of independence through protracted armed warfare involving large numbers of fighters and enveloping the citizenry in political choice and action. However, Tanzania gained independence without such warfare. Elsewhere, having lived through a still-born era of "mobilization," insecure rulers and military regimes lacking legitimacy have permitted the atrophy and decline of their dominant single-party systems.[11] Political participation has been discouraged.[12] Unable to control the popular political output, regimes have chosen to make politics a centralized, managed pheonomenon, divorced from popular participation. Regional differences would seem to matter here, as the Southern African states at least appear to be more populist and participatory, in a controlled sense. But the vitality of the elections in Nigeria, the earlier elections and the TANU/CCM (Chama Cha Mapinduzi) structure in Tanzania, and the vibrant press in Kenya and elsewhere demonstrate that participation is alive in other regions, too.

Finally, with regard to the capacity of state institutions to "perform" or to "deliver," there seem to be no discernible regional patterns. Regimes in all regions, of all political and ideological persuasions, seem equally inept, equally effective. In this regard regime performance is marginally affected by regional differences, if at all.

Thus, in general, West Africa, Equatorial Africa, East Africa, and the Horn muddled through their first decade and a half of independence with political-economic regimes verbally but not practically different from one another. For an outsider taking the long view, the tendency to ask, "What real difference does this make?" prevails.

Some of the second generation of leaders were different. Many achieved power through armed revolutionary struggle. In other cases the military coup was the vehicle to power (e.g., Ethiopia and Benin). For them, the ideological idiom was also a matter of political differentiation. But they were an "unestablished elite," very much rejected and opposed by the colonial power (Portugal), the settler minorities (Zimbabwe and South Africa), and the Western power structure in Europe and North America. Overall the revolutionaries lacked tolerance of compromise and moderation. They preferred coercion to co-optation and indecision, and they put forth exclusivist themes. Scientific socialism was the one true avenue to achievement. Ideological consistency and commitment were ostensibly imperative to give the revolution cohesion and direction.

No ideological mode has a monopoly on massive and systematic assaults on political freedoms. Such assaults are a function not of ideology but of political insecurity and personality defect. While most African regimes have been intolerant of open organized opposition, they have often chosen to co-opt rather than coerce opponents. Unestablished elites, perhaps less confident of their manipulative skills and more convinced of their ideological purpose, may still be slightly more inclined to turn to coercive devices.

In the larger order, the second wave of leaders such as Cabral, Machel, Dos Santos, Mugabe, and Tambo identified with a world system that appeared to provide an alternative to the international capitalist economy. If viewed as a historical process, independence and development defined scientific socialism as being more progressive or in the vanguard of their less adventuresome or less creative neighbors. Socialism symbolizes development and achievement, especially if one regards socialism as a qualitative rather than a quantitative state of grace. But socialist regimes were not entirely embraced by the rest of the socialist world, and Marxist-Leninists in Africa still preferred to exercise a measure of independent choice. As pragmatic political actors, they sought to maximize opportunities rather than to be taken for granted by either Super Power. Some saw scientific socialism as an intermediary position (domestically and internationally) rather than a total identification with what some feared as one of the Cold War poles. That socialists should take this line, especially in the violent cockpit of Southern Africa, would appear to demonstrate that African nationalism has reached a new plateau constructed on the promise of real change and the frustration with implacable minority resistance to the moral imperatives of the twentieth century.

The military coup is practically endemic to all regions of Africa. This is

not to say that the incidence of military coups is random. Insofar as coups
reflect the total social structural problems of a state there have been certain
social variables that contribute to social and regime instability and hence military intervention. Both social mobilization and the presence of a dominant
ethnic group have been found to be destabilizing.[13] To some extent this might
be regarded as a regional consideration in that certain sorts of geographical-
topographical factors contributed to the formation of larger or smaller ethnic
aggregations or more centralized or dispersed precolonial political structures.
Yet coups can also result from divisions within the armed forces that may not
necessarily reflect societal cleavages. Then again they may if society's strat-
ifications are replicated in its key institutions or if one group controls the governmental or political structure and a different group the military or segments
thereof.

West African states, probably because they have been independent longer,
and possibly because their ethnic-cultural divisions seem to cut horizontally
(east-west), seem to have endured a greater number of military coups. Military
factions have assumed power in a higher proportion of states and there have
been a larger number of takeovers per state. Only Senegal has avoided a coup.
But Equatorial Africa and the Horn are nearly as unstable, if not in numbers
of coups, then in the proportion of states so affected. There have been fewer
coups in East Africa, with only Uganda having been subject to direct military
rule. All three states have had armed forces mutinies, however.

Southern Africa has been relatively free of coups and coup attempts. The
Malagasy Republic alone has endured a military regime. This does not mean
that the armed forces are less of a political force in Southern Africa. For some
states the armed struggle for independence fostered an especially close working relationship between the ruling party and the armed forces. In others, the
elites, aware of the dangers of an underrewarded military and the lessons of
their brethren to the north, took measures to appease or outflank the armed
forces or in other ways to contain their political ambitions. The former High
Commission Territories, for example, waited years before they established armies, although they did possess paramilitary Police Mobile Units.

It might seem that the most obvious source of data about regional differences in Africa would emerge from the record of the numerous regional interstate organizations that have been created through the years. There were
thirty-five of these on the continent in mid-1983, many of them insignificant
and practically useless. Institutional overlap itself has become a barrier to further cooperation and integration. Thus because of diverse histories, composi-
tions, structures, and purposes, it is virtually impossible to compare regional
organizations with regard to their success or effectiveness.[14] States have
banded together for three main reasons: domestic politics, security, and eco-

nomic development. This process has been going on continuously since the first African states gained independence. A few organizations were even established prior to independence by the colonial regimes or by the European settlers. In such cases, these organizations were designed to facilitate colonial administration, to reduce the costs of colonial rule, to deflect black nationalism, or to further the interests and demands of the settlers. In addition, some regional interstate organizations had their genesis in collaborative interterritorial independence and liberation movements prior to securing independence. There are also the examples and influence of federal policies in British and French colonies. Most interstate organizations tend to be functional, often single-purpose, organizations. The narrower and less political the ends, the more likely the organizations are to survive. In order to compare regional organizational tendencies, a few examples will be given.

West Africa has been a breeding ground of regional organizations. Beginning in 1904 when the French created the federations of French West Africa and French Equatorial Africa to facilitate the administration of their extensive empires and to relieve the French Treasury of financial burdens that were assigned to the richer colonies, the pattern had been established. These federations were then adapted, after World War II, to serve as frameworks for limited representative government with regional assemblies based in Dakar and Brazzaville. In this capacity they contributed to the development of pan-territorial political parties, and to the realization that the federal principle favored some regional states and frustrated others. The French also established a number of regional functional organizations for diverse narrower purposes.

After independence, a distinct pattern of regionalism emerged in French-speaking Africa, one characterized by diversity, confusion, and continued dependence on France. There are some eleven regional organizations in francophone West Africa. They vary in the number of member-states in each organization, and in functions that sometimes overlap. The one constant has been that France has been able to manipulate these organizations to help France coordinate its own regional activities.[15] The West African inability to turn such regional organizations into agencies to promote intra-African cooperation is as much a function of their own political instability and economic weakness as it is of France's determination to remain the dominant European power in West Africa.

The British Colonial Office was not committed to common organizations for its holdings in West Africa. This was in keeping with a more pragmatic, ad hoc style of rule. Moreover, since these territories were noncontiguous, regional organization demanded greater and more costly coordination than could be supplied from London itself.

There are, of course, a few West African regional organizations that transcend linguistic, religious, and even ideological divisions. Some are narrow in scope and membership, such as the Chad Basin Commission (Cameroon, Chad, Niger, and Nigeria). This Commission has accomplished only small-scale projects and at one point was virtually moribund. Some are more inclusive, such as the Niger Basin Authority, with thirteen member-states. And some can be regarded as successful in that they have performed limited tasks usefully and established the groundwork for further cooperation. For example, the Mano River Union consisting of Liberia, Sierra Leone, and Guinea has survived since 1973. Even the violent military coup in Liberia in 1980 and small incidents on the borders between member-states have not seriously damaged the organization. Its aims are to promote joint agricultural and industrial production, trade, training, and the exploitation of natural resources. So far Union development and economic integration is most pronounced in trade and the elimination of tariff barriers between the two older members (Guinea joined in 1980), in road development, and in the training of middle-level civil servants. Despite governmental changes, coups, instability, and low economic performance in individual member-states, some of these organizations seem to survive (but not thrive), accumulating a patina of structure and continuity in the midst of a confusion of kinetic change.

At the broader, total West African level, the most significant attempt to sever neocolonial links has been the establishment of the Economic Community of West Africa (ECOWAS) in 1975. All fifteen (now sixteen) West African states signed that treaty and thereby created an organization to establish the largest customs union in Africa. The organization is rich in proposals, short on implementation. It seeks to liberalize trade; to facilitate the free flow of the factors of production, including the movement of people within the Community; and to encourage already existing regional organizations to merge their aims with those of ECOWAS (e.g., the francophone West African Economic Community [CEAO] and the Mano River Union). It has other elaborate development cooperative schemes for the region, but these are barely at the proposal stage. Instead, ECOWAS has seemed to have earned a reputation for the flamboyant life-style of its Secretariat rather than for practical accomplishments. By including Nigeria, Ivory Coast, and Senegal, states which hitherto had been wary of larger economic groupings, ECOWAS possesses the promise of economic success, but also the prospect of neocolonial influences, injected by way of economically larger "subimperial" states such as Nigeria or the Ivory Coast. The pattern of such states acting as points of penetration for global powers is not unimportant. Yet to fail to encourage regional approaches to common problems because of wealth and power asymmetries is to doom the region to perpetual weakness and conflict.

The Central African Customs Union (UDEAC) also faces this problem.

How can small and weak states resist dependence upon the industrial states of the northern hemisphere without becoming dependent on regionally dominant states? Chad, for instance, left UDEAC because it feared Camerounian power. Instead, it drifted into Zaire's sphere when it joined the Union des états de l'Afrique centrale (UEAC).

In the British colonies of East Africa there was hope, around independence time, that the East African Common Services Organization might provide a framework for greater cooperation and economic interaction between Kenya, Tanganyika, Uganda, and Zanzibar.[16] Some two dozen service bodies were firmly in place and most were quite effective. Three—the East African airways, railways and harbors, and posts and telecommunications—were self-financing. Others, such as the electricity supply commission, common currency, tariffs, research service, statistics, higher education, and the tourist travel association, were less successful. Some particularly optimistic observers, however, went so far as to see the EACSO as the first step toward the breakdown of state entities and the establishment of a larger regional state. Through neofunctionalist logic it was hoped that efficient and successful functional cooperation would lead to stronger interstate bureaucracies, the assignment of more functions to the regional organization, the attachment of greater loyalty to the larger entity, and eventually the withering away of the states and the strengthening of a new, more extensive central entity.

But this was not to be. The new governments, for various reasons, did not share a commitment to expanding the diverse roles of the EACSO. Although an East African Community was proclaimed in 1967, commonality and community were soon dissipated in a series of contentious disputes that led to the dismantling of various services, one after another. Applications for membership from Zambia, Ethiopia, Somalia, and Burundi were never approved and later events invalidated their efforts at geographical inclusiveness. By the early 1970s little remained, and by 1977 the EAC finally collapsed, with each member-state seizing what Community assets it could lay its hands on. The demise of the EAC was partly caused by the inordinate economic power of Kenya, partly a function of bureaucrats and politicians in each state resisting the surrender of services normally performed at state levels, and partly a result of genuine conflicting state and class interests in each member-state.

Much could be summed up in the phrase "the Nairobi mentality." Used by the non-Kenyans, it connoted a sense of superiority, a dislike of provincials, and an impatience with consultation. Kenya, for example, found it difficult to cooperate with Uganda and Tanzania on the matter of industrial planning, the attraction of foreign investment, and the location of industry. The node of growth around Nairobi was a natural attraction to foreign capital. Kenya felt that its sacrifice would be too great if it, in the interests of balanced Community-wide growth, discouraged investors and steered them to their partners. To Kenyans, "the Nairobi mentality" was rather a supersensitivity in Tanganyikans and Ugandans to the dynamism of Kenya's leaders. These conflicting interests were fostered and compounded by global powers that sought to extend their interests in the region by penetrating individual states and governments. The false promise of the early sixties foundered on the realities of political life in newly independent states. Yet to this day, the EACSO stands as a rare example of a regional organization that "worked," at least for a while, in transcending state boundaries by providing valued services. New talk of reviving the EAC has recently been heard in all three East African capitals.

Less successful, and clearly a creature of a colonial power willing to accommodate the demands of its settler population, was the Federation of Rhodesia and Nyasaland (1953–1963) in central Africa.[17] After Malawi and Zambia opted for independence and the Rhodesian-settler right wing gained ascendance, the breakup of the Federation followed. The Federation was designed primarily to serve Rhodesian industrial and commercial interests. Southern Rhodesian whites were keen to exploit Northern Rhodesia's copper wealth and to blunt black nationalism in the region. Because of the economic advantages to Rhodesia's whites, Salisbury's politicians were determined not to loosen their political hold on the north. Rewards and costs of federation were shared unequally and the federal organs dictated policy to member-states. Subsequent British governments realized these structural weaknesses. A British inquiry directed by Lord Monckton in 1960 concluded that African opposition in Malawi and Northern Rhodesia was too great and that the Federation could not survive without separate constitutional provisions for each territory. The Federation's collapse added another blemish to the record of federal collaborative schemes in Africa. Yet this failure did not discourage Africans for long.

The entente that is called the Front-Line States (Angola, Botswana, Mozambique, Tanzania, Zambia, and Zimbabwe) is not, in strict terms, a regional qua geographical organization.[18] However, if one is prepared to define region in terms of a response to a practical issue, i.e., the achievement of black rule in white dominated states, then the FLS have been able to coordinate policy and response quite well. Any state that is located on the "fault line" of Southern Africa and is willing to become directly engaged in assisting independence movements may ask to be included. It is a one-issue organization, to be sure, but the issue is absolutely central to the affairs of the continent. The FLS, as a relatively informal body that coordinates foreign policies, has achieved a remarkable record in supporting the demands first of black Zimbabweans and presently of South Africans and Namibians.

The economic counterpart of the FLS is the Southern African Development

Coordination Conference (SADCC).[19] Since April 1980 it has sought to foster functional cooperation along a broad range of economic and infrastructural issues. In one sense SADCC is an explicit challenge and alternative to the South African proposed and dominated Constellation of Southern African States and the actual networks of economic infrastructure in the region. In another and more important sense, however, it is a creative step, establishing and enriching new links, as well as severing old patterns of exchange. Because of a relatively quiet resolve, institutional and structural innovations, a willingness to divide labors equitably, and patience to "begin at the beginning" so to speak, SADCC seems to be achieving what other more flamboyant organizations have been unable to achieve. SADCC has sought not to burden itself with organization and bureaucracy. To begin with, its members (the six FLS plus Lesotho, Malawi, and Swaziland) set modest goals, content to strive for small victories. Subdued rhetoric marks SADCC's proceedings. Although SADCC has been largely dependent on Western sources of funding, members have managed to retain control of the pace and direction of a diverse program of projects.

Although superficially restrained, the sum total of SADCC's enterprise reflects an altogether radical program. No less a purpose is sought than the progressive divorce of black Southern African economic life from the pervasive wealth and infrastructural centrality of South Africa. The three member-states' governments that are not associated with the FLS, however, are less firmly committed to such a separation. The establishment of SADCC is, thereby, a declaration of intent to redesign the economic map of the region, but to do so by appealing to the national and state interests of member-states. Collective interests are not to be pushed at the expense of the sensibilities of individual members. As one analyst put it: "SADCC has resolved the knotty problems associated with any integration scheme by, in essence, running away from them. The much-heralded 'flexibility' attributed to SADCC is a euphemism for leaving each member free to pursue its own national interests."[20] Excessive centralization is also avoided, at some cost. SADCC's first years' activities would seem to be building cautiously to their collaborative ends, thereby suppressing or defusing the ideological tensions that might be expected to attend a developmental effort that involves Marxist and capitalist governing elites. For SADCC, coordination takes precedence over integration.

A second Southern African regional organization, the Preferential Trade Area for Eastern and Southern African States, was created in December 1981. From one perspective the PTA, with fourteen member-states, rivals SADCC. For another it complements SADCC, since it addresses tariff questions. All eligible non-SADCC states in the vicinity (except for the Seychelles and Madagascar) have joined the PTA. But not all SADCC members have opted for membership. Those SADCC members that seem to favor PTA are Lesotho, Malawi, Swaziland, Zambia, and Zimbabwe, all of which are landlocked. Four of the six FLS—Angola, Botswana, Mozambique, and Tanzania—seem skeptical of PTA. They see the PTA geographically dispersed, economically without focus, too bureaucratic, and a potential rival to SADCC. Since PTA is very much in its early stages, it is conceivable that it may succeed in attracting all regional actors into its ranks in the future.

In general, the African record with regional organizations is uneven, with far more failures than successes. It was particularly in the first years of independence that regional groupings failed, and this contributed to a distrust of regional solutions. Political instability does not facilitate long-range regional peace and planning. Ideologically motivated governments, insecure and distrusting, hardly favor sacrifice and cooperation. Since regionalism was at first seen as the logical organizational response to the inadequacies and legacies of colonial rule, regional organizations were expected to solve inherent problems that demanded major structural change. Quite naturally, they were not up to such expectations. Far from being facilitators of unity and development, regional issues tend often to contribute to contention and competition.

Occasionally, however, groupings have contributed to a reduction of regional tensions, and this accomplishment should not be minimized. But even the "success" stories, those organizations that have lasted or that served as forerunners for subsequent organizations, may have contributed most to enhancing the economic growth of dominant member-states, or of the core elites in key states. In Africa, the integrative potential of regionalism has yet to be realized. Although the single most advanced example of regional cooperation is from East Africa, that organization did not survive much beyond the period immediately after independence. West Africa has a mixed record of small successes and monumental flops. Since the balkanization of Africa is more complete in West Africa and Equatorial Africa, it stands to reason that West African regional cooperation, of necessity, had a tougher and longer road to travel than elsewhere.

Southern African states enjoy the benefit of having observed and learned from the tribulations of regionalism elsewhere in Africa, of having a powerful enemy state that serves as a rallying point, and of having no single regional actor (save South Africa and to a lesser extent Zimbabwe) that is dominant and thereby threatening. The goals are clear. The need is undeniable. The implacability of settler determination demands implacable resistance. SADCC can thereby coordinate and serve as a clearing house for a variety of economic programs and projects. So far, it appears to be progressing well.

Are there regional causes for these different patterns? Probably not. More likely it is a matter of timing—another "generation" of leaders—mature in the sense that they have learned from past mistakes. The stimulus to cooperation is obvious. Yet they are wary of moving too far too fast. They are willing to innovate organizationally to emphasize output and not structure. They are determined to succeed and not to be "used."

## III. What Causes Such Differences?

There are three major dimensions to the analysis that follows: (1) the geographical, (2) the temporal, and (3) the cultural. It is virtually impossible to disaggregate these dimensions or to say which is responsible for the differences that have been described in the preceding section.

The most apparent regional distinctions might be called geographic factors. It is fitting to begin the discussion with the most deterministic elements, those least subject to human change and intervention, such as climate, resource endowment, topography, and spatial relationships. These are givens which, to be sure, can be altered by human activity. Certainly their importance in social affairs can be augmented or diminished by conscious policy. But by and large, such deterministic features establish the parameters around which people must labor. Grand patterns of migration, economic structure, and cultural interaction in the long run are determined by geographical concerns. These factors in turn have an overarching effect on political structure and social organization. West African states, to take just one set of examples, reflect geographical givens by being divided into east-west striations or ecological zones of tropical rain forest, savanna, and sahelian desert, and the gradations and shadings between these zones. Thus, socially heterogeneous populations and economic variety are expected within states the boundaries of which run north and south. East Africa, because of highland areas climatically attractive to European settlers, assured that this social ingredient would shape life in Kenya and parts of other countries. The mineral riches of Southern Africa were an attraction to capital and to large numbers of European adventurers and entrepreneurs, just as the location of the Cape of Good Hope on the sea route to the Indies prompted the Dutch East India Company to establish a provisioning station there, with all the subsequent social history that followed. In many respects the present condition of many African peoples and entire regions can be traced to the fortuitous factors of geography.

Even before the independence struggles, before the coming of European settlers, investors, soldiers, and administrators, spatial considerations determined the extent and pattern by which African peoples became drawn into the world economy. "The chains of historical causation," as Barrington Moore has called them, could conceivably be traced deep into African history. The process is continuous and any analytical break in this ongoing process is bound to be arbitrary. But the fact remains that African peoples responded differently to efforts to incorporate them and the resources they commanded or sat astride. Degrees of subjugation reflected their abilities to resist and the importance of these peoples and territories as perceived by European governments and power elements. As Bernard Magubane notes, "The political economy in Africa can only be understood in terms of the relation of various African countries to the international power structure and the social classes this power structure reproduced within the dominated formations."[21] Geographical factors shaped those differential relations.

Contemporary history also prompts a confusion of explanations. Something as simple as the proximity of peoples and governments to zones of conflict (most particularly the settler-black conflict in Southern Africa) can have a profound impact on neighboring states. Zambia's economic difficulties, Angola's ongoing unrest, Zaire's nonperformance are to some extent shaped by their "front-line" situations. States in trouble are like fish in distress; they attract the Great Power "sharks" anxious to insinuate themselves into fluid situations, "targets of opportunity" as they have been called. The Horn and the Angola-Zaire-Namibia complex are two cases in point.

Thus because of the differential spatial links, climates, resource endowments, topography, and proximity to existing conflicts, Africa's regions have emerged with different social and political structures and perspectives. This ties in, at several points, with the temporal factor and with issues of timing and pace.

V. I. Lenin wrote of the "uneven development of capitalism" and Stalin of the "ebb and flow" of history.[22] What they were referring to, among other things, was to a temporal variable that reflects the ever-changing and divergent class and productive relations that prevail throughout the world at any one time and over time. These in turn lead to a spasmodic approach to revolution and development that affects various actors differently.

Some of the variety in contemporary political and economic life in Africa can be attributed to the timing of the decolonization process. Metropolitan powers saw their fortunes rise and fall at varying paces. But the impact of World War II fell similarly, though not uniformly, throughout black Africa. This in turn contributed to increased pressure from nationalist movements in the colonies. The result was that by the 1950s the British and the French were searching about for "honorable" ways to extricate themselves from the obligations of administration in Africa and Asia while at the same time trying to preserve for themselves in their respective colonies economic advantage and strategic and political influence if not control. The West was prepared to accept liberal transition provided it was not violent and provided the regimes established thereby continued to deal propitiously with the ex–metropolitan power. The fewest obstacles to such a transition were posed where few extenuating forces existed—only scattered or no settlers and limited valuable (strategic and economic) exploitable resources. West Africa was the logical starting place.

Naturally the metropolitan powers and the nationalist movements in Africa did not play out this scene on an empty stage. The Cold War contest between the United States and the USSR from around 1958 to the mid-1960s (in which the European states were not disinterested bystanders) established certain guidelines for the decolonization process. Part of the liberal thrust to the process developed because the Super Powers were emerging from self-tailored policy straitjackets associated with the two-camp image of world politics. There was no neutral or middle ground. Thus Stalinists regarded Gandhi as a "traitor," a "demagogue," and a bourgeois reformist. They called Nnamdi Azikiwe an "African Gandhi" and the author of a "colonial edition" of American pragmatist philosophy. Nkrumah was labeled a representative of the "big bourgeoisie" and his party a "screen covering the domination of English imperialism" in the Gold Coast.[23]

On the other hand, U.S. leaders, especially John Foster Dulles, expressed a mirror image of the situation. If you were not outwardly procapitalist (and few black leaders would openly admit to such politically damaging views) you must, ipso facto, be procommunist. These attitudes were self-defeating, as they served to alienate potentially cooperative Third World elites.

The European leaders and the Third World nationalists helped to remove such ideological blinders. As the Cold Warriors abandoned the two-camp image, they came to tolerate nonalignment and mixed economic systems and criticism from the Third World. Both Khrushchev and Kennedy modified the rigid foreign policies of their countries and contributed to the relatively calm acceptance of significant juridical changes in world affairs. They did not abandon the Cold War. Rather, they pursued their aims more flexibly.

As Cold War pressures relaxed in the 1960s, however, and detente between East and West took fragile root, so too did the march of African nationalism come face to face against the uncompromising colonialism of Portugal and the intense resistance of colonial settlers in Zimbabwe, Namibia, and South Africa. American interest in Africa declined as the United States became preoccupied with Vietnam and the Middle East. The USSR reduced its foreign policy commitments in Africa, too. Other than cleaning up a few of the "loose ends" of colonial rule, the struggle bogged down on the Zambezi and the borders with the Portuguese-ruled territories.

Once the wars of independence regained momentum, the USSR was into its military assistance mode; and the United States, although it took a stronger anticommunist line, was unwilling or unable to translate its rhetoric into practical policy. In this brief period between 1974 and 1979 new more militantly socialist and Leninist regimes were spawned. In Mozambique, Angola, Ethiopia, Guinea (Bissau), and eventually Zimbabwe regimes steeled in battle at first felt little need to compromise with their enemies or their less committed countrymen. Moreover, socialist bloc assistance, including military manpower from abroad, gave spine to their ideological line. Policies reflected the tangible armed assistance supplied by the socialist camp and the overt hostility shown them by the West. Out of conviction and expediency they sought alternative economic arrangements to facilitate a greater independence from world capitalism. The timing of their independence and the violent nature of the transition itself contributed to a changed mood in Southern Africa and in many of those regimes established during this half decade.

The Namibian and South African hostilities seem to be overshadowed among the Powers by world conditions that give these efforts low priority. The West, especially the United States, is preoccupied by the Middle East and Central America. The USSR is mired in a costly war in Afghanistan, economic problems at home, and a leadership succession contest not totally resolved, while its East European allies search for greater political and economic latitude. The Soviet Union will not lightly commit itself in Southern Africa if it feels that the Western world will challenge its policies directly. Not that world affairs alone can determine the outcome of wars for independence in Southern Africa. But they do define the context in which those struggles take place and, as such, they add to the challenges or lighten the burdens, depending on one's perspective.

Cold War configurations of power are important, but the global economic picture adds yet another ingredient. Resource scarcities, highlighted by OPEC's racheting upwards of petroleum prices, and periods of recession and growth have given added salience to industrial state/Third World state relations. In this milieu, Southern Africa takes on enriched importance. The global economy touches on Africa in a variety of ways. It affects investment patterns where Western firms and banks want to see stability. Investment is extremely sensitive to political considerations, with possible exceptions where there are scarce raw materials and where the regime guarantees a skilled and obedient work force, ideology notwithstanding. The inflated prices for a few vital commodities and the inability of more and more African states to feed themselves have made for a negative image in the West about African regime performance. The problems seem to be continent-wide. Except for a very few states blessed with raw materials in continual demand and scarce supply, no region of Africa has sustained itself well, or markedly better than other regions. The generally sluggish performance of the world's economy and the weak economic showing of Africa have the effect of homogenizing African regimes in the popular mind rather than accenting differences.

Linking the geographical and temporal dimensions is not easy. One possible mode of analysis might be found by focusing on spatial diffusion.[24] The two dimensions of space and time are central to diffusion theory. If ideas and innovations are to move across geographic space, they have to be transmitted. Additionally, the rate of movement can be influenced by intervening factors—mountain chains and cultural gaps, for examples. To overcome distance, carriers seek to offset barriers to diffusion.

There are two basic types of diffusion processes. First is what might be called contagious diffusion, by which ideas and things spread from one person to others nearby. In traditional societies, where long-distance communication and travel are difficult, most inexpensive innovations spread by contagious forms of diffusion. Changes among rural peasants are likely to be brought about in this fashion. We might point to the friction of distance which, of course, can be altered as technology lowers barriers.

However, pure distance and geographical barriers are not always the strongest influences in the diffusion process. Sometimes diffusion takes place with little apparent relationship to contiguity or proximity. It seems to jump around from one town to another or from one government to another, frequently missing the areas or potential recipients in between. Such diffusion processes are called hierarchical. Ideas tend to spread from city to city or from leader to leader or from key societal group to key societal group. All individuals and institutions are not equally receptive to innovation. Often, however, the actual diffusion process contains elements of both contagious and hierarchical transmittal.

As important political ideas are diffused throughout societies, contagion theory would seem to be more compatible with regional analysis than is hierarchical diffusion. Those physically close to an innovator or an innovation are more likely to adopt it. Immediately after the establishment of the Bolshevik state, West European leaders feared that fraternization of their soliders with members of the Red Army or with the rebel forces (as prisoners of war or during the truce period) might infect them with what they called the "Lenin virus." The Central Powers planned their dealings with Bolsheviks as if the Bolsheviks were dangerous and should be quarantined or isolated. Distance not only slows down the diffusion process, it weakens the potency of the ideas being diffused. Geographers call it a "distance-decay effect," and elaborate mathematical models have been constructed to measure and plot it. It is sufficient to indicate here that this type of research relating to regional analysis might usefully be undertaken, bearing in mind that contagion theory would be less applicable than hierarchical theory in explaining the sorts of political similarities and differences discussed here. Cultural barriers are as important as regional or spatial factors. The process of diffusion is a human process, not a mechanical one.

This leads into the final dimension for analysis of regional phenomena—the cultural and, most notably, the settler dimension. Easily exploitable economic resources, especially minerals, attracted European investors. Good soil and climate induced settlement from abroad. Strategically important topographical features led at first to enclave occupation and then settlement, some of which encouraged further penetration and occupation. European governments keen on solidifying their territorial claims sought colonists and rewarded them with land, passage, jobs, protection, and the opportunity to be socially, economically, and politically important. This in turn grew out of the historical context of the world and of particular European economies and the global competition for power and hegemony, as well as the individual colonist/settler motivations.

More important than the simple presence of large numbers of settlers and the social heterogeneity that such numbers entail is the profound impact that settlers had upon the metropolitan governments, their colonial policies, and the types of hierarchical structures established in the colonies. Great Britain, which may have recognized and abided by a paramountcy doctrine in, say, Uganda, seemed less committed to the principles of majority rule in Kenya or Zimbabwe. The settlers became at once an agent for colonial rule and a political force furthering their own interests. Although settlers often arrived at the instigation of the colonial power, cleavages soon opened, particularly when colonial settlers realized that the imperialists in Europe might abandon them if, by doing so, the European governments might prolong or expand long-term imperial interests by identifying with the emerging bourgeois nationalists in Africa.

Early independence was not granted out of some altruistic desire to allow majorities to be self-governing. The goal was to facilitate independence in order to modernize and prolong unequal relationships. Europe wanted to avoid protracted armed struggles that would be costly and that could be expected to harden anti-imperialist demands and possibly shepherd to power individuals and organizations resistant to neocolonial manipulation and penetration. Colonial settlers resisted the liberalizing policies. They undermined efforts to prepare blacks for power. They even declared independence unilaterally and fought to maintain minority rule.[25] Only by seceding from empire could the colonial settlers be "free" to repress and exploit more completely the majority of the population.

Colonial settlers concentrated in Southern Africa, thereby making them an identifiably regional phenomenon. Except for proportionately smaller numbers in Ethiopia, the Ivory Coast, Kenya, Senegal, Tanzania, and Zaire, the rest of Africa was spared European settlers (as distinct from soldiers, bureaucrats, and itinerant entrepreneurs).

Certainly Europeans brought with them skills and capital. Their presence helped to attract external investment. This would superficially seem to contribute to greater productivity and efficiency for states where they have been concentrated. But by far the greatest impact they have made is social. Colonists led colonial powers to modify and then adopt different philosophies of colonial rule. In Southern Africa social policy invariably reflected colonial settler dominance and black African subordinance. Such policies afforded little promise of peaceful change. As such, there seems to be a direct causal link between the presence of colonial settlers and delayed and particularly violent transitions to majority rule.

This did not, of course, discourage black peoples from pursuing the promised land of self-government. No less a figure than Tom Mboya insisted that African nationalist leaders had no desire to pursue a violent strategy toward independence. Rather they were driven to violence as a last resort by unbending colonial regimes supported by and supporting colonist kith and kin. "The reason is that, where there has been white settlement, there has been resistance to constitutional change and this has created more obstacles to nationalism."[26]

Colonial settlers may have been able to obstruct black rule in the short run. But in the long run they contributed to the estrangement of moderate leadership (from compromise with the dominant minority and from their own masses) and to the radicalization of the populace as a whole and of its emergent leaders. Chester Bowles, the former U.S. Ambassador to India, once asked the Governor-General of the Belgian Congo what it would take to put the Congo under communist rule. The Governor-General tersely replied: "One hundred thousand white European settlers." Bowles asked another Belgian official in the Congo what he would do about the Mau Mau problem in Kenya. "I would float a loan, buy the land, and move the white settlers out—even if it required all the NATO armies. If the settlers are allowed to keep control, they will bring all of Africa tumbling down about our ears."[27] To some extent the British eventually followed a similar line in Kenya. And what are the chances of the South African settler regime bringing "all of Africa tumbling down about our ears"? No wonder David Killingray was led to title his book about Europeans in Africa *A Plague of Europeans.*[28]

## IV. Conclusions

Despite problems of scope and focus, the important elements of African politics and history that might be regarded as regionally discernible have been identified. This discussion is not exhaustive, but rather seeks to shed light on important features of regional differences that have had an effect on contemporary Africa. It must be emphasized that the focus on regional differences is a bit forced, much like fastening on the importance of a decade or a century, or trying to analyze one country's foreign policy toward another state by discussing the data in isolation from the total picture. Categories imposed on phenomena that do not fall easily into those categories are artificial and sometimes analytically misleading. However, region does have efficacy and this chapter demonstrates the contexts in which this is so.

The differences between Southern Africa and the rest of the continent are most striking, particularly the majority resistance to minority rule and vice versa, the approach to regional organization and cooperation, the violence attending the decolonization process, and the persistence and continued presence of large numbers of whites still exercising authority and dominance—at least in South Africa and Namibia. Certainly it is understandable for peoples who have been ruled by a racial minority that virtually preaches capitalism and monopolizes the centers of capitalist wealth and power to blame capitalism for their powerlessness and to reject capitalism as a model for economic organization in their normative scheme. Growing out of the armed struggle for independence and majority rule has been a greater tendency to subscribe to Marxist-Leninist prescripts in the economic and political regimes established. As a result Southern African states (and other Marxist-Leninist regimes such as Benin, Ethiopia, and the Congo Peoples Republic) stand poised to make the transition to revolutionary transformation, or at least to be better prepared ideologically and temperamentally for it than have regimes pursuing less cohesive and consistent schemata for economic change. Anti-ideological programs of economic organization have, at best, led to a form of dependent development still closely linked to foreign capitalist governments and institutions.

The regional (qua spatial) variable is tied to the temporal variable, and at several points this linkage has been explicated. Indeed, in some respects there is an interactive link between the two—spatial differences led to temporal differences which led to spatial or regional distinctions, and so forth. Admittedly the problem has been approached inversely. The strategy should not have been to delimit regions arbitrarily and then look for similarities and differences. Ideally a scholar should try to identify and measure similarities and differences and then see if such common properties happened to coincide with regional or spatial categories. Had this been attempted it is probable that patterns of similarity and difference would have been even less regional phenomena and based more on other variables. However, that remains to be explored systematically.

Insofar as regions have a distinctive geographical character, and insofar as this contributes to cultural structures and behaviors that mark a region as different, the concept *region* has some analytical utility. Surely physical makeup affected the nature of precolonial political structures, the degree of penetration by outside forces, the extent of exploitation, the nature of economic life before and after colonization, the popular response to and resistance to colonial rule, the measure of precolonial and postcolonial social homogeneity and unity in a territory, the economic viability of a regime, and many other issues. In these senses region matters. To what degree? In what relationships to other factors? These are questions that have not been and probably cannot be answered satisfactorily at this stage of our scholarly odyssey.

## NOTES

1. The classic statement of this issue is J. David Singer, "The Level-of-Analysis Problem in International Relations," in Klaus Knorr and Sidney Verba (eds.), *The International System* (Princeton, N.J.: Princeton University Press, 1961), pp. 77–92.

2. Contrast this with the earlier literature on "non-Western systems," e.g., George McT. Kahin, Guy J. Pauker, and Lucien W. Pye, "Comparative Politics in Non-Western Countries," *American Political Science Review*, vol. 44, no. 4 (December 1955), pp. 1022–1041; Lucien W. Pye, "The Non-Western Political Process," *Journal of Politics*, vol. 20, no. 3 (August 1958), pp. 468–486; and comments on that article by Alfred Diament, "Is There a Non-Western Political Process?" *Journal of Politics*, vol. 21, no. 1 (February 1959), pp. 123–127.

3. See, for example, Ezekiel Mphahlele, *The African Image*, Rev. Ed. (New York: Praeger, 1974); Melville J. Herskovits, *The Myth of the Negro Past* (Boston: Beacon Press, 1958); and Jacques Maquet, *Africanity: The Cultural Unity of Black Africa* (New York: Oxford University Press, 1972).

4. Interestingly, the regional classifications of Africa used by the different world forecasting organizations do not, by and large, employ the traditional designations (e.g., West, East, Southern). Timothy M. Shaw and Don Munton, "Africa's Futures: A Comparison of Forecasts," in Timothy M. Shaw (ed.), *Alternative Futures for Africa* (Boulder, Colo.: Westview Press, 1982), pp. 37–92. Herman Kahn and A. J. Wiener, for example, wrote of Africa and Black Africa (excluding "Rhodesia, South Africa, and South West Africa"). The Bariloche Project in Argentina treats Africa as a whole, and Wassily Leontief uses just two categories: "Africa (tropical)" and "Africa (arid)." Only the World Integrated Model (Club of Rome, Mesarovic and Pestel) follows more traditional Breakdowns—West, Sahel, East, and Central. Yet the WIM plays fast and loose with these terms. The WIM includes Algeria, Gabon, and Nigeria in the "Middle East—Africa (oil producers)," a functional category based on resource development. It also groups South Africa not in Africa at all, but in a category labeled "other developed."

5. This author tried to come to grips with these issues in an Appendix to *Confrontation and Accommodation in Southern Africa: The Limits of Independence* (Berkeley: University of California Press, 1973), pp. 303–313.

6. The Economic Commission for Africa's West African grouping comprises the same states included here. What ECA calls Central Africa is called Equatorial Africa in this chapter. ECA includes the Sudan in a North African region, and it has no Southern African group. Instead, the states referred to here as the Horn and East Africa are subsumed under a category called East Africa, which earlier embraced all the independent black states of Southern Africa, too.

7. The case has been made that these regimes were far from radical. One early example of the critical literature is Bob Fitch and Mary Oppenheimer, *Ghana: End of an Illusion* (New York: Monthly Review Press, 1966).

8. See Kenneth Jowitt's distinction between resource and choice environments in "Scientific Socialist Regimes in Africa: Political Differentiation, Avoidance, and Unawareness," in Carl G. Rosberg and Thomas M. Callaghy (eds.), *Socialism in Sub-Saharan Africa: A New Assessment*. Research Series No. 38 (Berkeley: Institute of International Studies, University of California, 1979), pp. 133–173.

9. Claude Ake, "The Congruence of Political Economies and Ideologies in Africa," in Peter C. W. Gutkind and Immanuel Wallerstein (eds.), *The Political Economy of Contemporary Africa* (Beverly Hills: Sage Publications, 1976), p. 211.

10. Crawford Young, *Ideology and Development in Africa* (New Haven: Yale University Press, 1982), esp. pp. 13–21. A more quantitative effort to assess performance is David Wheeler, "Sources of Stagnation in Sub-Saharan Africa," *World Development*, XII, No. 1 (1984), pp. 1–23.

11. Immanuel Wallerstein, "The Decline of the Party in Single-Party African States," in Joseph LaPalombara and Myron Weiner (eds.), *Political Parties and Political Development* (Princeton, N.J.: Princeton University Press, 1966).

12. Nelson Kasfir, *The Shrinking Political Arena: Participation and Ethnicity in African Politics, with a Case Study of Uganda* (Berkeley: University of California Press, 1976).

13. Robert W. Jackman, "The Predictability of Coups d'etat: A Model with African Data," *American Political Science Review*, vol. 72, no. 4 (December 1978), pp. 1262–1275.

14. One such effort is: Timothy M. Shaw, "Regional co-operation and conflict in Africa," *International Journal*, vol. 30, no. 4 (Autumn 1975), pp. 671–688.

15. The eleven organizations are listed in Pearl T. Robinson, "The Political Context of Regional Development in the West African Sahel," *Journal of Modern African Studies*, vol. 16, no. 4 (December 1978), pp. 579–595; and Lynn K. Mytelka, "A Genealogy of Francophone West and Equatorial African Regional Organizations," *Journal of Modern African Studies*, vol. 12, no. 2 (July 1974), pp. 297–320. This article includes an excellent bibliography on the subject.

16. See Colin Leys and Peter Robson (eds.), *Federation in East Africa: Opportunities and Problems* (Nairobi: Oxford University Press, 1965); Thomas M. Franck, *East African Unity Through Law* (New Haven: Yale University Press, 1964); Joseph S. Nye, Jr., *Pan-Africanism and East African Integration* (Cambridge: Harvard University Press, 1965); and Christian P. Potholm and Richard A. Fredland (eds.), *Integration and Disintegration in East Africa* (Washington, D.C.: University Press of America, 1980).

17. See Patrick Keatley, *The Politics of Partnership: The Federation of Rhodesia and Nyasaland* (Harmondsworth: Penguin, 1963); Harry Franklin, *Unholy Wedlock: The Failure of the Central African Federation* (London: George Allen and Unwin, 1963); and Colin Leys and Cranford Pratt (eds.), *A New Deal in Central Africa* (New York: Praeger, 1960).

18. See Ronald T. Libby, "The Frontline States of Africa: A Small Power Entente," mimeo. (University of Zambia, May 1977); Robert S. Jaster, *A Regional Security Role for Africa's Front-Line States: Experience and Prospects*, Adelphi Papers No. 180 (London: International Institute for Strategic Studies, 1983); and Douglas G. Anglin, "The Frontline States and the Future of Southern Africa," in Lee Dowdy and Russell

Trood (eds.), *The Indian Ocean: Perspectives on a Strategic Area* (Durham, N.C.: Duke University Press, forthcoming).

19. Douglas G. Anglin, "Economic liberation and regional cooperation in Southern Africa: SADCC and PTA," *International Organization*, vol. 37, no. 4 (Autumn 1983), pp. 681–711; and Richard F. Weisfelder, "The Southern African Development Coordination Conference: A New Factor in the Liberation Process," in Thomas M. Callaghy (eds.), *South Africa in Southern Africa: The Intensifying Vortex of Violence* (New York: Praeger, 1983), pp. 237–266.

20. Anglin, "Economic liberation and regional cooperation," p. 704.

21. Bernard Magubane, "The Evolution of the Class Structure in Africa," in Gutkind and Wallerstein (eds.), *The Political Economy of Contemporary Africa*, p. 185.

22. V. I. Lenin, *Imperialism—The Highest Stage of Capitalism* (New York: International Publishers, 1939); and Historicus, "Stalin on Revolution," in Alexander Dallin (ed.), *Soviet Conduct in World Affairs* (New York: Columbia University Press, 1960), esp. pp. 160–162.

23. As quoted in Alexander Dallin, "The Soviet Union: Political Activity," in Zbigniew Brzezinski (ed.), *Africa and the Communist World* (Stanford, Calif.: Stanford University Press, 1963), p. 10.

24. R. Abler, J. Adams, and P. Gould, *Spatial Organization: The Geographer's View of the World* (Englewood Cliffs, N.J.: Prentice-Hall, 1970), esp. Chapter 11; and J. Hudson, *Geographical Diffusion Theory*. Studies in Geography No. 19 (Evanston: Northwestern University Press, 1972). Applying such ideas to issues more immediate to this study, see Kevin Cox and George Demko, "Conflict Behavior in a Spacio-Temporal Context," *Sociological Forum*, vol. 1 (1968), a study of agrarian riots in Russia from 1905 to 1970; and David L. Huff and James M. Lutz, "The Contagion of Political Unrest in Independent Black Africa," *Economic Geography*, vol. 50, no. 4 (October 1974), pp. 352–367, a study of military coups d'etat in sub-Saharan Africa between 1960 and 1972.

25. For a more expanded discussion of this point, see Kenneth W. Grundy, "Anti-Neo-Colonialism in South Africa's Foreign Policy Rhetoric," in Timothy M. Shaw and Kenneth A. Heard (eds.), *Cooperation and Conflict in Southern Africa: Papers on a Regional Subsystem* (Washington, D.C.: University Press of America, 1976), pp. 351–364; and Grundy, "Intermediary Power and Global Dependency: The Case of South Africa," *International Studies Quarterly*, vol. 20, no. 4 (December 1976), pp. 553–580.

26. Tom Mboya, *Freedom and After* (London: Andre Deutsch, 1963), pp. 50–51.

27. Chester Bowles, *Africa's Challenge to America* (Berkeley: University of California Press, 1956), p. 82.

28. David Killingray, *A Plague of Europeans: Westerners in Africa since the Fifteenth Century* (Hardmondsworth: Penguin Education, 1975).

CHAPTER 6

# The Military Factor in African Politics: A Twenty-Five-Year Perspective

*J. Gus Liebenow*

Despite the optimism of the late 1950s regarding the strength both of African political parties and of the parliamentary institutions through which they would operate following independence, events have eroded that euphoric prognosis. Considerably diminished is the ideal of an African public being regularly permitted to hold its political leaders accountable at all levels through open, freely contested, and fairly administered series of elections. Instead, the military coup d'etat has become the more recurrent instrument for changing top political leadership and for effecting dramatic changes in foreign and domestic policies in Africa. Some surviving single-party states have, indeed, permitted an element of electoral choice at the legislative level or have used the ritualistic occasion of an uncontested election as an opportunity for making significant changes in executive personnel and in national politics. Single-party states, however, are in the minority in Africa today, and states which permit legal opposition parties to function are an even smaller fragment of the whole.

Contrary to the earlier thought of both practitioners and scholars, the majority of African states have now experienced at least one successful military coup since independence; and a majority of that number have fallen victim to their second, third, or successive coups. The citizens of roughly half of the states have endured more years with some form of military intervention than periods of patently civilian rule. Despite early storm warnings, the scholarly reluctance to forecast military intervention as a recurrent feature of African political behavior persisted until the Nigerian and Ghanaian coups of early 1966. Until that point, the 1958 coup in Sudan, the Zaire mutiny of 1960, the assassination of President Sylvanus Olympio of Togo in 1963, and the rash of military mutinies in former British and French territories in 1964 were viewed as aberrations, which did not affect the long-term trend. It was indicative of the state of the scholarly art that neither the early single-country studies by James Coleman, David Apter, and others nor the several comprehensive surveys of African politics edited in the early 1960s by Gwendolen Carter, James Coleman and Carl G. Rosberg, or William Lewis made more than fleeting reference to the African military.[1] Even my own writings on Liberia in those edited volumes hardly suggested that the military would be a major challenger to the civilian elite who had governed that state since 1847.

Hoping to make amends for the absence of prescience with respect to the politicization of the military, Africanist scholarship has produced a virtual flowering of both broad- and narrow-gauged theories in an effort to explain and analyze the causes and performance of the African soldier in politics. In analyzing more than fifty cases of successful intervention and a greater number of abortive coups, one is struck by the idiosyncratic nature of civil-military relations in Africa. The conditions and identifiable causes of intervention vary considerably, as does the level within the military which provides the coup leadership. Despite the unique nature of African coups, some excellent studies based on single cases do suggest a more generalized pattern of behavior. Included in this category of studies would be Michael Lofchie's analysis of the 1971 coup in Uganda, which hypothesized that General Amin was acting as the agent of an economic class which saw its own corporate interests threatened as the meager resources of the society were dissipated on socialist experimentation.[2] Another case study, Richard Price's analysis of the 1966 Ghanaian coup, theorized that defense of military professionalism—as determined by the military itself—was a key factor in the army's turning against a civilian regime which had overstepped the bounds properly separating the civilian and military spheres of responsibility in a modern society.[3]

Two scholars with in-depth African experience early attempted to formulate theories of broader applicability to the sub-Saharan region. An intriguing causal explanation based upon an analysis of eleven African coups which occurred between 1963 and 1972 was proferred by Samuel Decalo.[4] He suggested that although general societal instability had to be taken into account, one of the strongest factors for military intervention related directly or indirectly to the personal ambitions or fears of specific key officers relative to civilian authorities. While it provides excellent post hoc analysis, the sui generis nature of the circumstances makes the Decalo thesis a difficult one to apply for predictive purposes.

A more thoughtful effort in exploring the various factors which have contributed to military intervention has emerged from the many works produced by Claude E. Welch, Jr., over the past two decades.[5] Welch has made a significant contribution to our understanding of the multiple "causes" of intervention as well as making preliminary efforts at establishing typologies for comparative analysis of civil-military relationships both in the Third World as well as in the more industrialized states. He has had some particularly significant insights to provide regarding the place of the military in the modernization process of African states.

It is increasingly apparent that the data on military intervention in Africa are not peculiar to that world region, even though there are many factors which differentiate sub-Saharan African politics from situations in Latin America, the Middle East, and Asia. Africa, for example, has lacked the class linkages among the politicians, military leaders, and landed aristocracy which have characterized many Latin American states. The persistence of colonial rule in Africa until the 1960s, furthermore, reduced in significance the issues of military professionalism, career mobility, and divergent ideologies which have marked civil-military relations in the Middle East and many parts of Asia. Nevertheless, Africanist scholars and comparativists with rich experience in the studies of the military in both the more developed societies and the Third World have attempted to formulate theories of global relevance. One of the most persistent in this effort has been Morris Janowitz, who early assumed that organizational and professional characteristics of the military as an institution were critical to our analysis of the causes of military intervention or nonintervention into the political arena.[6] Janowitz focuses on organizational format, skill structure and cadre lines, social recruitment patterns, professional ideology, and social cohesion within the military as factors of primary significance in our understanding of the politicization of the armed forces. Often posed in opposition to Janowitz's emphasis (although Janowitz denies the existence of a conflict) has been the contention of Samuel Huntington that the most significant factors in military intervention are found in the nature of the broader political, economic, and social structure of society within which particular militaries exist.[7]

The frequency with which coup groups have succeeded in toppling either a civilian regime or their own senior military colleagues should attest to the difficulties that both practitioners and scholars alike face in making educated guesses about "who, when, where, and why" with regard to military intervention in specific African countries. It is often the case, as Decalo has suggested, that the coup is a highly personalized affair. And indeed, the evidence regarding the variations in coup leadership manifest in the 1980 coup in Liberia (a Master Sergeant), the abortive Kenya coup of 1982 (a private), and the 1983 New Year's Eve coup in Nigeria (a Major General) suggests an even more highly capricious—and therefore unpredictable—quality associated with recent coup attempts. The "wild card" factor is all too persistent in African military interventions.

Rather than formulating a predictive theory of intervention, the purpose of this analysis will be fourfold. First of all, an effort will be made to explore the evidence from the past quarter of a century regarding the political role of the military in order to elucidate broad trends which can account for the general failure of civilian regimes, despite the optimism which surrounded political parties at the time of independence. Equally important is the related question of why there has been such general acceptance of military regimes by the African masses inasmuch as many of the initial conditions which encouaged earlier military intervention persist in Africa today. Secondly, this study will explore some of the basic problems which confront the African military when it has attempted to assume a governmental role in nation-building, directing economic development, and undertaking other political tasks. Thirdly, an effort will be made to evaluate the performance of military as against civilian regimes in carrying out the essential tasks of government in the new African countries. Finally, the recent Nigerian experience notwithstanding, an analysis will be made of the elements which must be addressed in making a successful transition from military to civilian regimes in Africa.

## The Weakness of Party Government as a Factor in Intervention

In exploring the many circumstances which appeared to have contributed to or encouraged the intervention of the African military in postindependence politics, the weakness of political parties emerges as a primary factor. African militaries, as we shall note shortly, are weak; but parties were weaker. In state after state, the civilian politicians who inherited the mantle of authority from the departing colonial administrators tended to overestimate their own strength and the role that parties had played in the demise of European colonial rule. There were cases, such as Kenya, Mozambique, Angola, Guinea-Bissau, and Zimbabwe, where massive and sustained armed confrontation by Africans against European settler minorities was the critical element in the success of the independence effort. During the late 1950s through the early 1970s, however, these are not representative of what was generally a fairly peaceful transfer of power in forty-five of the fifty African states, not that violence or the threat of violence were absent in the other cases. Without denigrating the efforts of African nationalists, however, there were other factors that compelled the European powers to face the inevitable and to attempt to withdraw from their colonial liabilities on terms most favorable to their own long-term economic, diplomatic, and other interests. Hence, I would suggest

that the independence of African states is significantly related inter alia to the
success of liberation efforts in India and Algeria; the victories of social labor
parties in the European colonial metropoles; the shrinking global military
commitments of Great Britain; the continuing pressure from within the United
Nations; and the anticolonial postures of the United States and the Soviet
Union.

Not only did party leaders overestimate their own role in terminating the
colonial presence, but they overestimated as well their organizational capacity
in controlling the postcolonial state. Some parties such as the NCNC and Action Group in Nigeria did demonstrate organizational strength even though
each was oriented to a particular region and cluster of ethnic groups. Elsewhere in Africa parties generally lacked experience in organizing tactics, and
the obstructionist policies and practices of colonial administrators had prevented the emergence of well-oiled party machines. Membership roles were
invariably inflated, the payment of dues was honored in the breach, and most
parties were plagued by the fact that the leadership tended to be more representative of the urban minority, of one religious faction, or of one or a limited
number of the several score of ethnic groups which had been arbitrarily included within the colonial state. While it is true that Pan-Africanism and anti-
colonialism were unifying ideologies to the point of independence, they were
of little value in instructing leadership with regard to the management of the
new state apparatus.

The pool of talent available to both run the state and continue the vital role
of the political party in galvanizing society with respect to nation-building,
economic development, and the other tasks was dangerously thin from the outset. Colonial educational policies had been marked by neglect where they
were not characterized by positive hostility to the concept of educating Africans to manage a complex modern society. The British and French only differed by degree from their Belgian, Portuguese, and Italian counterparts. The
absence of critical skills in the fields of public administration, medicine, engineering, diplomacy, and the general areas of economics and finance was appalling. Added to this legacy was the lower priority given by African nationalists
themselves to economics and other matters during the anticolonial struggle.
Kwame Nkrumah's dictum to "Seek Ye First the Political Kingdom. . . ."
meant that serious planning regarding the nature of the postcolonial economy
was long deferred. In any case, African politicians were by force of circumstances unequal bargaining partners during the transitional period relative to
the vested European economic actors.

These generalizations about the weakness of political parties vis-a-vis
military interventionists is further supported by the counterevidence from the
several categories of cases where the political party leadership has in fact en-

dured almost continuously since independence, despite threats of military intervention. The first category of states are those in which the party took on a military posture during the anticolonial struggle and not only galvanized the society with respect to the legitimacy of the new polity and its goals, but also, through its leadership, took steps to politically subordinate the military wing of the party. FRELIMO and ZANU are cases in point. The second category of cases deals with instances in which the party leaders, shortly after having achieved independence, took conscious steps to create a broad cross-regional, cross-ethnic, cross-religious grassroots party organization and to address the problems of economic—and particularly rural—development. Although the reasons and circumstances differ, there are parallels in the cases of Tanzania, Cameroon, Malawi, and Zambia. Finally, there are a series of states—largely in the francophone group (Ivory Coast, Senegal, Gabon)—in which the continuing presence of external military support early permitted African civilians to remain in control of the state irrespective of whether the party had remained vital or moribund or whether the party and state bureaucracies remained separate or fused.

### Perceptions of the Role of Force in Society

Undoubtedly as the counterpart to the nationalist leaders having overestimated the strength of their own party organizations was their tendency to underestimate the role of force which had been required in maintaining the colonial state. This led to the naively optimistic assumption that the use of military force would not be a significant sanction for authority in domestic politics or a significant element in the relations among African states once independence was achieved. The speech of Chief Obafemi Awolowo to the Calabar Congress in 1958—two years prior to Nigerian independence—was one of several instances in which a nationalist leader urged a policy of nonarmament for his country following independence.[8] Kwame Nkrumah of Ghana and Julius Nyerere of Tanzania (then Tanganyika) had also taken similar stances as did Awolowo's long-time Nigerian adversary, Nnamdi Azikiwe—albeit in a less emphatic manner. They were convinced that the spirit of Pan-Africanism at the continental level and the unity forged during the nationalist struggle at the territorial level would permit the new states to direct their energies to economic development, expansion of educational and health facilities, and the other more positive tasks associated with nation-building.

Only a few African nationalists were prepared to take their rhetoric in its full literal sense and dispense with the need for a national army. David Jawara of the Gambia, for example, took into account his country's geographical position as a defenseless "Jonah in the belly of the Senegalese whale" and elected to provide paramilitary duties to a slightly expanded national police force. Even this step, ironically, did not spare him the indignity of an abortive police-orchestrated coup in 1981. The leaders of Botswana, Lesotho, and Swaziland, mindful of their similar encirclement or near-encirclement by the Republic of South Africa also attempted to reduce their national military establishments to ceremonial size and role during the early postindependence era. While leaders elsewhere in Africa assumed more pragmatic stances after liberation regarding the need for some sort of military unit to serve both domestic and defense purposes, the initial tendency was to give a far lower priority to the military over other categories of expenditure in the national budgets. The neglected areas of health, education, natural resource development, and other programs had to come first. Soldiers, moreover, had not been accustomed to serving development roles in the colonial period and thus they were viewed by the civilian nationalists as exhausters of scarce resources in basically poor societies. When a budget crunch came, as it did in Togo in 1963, President Sylvanus Olympio's first instinct was to reduce the budgetary allocation for the military. Similarly the complaints of the mutinous armies in Tanzania, Uganda, and Kenya in 1964 and of the military leaders who toppled Kwame Nkrumah in 1966 was that the civilian regimes had drastically undermined military performance by failing to provide the army with better eqiupment, housing, uniforms, and other material.

The calculated efforts to downplay the political role that the military had played in maintaining civil authority in the European colonial state may be attributable to African civilians and soldiers alike having initially accepted the theory of the civilian supremacy model of civil-military relations. Military force was assumed to be at the disposal of civilian authorities and not an autonomous sanction available to the military directly. Curiously, the civilian supremacy model during the colonial era was not even strictly applied in Europe itself—as the de Gaulle intervention of 1958 should have demonstrated. In any event, it would be a radically distorted interpretation of Africa's distant as well as recent past to assume that the ideology of pacificism would find fertile ground in Africa. To argue that it could would constitute the reverse side of the stereotype which viewed Africa prior to the European-imposed peace as being a Hobbesian state of nature, with a "war of each against all." Historians, anthropologists, and others are providing evidence that the truth regarding resort to the sanction of force in precolonial Africa lay somewhere in between. Africans did indeed, for example, engage in long-distance trade and participated in religious, social, and other structures where cooperation prevailed over conflict as norms of behavior. On the other hand, there is a long history of interethnic combat being waged on a continuous if not an intermittent basis among many groups around the continent; the social structure of whole groups, moreover, such as the Ashanti in Ghana and the Zulu in South Africa was organized along rigid military lines with military values infusing all aspects of society.[9]

The pacifistic optimism of some nationalists also underplayed the role that force had played in subjugating Africa during the nineteenth and early twentieth centuries. While it is true that many societies capitulated without having had to be conquered, a number of societies over an extended period stoutly resisted the European imposition and were subdued only after the loss of countless lives and the destruction of the indigenous political, economic, and social systems. And it was in many instances African armies in collaboration with the small component of European officer and troops that were the real factor in the conquest of their fellow Africans.[10] In a number of cases, such as the Nandi of Kenya, full acceptance of European dominance came only after repeated punitive raids which involved a scorched-earth approach as well as the near-genocidal liquidation of men, women, and children.[11] Such punitive expeditions and the convincing use of the Maxim gun and other superior weaponry by European-directed armies were frequently sufficient example to convince other potential resisters of the futility of their actions.

The myth regarding the minimal role of force required in maintaining the European presence may be attributable to the relative absence of major armed confrontation in the period following the First World War until the Kenya uprising called "Mau Mau," which began in 1952.[12] Around the continent the military units of the groups that had collaborated with the Europeans in imposing colonial rule were quickly divested of their junior partnership role in the colonial relationship once conquest of neighboring groups had been completed. Traditional armies and regiments of young warriors were quickly disarmed and reduced to ceremonial roles. In most colonial territories, the military forces that maintained order for the colonial administration were recruited from outside the districts where they served and hence had no conflicting loyalties with respect to local traditional rulers. The colonial force, moreover, was remarkably small in size and normally armed only with rifles which were left unloaded until a crisis actually arose. Rather than being a continuing visible presence in every remote hamlet of the colony, troops were typically quartered at the district or regional headquarters.

Despite the paucity of men under arms, however, the colonial military was a mobile force which could be dispatched quickly to a troubled area. If the local force was insufficient to contain the crisis, reinforcements could be quickly brought in from neighboring territories or other parts of the empire. The infusion of troops directly from Great Britain—armed with the latest in terms of jet fighter planes and other modern weaponry—for example, was ultimately the crucial factor in suppressing the Kenya revolt of 1952–56.

And, of course, the Congo crisis of 1960 and the rescue operations carried out by British and French paratroopers during the spate of mutinies in 1964 provided adequate demonstration of the fact that the mere size of the local militia was not the only fact to be taken into account in analyzing the role that the sanction of force played in maintaining political authority.[13]

## Erosion of the Colonial Bargaining Strategy

A further factor limiting the ability of the new nationalist elites to maintain order and stability in the postcolonial state was the undermining or dismantling of the preceding colonial bargaining strategy that had been effective in securing the semblance of stability. This is not meant to suggest that the colonial administration was a neutral arbiter that stood aloof from the competing claimants for the limited human and material resources of the colonial territory. Indeed, the officers of the colonial state were anything but neutral whenever the vital interests of the European metropole, the empire as a whole, or the local settlers, merchants, missionaries, and other resident Europeans were directly challenged. There were, nevertheless, many occasions in which the administrators had to arbitrate conflict within the European community itself. This occurred, for example, when the needs of European mine owners, planters, and military recruiters in securing inexpensive manpower threatened the educational and proselytizing goals of the missionaries as well as the labor needs of the colonial administration itself in maintaining roads and other infrastructures. There was also an arbitrating role with respect to the growing conflicts between, on the one hand, those traditional authorities who continued to receive recognition by the colonial administrators and, on the other hand, the new groups of educated Africans who were needed at the lower or intermediate levels in staffing the colonial administration or assisting in the new European economic enterprises. Conflicts also arose between the aspirations of the burgeoning African merchant class and the better-financed Asian and Lebanese merchants who came in under the colonial umbrella. Admittedly—in its own interests—the colonial bureaucracy did provide negotiating machinery as well as carry out strategies of development that limited interracial, interethnic, and interregional competition and conflict. The policy of indirect rule, for example, was one way in which the British administrators around the continent hoped to limit and contain modernizing demands that could not be effectively regulated by the understaffed colonial bureaucracy. The "reserve" policy, which limited land settlement in an area to one ethnic group, was another.

Once the reins of power were tranferred to African nationalists, however, it was apparent that many of the previous participants in colonial politics, as well as in the economic and social transformation of colonial society, would either be forced out or compelled to assume a radically different role. European landowners in Kenya, for example, were compelled to emigrate or to reduce their holdings and largely to withdraw from the political arena if they chose to remain in Kenya. Asian entrepreneurs in East Africa and Lebanese in the West, in many instances, had their shops and other holdings subject to confiscation after previously having been harassed on the questions of citizenship, export of earnings, and other issues. The traditional as well as the appointed chiefs, moreover, were dismissed in Tanzania and Guinea for having collaborated too closely with the European colonialists. Thus, the nationalists felt no need to arbitrate with respect to many of their former opponents.

Even those, however, who had been part of the broad coalition to unseat the colonial administration found themselves challenged by the nationalists at the center. Politics took primacy over other legitimate types of activities, and the political nationalists increasingly turned against their fellow conspirators in the trade unions, the cooperative societies, the independent churches, student organizations, and ethnic political associations. Where the competing organizations were not actually banned or placed under severe restrictions, they were effectively subordinated to the dominant party or to the postcolonial state itself. Few new competitors were encouraged to appear on the scene. Consequently, in many new states the weakened condition of previous competitors to the political party leadership left only one other strong contestant in the field: the military. The continued presence, however, of a critical cadre of European officers in most postcolonial armies (Guinea in 1958 being an obvious exception) put the military into a different category. It was not necessarily viewed as an adversary, but as an institution which served at the pleasure of the new nationalist elite and could be brought into line by budget reductions and applying the lessons of the inherited civilian supremacy model. In Ghana, for example, Europeans still occupied key military posts in the early 1960s, and Kwame Nkrumah's oft-quoted admonition to the military cadets to refrain from political activity illustrates the strength of this self-deception.

## The Changed Nature of the Transitional Military Establishment

Although the nationalists did increasingly rely on the postcolonial military, the tendency for the nationalists during the anti-imperial struggle was to view the colonial military as an "alien" institution which could be effectively controlled by the party leadership once independence was achieved. This proved to be a critical mistake, but the basis of their reasoning, however, is understandable. The virtual monopolization by Europeans of colonial officer ranks and even of key noncommissioned positions in the French and Portuguese colonial armies provided very few career outlets in the military for the Africans who had been Western educated and exposed to modernization. Even Indians, Goans, and other third parties were frequently given preference over qualified Africans with respect to noncommissioned officer posts.

There were other reasons, as well, for the nationalists to regard the colonial military as an institution which was "alien" to the purposes of the nationalist movement. The colonial army generally had played a negative role in terms of African liberation, since it supported the colonial presence against guerrilla bands in Kenya, and against trade unionists, student strikers, and other "progressive" forces around the continent. More significantly, the rank-and-file and the few Africans who did qualify for noncommissioned rank overwhelmingly tended to be recruited from the areas of the country which had been least exposed to modernizing influences. Lord Lugard in Nigeria, for example, made it an explicit policy of government to draw heavily upon the less developed north for recruits in preference to the better educated and economically transformed Ibos and Yorubas in the south.[14] The conscious stereotyping of ethnic groups with respect to the military tasks that they were assumed to be most capable of performing had perpetuated ethnic segregation in the army. By contrast, the nationalists were attempting to transcend ethnic differences and embrace national or Pan-African concepts. The tasks of the military, furthermore, were viewed as being largely ceremonial when they were not overtly repressive and as such did not require an exceptional amount of education to be performed. Since the resort to the labor corvee had provided colonial administrators with a ready pool of free or cheap civilian labor, the colonial military was seldom called upon to perform road construction, bridge building, or other projects associated with development along the model of the U.S. Corps of Engineers. Finally, the conscious posting of soldiers to districts outside their ethnic homelands in order to avoid conflicts of loyalties with respect to the colonial administration had other consequences. It meant that the low prestige of the soldiers was further aggravated by the absence of family, ethnic, and other restraints upon abuses of authority by the troops.

The political nationalist failed to see that the colonial military was in fact an outlet for modernization for those who were overlooked in the European strategy for economic development or in missionary planning for location of schools and clinics. However low the salaries might have been or however primitive the facilities, the military experience involved the recruit in a cash economy, and there was undoubtedly a lot of processing of money within the military between the enlisted man and his home area. Since the officers were concerned about having a healthy force, the recruit was exposed to at least some of the rudimentary rules of modern sanitation and health. While the colonial officers were not interested in African college graduates, they did impart to the raw recruits from less-developed regions a certain level of literacy; typing skills and other forms of mechanical training; and the ability to drive and to repair motor vehicles. The army, moreover, exposed the enlisted man to the European or African language, which in many cases became the accepted lingua franca of a given territory. Furthermore, while the experience was not always transferable to other structures of modern society, the knowledge of bureaucracy, chain-of-command, and other imperatives for the successful functioning of the military could be put to use by the discharged veteran in civilian situations.[15]

In addition to the continuing transforming influences of the colonial military, developments during the final stages of colonial rule brought about dramatic changes. Perhaps in anticipation of the nationalist resistance activity which did not actually materialize, the British, French, and other colonialists had begun to introduce heavier armament, more modernized transport, updated communications facilities, and military aviation into the colonial army. Other changes as well were made in the character of the colonial army. Since the pool of non-African immigrants had slowed considerably after World War II, for example, increasingly Africans were provided with the higher level of technical education needed for military modernization. This meant not only higher wages but also a respectable career alternative for educated Africans. A few even qualified for officer training as independence approached. Since the colonialists were interested in retaining the friendship and commitment of this new cadre of African officers, they were frequently sent to Europe for training and given, upon their return, perquisites which rivaled those available to educated Africans in the civil service, the clergy, the schools, and other civilian structures.

### The Reliance of Party Nationalists on the Military

Having initially viewed the military as an unnecessary or at worst an alien institution, and then having viewed the postcolonial army as being automatically imbued with the ideal of subservience to civilian authority, the nationalists in many countries went on to commit one further critical error. The party leadership increasingly tended to rely heavily in maintaining its own shaky rule upon those two sanctions for authority—force and ritual—which are closely identified with the military. Inevitably this intensified the political role of the military at the expense of civilian authority.

Even Nkrumah, who had lectured most eloquently about the civilian supremacy model, increasingly relied on military ritual as a prop for his regime.

Mass rallies, the parading of tanks and other military equipment in Accra's Black Star Square (reminiscent of Red Square on May Day), the wearing of uniforms and ribbons, and the granting of chivalric honors gave a military flavor to what should have been civilian enterprises. The organization of the youth and workers into disciplined "brigades," the calls for heroism and sacrifice, and the constant reference to "the nation under siege" evoked military ritual and imagery in the maintenance of the new state against its enemies, both domestic and foreign.

In addition to military-like ritual, the civilian nationalists increasingly called upon the sanction of military force in dealing with a broad spectrum of political opponents. With respect to ethnic secessionists—such as the Ruwenzori movement in Uganda during the first Obote government—the resort to military action may have been understandable.[16] Less acceptable was the resort to military action by the leaders of the First Republic in Nigeria in moving against the Yoruba leaders who were challenging the nature of the federal political compact, but who did not seek the dissolution of the Nigerian state. A similar need for a political solution was required in the dispute between Obote and Buganda, even though the history of Baganda exclusivism is a long one. Equally questionable was the use of the army in many states in dealing with student demonstrations on university campuses or with labor leaders who were striking for improvements in the conditions of employment.

The use of the military to cope with political situations which realistically called for negotiation or arbitration had several major drawbacks. In the first place it revealed the very weakness of the civilian leadership and the political party in their professed roles as unifiers of the nation-state, calling into question the regime's legitimacy. The military, conversely, quickly came to the realization that its intervention was indispensable to the survival in power of the civilian nationalists. The military leadership and the troops, moreover, came to resent being thrust into bascially political situations where they had to bear directly the brunt of the hostility on the part of the suppressed dissidents instead of that hostility being directed against the flawed political leadership.

There were other dangers as well in relying upon the sanction of force in dealing with situations which should have been resolved through negotiation or more positive distribution of economic and physical rewards to a dissident group. In cases where there was a failure of military force in achieving its intended results, the army often turned upon the civilian authorities to justify its own inadequacies in dealing with guerrilla warfare. This occurred, of course, in Algeria in 1958 when the French paratroopers imposed de Gaulle upon the indecisive politicians of the Fourth Republic. And it was the primary justification for the military overthrow of the monarchy in Ethiopia in 1974, when it was obvious that the Eritrean secession movement could not be easily contained. Thus, in abandoning the course of political bargaining and opting to dissolve the poorly structured federal relationship between Ethiopia and Eritrea, the Emperor and his advisers by default made the military the one indispensable element in keeping the post–World War II state intact. They thereby sowed the seeds of their own destruction.[17]

### Signaling Civilian Vulnerability

Having once appreciated its mistake in augmenting the military's role with respect to basically political situations, the civilian nationalists further aggravated the relationship by signaling their fear of the political monster they had brought forth. Budget-cutting might, in a previous period, have been regarded as a genuine commitment to reallocate resources to health, education, and other programs neglected by the colonialists. After independence, however, it became a challenge to the corporate interests of the military, which had now come to enjoy a partnership role in the political arena. Although many of the early-hour justifications of African coups constitute pious rhetoric regarding defending the constitution or democracy, a significant portion of the post hoc rationale relates to salaries, uniforms, housing, and other narrow corporate interests of the military. While the military might not move speedily with respect to the loftier ideals, they demonstrated no hesitation in addressing their own basic needs.

Secondly, the civilian leadership in many cases took overt steps to limit the effectiveness of flamboyant military leaders who enjoyed a popular base, and the civilian leaders undertook to manipulate promotions and assignments within the military itself. An early case was noted by Richard Price in his book on the Ghanaian military. Price concluded that it was the military's resentment of Nkrumah's removal of the very popular General Ankrah from his position as Commander of the army that was one of the major precipitating causes of the 1966 coup. It was the politicians—in the thinking of the Ghanaian military leaders—who had violated the civilian-military compact by striking at the professional integrity of the army.[18] Samuel Decalo provides many other examples of civilians moving against military personalities, including the conflict which was coming to a head between Milton Obote and Idi Amin in 1971, just as Obote took off for Singapore.[19]

The patent manifestation of fear of the military on the part of the civilian leaders has often been signaled by the creation of independent military or paramilitary units which have the stated political mission of protecting the head of the regime. The creation of Nkrumah's President's Own Guard Regiment—which was recruited, trained, and equipped independently of the regular army—was a second professional irritant contributing to the 1966 coup in

Ghana. Military leaders not unexpectedly raised the question: against whom is the president being protected if the regular military is excluded from what it regards as one of its primary missions?

Even more challenging to both the integrity as well as the patriotism of the regular army has been the use of foreign troops to protect the leadership of the regime. Although it was undoubtedly warranted for the British to respond to requests from the heads of government of the three East Africa states in 1964, the intervention of British paratroops led to different long-run results in Kenya and Tanzania as opposed to Uganda. In the former states the incident led to the more effective subordination of the military to the state or the dominant party, after the mutineers had been dismissed or punished. In Uganda, the aftermath of the mutiny led to the establishment of an uneasy truce between the civilian and military leadership with the former going to extraordinary lengths to placate the military in terms of salaries and other perquisites.[20] The efforts at budgetary bribery following the British paratroop intervention, however, only served to reinforce the contempt of the military toward the Obote government and was a factor in the subsequent Amin coup.

Finally, we might cite reliance upon an external rescue force not as a direct factor in a coup, but as a factor which prepared the ground for the widespread acceptance of a military coup once it had occurred. Reference here is made to the 1979 rice riots in Liberia which occurred a year prior to the assassination of President Tolbert. During the demonstrations Tolbert called upon Guinean troops and planes to deal with the rice rioters after the Liberian military had largely refrained from action. It was the more politically subservient police that had fired on the unarmed demonstrators. The Guinean troops were soon withdrawn, but the general resentment of the use of alien troops in Africa's oldest republic became part of the year of ferment leading to the military coup of April 1980.[21] What differentiates Liberia from similar neighborly rescues is the fact that a Guinean rescue unit has remained in Sierra Leone after the coup attempt there in 1981, and a Senegalese force continues to provide protection to David Jawara of the Gambia following the 1981 police coup in that country. Thus, the continuity of civilian rule was maintained despite the resentment of the military regarding alien intrusions.

## Models of Civil-Military Relationships in Africa

In analyzing the extent of politicization of the military in the new African states, we must appreciate that the terms "military government" or "military intervention" cover a great variety of political relationships between the military and civilian authorities. Like the mythical walls between church and state in a liberal democracy or between government and the economy in capitalist-oriented societies, the political division between the domain of civil and military authorities even in a society committed to the civilian supremacy model is not hard and fast. The military, after all, is central to the political objective of maintaining the independence of the state community. Like other actors in society it makes political claims against the financial and other resources of the state in carrying out its primary mission. Conversely, regimes that are characterized as "military governments" in fact must normally either co-opt a wide range of civilian technicians or retrain soldiers to take on civilian skills in coping with the day-to-day concerns of society.

Similar caution must be used to avoid treating the military of a particular country as a monolith. In addition to the differences between the organization and roles of military as opposed to paramilitary units, there are service rivalries where an air force competes with an army for prestige and funding. Generational, regional, and ethnic imbalances further create tensions within the overall military group. In some cases, such as the January 1966 coup in Nigeria, senior officers have been effective in bringing most of their fellow officers as well as the troops along with them in taking control of government in the wake of a coup. Other interventions have found one segment of the military (such as the air force in the abortive 1982 coup in Kenya) acting unilaterally against a civilian government or even against their own senior officers in a military regime (such as the 1979 intervention of Flight Lt. Rawlings against the Acehompong government in Ghana). Occasionally, one segment of the military undertakes a preemptive coup against a civilian regime to forestall action by another segment of the military. This was apparently the case in the December 1983 action of General Buhari in terminating the tenure of the Shagari government in Nigeria.

Rather than as a bipolar model, which pits civilians against the military, the political relationship between civilian and military authorities is more appropriately analyzed in terms of a series of models along a continuum. Although they can be plotted along a line in terms of the degree of intervention of the military into the political affairs of a state, there is no suggestion that a given military group proceeds logically from one stage of the continuum to the next. Rather the continuum is posited for the purposes of cross-national comparative analysis and to assess changes in degree of intervention of specific military groups.

At one end of the continuum is the *civilian supremacy* model of civil-military relations. This is the model subscribed to by political leaders in Western-style democracies as well as in most Marxian socialist societies. Ironically, in addition to its being the norm in party-dominated African states, such as Tanzania, Senegal, and Malawi, it is publicly stated to be the ideal even by most military leaders in Africa who have succeeded in toppling well-

established civilian regimes. Essentially the civilian supremacy model requires that civilians, rather than the military, control decision making with
respect to the issue of war and peace, the determination of the size and general shape of the military establishment, the basic methods of recruiting both
officers and enlisted personnel, the allocation of major privileges and rewards
within the service, and, most important, the allocation of government revenues for the funding of all military and paramilitary activities. It is a model
that depends, for its proper functioning, upon the existence of strong independent political counterforces in the economy: schools, churches, professions,
and other areas of the private sector.

Subsequent models are arrayed along the continuum in terms of the duration and scope of military intervention into the political arena. The minimal
breach from the civilian supremacy relationship can be labeled the *watchdog*
model. This suggests an intervention which is both limited in time and calculated to achieve a specific objective, such as the assurance that the winning
party in a contested election will actually be installed in office. This is exemplified by the April 1968 noncommissioned officers' coup in Sierra Leone.
This action, the last of a series of coups which began a year earlier, put into
power the All People's Congress of Siaka Stevens. The latter had successfully
challenged the ruling Sierra Leone People's Party in the 1967 election but had
been denied the fruits of its victory by a preemptive military coup.[22]

The second level of military involvement in politics—the *balance wheel*
model—indicates a more extended intervention, with the military assuming
full authority with respect to all instruments of violence but leaving the running of government in the hands of bureaucrats, judges, educators, and others
who form part of a civil-military coalition. This model is represented by the
July 1966 Gowan coup against Ironsi in Nigeria and continued in effect until
the actual commencement of the Biafran civil war.

The next two models on the continuum represent an even further in-depth
and more pervasive involvement of the military in the running of the state.
This is based on the assumption that the co-opted civilians are creatures of
their own past and hence need to be either displaced or more closely supervised in order to achieve the objectives of the military intervention. The *direct
rule* model is the more conservative of the two, assuming that the solutions
which must be applied are more technical or technological rather than requiring a basic shift in ideology or a restructuring of the society. This position is
exemplified by the Nigerian military experience from the outset of the civil
war to the hand-over of authority in 1979. The more drastic version of in-depth
intervention is the *social transformation* model (Ethiopia, Benin, Congo-
Brazzaville), which assumes that there must be a complete break with past

values and institutions and a restructuring of society if it is to achieve its multiple goals of nation-building, overcoming of poverty, and popular democracy.

The last model on the continuum, the *atavistic* model represents a situation in which not only do military personnel penetrate every aspect of society, but military values and the so-called virtues of heroism, sacrifice, martyrdom through conflict, and blind obedience to authority become dominant in society. The obvious examples of this are Uganda under Amin and Equatorial Guinea under Macias Nguema. The atavistic model represents a calculated effort at creating disorder to root out all vestiges of civilized behavior. Amin was ultimately driven from power by the combined forces of Tanzanian regulars and Ugandan dissident refugees; nevertheless, the decades and even centuries of political relationships among the peoples of Uganda have been irreversibly destroyed. President Milton Obote presides over a radically different society and political system than the one from which he was excluded in 1971. The high cost which Uganda had to pay in terms of loss of hundreds of thousands of lives and refugees is too great a burden for any society.[23]

## The Mandate of the Military as a Governing Class

It has been one of the hard lessons of African politics that the military leaders who abandon the civilian supremacy model in favor of a greater degree of political intervention quickly discover that they have overestimated the depth of what they perceived as a popular mandate to govern, and immediately take on the mantle of guardian of the masses. The slogan of the Liberian Peoples' Redemption Council—"In the cause of the people, the struggle continues"—illustrates this presumption of a popular mandate. In most instances it was not the popularity of the particular military group per se that contributed to the acceptance of the coup, but rather the lack of popularity of the civilian or military leadership that had preceded them in office. To the extent, moreover, that the destruction of the preceding regime was broadly accepted, it has been perceived by the participants as a mandate which the military was obliged to share with other significant dissident groups in society. Thus, the very groups that had applauded the military intervention and provided it with popular acceptance are among the first to criticize any effort on the part of the military to give itself an unlimited mandate in terms of both time and scope of responsibilities. The lofty aims which the military initially proclaims soon give way to the pursuit of narrow corporate interests. Once the military, moreover, has proceeded beyond a narrow watchdog model, it sacrifices the neutral arbiter role which made it attractive to civilian dissidents in the first place. The military henceforward is perceived by its former co-

conspirators as one of the more firmly entrenched competitors in the pursuit of scarce resources and privilege in society.

The syndrome of popular disenchantment is well illustrated in the cases of Ethiopia, Ghana, and Liberia. The military Dergue in Ethiopia appeared to forget very quickly that it was the broad-based hostility of students, labor leaders, and peasants toward the regime of Haile Selassie—combined with discontent over the progress of the Eritrean war—that had brought the imperial system to its knees. Hence, when the Dergue attempted to carry out a radical transformation of society, instead of the more limited goals embraced by the students and the labor leaders, the latter manifested their loss of confidence in the military.[24] By that time, of course, the military was firmly in charge. Similarly, it was the market women who cheered most enthusiastically the second coming of Flight Lt. Jerry Rawlings during the New Year's Eve 1981 coup because of Rawlings's pledge to eliminate official corruption. Months later, however, these market people found themselves engaged in violent confrontation with Rawlings's troops who attempted to deal with the black market corruption which had become a way of life among the market vendors. Finally, a parallel exists in the advent of Master Sergeant Doe to power in Liberia in April 1980. The students, opposition political leaders, editors, clergymen, and others who had participated in the year of ferment leading to President William Tolbert's demise quickly found themselves chafing under the moratorium which the People's Redemption Council had placed on political activity during the first four years of military rule.

Ironically, it is the military itself, through the perpetuation of its tenure, that contributes most to undermining its own mandate. The commitment to the civilian supremacy model of civil-military relationships in Africa is not exclusive to civilian politicians. Indeed, it has become almost a sine qua non in the ritual of intervention that the coup leaders themselves in the early hours or days following their takeover of power publicly proclaim their commitment to an early return to civilian rule as soon as the factors which precipitated intervention have been eliminated. The frequency with which subsequent military leaders in Nigeria, Ghana, and elsewhere have undermined the efforts of their military predecessors in restoring civilian rule does not negate the general proclaimed preference for civilian rule.

## Organizational and Other Limits on Military Governance

The limits on the ability of the intervening military to control the machinery of state have been in many respects similar to the dilemma faced by the party leadership at independence, namely the need to rely upon others to provide the skills for economic planning, maintenance of the judicial system, and the other tasks of government. Just as the party leaders at independence initially had to rely upon expatriates, the military leaders following the coup have had to rely upon civilian bureaucrats, judges, teachers, and others in coping with the broad economic, social, and political questions that needed resolution. The specialized training and relatively insular experience of the military poorly prepared them for the tasks of governing. This was particularly the case where a *social transformation* model was envisioned, but it applied as well to the more limited instances of the *watchdog* or *balance wheel* models. Just as the departure of some experienced expatriate administrators at the time of independence had deprived the civilian nationalists of certain "institutional memories" required for the continued functioning of key ministries, similarly the assassination or departure of leading politicians impeded the ability of the military to effect a smooth consolidation of power. The modus operandi of the military, moreover, differs substantially from the rules and procedures which apply to civilian government. The military style of command through hierarchies is not readily adaptable to civilian politics. The latter requires constant negotiations among vested interests; trade-offs in vertical, horizontal, and oblique directions; and occasional recognition of failure as a healthy aspect of political behavior.

Taking on civilian tasks poses considerable risks for the military. Even if this involvement merely required military supervision of civilian performances, inevitably this diverted the top military leadership from its primary mission of running the military establishment to the more complex task of running the state. A number of things thus occurred which created internal tensions within the military. First of all, the easier access on the part of the top military to the new privileges associated with state power (as well as the extra-legal acquisitions of property) created a gulf between senior- and junior-grade officers as well as put distance between officers and the rank-and-file. Secondly, military leaders associated with governance of the state have been called upon from time to time to make decisions which may be in the interest of the larger community but do not necessarily satisfy the more narrow interests of the military. Thirdly, not all ethnic, religious, and other segments of society can be proportionally represented within the top military cadre. Hence, the appearance (if not the reality) of linkages of an ascriptive nature between the top brass and key ethnic leaders in the civilian sector creates ethnic tensions within the ranks of the military. In response to one or more of these developments, the collective nature of leadership, which may have characterized the initial coup group, ultimately gave way to one-man rule or governance by a narrowly based junta. Thus distance is put between the top leadership and its own primary constituency. Any one of the preceding factors may be a specific cause of the succession of coups that occurs within a single period of military governance.

## Comparative Tests of Military versus Civilian Performance

"THE LEGITIMACY ISSUE"

We have nothing approaching a truly scientific social science laboratory in which we can test the relative performance of civilian versus military regime.[25] The variables that must be taken into account range considerably even though most African states share a generalized situation of poverty, a recent history of colonial occupation, and a similar set of problems in nation-building. Even when comparing military and civilian rule within a single state, where the range of variables is thereby reduced, it is difficult to know when to start counting those developments or situations which must be credited to or charged against a civilian, as opposed to a military, regime. As previously noted, moreover, the range of models of civil-military relationships does inject a wide measure of uncertainty regarding crude analyses based upon more than fifty rather divergent cases of successful military intervention. Mindful of these problems, some broad generalizations can nonetheless be posited.

The first observation has to do with the frequent claims of military leaders that, despite the paucity of the numbers actually involved in a specific coup, military intervention has popular support. Thus, it is argued that military effort at governing has had a greater base of legitimacy than that of the civilians they displaced. What kind of test is being used to validate this claim? Dancing and demonstrations by jubilant market women at the announcement of a successful coup is not a reliable index. The very women, for example, who danced in front of Usher prison in Accra in January 1966 as Nkrumah's political prisoners were being released by the new military government were the same women who several days earlier had been photographed giving President Nkrumah a triumphal farewell as he went off to China for a state visit. The 1974 student demonstrations, labor strikes, and other kinds of anomic behavior that greeted the Ethiopian coup could not be read by the military Dergue that toppled the Emperor as an abiding test of its legitimacy. Indeed, within weeks the military had to turn against its fellow revolutionaries.

In considering the claims to legitimacy by various military governing groups, there are few objective tests by which to evaluate their claims of being more appropriate defenders of the society and its "constitution" than the civilians they have displaced. Neither is the military elected nor does it have its mandate confirmed in a postcoup election. By contrast, at least some of the party regimes do in fact periodically have their mandate to govern tested. In addition to those states which have long permitted or have recently introduced a system of multiparty competition (e.g., Botswana and Senegal), several single-party states have permitted competition to take place at the legislative level in a modified primary election system.

Aside from the referenda which military regimes have permitted with respect to acceptance of new civilian constitutions (usually on a take-it-or-leave-it basis), there are few instances in which a military has permitted a popular referendum on policies to be pursued by the military regime, let alone a referendum on its remaining in power. The closest thing to the latter was the referendum which the Ghanaian military provided in 1978 regarding its continuation in office as part of a unionist coalition of civilians and military leaders. Despite the many charges of a rigged vote, the military only managed to record a 56 percent favorable vote.[26]

In many instances the critical test of legitimacy of an African military regime is externally applied. Parallel to the OAU principle which upholds the sanctity of the inherited colonial boundaries of African states, a similar posture of "live-and-let-live" applies with respect to the acceptance of any governing regime. African leaders generally accord recognition to other African governing groups whether civilian or military, exemplary or outrageous, well-trained or deficient in the art of governing, supported by an elective majority or imposed by a handful of self-indulgent dissidents. It was a rare act for the Nigerian civilian leadership in 1980 to attempt to orchestrate a quarantine of the regime of Master Sergeant Samuel Doe following the assassination of President William Tolbert. Indeed, not only did Idi Amin secure official recognition of his regime, but he was actually elected Chairman of the OAU during the apex of his domestic atrocities. No one attempted to topple his government until he had actually invaded Tanzania. Citing another case, it was France, rather than other African states, that dethroned Emperor Bokasso in Central Africa. Once entrenched in power, military regimes, like the civilians they displaced, do not have to earn a sort of Wilsonian right of international acceptance.

"MAINTENANCE OF STABILITY"

A further aspect of performance evaluation relates to the claim that the military can better maintain order and stability in the new African states than can the civilians they displaced. Despite the superior direct control which military regimes exercise over the instruments of violence, there is no overwhelming evidence that they have done a more creditable job of providing the order and stability required for economic development or for the political consolidation required in forging a nation from among highly heterogeneous societies.

More frequently indeed, it is the military itself which is the major source of instability. This would include not only the *atavistic* models of military intervention provided by Idi Amin and others. It applies as well to those situations in which the very uncertainty and insecurity on the part of the coup leaders regarding the success of their intervention had led them to engage in significant destruction of property as well as the highly publicized and almost ritualistic killing of those identified with the previous order. Although the numbers were relatively limited, nevertheless the execution of previous military politicians by Jerry Rawlings in the Ghanaian coup of 1979 and the 1980 executions of thirteen Americo-Liberian civilian leaders following the Samuel Doe coup did provide the impression of a breakdown of public order. Even more broadly, the imposition of curfews and restrictions on movement and on political activities provides an increasing number of occasions where the military may—under the guise of maintaining order—exploit and extort the general public. By way of contrast, civilian regimes tend to place a higher priority upon educative, economic, group, and ritualistic sanctions. Military leaders tend to rely heavily upon the sanction with which they are most familiar—that of force. They secure the appearance of popular acceptance of their rule by securing a form of compliance based upon fear of physical reprisal.

### "ACCOMMODATING INTERETHNIC CONFLICT"

Although the military is one of the few continuing institutions associated with the entire colonial state, and although it claims to represent the defense of the whole nation against threats both domestic and external, the record of the military on accommodating interethnic conflict has been somewhat checkered. On balance the military does not appear to have been more effective than civilian regimes in reducing ethnic, religious, and regional conflicts or in balancing out the diverse claims against the state's limited economic resources. The military, moreover, cannot boast of a record superior to that of civilians in terms of maintaining the integrity of the original political boundaries. This has been part of a generally accepted compact which both civilian and military regimes alike have upheld under the Charter of the Organization of African Unity. Indeed, among the few instances in which efforts were made at secession (e.g., Biafra), or in which international boundaries were initially violated (e.g., the Somali incursions into the Ogaden and Uganda's attacks on villages in northwest Tanzania), a military governing group dominated the political scene.

On further analysis, moreover, the argument of the military which is based upon continuity from the colonial period is flawed. It ignores the fact that ethnicity was very carefully taken into account by the European administrators in the recruitment and assignment of Africans to the colonial army. It overlooks as well the fact that the colonial army supported the European bureaucracy rather than upholding the concept of an African national community.

Developments under civilian rule following independence further limited the ability of the postcolonial military to rise above its own ethnic problems. This was particularly the case where the departure of Europeans and the subsequent Africanization of the officer class brought advantages largely to those ethnic groups which had been more intensely exposed to mission education and other forces for modernization under colonial rule. These were often the same groups that dominated the political parties during the nationalist struggle. Career opportunities which had been viewed with disdain during the colonial period suddenly became—taking Uganda as a case in point—attractive to both the Baganda and the Lang'o educated elite. This turn of events was viewed with alarm by Idi Amin's group, the Kakwa (Nubi), whose home area had under British rule been generally neglected in terms of modernization but who had been systematically recruited as noncommissioned officers.[27] The Baganda and Lang'o officers were also suspect to the northern ethnic groups who were generally disproportionately recruited at the troops level. This situation was central to the understanding of the 1971 Amin coup. Similar examples of parallel interethnic tensions within the postindependence military can be cited from around the continent.

The intervention of the military into postindependence politics further exacerbated the preexisting ethnic imbalances. In the 1958 coup in the Sudan, for example, the northern Muslim Arabs expanded their influence under General Abboud to the detriment of the Nilotic Christian traditionalists within the military—setting the stage for the decade-long civil war. In Nigeria, the Igbo officers who were prominent in the January 1966 coup (and who had as a group escaped assassination attempts) moved too precipitously in promoting their co-ethnics to the vacated positions within the military. This aroused the suspicions of the Hausa-Fulani and representatives of other ethnic groups in the military, who subsequently effectuated the July 1966 coup against Ironsi and his fellow Igbos. Still a third case is that of Liberia, which, following the 1980 coup, found a disproportionate number of officer cadre coming from the Krahn and other southeastern ethnic groups. These were the ethnic groups that had been only recently exposed to modernization, but they were dominant within the group of eighteen noncommissioned officers who carried out the coup.

Even the two categories of cases which suggest that military forces are better able to achieve national integration than civilian political leaders are not unqualified successes in this regard. The first category consists of those instances in which the military wing of a nationalist political movement makes a conscious effort to transcend ethnic differences within its ranks. Rather than awaiting military victory, specific planning takes place during the military phase of the nationalist struggle regarding the nature of the civilian political system which will—inter alia—reduce ethnic considerations in decision making. Thus, an effort is made to emulate the Yenan experience of the Chinese Communist Party following the Long March. FRELIMO in Mozambique and SWAPO in Namibia are the African examples that come quickly to mind.

On the other hand, involvement in military action to achieve nationalist goals may actually harden ethnic lines. The fact, for example, that the Mau Mau Emergency was largely restricted to the Kikuyu and the related Embu and Meru groups provided the Kikuyu with an extraordinary claim to political preference over its ethnic competitors on the basis of its heroic efforts in challenging settler domination. In other cases where the ethnic base of resistance was broader, the absence of a unified military command and strategy on the part of those political groups fighting for liberation and control of the postcolonial state may actually exacerbate rather than ameliorate ethnic divisions within the new state. The ZANU/ZAPU split, reflected in the lack of coordination among the ZANLA and ZIPRA military wings, has perpetuated ethnic cleavage in postindependence Zimbabwe. And both the MPLA government and the challenging UNITA forces in Angola represent two different versions of broad ethnic coalitions forged under conditions of military combat.

The second category of cases—in which a military governing group appears to have done a more effective job in ameliorating ethnic conflict than was done by a preceding civilian regime—is virtually limited to one and possibly two examples. The lesser of these two is that of Burundi under the second military government, which Crawford Young suggests has made considerable strides in ameliorating the conflict between the Tusi and the Hutu caste groups. The conflict in Burundi previously had resulted in the deaths or exile of tens of thousands of Barundi. This case should receive greater research attention in the future. The better-documented case, of course, is that of Nigeria. The political system devised by the Nigerian military during the Biafran war and brought fully into existence in 1979 frontally addressed the question of ethnicity. The success of Nigerian military efforts at ethnic accommodation, of course, has been seriously flawed by the New Year's Eve coup in 1983. The coup dismantled the ingenious electoral system introduced by the military which limited participation to political parties with greater than regional appeal and which required a broad national mandate for one to be elected president. Other aspects of the military experiment in reducing ethnic tensions, however, remain in place despite the 1983 coup. The nineteen-state federal system, which broke up most of the larger ethnic groupings, continues to function with respect to management of public programs and the administration of justice at the state level. The national bureaucracy, moreover, was broadly recruited from among regions and ethnic groups during the last years of military rule, and this process has also continued, despite the coup. Of equal significance have been the continuity of military efforts to equalize economic distribution throughout the republic. The formula for sharing the oil revenues, for example, and the establishment of respectable universities in each of the nineteen states continue as monuments to the military's success in accommodating interethnic rivalry in Africa's most populous country.

Having acknowledged the example of the Nigerian military, however, it must be noted that several civilian regimes have been equally effective in dealing with the problems of ethnic and religious heterogeneity. The Revolutionary Party (the former TANU) in Tanzania, for example, has been a vital instrument in sublimating the differences among Tanzania's more than 120 ethnic groups. Nyerere's use of Swahili, the introduction of a radical development ideology, and the conscious efforts at regional equalization of economic benefits have all been factors in Tanzania's success in nation-building. Although the strategies and tactics differ substantially from those of Tanzania, other civilian regimes in Senegal, Cameroon, Kenya, and the Ivory Coast have also been able to achieve a kind of static tension among competing ethnic groups, with conflict being ameliorated as a by-product of a reasonable amount of success in economic development.

### "POPULAR CONTROL OVER GOVERNMENT"

Closely related to the question of ethnic accommodation is the question of establishing popular government. There is little evidence to support the proposition that the African military has been more effective than civilian regimes in providing an environment receptive to the survival of consociational democracy. On the contrary, the rejection by the Ghanaian military in 1982 and of the Nigerian military in 1983 of the experiments in democracy launched by their military predecessors just adds further fuel to the litany of failure on the part of military experiments in democracy around the continent. Conversely, there has been a steady widening of the base of permitted competition within several of the political party states. This has come either through challenges being permitted by opposition parties that do in fact compete and have their ballots counted or through encouraging effective challenges at the legislative level within many of the single-party states. Through voluntary resignations of heads of state, moreover, major changes in political directions have been achieved in Senegal and the Cameroons, with other retirements being considered elsewhere.

The denial of the democratic process, moreover, during periods of military intervention is not limited to the banning of political parties and elections. The restrictions are much broader, invariably involving a complete moratorium on all forms of political activity and legitimate discussion (as defined by the military); the imposition of curfews; the banning of independent newspapers and the arrest of journalists and editors; and the outlawing or restricting the activities of trade unions, cooperatives, churches, and other pluralistic institutions. This provides ample evidence of a general intolerance by the military of any form of political competition, let alone dissent. Confrontation of ideas, however, is the essence of pluralistic democracy. I am not suggesting that limits on civil liberties do not occur under civilian party regimes in Africa. It is rather the consistency of their application under military rule that undermines the military's professed commitment to democratic procedures. The modus operandi of the military, after all, dictates against the constant bargaining, open-ended discussion, and absence of closure, which are requisites of a functioning democratic system.

### "ACHIEVEMENT OF ECONOMIC DEVELOPMENT"

A substantial portion of the literature on the African military and economic development has been based upon certain theoretical assumptions about the modernizing disposition and capacity of the military. It is assumed that, unlike many other structures in African society, the new military is committed fully to modern technology as a necessary element in achieving effective defense and combat readiness.[28] Since indigenous or purchased technology is directly related to industrialization, it is further assumed that the military will place a high priority upon industrialization of African economies to ensure continued military preparedness. In contrast with churches, parties, and other institutions, the military as an institution is characterized by rational decision making; management by objectives; achievement orientation in the selecting and assigning of personnel to specific tasks; commitment to the idea of higher education—particularly in the technical fields; and conviction of the need to maintain a modern system of communications.

To the extent that the foregoing is true (and it is certainly questionable with respect to many African armies), all that it essentially confirms is that the military has a vested corporate stake either in (1) maintaining an industrialized economy which will itself produce the weaponry, communications system, transport, and other material needed by the military; or in (2) ensuring that the economy, through exports, will earn sufficient credits or secure enough funds through loans to pay a foreign source of needed military equipment. The attributes noted say nothing about the ability of the military to transfer its skills and attitudes to the governance of a national society or that it will be able to blend the various corporate demands (including its own) into a workable package for the maintenance of a healthy national economy and society. There is nothing in the training of military officers per se that makes them better qualified to comprehend the workings of complex industrial organizations, to cope with the problems of international finance, or to engage in the bargaining that must take place among the various participants in the market—whether that market is controlled or based on laissez-faire principles.

No objective indices of growth provide indisputable proof that a given society which has experienced both extended periods of military rule and extended periods under a civilian regime fares better under the former than it does under the latter. In any event, it would be difficult in most circumstances to delineate where one economic initiative ends or begins, whether the weather has been a factor, and what other considerations have to be taken into account. There have been very few single case studies which systematically address the performance of military regimes in an African country. One exception would be Donald Rothchild's appraisal of the Ghanaian experience during the second military intervention.[29] Rothchild notes the difficulties of controlling the variables which must be taken into account. Nevertheless, he confirms a rather negative judgment of economic performance. For the continent as a whole, certain gross data, however, suggest that civilian regimes fare better than military regimes. With respect to food production, for example, only seven of the forty-five states in sub-Saharan Africa are self-sufficient in food production. Of these seven states, six have experienced unbroken periods of civilian rule since independence.[30] Congo Brazzaville is the only exception, and it has a relatively small population. While the remaining African states break roughly evenly in terms of extended military versus extended civilian rule, the military-dominated states, such as Nigeria and Ghana, had mounted massive programs for "feeding the nations" under military rules but failed miserably in meeting production goals. One further interesting piece of data is the revelation that Uganda, having endured the disastrous economic chaos of the Amin military period, has managed to achieve dramatic increases in basic food production during the early years of Obote's Second Republic.

Other gross data which suggest better performance of civilian versus military regimes are contained in the 1983 IBRD figures for growth of production for thirty-four African states, listed in rank order. Of those states which have experienced unbroken civilian rule since independence or have experienced more years of civilian than military rule during the past decade, ten are in the upper half of the scale, and only four are in the lower half. Only seven of the states that have endured more years of military than civilian rule during the past decade (or since independence) are in the upper half of the scale, whereas twelve are in the lower half.

With regard to the waste of scarce resources on nonproductive activities, the record on corruption during periods of military rule is not demonstrably better than the record in those same countries under civilian rule. The second coming of Jerry Rawlings was directed against alleged corruption by civilians; the first Rawlings coup was directed against his predecessor military colleagues! Both civilian and military regimes in Africa experience periods of puritanical posturing regarding corruption, followed by periods of rampant rapaciousness. In the absence of hard data on corruption, the anecdotal material on civilian corruption tends to be as outrageous as the material on military misdeeds (such as the cement scandal under the Nigerian military). Aside from illegal exactions, the escalating costs of military weaponry, barracks, uniforms, and the associated perquisites have become increasingly significant factors in explaining national budget deficits, adverse balance of payments problems, and the possibility of default on repayment of loans. Once in power, military regimes have gone far beyond correcting the low economic status of the military vis-à-vis other sectors of society. At the time of transfer of power to civilian hands, the military has lacked the courage to bring the size of the military establishment down to the scale which would be reasonably required for defense. The Nigerian military was a significant case in point.

Furthermore, on the question of development, the military as a corporate structure has not been visibly associated with development projects or programs. The most significant use of the military in U.S. Corps of Engineers type projects has occurred under civilian, not military-dominated, regimes. Sékou Touré in Guinea—following the dramatic achievement of independence in 1958 and faced with having to absorb the Guinean troops who were summarily dismissed from the French army without their pensions—decided to put the returned veterans and the military to work on projects of value to the nation. Similarly, Nyerere, following the 1964 mutiny, subordinated the military to the national political party and involved the military in the economic transformation of Tanzanian society. In states where the military has enjoyed political authority, it has generally refused to involve troops in activities which are described as civilian, such as collecting the garbage in Lagos during a sanitation workers' strike. The only exceptions to this rule have occurred when the issue is a highly sensitive political one (e.g., the Nigerian troops did help conduct a census during the extended military period) or when a situation is regarded as a crisis matter, such as the use of Ghanaian troops in moving cocoa to market when vital export earnings from this mainstay of the Ghanaian economy had been threatened by lack of transport and fuel.

### Transition to Civilian Rule

Despite the popular sense of resignation, if not popular approval, which appears to greet many military interventions in Africa, in the long run the commitment to the general principle of civilian rule seems to be a deeply held one on the part of Africa's modernized sector. What is applauded is not military rule but the demise of particular civilian regimes associated with corruption or failure of economic growth. The military itself, moreover, recognizes the underlying preference for the civilian supremacy model by making an early pledge to restore civilian rule once the situation which led to the coup has been eliminated.

How then can the transfer of authority take place in a peaceful manner and with some assurance that the transfer will be permanent? Admittedly, we enter this discussion with more trepidation then we manifested before the 1983 Nigerian coup, particularly since the full post mortem has not yet been conducted on the overthrow of the Shagari government. Nevertheless, the procedures followed in the Nigerian transition seem worth restating, since it will probably be the course pursued by the new military there as well as continue to be the procedures followed in other states.

First of all, the transfer must be a genuine effort at restoring or refashioning civilian political institution. The "civilianization of the military" along the lines of Ataturk or Nasser and Sadat has not produced viable civilian supremacy models in the few places where this has been attempted in Africa. The titles have changed, but the military-created parties in Zaire and elsewhere do not function as genuine political parties. The emphasis in such regimes is upon the sanction of force rather than upon economic, educative, and other approaches to expansion of the base of popular participation in decision making.

A second requisite for successful transfer of authority is that the situations or issues which invited military intervention in the first place should be substantially resolved prior to the military withdrawal. The military is often able to impose a rational and mutually beneficial solution to a problem which has defied civilian agreement. The civilian negotiating leaders are often bound by the rigid and entrenched interests of their respective constituents and thus are unable to make those necessary concessions which might be regarded as a betrayal of vital interests. Thus, in Nigeria the military was able to provide a rational formula for the distribution of the revenues from oil in the eastern region and to cope with the problems of interethnic conflict by establishing a more workable federal system. Civilian politicians prior to the 1966 coup had been stalemated on these two fundamental questions.

Thirdly, if the transfer is to succeed, the military must work closely with the prospective politicians who will be expected to make the new political, economic, and social system function effectively after the transfer of authority. Civilians must be intimately involved not only in the broad issues but also in the mechanics of how the new system will function. The legitimacy of the process requires, furthermore, that a realistic timetable be established for the return to civilian rule, with a series of incremental target dates determined and fairly faithfully adhered to.

Fourthly, success of the civilian restoration requires that the military engage in the complicated self-denying act of consciously sharing power with other elements in the society. Not only would this require that the military reduce its mission to one adequate to the defense of the nation, but it also requires that the military avoid even the appearance of entrenched clauses or informal understandings which would give legitimacy to a future military intervention. Paralleling a reduction of its own political role, the military must be committed to a process which effectively permits respected civilian politicians—without regard to their previous roles—to participate in politics. And the base of institutionalized pluralism within the society must be expanded and strengthened with trade unions, cooperative societies, universities, churches, independent presses, and other forms of social and economic structures serving as strong, effective counterpoints to the strength of both the military and the political parties.

One final caveat regarding the return to civilian rule relates to the extent of external funding and support for the military in particular African countries.[31] During the early postindependence era the continuing external linkages with Britain and France, for example, proved during the rash of mutinies in East and West Africa to be a factor in averting a military takeover or guaranteeing a speedy return to civilian rule. An even more recent case was the intervention of the French military in the overthrow of the former Colonel Bokasso, who had restyled himself Emperor of the Central African Empire. The long-term effect of these external linkages, however, has been to place the military at the center of the political struggle over the allocation of scarce resources. The increasingly high cost of modern weaponry and military technology as well as the perpetuation and expansion of the package of material benefits which the new military enjoys cannot be met from domestic production alone. They require loans, gifts, and other outlays from foreign sources. Aid from the Soviet Union to Africa has long been heavily oriented to military over other forms of economic aid, and the American assistance programs are increasingly skewed in that direction. Having become accustomed to imported weaponry, the military is reluctant to turn over the reins of power to civilian regimes that have educational, health, and other priorities with respect to the use of scarce resources. This problem is particularly acute where the military governing group is engaged in one or more instances of rebellion and can only survive because of massive infusions of outside military assistance—whether from the East, the West, or the Libyans. There comes a point, however, as is certainly true of Ethiopia today, when the question arises as to whether the beleaguered military governing class has invited in a new colonial governing class. No matter what the intentions with respect to reestablishing civilian rule, the options are severely limited.

## NOTES

1. Gwendolen Carter, ed., *African One-Party States* (Ithaca, N.Y.: Cornell University Press, 1962); James S. Coleman and Carl G. Rosberg, eds., *Political Parties and National Integration in Tropical Africa* (Berkeley, Calif.: University of California Press, 1964); Gwendolen Carter, ed., *Five African States: Responses to Diversity* (Ithaca, N.Y.: Cornell University Press, 1963); William H. Lewis, ed., *French-Speaking Africa: The Search for Identity* (New York: Walker, 1965); Gwendolen Carter, ed., *National Unity and Regionalism in Eight African States* (Ithaca, N.Y.: Cornell University Press, 1966).

2. Michael Lofchie, "The Uganda Coup—Class Action by the Military," *Journal of Modern African Studies*, vol. 10 (1972), pp. 19–35.

3. Robert M. Price, "A Theoretical Approach to Military Rule in New States: Reference Group Theory and the Ghanaian Case," *World Politics*, vol. 23 (April 1971), pp. 399–430; "Military Officers and Political Leadership," *Comparative Politics*, vol. 3 (April 1971), pp. 361–379.

4. Samuel Decalo, *Coups and Army Rule in Africa* (New Haven, Conn.: Yale University Press, 1976).

5. Cf. Claude E. Welch, Jr., *Soldier and State in Africa* (Evanston, Ill.: Northwestern University Press, 1970); "The African Military and Political Development" in Henry Bienen, ed., *The Military and Modernization* (Chicago: Aldine, Atherton, 1971); (with Arthur K. Smith) *Military Role and Rule: Perspectives on Civil-Military Relations* (North Scituate, Mass.: Duxbury Press, 1974).

6. Morris Janowitz, *Military Institutions and Coercion in the Developing Nations*, rev. ed. (Chicago: University of Chicago Press, 1977).

7. Samuel P. Huntington, *Political Order in Changing Societies* (New Haven, Conn.: Yale University Press, 1968).

8. Richard Sklar, *Nigerian Political Parties: Power in an Emergent African Nation* (Princeton, N.J.: Princeton University Press, 1963), pp. 280ff.

9. Donald R. Morris, *The Washing of the Spears: A History of the Rise of the Zulu Nation Under Shaka and Its Fall in the Zulu War of 1879* (New York: Simon and Schuster, 1965).

10. Michael Crowder, ed., *West African Resistance: The Military Response to Colonial Occupation* (London: Hutchinson, 1978).

11. Lewis J. Greenstein, "Africans in a European War: The First World War in East Africa, with Special Reference to the Nandi of Kenya," Ph.D. thesis in History, Indiana University, Bloomington, 1975.

12. Carl G. Rosberg and John Nottingham, *The Myth of "Mau Mau": Nationalism in Kenya* (Stanford, Calif.: Hoover Institution, 1966).

13. Henry Bienen, "Public Order and the Military in Africa: Mutinies in Kenya, Uganda, and Tanganyika," in Henry Bienen, ed., *The Military Intervenes: Case Studies in Political Developments* (New York: Russell Sage Foundation, 1968), pp. 35–69; Crawford Young, *Politics in the Congo: Decolonization and Independence* (Princeton, N.J.: Princeton University Press, 1965); and Ernest Lefever, *United Nations Peacekeeping in the Congo, 1960–64* (Washington, D.C.: Brookings Institution, 1966).

14. Lord Frederick J. D. Lugard, *The Dual Mandate in British Tropical Africa* (Edinburgh: 1922), p. 577. Cf. also John Barrett, "The Rank and File of the Colonial Army in Nigeria, 1914–18," *Journal of Modern African Studies*, vol. 15 (March 1977), pp. 105–108.

15. Several interesting studies of army veterans in Africa suggest that they did not play a modernizing role in society once they had returned to mufti. Cf. Eugene P. A. Schleh, "The Post-War Careers of Ex-Servicemen in Ghana and Uganda," *Journal of Modern African Studies*, vol. 6 (1968), pp. 203–220; G. O. Olusanya, "The Role of Ex-Servicemen in Nigerian Politics," *JMAS*, vol. 6 (1968), pp. 221–232; and Rita Headrick, "African Soldiers in World War II," *Armed Forces and Society*, vol. 4 (May 1978), pp. 501–526.

16. Nelson Kasfir, *The Shrinking Political Arena: Participation and Ethnicity in African Politics, with a Case Study of Uganda* (Berkeley, Calif.: University of California Press, 1976).

17. Marina and David Ottaway, *Ethiopia: Empire in Revolution* (New York: Africana Publ. Co., 1978).

18. Robert Price, loc. cit.

19. Decalo, "The Politics of the Personalist Coup," op. cit., pp. 173–230.

20. Lofchie, loc. cit.

21. J. Gus Liebenow, "Liberia: The Dissolution of Privilege," Parts 1–3, *American Universities Field Staff Reports*, 1980, pp. 39–41.

22. Cf. Thomas S. Cox, *Civil-Military Relations in Sierra Leone: A Case Study of African Soldiers in Politics* (Cambridge, Mass.: Harvard University Press, 1976).

23. Tony Avirgan, *War In Uganda: The Legacy of Idi Amin* (Westport, Conn.: L Hill, 1982).

24. Edmond J. Keller, "The Ethiopian Revolution at the Crossroads," *Current History*, vol. 83 (March 1984), pp. 117ff.

25. Several interesting efforts in this direction are found in Robert W. Jackman, "Politicians in Uniform: Military Governments and Social Change in the Third World," *American Political Science Review*, vol. 70 (December 1976), pp. 1078–1097; Eric A. Nordlinger, "Soldiers in Mutfi: The Impact of Military Rule Upon Economic and Social Change in the Non-Western States," *American Political Science Review*, vol. 64, (December 1970), pp. 1131–1148; and R. D. McKinlay and A. S. Cohan, "A Comparative Analysis of the Political and Economic Performance of Military and Civilian Regimes: A Cross-National Aggregate Study," *Comparative Politics*, vol. 8 (October 1975), pp. 1–30.

26. Cf. Ronald Rothchild, "Military Regime Performance: An Appraisal of the Ghana Experience, 1972–78," *Comparative Politics*, vol. 12 (July 1980), pp. 459–479.

27. Aidan Southall, "General Amin and the Coup: Great Man or Historical Inevitability?", *Journal of Modern African Studies*, vol. 13 (1975), p. 89; and Ali Al'Amin Mazrui, *Soldiers and Kinsmen in Uganda: The Making of a Military Ethnocracy* (Beverly Hills, Calif.: Sage Publications, c. 1975).

28. Cf. Henry Bienen, "Armed Forces and National Modernization: The Continuing Debate." Paper presented to First Wharan Gdae International Symposium, Korea Military Academy, Seoul, September 21–22, 1981.

29. The six civilian-dominated states include the Republic of South Africa, Zimbabwe, Malawi, Kenya, the Ivory Coast, and Cameroon. The military regime state is Congo Brazzaville.

30. The *IBRD World Development Report*, 1983.

31. Cf. Frank M. Chiteji, "Superpower Diplomacy: Arming Africa," *Current History*, vol. 83 (March 1984), pp. 125ff.

CHAPTER 7

# Africa's Agrarian Malaise

*Michael F. Lofchie*

After twenty-five years of independence, it has become unmistakably clear that Africa's agricultural sector is not developing. This basic fact is solidly established by a wide variety of economic indicators and is universally acknowledged by observers at all points on the political spectrum. In many countries, agricultural stagnation is so pronounced that it poses fundamental constraints on the possibility of development in other spheres of economic life. Agricultural decay and sluggish performance in the industrial and commercial sectors relate to one another as cause and effect. Together, these threaten to undermine the social fabric of Africa's still fledgling national political systems.

The exact extent of this malaise is almost impossible to determine, for entire subsectors of the agricultural economy are practically beyond the reach of research and measurement. Astonishingly little is known, for example, about the precise dimensions of subsistence agriculture and what proportion of peasant production is actually consumed at home. Even less is known about the size of Africa's flourishing parallel, or illegal, economies beyond the fact that they often supply a very high percentage of urban and rural food requirements. Nor is there adequate information about the volume of production and trade in legal but unregulated (and therefore unmeasured) agricultural commodities. Add to these factors the fact that African governments sometimes exaggerate the extent of the agricultural crisis in order to qualify for food aid, and it is not surprising that at least one experienced observer doubts that a major crisis exists.[1]

The evidence that is available, however, points overwhelmingly in the direction of a serious and deepening agrarian malaise. The most visible symp-

The author wishes to thank the Academic Senate of the University of California, Los Angeles, the Presiding Bishop's Fund of the Episcopal Church, and the Africa and Middle East Bureau of the U.S. Department of Agriculture for financial support to conduct research on African rural development.

tom of this malaise is declining per capita food production. According to a major study by the U.S. Department of Agriculture, "Sub-Saharan Africa is the only region of the world where per capita food production declined over the past two decades."² With a population growth rate of approximately 3 percent per year, Africa managed only a 2 percent increase in food production during the 1960s and 1970s. Although this shortfall may at first appear relatively minor, the net effect was that by the end of the 1970s, per capita food production was only about four-fifths of its 1961 level. Africa's failure to maintain a balance between food production and population increase contrasted markedly with the experience of other developing areas such as Asia and Latin America, both of which managed to achieve per capita increases in food production during the same period.

Failure in the food-producing sector has ominous implications. It threatens to further undermine nutritional levels, especially in regions where caloric intake is already marginal or submarginal by international standards. Where long-term cyclical deterioration is compounded by crop losses due to drought or other disastrous events, the results are calamitous. Famine has rapidly become the most common symbol of African life to the external world, replacing other historically entrenched stereotypes. It is unutterably tragic that the imagery of starvation, unlike the imagery it has replaced, corresponds all too closely to reality for much of the continent's agrarian hinterland.

Food shortfalls necessitate grain imports and these increasingly pose a staggering financial burden on countries whose foreign exchange reserves are already badly depleted by other pressures. The U.S. Government's agricultural study estimates that Africa's imports of cereal grains roughly tripled from 1960 to 1979. Because of price increases, however, the net real cost of these imports increased about sixfold during this period.³ Occasionally, African countries have been compelled to enter the world market for cereals at a moment when Western grain reserves were under especially great pressure; for example during the period of massive Soviet purchases in 1973–74 or the North American drought of 1983. These occasions exact a particularly burdensome financial toll, often bringing even relatively solvent countries to the edge of bankruptcy.

There is little reason to believe that the need for food imports will alleviate in the near future. For no substantial improvements in the agricultural sector are discernible which give any evidence that food production is likely to overtake population increase. Indeed, even the best-case scenarios depict a continuing increase in food imports throughout the remainder of this decade, with at least one study suggesting a further tripling of import levels by 1990. International aid organizations have quietly dropped the fiction that food deliveries to Africa are the result of episodic events (droughts, wars, crop blights) and now publicly acknowledge that food assistance is a long-term necessity, the product of fundamental structural malaise. This change in viewpoint has been closely coupled with a tendency to treat food aid less and less as humanitarian assistance whose costs will be borne by the donor and more and more as a straight market transaction whose costs will be borne by the recipient countries.

The development implications of growing food imports require little elaboration. Food requirements will tend increasingly to "crowd out" the purchase of other necessities vital to long-term development, including capital goods, spare parts, raw materials, and energy. Imports which could increase employment, add to per capita production, improve the general quality of life, and enhance the revenue base for vital governmental services become displaced as a consequence. Food imports have no beneficial development impact upon a society; their sole purpose is to avert starvation. Even the most ardent advocates of the "food for work" model of food assistance would not see this program as a worthy substitute for importing the wherewithal for an industrial program. Food imports require African governments to confront the cruelest form of political choice: food imports now to avert immediate starvation or vital goods for the industrial sector to avert unemployment and more gradual deprivation.

Africa's agrarian malaise extends, as well, to the export sector. Once differentiated from the food-producing sector by relatively robust performance even during extremely difficult periods such as droughts, Africa's export-oriented agriculture is now increasingly characterized as "sluggish" and "stagnant." The World Bank's Report entitled "Accelerated Development in Sub-Saharan Africa" characterized the situation in the following terms:

> By the end of the 1970's, agricultural exports were no greater than the early 1960's. In fact, a modest rate of increase of 1.9 percent a year in the 1960's was offset by an equal decrease in the 1970's. In terms of volume, the only crops registering gains were coffee, cocoa, tea, sugar, and cotton. . . . As a consequence, Africa's share of world trade declined for most of these commodities. While world trade in those commodities exported by the Sub-Saharan countries grew in volume by 1.8 percent a year, and 3.3 percent in value (constant prices) over the two decades, the growth rates of exports from Africa were zero and 1.8 percent respectively.[4]

As in the case of food crops, then, Africa's performance in the export crop sector has fallen markedly behind that of other developing areas. And increases in real earnings from agricultural exports have failed even to keep pace with the rate of population growth.

Poor performance in the export sector of agriculture links directly to Africa's overall crisis of development. Because agricultural exports are a vitally important source of foreign exchange, stagnation in this sector is largely accountable for the deep scarcity currently experienced by virtually every African nation. Indeed, serious shortages of foreign exchange afflict even the major oil-exporting countries, for these appear to have been especially susceptible to a deterioration of export agriculture. The stagnation of export agriculture can also be counted as fundamentally responsible for the failure of industrialization, for this sector was counted upon to generate the financial resources necessary to launch an industrial revolution. Some observers link the deterioration of export agriculture indirectly to the current food crisis, arguing that food grains would not be in scarce supply if there were financial resources available to purchase them on the world market.

The causes of Africa's agricultural crisis are the subject matter of this essay. This is a daunting task. For although it is possible to isolate major continent-wide trends, Africa's agricultural economies are so complex and diversified that no single explanatory theory can possibly suffice. The most fruitful approach may be to set forth several broad categories of explanation that, taken collectively, can begin to illuminate the pathology of agrarian malaise. It is useful to consider three: (1) physical and environmental constraints; (2) external constraints; and (3) internal factors, e.g., national policies affecting agriculture.

## Physical Constraints

Tropical environments are generally unsuitable for intensive agricultural development. Early theories that the agricultural sector could furnish the resources to stimulate development in other sectors were dubious on this basis alone. It is instructive at this point, some twenty years since the publication of Rene Dumont's classic *False Start in Africa*, to recall his opening remarks. "None of the great economic powers—Europe, the United States, China or Japan—has developed under tropical conditions."[5] For, despite their often lush appearance, tropical regions are most often characterized by poor and badly depleted soils, by inhospitable climate, and by diseases which ravage human, animal, and crop populations.

Physical constraints provide the most fruitful point of departure for understanding Africa's agrarian malaise, if only because observers unmindful of these constraints have sometimes made outlandish statements about the continent's agricultural potential. Who has not heard, for example, that this or that country, region, or district has the potential, properly cultivated, to become the "breadbasket" of Europe, the Middle East, or some other world area. Such notions could be easily dismissed were it not for the fact that the underlying point of view continues to produce disastrous policies. The notion of proper cultivation has generally been interpreted to mean capital-intensive, temperate-zone agricultural methodologies; and Africa's rural landscape continues to be pervaded by policymakers who believe, despite evidence to the contrary, that this methodology will lead to agricultural development.

The vast majority of the land area where cultivation can take place in Africa is not well suited to intensive agricultural development. For African soils are typically thin, badly deficient in important crop nutrients, and low in organic content.[6] As a result, they are highly vulnerable to such damaging processes as desertification, erosion, and laterization. Similarly, Africa's rainfall patterns are more often than not characterized by extremes of high and low precipitation and by a confounding degree of unpredictability from one season to the next. Africa's physical environment has proved so fragile that its susceptibility to ecological deterioration must now be reckoned among the major constraints on agricultural development. This is not the place for an extended treatment of Africa's contemporary environmental problems, but a schematic approach may help to illustrate the close relationship between environmental fragility and the current agrarian crisis.

Before attempts to introduce modern agriculture, much of the African landscape was characterized by a perennial ground cover consisting of forests, indigenous year-round grasses and shrubs, or some combination of these. The ground cover performed a number of ecologically vital functions. It sustained the soil base by forming a protective mulch composed of leaf litter and fallen grasses. This shielded the topsoil from direct exposure to the baking sun and insulated it from the impact of direct bombardment by heavy tropical rains. The mulch was also important in providing the soil with its nutrients: through the process of microbial decay it became decomposed organic matter that interpenetrated the soil beneath. Insofar as Africa's premodern physical environment can be currently reconstructed, then, the tropical soils were able to sustain a dense biomass. But this was only possible because of a delicate balance between the decomposition of surface vegetation and the growth of new plant materials.

It would be naive to assume that traditional African agriculture was perfectly suited to this physical environment. But there is much reason to believe that its environmental impact was minimal, especially when compared to much that has occurred since. Because population densities were low, much of the land area simply remained untouched for long periods of time. Where settled agriculture did occur, it frequently involved shifting cultivation that allowed long fallow periods during which the fields could recover. And perhaps most importantly, because traditional agricultural technology was relatively elementary, its use did little to damage or remove the preexisting vegetative cover. Unstable as the tropical milieu may have been, the carrying capacity of the land seems to have been adequate to the demands placed upon it by its human population.

Agricultural practices introduced during the era of European colonialism have contributed to the decline of Africa's physical environment in a variety of ways. Some have to do directly with the introduction of certain crops and methods of cultivation that were not at all suitable for Africa's soils or climate. Crops which involve an annual cycle of planting and harvesting have proved to be especially harmful, for their introduction has commonly involved land clearing which strips the soil of its original cover, thereby interrupting the natural cycle of organic replenishment.[7] This is especially visible in areas where cotton, groundnuts, and tobacco have been introduced. These crops make especially heavy demands on the soils' nutrients and the loss of fertility is particularly quick. But similar trends can be observed in areas allotted to corn and wheat.

European rule had a number of additional effects on the physical environment. These were largely indirect in character and had to do with the impact of population increases induced by the introduction of bioscientific medicine. By the middle of this century, Africa's population had grown to the point where traditional agricultural patterns could no longer be sustained. Land areas whose vitality for agricultural purposes had depended upon long fallow periods between intervals of use had to be brought under annual cultivation, with disastrous effects on their arability. Exhaustion of the soil is now so widespread that it makes a good deal of sense to attribute some of the decline in Africa's per capita food production to the deterioration of the land base brought about by overuse.

This aspect of the decline of the physical environment has had profound social consequences. To maintain levels of production, rural producers have had to turn increasingly to the use of fertilizers and other purchased inputs. As they become more and more dependent upon and indebted to urban suppliers, farmers are increasingly compelled to surrender economic jurisdiction over their harvests and farms. As land and crops become collateral for debt, their ultimate ownership reverts increasingly to absentee organizations and individuals. This process may have a great deal to do with one of the great paradoxes of food deficits in Africa: namely, that they occur far more frequently among peasant populations in the countryside, where food crops are grown, than among the poorer populations in the cities, who must purchase food in the marketplace.

Africa's physical environment has also been stretched beyond its carrying capacity by the tendency of greater and greater numbers of rural dwellers to settle in marginal land areas. In some instances this is a matter of deliberate policy as governments confronted with desperate overcrowding in the high-potential areas have been forced to move their landless rural populations onto settlements in regions which hitherto did not support agricultural activity. But in most cases, it is simply the outcome of a desperate search for physical survival.

The movement to marginal lands sheds fundamental light on a key aspect of Africa's contemporary agricultural crisis. It explains why drought seems suddenly so commonplace as the cause of agricultural failures: by definition, marginal lands are areas where rainfall is at best unpredictable and, in fact, in most cases quite predictably unlikely to sustain successful agricultural activity. The settlement of marginal areas also explains why agricultural breakdowns are highly regional in many countries, with disaster in some districts occurring almost side by side with ample production in others.

The hidden time bomb of environmental deterioration in Africa is deforestation, a process that began early in the colonial era when forests were cleared to make way for export crops. In a sense, this process continues today as African countries, hard-pressed for foreign exchange, turn to timber exports as one means of generating hard currency to pay their debts to Western nations. Internal use is also a major threat. Charcoal is still Africa's most common cooking fuel and, for certain countries, a source of foreign exchange as well. The cumulative result of these pressures has been a deep intrusion into Africa's once nearly ubiquitous forest cover. In some countries (Kenya and Ivory Coast), the results of this process on rainfall patterns and on the level of the underground water table are already measurable. The agricultural consequences of deforestation may, in the long run, prove greater than those of any other environmental problem. For, once removed, the forest canopy, so vital a part of the continent's ecological system, is all but impossible to restore.

In reflecting broadly on the relationship between physical environment and agricultural development, it is difficult to avoid the conclusion that the Western developed societies referred to by Dumont were possessed of a set of singularly propitious natural advantages. These included the following: (1) a dense and relatively rich soil base; (2) a generally temperate climate that included a relatively long summer growing season followed by a winter frost that reduced substantially the incidence of human, animal, and crop diseases; and, (3) moderate and, more importantly, highly predictable rainfall patterns from one year to the next. This unique set of conditions did much to facilitate the emergence of highly productive large-scale agriculture characterized by the intensive cultivation of wheat, corn, and other cereals. Agricultural growth set the stage for the process of overall social modernization. Early theorists who speculated on the ready transferability of Western models of development to tropical areas would have done well to consider the implications of these major environmental differences.

The portentous implication of Africa's environmental predicament for future agricultural development is that it appears to rule out both a return to earlier models of cultivation and the continued application of the Western model as solutions to the current crisis. Sheer population pressures alone make it impractical to consider a return to any system which requires that large areas of land be left uncultivated for long periods of time. At this point, however, it seems almost equally impractical to consider further applications of the capital-intensive, temperate-zone model. For the experience of this system has almost uniformly been one of temporary, highly localized, and extremely expensive increases in production virtually certain to be offset in the long run by further deterioration of the physical environment. Unless an agricultural system more wholly suited to Africa's environmental circumstances can be developed, it is difficult to envision any other future than one of continuing environmental decay accompanied by a corresponding need for food imports.

### External Constraints

The externalist approach to Africa's agrarian crisis stresses the primacy of root causes which lie outside the boundaries of the continent and are, therefore, beyond the policy reach of national governments. The broadest and most all-encompassing theoretical statement of this viewpoint is to be found in that theory, or, more properly, complex of theories, concerned with underdevelopment. This theory, sometimes referred to as core-periphery theory or dependency theory, has been the subject of an encyclopedic and highly variegated literature, as have its merits and shortcomings. Thus, it is unnecessary to describe once again the theoretical positions of such diverse scholars as Paul Baran, Walter Rodney, Immanuel Wallerstein, Samir Amin, and Arghiri Emmanuel, to mention only a few. But it would be impossible to understand that externalist approach to Africa's agrarian malaise without reference to their viewpoint. For it does furnish us with the most cogent elaboration of the viewpoint that the basic constraints on agricultural development lie in the character of the continent's dependence upon the global trading economy.

Externalists believe that it makes little sense to treat the current agrarian crisis as if it were separate from the overall problem of national poverty in African nations. From their perspective, agricultural stagnation is merely one part of the larger picture which includes the failure of industrial and commercial development as well. Since these are conceptualized as parts of an interlocked pattern, externalists believe in the need for a single theory to explain both rural and urban poverty. They reject the proposition that the agrarian crisis can be treated through an explanatory framework whose terms of analysis are separate from those used to understand the lack of industrialization or the weakness of the commercial sector.

The point of departure for this theory is the view that the global economy can be divided into two categories of countries, core and periphery. The core consists of the advanced industrial societies of Western Europe and North America, plus Japan. The developing countries of the world, especially those of Africa, Latin America, and south and southeast Asia form the periphery. The central proposition of this theory asserts that the industrialized countries have been able to attain their development precisely because of their capacity to exploit—that is, extract an economic surplus from—the periphery. In a nutshell, the wealthy nations have developed because, through the mechanism of colonial control, they were able to siphon off the economic resources of the poorer ones. And, conversely, the underdeveloped countries are poor because their wealth has been removed to finance industrialization elsewhere.

It is virtually impossible for the nations of the periphery to break this pattern. For the industrial core continues to wield a set of control mechanisms that enable it to subordinate the economic life of the poorer countries to its own interests. The principal basis of control is the essentially compliant nature of political elites in the Third World, often referred to in the literature on development as "comprador" or "auxiliary," that is, collaborationist. The West's monopoly of advanced science and technology is also important since peripheral nations are utterly dependent for these upon Western powers, as they are for the capital to finance such minimal development as does occur. Multinational corporations provide the West with additional leverage since they are especially adept at extracting economic resources from the Third World without the need for formal colonial protection. The end result is that Third World countries must accept the structure of the world economy as a given, wholly beyond their jurisdiction to change.

The persistent poverty of African Third World countries is determined, according to this theory, by the fact that they participate in the global economy almost solely as exporters of primary agricultural products and importers of finished goods. Drawing heavily on classical economic ideas, theorists of underdevelopment argue that the relative value of commodities is determined by the amount of labor involved in their production. Their presentation of this argument, known as the theory of "unequal exchange," is intended to convey the fundamental economic disadvantage suffered by exporters of primary products.[8] Since the goods that African countries sell on world markets are largely unaugmented in economic worth by an intensive infusion of human labor, they are of intrinsically less value than the manufactured goods being imported. For this reason, African countries can never create or retain an economic surplus large enough to finance the growth of the agricultural sector or the capitalization of an industrial sphere.

Some observers believe that this condition worsens over time and that the terms of trade are shifting steadily against Third World countries. They believe that if the basic presupposition of the theory is true—namely, the labor theory of value—then industrial progress in Western societies can only exacerbate further the gap between the value of their manufactured goods and the primary products exported by countries in the periphery. Thus, the concept of declining terms of trade has been used to explain not only the widening gap between industrial and Third World areas, but the actually worsening economic conditions in major portions of Africa. The essential idea is fairly simple: given levels of exports purchase less and less in the way of imported items from abroad. Not only must exports increase steadily merely to maintain a given level of imports, but population growth means that even steady volumes of imports are divided among ever larger numbers of persons.

An important part of the theory of underdevelopment pertains directly to conditions in the agricultural sector. The operative concept is agrarian dualism. This idea suggests that since the economic systems of peripheral countries are shaped fundamentally by their dependency upon the core and by their role as exporters of primary products, the structure of the agricultural sector has come to be heavily skewed to favor the production of goods for foreign markets.[9] A sharp dichotomy has arisen between export-oriented agriculture, often based on the plantation system, and production for local markets, typically based upon peasant farming. Colonial and postcolonial agricultural policies alike are said to have benefited the export enclave at the expense of food production for domestic consumption.

The concept of agrarian dualism elaborates richly upon this dichotomy. Export agriculture is based upon large-scale units of production, typically held under private or corporate ownership, and is afforded the widest possible array of governmental inputs including extension services and a well-developed infrastructure. Highly capitalized, the export sector partakes of the most modern advances in productive techniques, including high-yielding hybrid seeds and the most scientifically advanced types of fertilizers, pesticides, and systems of cultivation. Transportation, marketing, and storage facilities are readily available as are a number of vitally important "soft" services such as credit, insurance, and market analysis. In many African countries, export agriculture is the closest available approximation of an industrial process and its importance is underscored constantly by figures which reveal its immense contribution to GDP and to governmental revenues.

The peasant sector, by contrast, often presents an image of deliberate and systematic neglect. Units of production are small, sometimes fragmented, and almost always held under communal tenure, a system which, whatever its many merits, is generally regarded as a disincentive to investment in the land. Vital governmental inputs such as extension services and infrastructure are conspicuous by their absence as is the use of modern agro-scientific methods. Farm to market roads frequently consist of little more than bicycle tracks or footpaths and the use of hybrid seeds, pesticides, and chemical fertilizers is extremely rare. Since most of what is produced is consumed at home rather than sold on the market, there is little opportunity for capital accumulation. The most typical technology is the hand-held hoe; animal-drawn equipment is used only occasionally, and fossil-fuel-driven machinery is virtually nonexistent. If the export sector approximates a modern industrial system, peasant production of food crops for local consumption represents an archaic cottage industry, a technological throwback to precolonial systems of production.

In the theory of underdevelopment, the flourishing of export agriculture and the impoverishment of the peasant sector are related as cause and effect. For despite extensive capitalization, the plantation form of agricultural production is labor intensive and, to function profitably, requires a ready supply of seasonally available, low-cost labor. The peasant sector was the only possible source from which this labor could be drawn. But to induce peasants to make their labor available, their living conditions had to be worsened to the point where wage employment, even at abysmally low wage levels, became necessary for survival. In this view, the degradation of the peasant sector of the agricultural economy is not the mere accidental by-product of colonial and postcolonial neglect, but the intended consequence of governmental policies designed to produce a labor supply for the export enclave.

The most effective of these policies has been low producer prices for peasant-grown foodstuffs. This policy accomplishes several closely related objectives. It not only compels peasant farmers to accept wage labor as a supplemental source of cash income, but insofar as the cost of food is a basic determinant of wage levels, it facilitates a low wage level on the exporting farms. By making cheap foodstuffs available in the urban sector, this policy also lowers the level of urban discontent and subsidizes the material life-style of middle- and upper-level elites. The policy of low food prices has been so widespread that observers of all points of view are virtually unanimous in their conviction that it is a fundamental cause of the continent-wide problem of food deficits. Lacking any real incentive to participate in the official marketplace, peasant food growers have simply withdrawn further and further into a subsistence-type life-style or channeled their energies into parallel markets where their production does not appear as part of governmental statistics on available food production.

Food pricing policies inherited from the colonial era have today placed African governments in a terrible dilemma. To raise food prices might well solve the problem of food deficits by encouraging increased production and marketing on the part of peasant growers. But since most African states are not in a financial position to subsidize food prices for their nonagricultural populations, this could easily launch a wave of urban inflation that would seriously destabilize already fragile political systems. And there is a further concern that added emphasis on food production might contribute to further stagnation in the export sector of agriculture.

The theory of underdevelopment also presents an important point of view about the weakness of export agriculture, suggesting that although this sector has enjoyed an impressive range of supportive inputs, it is by no means their ultimate or major beneficiary. For the role of agricultural exports is to generate profits for Western business: its beneficiaries are the multinational processing and merchandizing firms which handle such commodities as coffee, tea, cocoa, cotton, palm oil, and sisal. Since the key to these companies' profitability is a supply of low-priced primary goods, they have a powerful incentive to push primary agricultural prices downward. In some instances this is facilitated by the fact that they have an ownership share in the farms which produce their goods. But even where this is not the case, the leverage they enjoy through their monopoly of access to the international marketplace enables them to acquire the products they need on the most advantageous possible terms. The end result is that the profits from export agriculture do not remain at home to finance a broad-gauged pattern of growth and development, but, instead, travel abroad where they contribute to the further advance of already well-to-do core societies.

Despite its many important insights, the theory of underdevelopment is not, finally, either conceptually or empirically persuasive as an explanation of Africa's agrarian malaise. For its all-inclusive generality, in certain respects a source of strength, also gives rise to serious doubts as to its overall conceptual and empirical accuracy. The theory has proven vulnerable to criticism on a variety of fundamental grounds. There is much reason, for example, to discount its bimodal division of the world into core and peripheral societies as grossly oversimplified and to suggest the need for a more sophisticated system of classification that takes into account the almost infinite variety of shadings between development and dependency. An analytical model that treats the agricultural sectors of such utterly dissimilar countries as Tanzania and Nigeria or Ivory Coast and Upper Volta as if their problems stemmed from a common source is not only doubtful on the face of it, it is also potentially harmful in obscuring the factors which account for the considerable economic differences between these societies.

Observers have also demurred at the theory's conceptualization of political leadership as comprador and called attention to the extent to which some African elites compete with Western economic interests to acquire wealth on their own.[10] In this perspective, the postcolonial African state cannot be accurately understood simply as a vehicle for the transmission of capital overseas. For control of the state apparatus can equally facilitate the interests of those who wish to constrain the role of international capital in order to gain an autonomous financial base. There are vast differences in the extent to which African states allow their political elites to accumulate capital by investing in the agricultural sector. And these differences often help account for the wide variation in agricultural performance from one country to the next.

The externalist approach to Africa's agrarian malaise is also vulnerable to criticism of its two most fundamental economic propositions, the expropriation of the economic surplus by Western societies and the concept of unequal exchange. Despite its centrality, the doctrine of expropriation of the surplus is seldom argued evidentially. With the exception of a handful of authors such as Pierre Jalee and Rafael Kaplinsky,[11] the case is principally left to rest on an extremely doubtful interpretation of Western history: namely, that the wealth of industrial nations has come about through their pillage of the agricultural surplus from peripheral regions.

Observers of all theoretical persuasions could readily agree that African agriculture has been mined for an economic surplus both during and since the colonial period and that this factor, more than any other, is at the basis of the current agrarian crisis. But there is compelling reason to believe that this surplus has not been transmitted overseas but that it has been absorbed internally, where it has gone to finance a host of political and economic activities. The strongest evidence to this effect is the very great discrepancy between producer prices and world market prices for both export and food crops that has existed since the very beginning of state intervention in these markets. There is a very real sense in which the differential between these two sets of prices is Africa's agricultural surplus. And this surplus, or at least the lion's share of it, appears to have been consistently utilized within Africa.

It would be impossible here to inventory all of the internal uses of the agricultural surplus but it is instructive to identify certain major ones as a means of casting further doubt on the view that this surplus has been extracted by Western nations. Much of it has gone to provide the financial basis for the colonial and postcolonial state, including its parastatal organs, and to pay for the provision of its social services including health, education, police, and infrastructure. One of the more harmful features of Africa's colonial legacy has been the tendency to set administrative salary scales at levels commensurate with those paid in the European metropoles. This policy, inherited from colonial governments which sought to provide economic incentives to European administrators, has resulted in a hugely expensive state machinery. The costs of government in Africa are so great that one political scientist views them as a basic cause of economic deterioration.[12]

A sizable proportion of the agricultural surplus is also used to finance the life-style patterns of middle- and upper-class elite groups which, in some countries, enjoy a level of personal consumption that is utterly disproportionate to the economic capacity of their society. Where corruption is prevalent, it, too, would draw partially on the agricultural surplus, often with devastating effects on bureaucratic and economic performance.[13] There is growing documentation that the economic surplus generated by the agricultural sector has also provided at least a part of the basis for capital accumulation by Africa's new "national" bourgeois classes. In recent years, the agricultural surplus, especially the foreign exchange earnings from agricultural exports, has gone to finance prestigious but enormously costly activities such as national airlines and diplomatic missions abroad. Today, enormous sums are spent to finance national armies whose costs in local and hard currencies exceed calculation. This ensemble of uses for the economic surplus generated by the agricultural sector may, in the end, be far more accountable than diversion to Western recipients for the depletion of Africa's agricultural base.

A second point of vulnerability in the economics of the externalist approach to Africa's agrarian crisis has to do with the concept of unequal exchange or, more precisely, declining terms of trade. It is virtually an article of faith among innumerable observers of contemporary Africa that the continent has suffered terribly from the declining purchasing power of its primary exports, especially agricultural exports. Some feel that this factor alone can largely account for the severe foreign exchange constraints which, today, not only inhibit the process of industralization, but cripple the agricultural sector as well. The argument to this effect is simple and straightforward: due to the fact that the costs of industrial goods rise disproportionately to the real-price increases for agricultural commodities, Africa has become gradually starved of the imported inputs necessary for economic buoyancy. This conviction is so widespread that it is at the basis of intensive efforts to reform the entire system of international trade and tariffs so as to tilt the balance of benefits more in favor of Third World exporters.

The World Bank has fundamentally challenged this belief in its highly influential volume *Accelerated Development in Sub-Saharan Africa: An Agenda for Action* (hereafter, the Berg Report). According to this extremely well-documented study, "most African countries, other than mineral producers, experienced favorable terms of trade during the 1970's." The Berg Report goes on to suggest that "past trends in the terms of trade cannot explain the slow economic growth of Africa in the 1970's because for most countries . . .

the terms of trade were favorable or neutral." It concludes that the major cause of the continent's severe foreign exchange shortages is "nearly stagnant or declining export volumes for the continent as a whole during the 1970's." [14] Although the huge price increases for oil imports did have an enormous effect, especially in the late 1970s, the root cause of the continent's difficulty, according to this analysis, lay in its inability to maintain its 1960s share of nonfuel exports by developing countries.

The Berg Report's analysis of terms of trade posed such a fundamental challenge to widely accepted views of this issue that it seemed especially important to reexamine some of the available evidence before accepting the Report's controversial conclusion. [15] The results of this research may be summarized as follows:

1. The literature on terms of trade is extraordinarily opaque, and may provide a classic example in the social sciences of how statistical evidence can be manipulated to sustain very different conclusions. The results of a terms of trade survey can be made to vary widely depending upon such factors as the time period chosen, the mix of commodities used for comparison and the weights assigned to each, the method used to determine prices and currency exchange rates, and the particular definition of terms of trade employed. Any conclusions about changing terms of trade over time, therefore, must be treated with great caution.

2. The specific evidence we gathered about five African countries since independence was generally consistent with the analysis of terms of trade in the Berg Report.

   a. The next barter or commodity terms of trade for three agricultural exporters—Kenya, Tanzania, and Ghana—improved slightly during the period since independence. This is especially true if the evidence employed is confined to industrial imports and imports of petroleum products are omitted.

   b. The terms of trade for two minerals exporters—Liberia and Zambia—declined markedly, especially for Zambia which, due to its landlocked status, faces high transportation costs for both imports and exports.

   c. If the cost of petroleum products is included in the tabulations, all five countries suffered sharp momentary declines in their terms of trade in the mid 1970s and again between 1979 and 1981. In sum, the theoretical argument that Africa has suffered a deterioration in its terms of trade with the West lacks an evidential basis. It is all but impossible to attribute the current agrarian crisis to declining terms of trade for agricultural products.

3. All the countries we examined showed a considerable tendency toward sharp short-term fluctuations in their terms of trade since independence. This factor, which is not examined at all in the Berg Report, could be expected to have a disruptive impact on a country's economic stability and, thereby, lessen its prospects for sustained economic growth.[16]

Despite these serious limitations, the theory of underdevelopment continued to be highly appealing to scholars and political activists.[17] The reasons for its popularity are not difficult to discern. Its sweeping synthesis of historic, political, and economic factors endows it with an intellectual breadth unmatched by most other contemporary approaches. Moreover, in dealing with the all too obvious failure of economic development, it achieves a strikingly realistic quality, especially when contrasted with the more optimistic but retrospectively naive assumptions of the independence era. Observers have also been attracted by the theory's humanistic features, its concern with the ease with which small and powerless countries can be taken advantage of by large and powerful ones and with the tendency for politically dominant elites to enrich themselves at the expense of the masses in developing societies.

The theory of underdevelopment has further contributed by generating a heightened sensitivity to features of the international economic environment that are inhospitable to African development. These include new forms of protectionism by Western governments such as tariff systems that discourage export-led industrialization by imposing duties that escalate sharply with the degree of manufacturing of the product and the numerous technical barriers, such as "anti-dumping" laws, that can also be used to reduce the volume of trade with developing nations.[18] A World Bank economist has also called attention to the problem of low demand elasticities for Africa's primary agricultural exports. This factor alone raises serious questions about the feasibility of the export-led growth strategy advocated in the Berg Report. For it suggests that even sharp price cuts for such commodities as coffee, cocoa, or cotton are not likely to increase the demand for these items in the importing nations.[19] Moreover, the very same devaluation that would lower the prices of Africa's agricultural exports, possibly to no effect on export volumes, could have a substantial negative impact on agricultural output by increasing the cost of imported inputs such as heavy equipment, pesticides, and chemical fertilizers.

Aid programs that consistently give high priority to capital-intensive projects could also be cited as examples of external policies deleterious to development. For these often create recurrent financial and administrative burdens that are simply beyond the means of host governments. They also tend to worsen the severity of the foreign exchange crisis by requiring large amounts of imported parts and supplies.[20] A theory focusing on these kinds of external factors could well construct a persuasive case that external factors have a significant, if as yet indeterminate, impact in deepening the agricultural crisis.

The theory of underdevelopment has set the terms of debate about the roots of Africa's agrarian malaise, and certain of its concepts continue to inform the literature on this topic even while others are subject to searching criticism. Its vivid depiction of the duality between peasant and export-oriented agricultural systems, emphasizing the deliberate impoverishment of peasant producers, continues to provide scholars with a compelling explanation of the continent's intractable food crisis.[21] And its insistence that the social changes brought about by capitalist agricultural practices have reduced the capacity of societies to respond effectively to economic crisis has also found powerful theoretical support.[22]

Reduced to a single proposition, underdevelopment theory suggests that today's agricultural crisis is rooted in the fact that the vital economic interests of agriculture have been suppressed so that its profits could be milked off to provide financial benefits for other economic spheres. This is a viewpoint that far more conservative theoreticians find difficulty in criticizing. Virtually all of today's remedial policies, including those suggested by internally oriented analysts, start from the same premise, namely, that the most critical immediate need is to redirect the balance of economic benefits back toward rural society.

## Internal Constraints

The internalist approach to Africa's agrarian crisis focuses centrally on the policies of African governments, and its core proposition holds that these policies have been systematically biased against the agricultural sector. The essential argument is fairly straightforward: today's agrarian crisis arises out of a set of policies designed to suppress the economic interests of agriculture in order to finance development in other sectors of the national economy. This point of view is systematically set forth in Robert Bates's excellent volume *Markets and States in Tropical Africa.*[23] Because Bates's work incorporates many of the major tenets of internalist thinking, it is especially useful as a leading example of this intellectual genre.

Since colonial times, according to Bates, African governments have intervened in the markets that affect rural producers in ways that pose fundamental disincentives to agricultural production. The first and most important of these markets is that for the crops that farmers produce for export. Here, Bates shows, governmental agencies such as parastatal marketing boards have consistently set producer prices at levels far below those which prevail internationally or below what farmers would have received had agricultural markets been able to operate freely. Producers of export crops have been especially poorly treated, and Bates demonstrates that "in most instances, they obtained less than two thirds of the potential sales realization, and in many cases, less than one-half."[24] Food producers, too, have been compelled to accept far less than retail price levels for their staple crops.[25] Bates's evidence for these points provides stunning confirmation of the extent to which African governments have skimmed off the agricultural surplus to finance nonagricultural, typically urban, projects.

African governments have also intervened extensively in the market for goods which rural producers seek to acquire as consumers, driving upward the price levels of these items. Virtually all African states have, to some degree, sought to foster a process of urban industrialization through a policy of import substitution. Typically, the new industries have concentrated on the production of basic consumer goods such as cotton cloth, wearing apparel, household utensils, small tools, farm implements, and daily sundries. The conception that these are infant industries which require immunity from competition during the period of their incubation has led to such protective policies as high tariff barriers, quotas or outright bans on imports, legalized monopolistic access to local markets, tolerance for inefficiency in management and production on the grounds that these are inevitable during the learning period. It has also led to acceptance of high prices justified as necessary to finance further capitalization. The effect of the policy of import substitution and the trade restrictions which inevitably accompany it has been to force the price of many locally produced consumer goods far higher than that for equivalent imported items, catching the rural population in an economic vise between artificially low prices for farm products and inflated price levels for day-to-day necessities.[26]

Governmental intervention has also had a decided negative effect on a third market of vital importance to farmers, that for essential agricultural inputs such as fertilizers and pesticides. Although African governments often seek to make these goods more generally accessible by subsidizing their prices, the available evidence suggests not only that this policy has been unsuccessful, but that its results have frequently been entirely the opposite of those intended. The reason is not difficult to discern. Due to artificially low prices, subsidized inputs are frequently subject to great scarcity. This permits the bureaucracies entrusted with their distribution to engage in corruption and favoritism: the subsidized goods can then be obtained only by a small elite stratum of farmers, those with close political ties to the agrarian bureaucracy or the governing class.[27] When this occurs, the vast majority of agriculturists,

those intended to benefit from low-priced inputs, have only limited access or
none whatsoever.

Observers at the field level have also reported that the bureaucracies responsible for distributing subsidized inputs are subject to great inefficiency
and that their deliveries of fertilizer and other goods are frequently too late for
effective use. Governmental regulation of agricultural inputs is almost always
part of a larger programmatic undertaking which seeks to alter the overall pattern of agricultural production. Such programs appear almost inevitably to
generate intense friction between government officials and their producer cli-
enteles and the resulting drop in farmer morale has invariably been reflected
in disappointing production figures for the projects involved. As a general
proposition, then, it is difficult to avoid the conclusion that governmental intervention in the market for agricultural inputs is a failed policy, one that has
led directly to inefficiency and corruption and indirectly to poorer levels of
performance by the agricultural sector.

Other government policies have affected the agricultural economy more
subtly, but with no less depressing results. Of these, one of the most conse-
quential has been the widespread governmental preference for large-scale
projects as the means to increase agricultural production instead of policies
that would do so in more universalistic ways such as improving farmer incentives through increased producer prices. Since large-scale agricultural
projects in Africa are typically established as state farms in cooperation with
external donors, their costs of production tend to be heavily subsidized by
state treasuries. As a result, they characteristically involve African governments in a damaging and somewhat unfair competition with their own farming
communities. Not only is it inevitable that state farms compete with private
farmers in the marketplace for agricultural inputs, but, since they are not constrained to market their products at price levels which reflect production costs,
they compete with private farmers in the sales marketplace as well. The policy preference for state agricultural projects, then, contributes in several ways
to the agrarian malaise; by forcing up the cost of inputs, by forcing down the
market price of farm products, and, in a somewhat more diffuse fashion, by
diverting agricultural resources away from a society's efficient producers to
less efficient farming systems.

Of all the governmental policies which have a negative impact upon the
agricultural sector, none is more devastating in its effects than the continent-
wide tendency of African states to overvalue their currencies' exchange rates.
For this practice sets in motion a whole set of powerful disincentives to agricultural growth.[28] Its most conspicuous effect is to subsidize the material life-
style of urban consumers at the expense of rural agriculturalists by lowering
the cost of imported goods. For Africa's urban elites have grown heavily de-

pendent upon a host of foreign goods ranging from automobiles and expensive household appliances to innumerable smaller items such as foods and wearing apparel. Since the foreign exchange used to finance these imports is normally generated by agricultural exports, the exchange rate policy results, in practice, in a kind of low visibility income transfer from rural agriculturists to the urban middle and upper classes. It is not at all surprising that Africa's cities continue to attract a rural influx and that this results, not at all paradoxically, in the fact that many African countries now experience simultaneous urban employment and a labor bottleneck in the agricultural sector.

Overvalued exchange rates have also had a substantial impact in suppressing local food production. Since the cost of imported foodstuffs is cheapened along with that of other foreign goods, it is not at all uncommon for Western grains such as wheat, corn, and rice to be less expensive in African cities than the same items, or equivalent food staples, produced by local farmers. When these grains enter local markets as food aid rather than on the basis of direct sales, their cost to local consumers is lowered even further and there is an even greater tendency to undermine the price structure of locally produced goods. The disincentive effect on local production is sometimes so great that it launches a cycle of ever increasing dependency upon food imports from abroad: local farmers find it increasingly difficult to compete in markets dominated by artificially cheapened imports, and urban populations become more and more acclimated, in terms of diet as well as economics, to inexpensive foreign grains. Since cheap food in the cities is one of the key props of fragile regimes, African governments find it politically impossible to disentangle themselves from exchange rate practices that undermine the economic basis of their own food growers.

The effect of overvalued exchange rates on export agriculture has been even more disastrous. For the producer price paid to export farmers tends to be a direct function of the ratio at which foreign exchange converts into local currency; the fewer units of local currency obtained by a marketing board per unit of foreign exchange earned for a commodity (overvaluation), the less it is able to pay its farmer clientele. Thus, overvaluation helps explain why so many African marketing boards have been unable to pay their farmers for long periods of time, or pay only a fraction of the official producer price, while others have had to turn to such questionable devices as certificates of credit. An unrealistically high exchange rate can easily result in the fact that, after the administrative and operating costs of a marketing agency have been provided for, there is simply no balance of local currency remaining with which to pay the farmers.

It has become a commonplace in the literature on Africa's agricultural crisis to attack the marketing boards for inefficiency, waste, overstaffing, and blatant mismanagement. And there is undoubtedly an overabundance of evidence to sustain these criticisms. But it is well to remember that Africa's parastatal marketing agencies are obliged to operate within a system of official exchange rates that fundamentally constrains the return they are able to provide to farmers. Not even the most efficient system of management could overcome the economic distortion that accompanies an overvaluation on the magnitude of fifty to several hundred percent.

Summing up these policies, it is no exaggeration to suggest that the interventions of African governments in the agricultural sector add cumulatively to a system of potent economic disincentives. Not only is it not surprising that agricultural production has dropped appreciably since independence, there is also no mystery as to why so much of what is produced evades governmental attention in parallel or unregulated markets. The debate over Africa's agricultural crisis does not need to pause even briefly over the issue of peasant rationality and market responsiveness. There is overwhelming evidence that African farmers respond with acute sensitivity to price fluctuations in the marketplace for their goods. Today's agrarian crisis has nothing to do with a peasant cultural preference for value systems that induce other than market-responsive behavior. It can be explained almost entirely as the outcome of a set of governmental policies that are eliminating the economic incentives for agricultural production.

The challenging question is why governments have persisted in these policies despite their evident failure. One possible explanation is that political leaders continue to be wedded to development theories that view the agricultural sector as the wellspring out of which broader economic growth can be financed. Such theories were prominent when the first generation of nationalist leaders began its ascent to power, and many of today's key administrative officials were also schooled in this approach to development. Academics and professional development experts alike believed that export agriculture would function as a growth-leading sector by generating foreign exchange and by creating employment opportunity in burgeoning feeder services such as transportation and storage. There was even a notion of economic recycling embedded in this theory, namely, the assumption that once urban industrialism had been launched, the profits it generated could be returned to agriculture to finance future agricultural development. Today's dismal reality now seems light years distant from this almost utopian vision of the African future. But even so, it is not wholly unreasonable to ask where agricultural countries can obtain the capital for broader national development if not from the agricultural sector.

A more plausible explanation of government policies that suppress agriculture focuses on the impact of powerful pressure groups on state action.

A whole array of politically potent social groupings benefits from the current arrangement and the leverage they can bring to bear endows on economically unsound policy with a solid basis in the logic of political survival. The list of pressure groups includes, most prominently, the total ensemble of urban constituencies which have a stake in policies that produce a relatively cheap food supply, including the members of Africa's fledgling working classes and the proto-industrialists whose wage bill is lowered when inexpensive foodstuffs are plentiful. The most powerful groups, however, given their political volatility, are the legions of salaried employees of public and private sector bureaucracies who have the purchasing power of their wages buoyed up substantially by policies that lower the cost of a host of imported consumer goods in addition to food items. The material life-style of Africa's new urban elites would be all but impossible were it not for policies that treat the foreign exchange earned from agricultural exports as if it were an economic fringe benefit for the middle and upper classes. Since urban inflation, not rural poverty, is the great destabilizer of African regimes, governments that wish to survive are compelled to treat agriculture as if it were an inexhaustible resource.

Whatever the origin of these policies, their persistence in the face of mounting evidence of massive agricultural collapse has convinced all but a tiny handful of observers that governmental intervention in the agricultural sector diminishes the prospects for its development. There is a growing conviction that the free market can do a better job of setting prices, allocating resources, spurring productivity, and, indeed, improving rural incomes than the existing policy framework. This new consensus is vividly reflected in the analysis of African agriculture presented in the Berg Report; and, partly due to the enormous impact this study has had, it has already come to dominate the prescriptive remedies put forward by any number of donor organizations including the World Bank and USAID. Representatives of these organizations have become convinced that the relatively unrestricted aid and lending policies of the past have enabled African governments to mask over the real extent of the damage done to agriculture by their statist approach. The result is that African governments now find themselves confronted with a new and powerful source of pressure on agricultural policy, the donor community. Increasingly, donor organizations whose leverage is considerable due to the critical need for external assistance, exert the weight of their leverage almost entirely in the direction of policy changes that would free the agricultural marketplace.

This sort of pressure is nowhere more evident than in the lending policies of the International Monetary Fund (IMF). Though technically not an aid organization at all, but rather an international credit institution engaged in making hard currency loans to countries which are experiencing serious debt crises, the IMF has in recent years taken on a degree of importance that far transcends its limited role.[29] Due largely to the fact that the economic analysis underlying its loans so perfectly embodies the new anti-interventionist, free-market consensus, the IMF has increasingly become a bellweather for other donor agencies. Any number of international aid organizations now wait to see whether a given country has come to terms with the IMF and attach this as a condition before proceeding with their own assistance programs. The role of the IMF in developing areas has now become so great that it has introduced its own terminology into the lexicon of development theory. Structural adjustment, the declared rationale behind many IMF loans in the Third World, is the current metaphor for a changeover from state economic regulation to a free-market approach to the development process.

For the economic analysts of the IMF, the current crises of African nations stem from two closely intertwined patterns of governmental mismanagement, excessively high deficit spending and overregulation of the marketplace.[30] Large budget deficits, incurred principally to finance costly and unproductive social services and dealt with almost entirely by increasing the money supply, tend to be enormously inflationary. Pressured by the political dangers of this inflation, governments have responded by overvaluing their currencies and by intervening frequently to control internal markets. The result of these policies has not only been huge trade deficits and critical foreign-exchange shortages, due to underpricing of imports and the disincentive effect on export-oriented industries, but severe distortions of the internal economy marked by inefficient pricing of capital, labor, and commodities. In this point of view, the cure for economic pathology lies in a series of internal reforms designed to free the marketplace of the burden of governmental intervention and allow the natural processes of price setting to bring about economic health.

To achieve this goal, the IMF characteristically attaches a set of stringent conditions to its loans and offers a given loan only in a phased sequence so that compliance with its conditions can be carefully monitored. Of the many conditions employed by the IMF, the following have the greatest bearing on the agricultural sector.

1. *Devaluation*. The IMF almost invariably insists that its borrower countries reduce their currencies' exchange rates promptly to levels that more accurately reflect realistic international values.
2. *Reduced budget deficit as a percentage of gross domestic product*. This condition follows naturally on the first and reflects the conviction that if inflation, brought about by high deficits, is allowed to continue, currency exchange rates will once again be thrown out of alignment.
3. *Free agricultural marketplace*. IMF economists believe strongly that agricultural prices should be allowed to rise toward free-market levels

and they therefore characteristically require either that parastatal agencies be removed entirely from the process of acquiring and vending agricultural commodities or that their role be severely reduced.

The critical question is whether the implementation of these requirements will produce significant improvements in the performance of the agricultural sector. Supporters of IMF policies point to the need for improved producer incentives and argue that, without the IMF, there is little possibility of their being achieved. For Africa's agricultural producers on their own generally lack the political influence necessary to induce basic changes in governmental policy. In this perspective, IMF conditionality has given political weight to economic reforms that will benefit hitherto powerless peasant communities. There is a strong belief that devaluation, combined with the elimination of controlled producer prices and the removal of wasteful and inefficient parastatals from the agricultural marketplace, will result in a number of important economic gains, the most important of which is increased producer prices. And since African agriculturists are demonstrably price-responsive, this change ought to induce measurable increases in marketed outputs.

Critics of the IMF approach generally focus their reservations on the political and economic implications of an essentially free-market strategy. As Nigeria's recent experience demonstrates, African governments are not institutionally well equipped to sustain rising levels of urban discontent: the political price of a freer market in the agricultural sector may well be a heightened incidence of military intervention or increased repression by civilian regimes. In the countryside, it is not difficult to envision the possibility that an agricultural free market would quickly result in higher and higher levels of landlessness. For rising agricultural prices, and the generally liberal economic environment associated with them, would make agriculture an attractive arena for capital investment. And this has historically been associated with increased mechanization and the consolidation of peasant farms into larger and larger units of production. The rural consequence of an agricultural free market is all too likely to be heightened deprivation for untold numbers of marginal peasant producers.

Concern about the IMF strategy also focuses on its highly selective approach to the agrarian crisis, the somewhat singular absorption with producer prices and the accompanying tendency to neglect other facets of the problem of falling marketed outputs. First-hand observers of the African agricultural scene point out repeatedly that increases in producer prices, however fundamental these may be, may have no effect whatsoever unless accompanied by a number of other improvements in the economic environment in the countryside. In any number of African countries, for example, the rural infrastructure has deteriorated so badly that it is almost physically impossible for farmers to transport their goods to marketing centers. In others, farmers hesitate to participate in the cash marketplace out of sheer personal insecurity, the danger of robbery by soldiers or bandit gangs. And in countries where foreign exchange shortages or other economic difficulties have constricted the supply of consumer goods, increased producer prices have only the most minimal effect. For cash income is not an incentive without opportunities to spend it in ways that improve the quality of life. Unless the process of agrarian reform addresses these and a number of other questions, no amount of price increase will improve the level of marketed agricultural production.

Perhaps the most serious shortcoming of the IMF approach, however, is the lack of a comparative perspective and the resulting tendency to ignore the immensely important role played by governments in countries which have achieved successful agricultural economies. In the United States, Canada, and Western Europe, governmental intervention is absolutely critical in sustaining high levels of productivity. Throughout most of these countries, governments not only participate actively in the regulation of producer prices, but also undertake a host of other critically important functions including the provision of vital inputs such as research, pest control, and systems of irrigation. An inventory of governmental interventions in the agricultural sectors of these countries would be virtually endless and would extend from the regulation of production at the farm level to the subsidization of exports to overseas markets.

The theoretical implication of this comparison is of utmost importance. It suggests that the issue of state involvement in agriculture needs to be defined in wholly different terms than those set by the IMF and the donors which follow its lead. These donors have now concluded, almost unanimously, that because current patterns of state involvement in the agricultural sector have helped to produce the current crisis, the remedy lies in a wholesale withdrawal of government from the rural economy. But the relationship between state involvement and agricultural recovery is not a simple matter of interventionist versus noninterventionist strategies. It is a far more complex issue that requires careful differentiation between effective forms of intervention and those that tend to damage the performance of the agricultural sector.

African governments are now caught between two powerful sources of pressure on agricultural policy. On the one hand are the volatile urban constituencies which have formed such an effective lobby for current statist policies and which continue to agitate blatantly against any changes that might unleash inflationary trends in the cities. On the other hand, governments confront mounting pressure from the international donor community which, on the whole, proposes freeing the agricultural marketplace as a necessary first step toward a solution. Although the available evidence is by no means complete or unambiguous, it is difficult to believe that the IMF prescription would not substantially improve the performance of the agricultural sector.

The available evidence does suggest that capitalism has the capacity to stimulate African development and, over time, to improve the material conditions of its peoples. This is not to suggest that the course of capitalist history is one of smooth, uninterrupted progress. In his powerful critique of dependency theory, Colin Leys does well to remind us of how unrealistic it would be to suppose that "capitalist development (in Africa) could be expected to unfold without the inequalities and unevenness, the instability, crises, (and) unemployment . . . that have characterized early capitalism elsewhere. . . ."[31] But even a progress marred by such events is better than no progress at all, and thus a major improvement over twenty-five more years of agricultural stagnation.

## NOTES

1. Sara S. Berry, "The Food Crisis and Agrarian Change in Africa: A Review Essay," *African Studies Review*, Vol. 27, No. 2, June 1984, pp. 59–112.

2. United States Department of Agriculture, *Food Problems and Prospects in Sub-Saharan Africa: The Decade of the 1980's*, p. iv. See also Cheryl Christensen and Larry Witucki, "Food Problems and Emerging Policy Responses in Sub-Saharan Africa," *American Journal of Agricultural Economics*, Vol. 64, No. 5, December 1982, and Carl K. Eicher, "Facing Up to Africa's Food Crisis," *Foreign Affairs*, Fall 1982.

3. *Food Problems and Prospects*, pp. 4–8.

4. The World Bank, *Accelerated Development in Sub-Saharan Africa: An Agenda for Action* (Washington, D.C., 1981), p. 46.

5. Rene Dumont, *False Start in Africa* (New York, 1969), p. 25.

6. A. de Vos, *Africa, The Devastated Continent* (The Hague, 1975), pp. 20–22. See also David Janzen, "Tropical Agroecosystems" in Philip Abelson (ed.), *Food: Politics, Economics, Nutrition and Research* (American Association for Advancement of Science, 1975), pp. 103–110.

7. Mark Freudenberger, "Physical Constraints to Agricultural Development in Tropical and Semi-Tropical Zones of Africa" (African Studies Center, Food and Agriculture Project, 1983).

8. See, for example, Arghiri Emmanuel, *Unequal Exchange: A Study of the Imperialism of Trade* (New York, 1972).

9. For an extensive treatment of the academic debate over this concept, see Institute for Development Research, *Dualism and Rural Development in East Africa* (Copenhagen, 1973).

10. The best theoretical statements of this position are Richard L. Sklar's articles "The Nature of Class Domination in Africa," *The Journal of Modern African Studies* (Cambridge), Vol. 17, No. 4, December 1979, pp. 531–552, and "Postimperialism: A Class Analysis of Multinational Corporate Expansion," *Comparative Politics* (New

York), October 1976, pp. 75–92. An excellent empirical study of the emergence of national capitalism is Nicola Swainson, *The Development of Corporate Capitalism in Kenya, 1918–1977* (London and Berkeley, 1980).

11. Pierre Jalee, *The Pillage of the Third World* (New York, 1968) and *The Third World in World Economy* (New York, 1969). See also Rafael Kaplinsky, "Capitalist Accumulation in the Periphery: The Kenyan Case Re-examined," *Review of African Political Economy*, No. 17, January–April 1980, pp. 83–105.

12. David Abernethy, "Bureaucratic Growth and Economic Decline in Sub-Saharan Africa: A Drama in Twelve Acts" (Boston, African Studies Association, 1983).

13. David J. Gould and Jose A. Amaro-Reyes, *The Effects of Corruption on Administrative Performance: Illustrations from Developing Countries*, World Bank Staff Working Papers, Number 580 (Washington, D.C., 1983).

14. *Accelerated Development in Sub-Saharan Africa*, pp. 18–19.

15. The African Studies Center at UCLA maintains a modest research project on African rural development, the Food and Agriculture Project. Research assistants in this project were asked to compile statistics on terms of trade available from the International Monetary Fund, UNCTAD, and the U.N. Statistical Office, as well as other literature, and to prepare tabular and graphic material that would help assess the accuracy of the World Bank's interpretation. Five countries were chosen for intensive analysis: two minerals exporters, Liberia and Zambia, and three agricultural exporters, Kenya, Ghana, and Tanzania. We are also indebted to Dr. Alan Buckley of Getty Oil Company for making available a private collection of materials on terms of trade.

16. The author is especially indebted to Professor Sayre Schatz of Temple University for this observation.

17. For further critical treatment of the economic presuppositions of dependency theory, see Colin Leys, "African Economic Development in Theory and Practice" in *Daedalus*, Spring 1982, esp. pp. 103–107. See also Martin Staniland, *The Underdevelopment of Political Economy*, ACIS Working Paper No. 32, Center for International and Strategic Affairs, University of California, Los Angeles, 1981.

18. See, for example, Douglas R. Nelson, *The Political Structure of the New Protectionism*, World Bank Staff Working Papers, Number 471 (Washington, D.C., 1981).

19. Shamsher Singh, *Sub-Saharan Agriculture: Synthesis and Trade Prospects*, World Bank Staff Working Papers, Number 608 (Washington, D.C., 1983).

20. For an excellent discussion of this entire problem, see E. Philip Morgan, "The Project Orthodoxy in Development: Re-evaluating the Cutting Edge," in *Public Administration and Development*, Vol. 3 (1983), pp. 329–339.

21. See, for example, Richard W. Franke and Barbara H. Chasin, *Seeds of Famine* (Montclair, 1980).

22. Michael Watts, *Silent Voice: Food, Famine & Peasantry in Northern Nigeria* (Berkeley, 1983).

23. Robert H. Bates, *Markets and States in Tropical Africa: The Political Basis of Agricultural Policies* (Berkeley, 1981).

24. Ibid., p. 29.

25. Ibid., chapter 2. See also Christensen and Witucki, op. cit., p. 893.

26. For an excellent criticism of import-substitution policies in Africa, see Michael Roemer, "Economic Development in Africa: Performance since Independence and a Strategy for the Future" in *Daedalus*, Spring 1982, p. 138.

27. Brian C. D'Silva and M. Rafique Raza, "Integrated Rural Development in Nigeria: A Case Study of the Funtua Project" (Unpublished manuscript, 1980).

28. *Accelerated Development*, pp. 26–67.

29. G. K. Helleiner, "The IMF and Africa in the 1980's," International Finance Section, Department of Economics, Princeton University, *Essays in International Finance*, No. 152, July 1983.

30. Bish Sanyal, "The IMF Logic" (African Studies Center, Food and Agriculture Project, 1984).

31. Leys, op. cit., p. 104.

CHAPTER 8

# Urban Growth and
# Rural Development

*Goran Hyden*

## Introduction

In 1980, about 72 percent of Africa's total population of approximately
400 million still lived in the rural areas. Despite the fact that Africa had the
world's highest rural-urban migration rate between 1960 and 1980, it remains
today the least urbanized of all continents.[1] Less than twenty cities are estimated to have at least a million inhabitants. Furthermore, the rate of growth is
disproportionately concentrated to the metropolitan centers, with the remaining components of the urban system experiencing a much less dramatic
growth.

Another reality of Africa twenty-five years after independence is a high
incidence of unemployment, underemployment, and increasing mass poverty.
For example, out of a total of 33 million people that were added to the African
labor force during the 1970s, as many as 40 percent found no access to remunerative employment. Some have subsequently entered the informal sector
as self-employed, but with growing numbers of school leavers flooding the
labor market every year unemployment and underemployment remain prominent features of the economic scene in Africa. So does the exceptionally high
dependency ratio of nearly three people per employed person.

This state of affairs is particularly alarming against the backdrop of a disappointing performance in agriculture on the continent, as detailed and further discussed by Lofchie in Chapter 7. For the whole decade of the 1970s,
when the African population was expanding at an average of about 2.8 percent, total food production on the continent was rising by no more than
1.5 percent. By 1980 food self-sufficiency ratios had dropped from 98 percent
in the 1960s to around 86 percent, implying that, on average, each African
had 12 percent less homegrown food in 1980 than twenty years earlier.[2] Aver-

**188**

age per capita food consumption in Africa in terms of calories remained almost stagnant at about 2,197 calories in the late 1970s as compared with 2,115 calories in the early 1960s.

A principal cause of the food crisis, besides the exogenous problems of drought and desertification, is the continued low productivity of African agriculture. For example, while the world average for the output of cereals is about two tons per hectare, Africa's average is only half that figure. For all roots and tubers, average productivity per hectare has remained stagnant at around seven tons compared to a world average of eleven tons per hectare. Africa's fertilizer consumption levels stand at only three kilograms per hectare of agricultural land, while the equivalent figure for Latin America and Asia is respectively over eight kilograms and twenty-six kilograms.[3]

At the same time, Africa is forced to cover its widening food deficit through imports. Between 1970 and 1980, the volume of total food imports increased by an average annual rate of 8.4 percent. Food aid to Africa reached 1.5 million tons in 1980; but that same year imports of food grains alone amounted to 20.4 million tons, costing the countries on the continent more than $5 billion, excluding the heavy ocean freight costs.[4]

While these figures in themselves are a cause for serious worry, the most disturbing aspect is that the outlook for the future is today much bleaker than at the time of independence. Development strategies pursued in the last twenty-five years have in most African countries failed to cope with the constraints to development present on the continent and have in some instances reduced the scope for progress. In this review of urban and rural development, therefore, it becomes necessary to take a critical look at past approaches and assess what changes in strategy may be considered for the future.

### The Normative Setting of Past Strategies

Twenty-five years ago independent Africa was born into a world characterized by its faith in progress. Captivated by scientific and technological success, the postwar generations in both the East and the West had lost their sense of proportion, thrown caution to the winds, and dismissed as unfounded pessimism all realistic references to man's natural limits. The sense of "Prometheus unbound," i.e., man's notion of unlimited scope in improving his functional skills for the purpose of satisfying human needs and of gaining increased control over his destiny, was imbuing liberal and socialist groups alike. Against the backdrop of this almost religious faith in secularization through the expanded uses of science and technology, keeping overseas colonies in political bondage was no longer necessary. Just as the United States and Europe had abolished slavery at the initial spread of this positivist outlook a hundred years earlier, they were not extending freedom to their colonial territories.

It is no coincidence that, in Portugal and Spain where the cult of the sciences and technology was least developed, this process was slower and completed only after a struggle leading to a social and political transformation not only of the colonies but of the metropole itself. The result, particularly in the case of Portugal, was a close collaboration between the country's emerging political organizations and the liberation movements in the colonies. The Marxist-Leninist position of the ruling parties in Lusophone Africa reflects this close association with prevailing European philosophical tendencies.

While influential critics of Western positivism like Marcuse[5] and Habermas[6] acknowledge its peculiar origin in bourgeois society, they also detect a similar "superman" mentality in communist countries. Marxism, after all, as Schumpeter reminds us,[7] was the creation of the bourgeois mind. In Marx's notion that the dynamic motion of matter is reflected in our mind in the form of dialectical laws which science is able to explore lay a similar optimism that man is capable of absolute knowledge of the world and able to gain absolute control over it. In the dialectical scheme, issues such as the subject-object problem, determinism and indeterminism, the thing-in-itself, matter, mass and energy, the problems of absoluteness and relativity, infinity and finiteness, continuity and discontinuity, would no longer baffle scientists and philosophers. The world is one; nature and man, science and history are referred to one another by the dialectical motion of matter, Marx argued. In this perspective it has proved only too easy to ascribe the existence of unsolvable problems in contemporary science and philosophy to a wrong approach or "false consciousness."

Thus, whether looked at from a liberal or a Marxist perspective, the East and West in the 1950s and 1960s shared a view of the world guided by unbounded optimism and an almost religious faith in progress. In either perspective, the finite, temporal, and historical nature of man's position in society was lost. To the liberal positivist, history had become irrelevant and thus superfluous. His Marxist counterpart had placed himself above history, thus confirming the impudent pride and immodesty that characterized the world into which the African nations were born. With independence Prometheus moved to Africa—more unbound than ever—in search of new victories.

Appreciation of this ahistorical perspective on the contemporary world is necessary in order to understand Africa's current predicament. Whether through "modernization" or "revolution," the prevailing strategies of development have called upon Africa to initiate contemporary models derived from historical experiences very different from its own. The first twenty-five years of independence in Africa have been a period of endless and sometimes shameless experimentation, with the continent being treated much like an empty box. Pet notions from both the East and the West have been applied to Africa with a view to bringing it into the mainstream of world development. As a part of the "periphery" of the world economic system, its own development problems have been conceptualized in terms reigning at the center. Thus, for instance, with little or no regard for prevailing modes of production and organization on the continent, trends and events have been interpreted primarily in terms of a battle between capitalist and socialist forces. In these circumstances, it is not surprising, as Hart notes,[8] that "development" in Africa is a world of words and numbers that bear little relationship to the material and social realities of the continent. Africa has been brought up to adulthood with little respect for its own dynamics and abilities. Twenty-five years after its birth independent Africa is consequently ill equipped to cope with the problems and constraints affecting its future progress. Prometheus has increasingly found himself bound and paralyzed.

## The Historical Realities of Rural Development

A factor of special significance to development in Africa is the absence of a feudal tradition. Although there has been an academic debate about the extent to which that statement is true,[9] there is general consensus that patterns of land ownership and utilization in sub-Saharan Africa are different from those found elsewhere. Yet only recently has this point been more closely examined in the context of a political economy approach. One of the first analysts to stress the historical significance of this point, Jack Goody, argues that in the absence of wheel, plough, and all other concomitant aspects of the "intermediate technology," sub-Saharan Africa was unable to match the development in productivity and skills, stratification and specialization, that marked the agrarian societies, e.g., of early medieval Europe or the Far East.[10] Even in those African societies where feudal tendencies became discernible, e.g., among the Baganda in Uganda,[11] the Ashanti of Ghana,[12] and in imperial Ethiopia,[13] they lacked a feudal technology to develop and sustain such systems. This structural difference is of particular importance for understanding why African agriculture even now is not performing as well as in other parts of the world.

### THE STRUCTURAL AUTONOMY OF THE PEASANT

The absence of a feudal technology has left African agriculture structurally simple and in some respects backward. Production technology has only recently enabled farmers in Africa to move beyond the small landholding. The bulk of the production units are still small private plots allocated according to customary land tenure rules. Each such unit is characterized by a rudimentary division of labor; and, because there is no product specialization, there is very little exchange between these various units. There is no structural interdependence bringing them into reciprocal relations with each other and leading to refinement of the means of production. Given their simple technology and the lack of variety of product among the households, producing the basic necessities and meeting the basic social needs are, for the bulk of Africa's rural households, time-consuming tasks. The scope for a surplus product, and thus for class division, is limited. Because there is no systematized body of knowledge underpinning the mode of production, it is characterized by fragmentation and, at the level of each unit of production, a high degree of autonomy. Production is normally cleverly adjusted to local conditions and often compatible with ecological potentials, but man's relation to nature in this situation is one of symbiosis rather than manipulation.[14] This mode of production does not give rise to a very elaborate superstructure; and, most importantly, because of the almost total absence of technological interdependence, the peasant household does not really depend for its own reproduction on the contribution by members of other social classes.[15]

Although African peasants in the last hundred years have been drawn into the capitalist world economy as commodity producers and there has been an accompanying privatization of land tenure, this exposure to capitalism, at the level of exchange commodities, hardly warrants the conclusion which so many political economists have drawn,[16] that sub-Saharan Africa has been effectively subjugated to the demands of a capitalist mode of production (see Lofchie, Chapter 7, "External Constraints"). At the level of production, by contrast, technology has changed little; and, as a result, both forms and organizations of labor have remained very much the same.

Because capitalism has hardly more than begun to transform the relations of production, it would be wrong to imply that the instruments of production have been brought under its sway. With no evidence of new social forms of labor developing and free petty landownership being available to the vast majority of rural producers, it seems more helpful to think of rural Africa in terms of still being under the influence of a precapitalist, peasant mode of production. Certainly, studies from all corners of the continent confirm that farming in Africa is embedded in a multiplicity of occupations and tasks.[17]

Because Africans farm only part of the year and do a great many other things both during the farming season and after it, the scope for productivity gains under present forms and organization of labor is very limited. While African peasant farmers no doubt demonstrate responsiveness to price incentives, it would be wrong to assume, as does for instance the World Bank Report on African development,[18] that significant aggregate production gains could be made by making prices more attractive (see also Lofchie, Chapter 7, "Internal Constraints"). Without suggesting that pricing policy is wholly unimportant, it must be recognized that in many African countries nonagricultural activities are often viewed by peasants as potentially more remunerative than agricultural specialization. As Gellar has demonstrated for instance in Senegal,[19] higher producer prices for certain crops do not in themselves provide sufficient material incentives to induce peasants involved in a myriad of activities to specialize in producing more of the crops which the government wants them to produce. While new agricultural policies no doubt are needed throughout Africa, it must also be recognized that prevailing technology and forms of labor constitute real constraints to any drastic improvement in agricultural production. Overcoming these constraints will be facilitated more by reliance on market than on bureaucracy, but even with a more open economy, there will be no "quick fixes."

To be sure, the extent to which a peasant mode of production still dominates rural Africa varies from one country to another and often within single countries. The most important variations from this pattern tend to exist in countries like Kenya and Zimbabwe, where the presence of a significant settler population has helped to bring about a capitalist economy with more extensive local roots. In these countries, capitalism is more than just a few limited enclaves. The capitalists, initially only foreigners but later also an increasing number of Africans, have uprooted many producers from their land and managed to institutionalize the underpinning of a capitalist mode of production with the result that agricultural productivity in these countries has improved significantly. With labor specialization and resultant class differentiation has also come greater scope for domestic capital formation and generation of a surplus product.[20]

In most of the African countries, however, where the peasant mode still retains strong influence, the ability of the rulers to extract a surplus product is seriously confined by the structural autonomy of each production unit.[21] In these economies, the conditions for appropriating the surplus are quite different from those of other systems. Under feudalism or capitalism, for instance, such appropriations are made in the immediate context of production either on the landed estate or in the factory. In those systems the state is functionally and structurally linked to the productive demands of the economy and as such is an effective instrument of influencing societal trends. The submerged classes have no recourse but to respond to the dictates of the system at large. Since they do not own the means of production but only serve them, members of these classes are effectively captured by the system.

This analogy, however, is not very helpful, at least at this point in time, for an analysis of the African political economy, because the relations emerging in the peasant mode of production are qualitatively different. As the productive and reproductive needs of the peasants can still largely be met without the support of other social classes, relations between those who rule and those who till the land are not firmly rooted in the production system as such. Instead, appropriations by those in control of the state are made in the form of taxation and constitute simple deductions from an already produced stock of values. These are tributary rather than productive relations, and they imply a much more limited degree of societal control. In a historical perspective, this relative autonomy of the peasant producers is not unique. In Imperial China, for instance, the government and the upper classes performed no function that the peasants regarded as essential for their way of life. Hence the link between rulers and ruled was weak and largely artificial, liable to snap under any severe strain, as Barrington Moore underlines.[22] Also in India, at least up to this century, central authority was in a substantial measure superfluous to production and social reproduction in the rural areas.[23] Still the situation in either China or India differed in that both societies had developed a local gentry that controlled the peasantry. This class was instrumental in obtaining the economic surplus out of the peasantry and was essential to regime stability and system's maintenance.

In sub-Saharan Africa, by contrast, there exist no such landlords to serve as intermediaries between central authority and rural producers. The inevitable consequence is that the state in Africa is structurally removed from the mainstay of agricultural production. It sits suspended in "mid-air" over society,[24] and as such it is the opposite to Orwell's notion in *1984* where the society is totally absorbed into the state.

Being structurally superfluous from the point of view of the individual producer, the state is inevitably looked upon with suspicion by the peasant. Public policies aimed at changing his production system are received with mistrust and often passive resistance. Because he owns the land, or at least has the undisputed right to till it, his ability to escape policy demands is much greater than that of a tenant under feudal rule or a worker under capitalism. In that respect, his situation resembles more that of the pastoralist (although the latter's autonomy of a given macroeconomic system is likely to be even higher). Looking back at the first twenty-five years of agricultural development policy in postindependence Africa, this unique ability of the peasantry to withhold support of the rulers is perhaps the most important lesson learnt. It is a major reason why virtually all African governments have become so uncomfortably dependent on external sources of funding. Contemporary governments are not much different from the rulers of the more elaborate regime structures of the precolonial era, e.g., in West Africa, who supplemented their surplus by obtaining income from other sources, notably long-distance trade.[25] Foreign aid is its modern surrogate.

THE STUNTED BOURGEOISIE

Another respect in which the absence of feudalism in Africa is important to contemporary development is its effects on the self-image of the emerging African bourgeoisie. In other societies the bourgeoisie has developed in confrontation with a more reactionary class of landlords who have seen the principles of capitalism as a threat to their own position of power. By eliminating feudalism and the vestiges of precapitalist formations associated with it, the bourgeoisie has been allowed to perform a progressive function. Being the product of a long course of development, a series of changes in the modes of production and exchange, the bourgeoisie, as Marx and Engels stress in the Communist Manifesto,[26] has historically played a most revolutionary part by putting an end to all feudal, patriarchal, and idyllic relations. This historically progressive role has been recognized in Europe, Asia, and Latin America as an integral part of the development of these societies. Even socialists would admit that, without the simplifications of class antagonisms that the bourgeoisie is able to bring about, their own task of building a new society would be impossible. In sub-Saharan Africa, by contrast, the emerging local bourgeoisie has never been allowed to perform this function. With no feudal class to overthrow and without much strength of its own, this group of people is not finding it easy to realize its historical mission.

Against this background, it is not surprising that the predominant trend in the literature ever since Fanon[27] and Dumont,[28] who were the first to curse the African bourgeoisie, has been to demonstrate its shortcomings and weaknesses. There has been virtually no encouragement of bourgeois aspirations, and those who have engaged in capitalist practices have usually had to do so against or in spite of official policies with the risk of being caught as saboteurs or traitors. It is in this atmosphere that anticolonial leaders like Amilcar Cabral of Guinea-Bissau found support for the proposition that the bourgeoisie in Africa had to commit "suicide" as a class by joining the peasants and the workers.[29]

Because the African bourgeoisie is in ascendancy rather than a fully matured class, it tends to generate opposition primarily from those groups who have a vested interest in the precapitalist structures. Thus, while much of the criticism of the bourgeoisie in Africa has been pursued in the name of a proletariat, its actual origin has been as much from the right, i.e., from a precapitalist foundation. Rather than facilitating or accelerating a social transformation after independence, the anticapitalist policies have generally rendered progress more difficult. We know from the historical experience of other societies that capitalism, by attacking the principles of premodern society, generates its own counterrevolution.

A case in point is the famous counterrevolution in Vendée which was an ongoing protest against bourgeois values in France from 1793 to 1832. The counterrevolutionary area was one where commercial agriculture had not yet penetrated society but constituted a potential threat to smallholder producers. Peasants were long since used to a relatively high degree of autonomy and agricultural techniques had remained stagnant. The main thrust of this counter-revolution was anticapitalist, and the prime targets were merchants and manu-facturers in nearby towns and those scattered through the countryside of the Vendée itself.[30]

In retrospect, Africa's anticapitalist policies can similarly be categorized as counterrevolutionary as they have undermined the efforts to enhance pro-ductivity and improve the organization of activities essential to societal prog-ress. In fact, in many countries labor productivity has declined and essential services broken down.[31] The implications of anticapitalist policies have been particularly harmful where they have been combined with (1) an expansion of social development programs without consideration of what the economy can afford and (2) an attempt to deal with the peasantry through an oversized bu-reaucracy rather than the market.

To understand why there has been such a strong desire to provide universal education, primary health care, and other related social development mea-sures, it is important to remember that the rulers in contemporary Africa do not have direct control over the majority of the population to the extent that we know it from more advanced economies where everybody is dependent on the macroeconomic structures in place and rationalizes his or her behavior in re-sponse to the constraints and opportunities of the prevailing system. Where the producers constitute a multitude of small peasants with only a marginal dependence on the macroeconomic system, their behavior and actions are not very predictable.

The rulers have few levers to apply in order to obtain compliant behavior. One means that has been extensively attempted by African governments is to "buy" the support of the rural producers by providing them with social wel-fare measures deemed to be popular among the peasants. Educational facili-ties, primary health care, fresh water supplies, and other similar projects have been extended to the rural areas at very high cost and in a manner that raises the question whether this pronounced preference for a "basic needs" strategy is primarily in the interest of the masses or those in power. This is particularly the case where such facilities have been constructed regardless of local inter-est and without a matching self-help contribution by the local community. It has worked best in those cases where, as Holmquist shows, the policy has been in response to strong local pressures.[32]

Regardless of circumstances, however, the macroeconomic consequences have been inflationary. For a long time, African governments could depend on generous foreign aid to boost these welfare programs; but, as they have expanded, neither foreign nor local funds have proved sufficient to keep these programs going. The inevitable consequence has been a serious decline in public education standards with schools lacking even basic equipment and teachers not being paid their salaries on time. In rural health clinics, the same trend is discernible: no drugs and low staff morale. In the rural water development programs, pumps and pipes break down without anybody caring or being able to repair them effectively. A growing tendency among the rural population has consequently been to withdraw from the official system: return to illiteracy; visit the traditional *mganga* (doctor); and rediscover the old water-hole (even if the quality of the water might be much lower than in the government-provided pipe).

The cost implications of an approach based on the notion of buying the political support of the peasants might have been less disastrous had the rulers been successful in improving rural productivity. What confounds the difficulties facing African countries today, however, is the prevailing tendency of dealing with the peasant economy through inert state bureaucracies. Being structurally and functionally removed from the predominant production systems of rural Africa, this strategy of depending on a bureaucracy rather than the market is inherently counterproductive.

Since the early 1960s governments in Africa have tried to cope with the "peasant problem" by rearranging the circumstances under which it can be solved. The most common but also least drastic has been the creation of cooperative institutions that bring the peasants together into more manageable entities. This policy was tried by the colonial authorities and proved selectively successful, primarily in those areas where the conditions for agricultural growth existed.[33] Postindependence efforts, however, to extend cooperatives to all corners of a country, irrespective of economic opportunities and financial feasibility, have proved largely ineffective: these organizations have either failed to take off or have been appropriated by a small group of well-to-do farmers for whom cooperation makes sense from a service and marketing point of view.[34] All the same, there is sufficient evidence from various parts of the continent to suggest that cooperatives are viable institutions under certain conditions, notably in a functioning market economy that provides incentives for peasant farmers to break out of their isolated production systems. Prevailing policies, however, have ignored this point and instead concentrated on how the peasants can be made more malleable to strategies of rural development induced or enforced from above by public bodies. Encouraged by institutions like the World Bank, a number of governments in Africa adopted what was in the 1960s referred to as the "transformation" approach to agricultural development, implying the creation of separate settlement schemes to which specially recruited farmers would be invited. In Tanzania, for instance, these settlements proved expensive failures and were soon abandoned by the government,[35] only to be resurrected a few years later under a new guise: the *ujamaa* village. Faced with a rural population living in scattered homesteads often far from each other, government officials were genuinely concerned with how all these people could be reached with inputs and services. Following a promising start characterized by select willingness to move into villages and adopt the policy of communal production, the strategy soon backfired as overambitious officials applied force to move peasants into such villages. Although the communal production requirement was eventually dropped, during the mid-1970s all rural producers were "villagized." As several studies have demonstrated, peasants were often moved to land which was qualitatively inferior to that they used to cultivate or had to accept cultivation of land that was a considerable distance from their houses.[36] Although some settlements have succeeded, e.g., in Kenya where their production was boosted by incentives to produce for the growing Nairobi market, most such ventures, even when tightly managed, have been faced with great difficulties.[37]

Sensing the difficulty of raising agricultural production through dependence on the peasants only, many governments have tried to get around it by creating large-scale farms. Ever since Nkrumah attempted this strategy in Ghana with a view to producing a greater public surplus than could be accomplished in the context of small-scale peasant farming,[38] it has proved a costly failure. State farms have turned out particularly wasteful in Africa where the material conditions for such type of farming are largely nonexistent: no indigenous experience of large-scale farming and thus no technical know-how or labor discipline and organization required to keep such ventures going.

In general, the result of two decades of rural development policies in Africa has been the creation of a gigantic state apparatus, which due to its failure to raise rural productivity has increasingly become a liability to society. Rather than generating new capital it has become a predator, living off society's meager resources. With growing size and inefficiency, the state has appropriated an increasing share of the agricultural surplus, thus encouraging the peasants to use their exit option. Attempts to cope with this problem through administrative reform, including decentralization, have proved at best marginally effective and, in some cases,[39] have turned out counterproductive. A major review of rural development policies and projects in different parts of sub-Saharan Africa demonstrates convincingly that the public provision of services and inputs for development through government bureaucracies has generally met with little success.[40]

Through the public management of economic resources, as Bates emphasizes in his analysis of agricultural policy in Africa,[41] the bureaucracies have institutionalized a structure of relative advantage—a structure within which

they themselves occupy positions of privilege and power. This cadre of officials—often referred to as the "bureaucratic bourgeoisie"[42]—constitutes the
single largest component of the governing class in African countries. To the
extent that they have developed true bourgeois aspirations, this group of people
makes up a highly stunted and lopsided class. Consisting mainly of administrators and professional people, it operates without the dynamic support of
indigenous manufacturers and merchants.

Unlike Eurasia, Africa never developed its own class of manufacturers,
and during the colonial time foreign investments were given priority over the
development of a local capitalism. Even where a local merchant tradition exists, as in West Africa, its potential has not been tapped for development purposes. Because development strategies in most African countries since independence have been generally anticapitalist, the emerging bourgeoisie has
been fed mainly through its administrative and professional cadres. The increasingly parasitic image of this group of people has contributed toward giving the bourgeois class in Africa a bad name and has tended to reinforce the
misguided belief that the solution to the problem of a stunted bourgeoisie is
more socialism.

Failure to improve productivity on the land and the emergence of a "preda-
tory" state are the principal causes of stagnation in rural Africa. These factors
also explain why the official economy of most African countries is already
being subverted from within as more and more people, out of frustration with
the overregulated system, turn to black-market arrangements or resort to the
"economy of affection" to work out satisfactory microeconomic arrangements.[43] Through these alternative economies people are generally able to
find means of surviving, and by denying or withholding support of the official
system they are subverting the position of those in power.

While governments have tried to curb black-market activities by launch-
ing campaigns against "economic saboteurs,"[44] their ability to deal with the
phenomenon effectively is limited under present circumstances when supply
of commodities falls far short of demands. Even more difficult to control is
the economy of affection through which complex bonds of affinity promote
a considerable flow of public resources. The deviation of such resources
through invisible and intractable channels has in most African countries
placed state and society on a collision course.

What is happening in Africa today can best be described as a "silent"
guerilla war launched against those who are responsible for trying to capture
the peasants by overextending the state and, in the process, making it inopera-
tional. Using the peculiar structural safeguards inherent in the peasant mode
of production and its economy of affection, these silent fighters are likely to
have the capacity to outlast those in control of the sinking state. Sensing their

accelerating submergence, many African governments now see a more generous flow of foreign aid as the only solution to their predicament. While such
assistance might provide temporary relief, it also increases the danger of these
governments engaging in further self-destruction by multiplying hasty public
schemes that yield little and the peasants can ignore.[45] This is only going to
inflict further blows on the self-image of the already stunted bourgeoisie and
prolong Prometheus's bondage on the continent.

## The Experience of Urban Growth

In revolutionizing the means of production in other parts of the world
Prometheus has depended heavily on the social space and social dynamic provided by an urban environment. As the literature reveals, it is a very old observation that man thinks, feels, and responds differently in the city than outside it.[46] Ancient men perceived and valued the special properties of their
cities. In ancient Egypt, for instance, fathers had a special interest in getting
their children to learn to write and take up "white collar" tasks of scribes in
the imperial bureaucracy rather than suffer the privations of humbler occupations. In nearby Babylonia, social ascent through urban occupations was
strictly controlled with a view to emphasizing the privileged nature of urban
life. When the Jews were carried off into Babylonian captivity, they were permitted considerable freedom but were carefully excluded from access to the
priestly schools and the political positions associated therewith. In ancient
China the desirability of the urban roles is indicated by the patience, and hard
work the individual was willing to devote in preparation for the civil service
exams and the extent to which his family and clan might finance his training
for the mandarinate. In classical Greece the citizen was proud of his membership in the city, and he took this quality as a distinguishing difference between
himself and the barbarian. Similar attitudes and evidences of civic pride differentiated the denizen of Rome.

The centrality of the city to the destiny of man has also been a major
theme in sociological research. Writing as one of the first "urban sociologists," Georg Simmel pointed out, at the turn of the century, that metropolitan man is subject to an unusual volume of stimulation and he develops a
mentality protecting himself against elements in his environment which would
uproot him.[47] His view of urban man was that he must react with his head
rather than his heart—to yield to deep emotional reactions is to be crushed.
His environment intensifies his awareness, not his feeling, leading to a dominance of intellectuality which extends in many directions with the specialization of the urban environment. The institutions of the city, characterized by

the dominance of a money economy and intellectualism, confirm its mentality. The very complexity of life in the city reinforces punctuality, calculability, and exactness and leads to a matter-of-fact attitude in dealing with men and things. Writing a few years later, using a different vantage point, Oswald Spengler confirmed the notion of the city as a "state of mind," a body of customs, traditions, and organized attitudes quite distinct from those found in the countryside.[48] The roots of human life are always in the soil. Only in the cities do men disengage themselves from such roots. The urban man is an intellectual nomad, quite homeless, a microcosm, as intellectually free as the nomad is sensually free, he said. World history is city history.

Although the notion of the city as the pace-setter has dominated sociological theory, other interpretations of the city have been important too. Ever since the days of ancient Greece philosophers and writers have been suspicious of the city. Aristotle and Plato, for instance, held the middle classes— typical urban strata—in contempt and wished to subordinate them to warriors and philosophers. Private property, i.e., urban alienable property, was suspect and money thought to be dangerous. The location of the city on the sea was thought to be a mistake. Their own choice for a city was Sparta, hardly a true city but a permanent open military camp. A similar reaction against the city emerged in Europe in the nineteenth century among writers like Nietzsche who not only hated the punctuality and exactness of the metropolis but extended the same aversion to the money economy and the intellectualism of modern existence and science.[49] Other criticisms of the city include its tendency to generate social relations characterized by superficiality and anonymity. Freedom from personal emotional control of intimate groups leaves city residents in a state of *anomie* (a kind of normlessness), argued Durkheim.[50] The transitory and segmental character of urban social relations has since been used to explain the social decay and misery that city life also tends to generate.

### NO URBAN PROLETARIAT

It may be useful to analyze African urbanization against this broad theoretical background. Although Africa, like any other continent, had its early civilizations, its own agricultural systems were never developed to the extent of sustaining urban growth of any significance. Wherever important cities developed, as along the trade routes in West Africa and the coast of Eastern Africa, such growth was the result of surplus appropriation from trade rather than production on the land. Precolonial urban conglomerations, therefore, tended to be of two kinds: (1) trading enclaves with relatively little or no structural linkage to the countryside and (2) concentrations of people living together for defensive or ecological reasons but practicing agriculture as their main preoccupation. While an urban mentality, as opposed to a rural one, did characterize the trading towns, neither type had much impact on development beyond its immediate hinterland.

The colonial powers accelerated urbanization by creating for administrative purposes their own town or building "new towns" adjacent to existing urban settlements. In their scheme of things, the towns were primarily for the Europeans and immigrant minorities, mainly Arabs and Asians, invited to conduct commerce. As these urban settlements grew and became centers of local manufacturing, the demand for African labor increased. Getting the Africans to leave their rural environment, however, proved difficult. The urban areas were alien to the Africans; working conditions and pay were poor; and residence in towns tended to expose the Africans to all kinds of humiliating restrictions.[51] Unwilling to improve the living conditions and wages of African workers, colonial regimes turned to coercive measures to secure an adequate labor force. Initially they used compulsory labor, but since it tended to offend the sensibilities of metropolitan legislators and opinion leaders (except in Portugal and Spain) this method was soon abandoned in favor of taxation. This indirectly coercive measure was seen as the most appropriate in many colonies to get the men on the land to leave their residences for purposes of seeking work. To ensure reasonable stability in the labor force, the urban Africans were often long-distance migrants who were sufficiently removed from social networks and productive alternatives and thus by virtue of circumstances dependent on their urban jobs.[52]

The colonial towns reflected urban perceptions held by their European residents. To ensure their efficient administration, urban migration was strictly controlled and residence segregated along racial lines with only Europeans having access to low-density housing areas. The African immigrants were confined to the high-density areas. In the case of workers, many came alone, leaving their family on the land, and were often forced to stay in specially built housing estates. Community facilities were provided according to the principle of ability to pay, which meant that the provision, e.g., of tarmac roads and sewers, was confined to the high- and middle-income residential areas where very few Africans lived. In the high-density residential zones where the low-income (primarily African) groups lived only dirt roads and primitive forms of sanitation would be provided.[53] The more pervasive the European presence the more conspicuous the segregation and regimentation in the urban areas tended to be. Thus, for instance, the colonial towns of East and Southern Africa, notably Nairobi and Harare (Salisbury), were much more "European" in outlook and layout than those in West and Central Africa (with the exception of Dakar), where white settlement and control was more marginal.

The European colonizers tried their best to create an African working class who reflected the values and orientation of an urban proletariat. This task, however, proved very difficult because, unlike Europe, there was no surplus agricultural labor in Africa ready to take up industrial employment. Africans employed in the urban areas generally retained ownership of their land and thus a desire to retire in the rural areas. Rather than developing a distinct urban outlook African workers sustained close rural connections. Most urban residents formed clubs or associations with a view to satisfying social and economic needs of those left on the land.[54] The social networks and organizations that had grown out of the economy of affection in the rural areas were extended to the urban areas during the colonial period.

Rather than seeking their salvation in trade union or political movements, many of the urban Africans developed their anticolonial orientation in improvement associations, independent churches, and other similar organizations linking them to their respective rural communities. As Hodgkin[55] and Skinner[56] have shown, these organizations constituted the precursors of the nationalist movements and helped to shape their populist outlook. Some of the messianic cults that developed among urban Africans had a radical message and scared the colonial authorities. Vittorio Lanternari argues, for instance, that these cults were "religions of the oppressed," embodying a vision of the future in which the white-dominated social order is inverted.[57]

Although the European colonizers with their capitalist outlook set the stage for the development of a working class in the urban areas, it was the prevalence of organizational mechanisms derived from the precapitalist formations in the countryside that provided the basis for an anticolonial reaction also in the urban areas. Although the Europeans tried hard to institutionalize capitalist relations of production, the Africans, through their access to an alternative livelihood in the rural areas, tended to slip out of their control. There were few African nationalists who, like Tom Mboya,[58] made their political career within the formal urban structures, e.g., trade unions. The prevailing tendency was to resign from employment and carry on the battle outside such structures. Thus, the nationalist movement (or movements if there were more than one) tended to become the home of people with very different backgrounds and opinions but having one objective in common: the removal of the foreign rulers. In the struggle for independence it was possible to achieve consensus among all these groups by adopting a populist stand juxtaposing colonialism to capitalism. Although often pursued in a socialist language, the nationalist movements tended to revive the precapitalist orientations that had survived colonialism.

Against this background it is doubtful whether it is correct to argue, as, e.g., Sabot does,[59] that the urban labor force in the postindependence period has become firmly committed to wage employment and such essential features of a stable labor force as industrial discipline. The experience in Tanzania and other countries after independence indicates that it is not difficult to undermine the structures that cause the separation of individuals from their means of production and thus help to stabilize the urban-based labor force.[60] Workers, like other urban dwellers, continue to fulfill their customary obligations within the economy of affection because they see it as offering more security and comfort than the more blunt social realities of urban industrial life.

For most people, urban migration is not a unilinear process but a circulation between village and town. An interesting point worth further study is what the effects on urban migrants are of the size of town and the peculiar atmosphere that may prevail. In her study of Ghanaian workers, Margaret Peil suggests that Tema, though smaller than Accra or Kumasi, is more "urbanized" in a sociological sense because it is a new town created for industry where almost everybody is a stranger and where impersonalism is much stronger than in the more established cities.[61] Are workers in such "new" cities more or less likely to retain a rural orientation as a safety measure than residents in established cities where the social networks of the economy of affection facilitate incorporation into a new type of residence and work?

Although we need to know more about urban workers, whether in the formal or the informal sector, studies from all corners of the continent indicate that the urban dwellers use their savings for investment in the rural areas or for support of relatives in their respective home communities.[62] This overwhelming evidence is hardly proof of a proletarian orientation. Elkan's observation from 1960 that it is wrong to equate the growth of towns in Africa with the growth of an urban proletariat seems as valid today as it did then.[63] In fact, in many countries, e.g., Ghana, Uganda, and Tanzania, where the urban economy has more or less collapsed in recent years, the tendency among urban residents to retain and develop their rural connection has been reinforced. More and more urban residents have become dependent on being able to derive income from cultivating land or keeping cattle in order to sustain their urban-based livelihood. The inability of a growing number of Africans to sustain such a livelihood is an indicator of the present economic crisis in Africa.

THE WANING SOCIAL SPACE

As indicated in the beginning of this section, urbanization is a force capable of accelerating social transformation. Although it is associated with its own costs, it has the advantage of creating the social space necessary for creativity, initiative, and entrepreneurship. The colonial authorities recognized the progressive potential of the city, but it was only in the period after the second World War that they began to consider integrating Africans more fully into urban life. In East Africa, for instance, a special Royal Commission recommended in 1955:

> The towns are the centres of social and intellectual life, of economic enterprise and political activity. It is essential to break down the barriers which prevent Africans from full participation in the life of the towns. The African must come to regard the towns as places which fully provide him with an outlet for his courage, ability and initiative.[64]

These measures came too late, and those Africans who had looked forward to making better use of their creativity in the towns were generally unable to carry the day against those who had assembled behind the populist flag in the nationalist movement and who saw circumscription of private accumulation as the key to postindependence success. Thus political leaders have tended to castigate urbanization as a source of social problems and have taken steps to reduce the new social space on which progress could be generated. By preempting or at least deliberately containing the development of an entrepreneurial class based in the private sector and instead confining the bulk of local talent to the public sector, African governments have placed a harmful straitjacket on the budding local bourgeoisie. To be sure, with the exodus of the Europeans at independence, Africanization of the public service became a necessary priority, but in many countries this measure was carried out without much consideration of the need to diversify the opportunities for entrepreneurial people. Not all hired in the public service were ready to accept the regulations proscribing private accumulation of wealth and some engaged against the law in activities that enabled them to realize their genuine class interests more effectively. This conflict of interest has created a serious political dilemma throughout sub-Saharan Africa. Some leaders have been ready to overlook the tendency of their public servants to divert public funds for private use or devote time to pursuit of private business as long as they themselves, like the medieval kings of Europe, can exercise direct control of the public purse.[65] This method of dealing with the undespairing bourgeoisie has inevitably lowered public confidence in government. The personal enrichment in which politicians and public servants have engaged has contributed to political instability and deteriorating public management. Because governments tend to change frequently—usually through unconstitutional means—leaders have been only too anxious to deplete the public purse for their own benefit.

Rather than facilitating an exit of officials with a true bourgeois ambition out of the public service, most African leaders concerned about the political consequences of diversion of public funds for private uses have imposed restrictions on their public servants. Some governments have adopted special leadership codes that make a virtue of puritanism and selflessness. While this type of public ethic strikes a sympathetic cord in both liberal and socialist circles, the question must be asked whether it is historically appropriate for contemporary Africa. In other parts of the world the development of such an ethic has taken a long time and has been spearheaded by groups in society capable of demanding such behavior of the public service. These groups have been based in private business, trade unions, and voluntary movements for whom a reliable public service, serving as the "executive arm" of the dominating interests in society, has been a political necessity. Thus, the historical experience suggests that the road to a public morality based on the notion of the government as a servant of the people has gone via the growth of the private and voluntary sectors. The attempt by many African governments to accomplish the same goal by skipping a capitalist stage of development has reduced their chances of development. The dilemma facing these countries is that in the absence of indigenous manufacturers and merchants, the public sector is being asked to perform entrepreneurial roles for which it is not equipped. Even if the officials are honest and entrepreneurial, there is a natural tendency for the public sector to engage in schemes and projects that are costly and tend to be guided by political rather than economic and financial criteria. By reducing the latter to secondary importance, policies rarely bear a relation to the local resource base and thus perpetuate the position of the state as suspended in mid-air over society. Instead of developing capitalist relations of production that produce a new social consciousness and dynamic, these governments have reinforced the precapitalist foundation of society that depends on tributary relations, i.e., the right to "milk" the peasants through taxation of their already produced stock of values.

There are of course differences among African countries. The sheer force of capitalist penetration in the wake of Nigeria's oil boom has generated a local bourgeoisie anxious to set the terms of the country's development. In Kenya, the deliberate policy of providing incentives for Africans to enter commerce has also produced a relatively strong urban bourgeoisie. In most African countries, however, politicians and bureaucrats have failed to generate public capital; and as a result they have reinforced the image of the town as a parasite. Rather than realizing that the bureaucrats and politicians cannot survive in the urban areas—let alone develop the country—without the complementary contributions by merchants and manufacturers, the anticapitalist and anti-urban bias has led many governments to believe that the solution lies in more socialist militancy and puritanism. The local bourgeoisie, the only class capable of bringing about a social transformation of contemporary African society, is still being hindered in many countries from developing the strength that enables it to pursue its historical mission. The implications of the anticapitalist policies pursued have not been to produce a more socialist society—the capitalist foundation has been too weak to permit such a transformation—but to reduce the social dynamic of those forces in society that provide the very fuel of socialist development.

The result of this trend of development is that Africa's urban areas are allowed to grow without producing the economic foundation or social space that enables them to serve as pacesetters of society. A specifically urban culture has yet to develop in Africa where up to this time the precapitalist values embodied in rural society tend to permeate social behavior and interactions in the towns. The lineage remains, as Hart calls it,[66] a "fertility machine" that is being fueled through injections from the urban areas. The urban elite still actively supports a wide circle of lower-class kinsmen. The tendency to detach oneself from such relations is very rare. Thus, even in the urban areas nucleation of the family with its ensuing flow of wealth from parents to children, rather than the opposite way around, as practiced within the economy of affection, is far from being a common demographic pattern.[67] Furthermore, the prospect for institutionalizing such behavior in the near future is low because public social security schemes are functioning so poorly that urban families are reluctant to abandon their predominant profertility behavior.[68] Thus, for instance, policies aimed at stabilizing family life of Africans living in urban areas by providing them with better and more adequate housing have been undermined by the deteriorating management of those public institutions with a potential of influencing demographic and other social behavior of urban residents.[69]

At the same time, it must be recognized that, in spite of the waning social space in the urban areas, there are Africans who struggle to survive and flourish in this inhospitable environment. Marris and Somerset, for instance, have demonstrated how in Kenya (where the climate is generally more hospitable than in many other countries) African entrepreneurs are emerging as demographic and economic innovators as a result of both opportunities and frustrations suffered in their relations with public authorities.[70] Although kinship obligations may not, as Beveridge and Obershall argue,[71] be a significant factor in determining success or failure of individual business ventures, it is clear that in a broader political economy perspective, reduction of such obligations matters.

## Perspectives on the Future

The analysis in this chapter has tried to demonstrate that by placing themselves above history in a self-confident fashion, policymakers in Africa during

the first two decades of independence have relied on strategies and policies
that are largely out of tune with Africa's own processes and resources. If governments wish to enhance their capacity to reverse the deteriorating trends in
both urban and rural areas they probably have to follow the example of the
Chinese leaders who, in rejecting what they call "irresponsible leftist thinking,"[72] have adjusted the country's economy to national capabilities. In considering new strategies that better recognize the material realities of the continent, the African experience suggests a shift in position (1) from reliance on
the bureaucracy to the market, (2) from top-town to bottom-up approaches,
(3) from formal to the informal sector, and (4) from rural to urban development priorities.

### FROM BUREAUCRACY TO MARKET

Expansion of state control was an understandable ambition in postindependence Africa as political leaders tried to curtail the impact of foreign orientations and interests developed in the colonial era. Twenty-five years after
independence, however, it is increasingly clear that, if carried too far, political
and administrative interventions in social and economic interactions are self-
defeating. Concentration of public resource allocation to government and its
various agencies intensifies political rivalry and introduces criteria of policymaking that have little to do with economic and managerial feasibility. Such
concentration also holds back the emergence of a public morality that guarantees responsible governance by reinforcing the notion that the state realm is an
arena where one tries to make as large gains as possible for oneself and one's
group or community.[73] Taking advantage of politicized relations of affection,
public funds and other resources are diverted for uses that undermine effective
public management.

Bureaucratic control over agricultural production, as Lofchie also shows
in Chapter 7, has tended to alienate the peasant producers and encourage their
inclination to withdraw from participation in public programs. In societies
where the state is not functionally and structurally linked to the prevailing
rural production systems, governments are likely to find that only by an imaginative and foresighted use of a market-economy approach will the peasants
in the long run allow themselves to be captured by the official system of
governance.

An increasing number of African governments are now accepting this
point, but it must be stressed here that what is needed is much more than better
producer prices for agricultural crops. Attention must be paid to a whole bat-
tery of macroeconomic policies that provide stimulus for private and community initiatives both in the rural and urban areas. Experience from countries
like Kenya and Zimbabwe suggests that effective management of urban-based

manufacturing and service institutions has great pay-offs in the rural areas. The agricultural sector in these countries has functioned relatively well because governments have allowed the local bourgeoisie to diversify and thus develop talents sufficiently broad to deal with the challenges of specialization and differentiation in both rural and urban areas. The African bourgeoisie, however, remains undeveloped and lopsided in most countries, and any shift from reliance on bureaucracy to the market must be accompanied by measures aimed at promoting indigenous manufacturing and merchant talent, whether located in the towns or in the countryside.

FROM TOP-DOWN TO BOTTOM-UP APPROACHES

Strategies and policies for development have so far been designed primarily with government interests in mind. Very little attention has been paid to how public interventions tally with the priorities of potential beneficiaries or target groups. National development policies, particularly in the rural sector, are more likely to succeed in winning popular support in the future if they are compatible with and complement strategies pursued by local actors. Because these strategies tend to vary markedly due to regional, ethnic, and ecological variations as well as different priorities, policies need to be flexible. The notion that there is an official "blueprint" that can and must be implemented to the last letter in every corner of the country has proved disastrous and should be replaced by a greater concern to provide stimulus and a supportive milieu in which local initiatives can flourish. As Gellar concludes in his study of Senegal, the establishment and support of rural markets may produce more tangible results than streamlining extension services or decentralizing government-controlled rural credit schemes.[74] Also important for any attempt to promote rural progress in the years ahead is the development of nongovernmental organizations that can aggregate the demands from below and articulate them in public policy arenas. Such organizations would also enable government programs to become more effective by providing additional capacity for implementation.

Encouraging results are available in both Kenya and Zimbabwe from efforts to let local initiatives sprout. Whether through local savings, as in the case of the Savings Development Movement in Zimbabwe, or through self-help contributions for education and other forms of social development, as in the case of the *harambee* movement in Kenya, peasant households have demonstrated that in spite of their relative poverty, they are capable not only of developing their own communities but of making a contribution to national development as well.

### FROM FORMAL TO INFORMAL SECTOR

Thinking about development in Africa has so far been confined to the formal sector. Official statistics generally leave out the rapidly growing informal-sector activities and policymakers have shown but marginal interest in the question of how the resource potential of the informal sector may be mobilized. At a time when wage employment in the urban areas is stagnant or on the decline, a growing number of people, particularly school leavers, engage in self-employment in nonregistered service or income-generating activities. Thus, the informal sector serves as a significant safety valve, reducing social tension and providing productive outlets for a growing number of people. Most people in the informal sector, however, continue to work in isolation and without much recognition by policymakers. A study of informal-sector training in Kenya[75] highlighted the important contribution toward skills development that informal-sector apprenticeship makes. Judging from such data, there is little doubt that greater support for the training and development work of the informal sector could have considerable payoff in most African countries.

Another forgotten dimension of the informal sector is the extensive resource flow that takes place between the urban and the rural areas. There is now plenty of evidence from various parts of the continent to the effect that remittances by urban migrants play a crucial role in rural development.[76] Although such remittances tend to become a substitute for income from agricultural production in areas where ecology, climate, or other factors limit the latter's profitability, they serve investment purposes in other parts of Africa. The average urban migrant in Africa still plans to retire on his farm, and as a result he tends to use his urban experience to modernize farming practices.[77] As long as this unofficial redistribution of income and resources from the urban to the rural areas remains prominent, governments will better serve rural progress by facilitating such transfers rather than making their own attempts at agricultural modernization through an inept extension service. Thus, for instance, the existence of a country-wide, reliable system of remitting funds through local post offices may contribute more to rural development than formal credit schemes operated by official cooperative societies.

### FROM RURAL TO URBAN DEVELOPMENT PRIORITIES

African policymakers have spent much more time to date thinking about rural as opposed to urban development, yet the bulk of public funding has gone to support urban growth. As typically manifest in controls of food prices, tax benefits, subsidies, and public investments as well as services, government policies reflect an urban bias. Judging from official government budget and national accounts figures only, it is easy to draw the conclusion, as for instance Michael Lipton does, that the principal contradiction in Africa is between townsmen and farmers.[78] This outlook has made most African policymakers treat urban migrants as a problem and a burden rather than an opportunity. Rural development, therefore, has become important as a means of stemming migration to the towns. A recent study of rural development interventions in Third World countries over the last two decades, however, shows that agricultural development, the provision of training and educational facilities in the rural areas as well as other measures to enhance rural progress, do not stem but in fact reinforce urban migration.[79] The question must be raised, therefore, whether direct public investment in the rural areas is warranted on the scale attempted so far. The degree to which capital formation and resource redistribution benefiting the rural areas take place through unofficial channels should not be underestimated, nor should the readiness of rural communities to engage in development activities on their own. Governments may be better off in the future if they recognize these features of the development scene and try to promote rather than preempt them.

African leaders need to abandon their ambivalent attitude toward the city and develop more imaginative urban development policies, if only to ensure that Africa's projected urban population of 472 million by the year 2008 won't be living in conditions of unbearable squalor.[80] A study by Inkleles and Smith indicates that Third World cities have so far failed to serve as effective modernizing agents.[81] One reason, at least in the African context, may well be that the official approach has been characterized by the provision of subsidies to urban dwellers rather than incentives for investment. Although urban investments may initially be higher than in the rural areas, the public costs of urbanization, as Linn shows,[82] are likely to be offset by better results—both in town and village—provided the urban subsidies are gradually reduced. The frequently expressed concern with growing rural-urban income differentials is not only exaggerated but often also misplaced. The returns on investments in the urban areas—not only the capital city but other strategic growth centers as well—that safeguard adequate social space for initiative and change are likely to be greater for townsman and villager alike than equivalent public investments targeted on the rural areas alone. The road to rural development in Africa, therefore, may well go through urban investments. The risk of such a strategy producing an increased polarization between town and countryside is likely to be mitigated as long as urban residents retain their interest in land ownership and membership in their home community.

It is of course true that the long-term effect of a successful urban development strategy will be to curb the rural orientation of the urban dwellers and, as they cut the affective ties with their home communities, substitute relations that bring capital and labor into socially productive conflicts. Such a transformation is likely to enhance national productivity and provide the scope for public investments to mitigate the risks of a growing polarization between town and countryside in the future. The most important effect of that transformation, however, may be Prometheus's emancipation and thus his ability to perform for Africa the same historical role he has done in other modernizing societies.

## NOTES

1. Economic Commission for Africa, ECA and Africa's Development 1983–2008: A Preliminary Perspective Study (Addis Ababa, Economic Commission for Africa, 1983), p. 7.

2. Ibid., p. 8.

3. Food and Agricultural Organization, *Agriculture Toward 2000* (Rome, Food and Agricultural Organization, 1979), Table 4.5.

4. ECA, op. cit., p. 9.

5. Herbert Marcuse, *Soviet Marxism* (London, Routledge & Kegan Paul, 1958), and by the same author, *One-Dimensional Man* (Boston, Beacon Press, 1968).

6. Jürgen Habermas, *Toward a Rational Society: Student Protest, Science and Politics* (Boston, Beacon Press, 1970).

7. Joseph A. Schumpeter, *Capitalism, Socialism and Democracy* (London, Unwin University Books, 1952), p. 6.

8. Keith Hart, *The Political Economy of West African Agriculture* (Cambridge, Cambridge University Press, 1982), p. 105.

9. Two early contributions that set the note of this debate were J. J. Maquet, *The Premises of Inequality in Ruanda* (London, Oxford University Press, 1961), and I. I. Potekhin, "On Feudalism of the Ashanti," paper read to the International Congress of Orientalists, Moscow, 1960.

10. Jack Goody, *Technology, Tradition and the State in Africa* (London, Oxford University Press, 1971), p. 76.

11. This claim was originally made by J. Roscoe in his extensive study *The Baganda* (London, Macmillan, 1911) and has been made subsequently by Marxists and non-Marxists alike: see, e.g., contributions to Lloyd A. Fallers (ed.), *The King's Men* (London, Oxford University Press, 1964), and Mahmood Mamdani, *Politics and Class Formation in Uganda* (New York, Monthly Review Press, 1976).

12. R. S. Rattray, *Ashanti* (London, Oxford University Press, 1923).

13. Richard Pankhurst, *An Introduction to the Economic History of Ethiopia* (London, Oxford University Press, 1961).

14. For a discussion of this argument, see Florian Znaniecki, *The Social Role of the Man of Knowledge* (New York, Octagon Books, 1965). A case study from precolonial and colonial Africa is provided by Helge Kjekshus, *Ecology Control and Economic Development in East African History* (Berkeley and Los Angeles, University of California Press, 1977).

15. For an elaborate analysis of this point, see Barry Hindess and Paul C. Hirst, *Pre-Capitalist Modes of Production* (London, Routledge & Kegan Paul, 1975).

16. This is the prevailing assumption, e.g., in the textbook edited by Peter C. W.

Gutkind and Immanuel Wallerstein, *The Political Economy of Contemporary Africa* (Beverley Hills, Sage Publications, 1976).

17. For two West African case studies, see Polly Hill, *Rural Hausa: A Village and Setting* (Cambridge, Cambridge University Press, 1972), and John C. Caldwell (ed.), *Population Growth and Socio-Economic Change in West Africa* (New York, Columbia University Press, 1975). A "state-of-the-art" contribution on the subject is made by Jane Guyer in her paper "Household and Community in African Studies," *African Studies Review*, Vol. xxiv, Nos. 2/3 (June–September 1981) pp. 87–138. A statement from a Marxist point of view is contained in a volume edited by David Seddon, *Relations of Production: Marxist Approaches to Economic Anthropology* (London, Frank Cass, 1978).

18. World Bank, op. cit., pp. 55–58.

19. Sheldon Gellar, "Rural Development Policy and Peasant Survival Strategies," unpublished paper, Princeton University, February 1984, p. 10.

20. See, for example, Michael Cowen, "Commodity Production in Kenya's Central Province," in Judith Heyer, Pepe Roberts, and Gavin Williams (eds.), *Rural Development in Tropical Africa* (London, Macmillan, 1981), pp. 121–142.

21. Hart, op. cit., argues with reference to West Africa that "no matter what violence may have been inflicted on the indigenous population, the forms of commodity production are still overwhelmingly precapitalist" (p. 113).

22. Barrington Moore, Jr., *Social Origins of Dictatorship and Democracy: Lord and Peasant in the Making of the Modern World* (Harmondsworth, Penguin Books, 1967), p. 205.

23. Ibid., p. 339.

24. Goran Hyden, *Beyond Ujamaa in Tanzania: Underdevelopment and an Uncaptured Peasantry* (London, Heinemann, and Berkeley and Los Angeles, University of California Press, 1980).

25. Catherine Coquery-Vidrovitch, "The Political Economy of the African Peasantry and Modes of Production," in Gutkind and Wallerstein, op. cit., pp. 90–111.

26. Karl Marx and Frederick Engels, "Manifesto of the Communist Party," in Karl Marx and Frederick Engels, *Selected Works*, Volume 1 (Moscow, Foreign Languages Publishing House, 1962), pp. 21–65.

27. Frantz Fanon, *The Wretched of the Earth* (Harmondsworth, Penguin Books, 1968).

28. Rene Dumont, *False Start in Africa* (London, Andre Deutsch, 1966).

29. For an analysis of Amilcar Cabral's thought on this subject, see Henry Bienen, "State and Revolution: The Work of Amilcar Cabral," *Journal of Modern African Studies*, Vol. 15, No. 4 (1977).

30. Moore, Jr., op. cit., pp. 92–101.

31. Although statements made by political leaders tend to admit decline in labor productivity, few studies have actually examined its scope. One exception is a study by the Polish economist Jerzy Jedruzek of Tanzania. See his "Economic Efficiency and the Process of Development," Economic Research Bureau, University of Dar es Salaam, October 1978.

32. Frank Holmquist, "Class Structure, Peasant Participation, and Rural Self-Help," in Joel Barkan and John J. Okumu (eds.), *Politics and Public Policy in Kenya and Tanzania* (New York, Praeger Publishers, 1979).

33. For an overview of development of cooperatives in East Africa, see Goran

Hyden, *Efficiency versus Distribution in East African Cooperatives* (Nairobi, East African Literature Bureau, 1973).

34. There are several studies from various African countries that highlight these problems, e.g., Roger King, "Cooperative Policy and Village Development in Northern Nigeria," in Heyer, Roberts, and Williams, op. cit., pp. 259–280; John S. Saul, "Marketing Cooperatives in a Development Country: The Tanzanian Case," in Peter Worsley (ed.), *Two Blades of Grass* (Manchester, Manchester University Press, 1969), pp. 347–370; A. Z. Mutaha et al., *Cooperatives in Tanzania: Problems of Organization* (Dar es Salaam, Tanzania Publishing House, 1976); C. E. F. Beer, *The Politics of Peasant Groups in Western Nigeria* (Ibadan, Ibadan University Press, 1976); and C. Stephen Lombard, *The Growth of Cooperatives in Zambia 1914–1971* (Manchester: Manchester University Press for Institute of African Studies, University of Zambia, 1971).

35. For an account of the settlement experience in Tanzania, see Lionel Cliffe and John S. Saul (eds.) *Socialism in Tanzania*, Volume 2 (Nairobi, East African Publishing House, 1974), pp. 131–140. For another interpretation, see John Nellis, *A Theory of Ideology: The Tanzania Example* (Nairobi, Oxford University Press, 1972).

36. There are several studies of Tanzania's *ujamaa* village experience. See, e.g., Michaela von Freyhold, *Ujamaa Villages in Tanzania: Analysis of a Social Experiment* (London, Heinemann Educational Books, 1979); Jannik Boesen, Birgit Storgård Madsen, and Tony Moody, *Ujamaa—Socialism from Above* (Uppsala, Scandinavian Institute of African Studies, 1977); Dean McHenry, Jr., *Tanzania's Ujamaa Villages: The Implementation of a Rural Development Strategy* (Berkeley, University of California, Institute of International Studies, 1979); and Andrew Coulson, "Agricultural Policies in Mainland Tanzania 1946–1976," in Heyer, Roberts, and Williams, op. cit., pp. 52–89.

37. Robert Chambers, *Settlement Schemes in Tropical Africa* (London, Routledge & Kegan Paul, 1969).

38. For an analysis of the Ghanaian experience, see Frances Hill, "Experiments with a Public Sector Peasantry: Agricultural Schemes and Class Formation in Africa," paper presented to the African Studies Association Conference, Boston, November 1976.

39. For a discussion of the problems of administering development in Africa, see David K. Leonard and Dale Rogers Marshall (eds.), *Institutions of Rural Development for the Poor* (Berkeley, University of California, Institute for International Studies, 1982), and Jon R. Moris, *Managing Induced Rural Development* (Bloomington, Indiana University, International Development Institute, 1981).

40. Heyer, Roberts, and Williams, op. cit.

41. Robert H. Bates, *Markets and States in Tropical Africa* (Berkeley and Los Angeles, University of California Press, 1981), p. 121.

42. This term was first coined by Issa Shivji, *Class Struggles in Tanzania* (London, Heinemann Educational Books, 1975).

43. The concept *economy of affection* originally used in the present author's book *Beyond Ujamaa*, op. cit., refers to the various networks of support, communications, and interaction among structurally defined groups connected by blood, kin, community, or other affinities. It links together in a systematic fashion a variety of discrete social and economic units which in other regards may be autonomous, thus giving rise to economic flows and exchanges based on criteria other than those guiding economic behavior in a capitalist or a socialist type of economy.

44. Such campaigns were conducted, for instance, in Mozambique and Tanzania during the early half of 1983.

45. This point is further analyzed by Hart, op. cit.

46. For an overview of the city in historical perspective, see Max Weber, *The City* (New York, The Free Press, 1958).

47. See the volume translated by Kurt Wolff, *The Sociology of Georg Simmel* (Glencoe, The Free Press, 1950), pp. 409–424.

48. Oswald Spengler, *The Decline of the West* (New York, Alfred Knopf, 1928), two volumes.

49. Weber, op. cit., p. 33.

50. Emile Durkheim, *The Division of Labor in Society* (New York, The Free Press, 1964).

51. On the history of urban growth in Africa, see, e.g., B. Thomas, "On the Growth of African Cities," *African Studies Review*, Vol. XIII, No. 1 (1970), pp. 1–8; also Richard Sandbrook, *The Politics of Basic Needs: Urban Aspects of Assaulting Poverty in Africa* (London, Heinemann Educational Books, 1982), pp. 33–76.

52. For a general overview of the question of forced labor, see E. J. Berg, "The Development of Labor Force in sub-Saharan Africa," *Economic Development and Cultural Change*, Vol. XIII, No. 3 (1965), pp. 394–412. For a case study of Tanzania, see Justinian Rweyemamu, *Underdevelopment and Industrialization in Tanzania* (Nairobi, Oxford University Press, 1973), esp. Ch. 1. On the question of long-distance labor, see M. A. Bienefeld, "Trade Unions, the Labor Process and the Tanzania State," *Journal of Modern African Studies*, Vol. 17, No. 4 (1979), pp. 553–593.

53. The policies of the British authorities in East Africa are analyzed in various contributions to John Hutton (ed.), *Urban Challenge in East Africa* (Nairobi, East African Publishing House, 1972).

54. See, e.g., Kenneth Little, *West African Urbanization: A Study of Voluntary Organizations in Social Change* (Cambridge, Cambridge University Press, 1965); Immanuel Wallerstein, "Voluntary Associations," in James S. Coleman and Carl G. Rosberg (eds.), *Political Parties and National Integration in Tropical Africa* (Berkeley and Los Angeles, University of California Press, 1966), pp. 318–339; S. Ottenberg, "Improvement Association among the Afikop Ibo," *Africa*, Vol. XXV, No. 1 (1955); William A. Shack, "Notes on Voluntary Associations and Urbanization in Africa, With Special Reference to Addis Ababa, Ethiopia," *African Urban Notes*, Series B, No. 1 (Winter 1974/75); and Peter Koehn and Sidney R. Waldron, *Afocha: A Link Between Community and Administration in Harar, Ethiopia* (Maxwell School of Citizenship and Public Affairs, Syracuse University, 1978).

55. Thomas Hodgkin, *Nationalism in Colonial Africa* (London, Frederick Muller, 1956).

56. Elliot P. Skinner, "Voluntary Associations in Ouagadougou: A Re-appraisal of the Function of Voluntary Associations in African Urban Centers," *African Urban Notes*, Series B, No. 1 (Winter 1974/75).

57. Vittorio Lanternari, *The Religions of the Oppressed: A Study of Modern Messianic Cults* (New York, Mentor Books, 1965), esp. pp. 240–244.

58. For an excellent biography of Mboya, see David Goldsworthy, *Tom Mboya: The Man Kenya Wanted to Forget* (Nairobi, Heinemann and New York, Africana Publishing Corporation, 1982).

59. Richard Sabot, *Urban Migration in Tanzania*, Volume II of the National Urban

Mobility, Employment, and Income Survey, Economic Research Bureau, University of Dar es Salaam, September 1972.

60. In the spirit of the populist ethic reigning in Africa after independence it has been common, particularly in countries committed to a socialist strategy, to encourage workers to challenge management authority in organizations on the ground that such a move constitutes part of their "liberation." Workers have no doubt taken advantage of this opportunity, but it has generally been at the cost of productivity and the refinement of the means of production. The inevitable outcome of this effort, therefore, has been reversal to a very authoritarian management style as a means of restoring labor discipline and enhancing productivity. For an analysis of this phenomenon, see Issa Shivji, op. cit.; also Hyden, *Beyond Ujamaa*, op. cit., Ch. 6.

61. Margaret Peil, *The Ghanaian Factory Worker: Industrial Man in Africa* (Cambridge, Cambridge University Press, 1972), Ch. 6.

62. Cf., e.g., John C. Caldwell, *African Rural-Urban Migration: The Movement to Ghana's Towns* (New York, Columbia University Press, 1969); John C. Mitchell (ed.), *Social Networks in Urban Situations* (Manchester, Manchester University Press, 1969); Joyce Moock, "The Content and Maintenance of Social Ties Between Urban Migrants and Their Home-Based Support Groups: The Maragoli Case," *African Urban Studies*, Number 3 (Winter 1978–79); Thomas Weisner, "The Structure of Sociability: Urban Migration and Urban Ties in Kenya," *Urban Anthropology*, No. 5 (1976), pp. 199–223; and Sandbrook, op. cit.

63. Walter Elkan, *Migrants and Proletarians: Urban Labour in the Economic Development of Uganda* (Oxford, Oxford University Press, 1960).

64. Great Britain, *East Africa Royal Commission 1953–55 Report*, Cmd 9475 (London, H.M.S.O. 1961 ed.) p. 250.

65. There is also evidence that some leaders may encourage their followers to make private gains from the public purse. See, e.g., David J. Gould, "Disorganization Theory and Underdevelopment Administration: Local 'Organization' in the Framework of Zairean National 'Development'," paper presented at the Joint Meeting of the African Studies and Latin American Studies Associations, Houston, Texas, November 1977.

66. Hart, op. cit., p. 133.

67. John C. Caldwell, "Toward a Restatement of Demographic Transition Theory," *Population and Development Review*, Vol. 2, Nos. 3–4 (September–December 1976), pp. 321–366.

68. For a case study of Kenya, see Thomas E. Dow, Jr., and Linda H. Werner, "Prospects for Fertility Decline in Rural Kenya," *Population and Development Review*, Vol. 9, No. 1 (March 1983), pp. 77–97.

69. For a case study of this issue, see Richard Stren, "A Survey of Lower Income Areas in Mombasa," in Hutton, op. cit., pp. 97–116.

70. Peter Marris and Anthony Somerset, *African Businessmen* (London, Routledge & Kegan Paul, 1971).

71. Andrew A. Beveridge and Anthony Oberschall, *African Businessmen and Development in Zambia* (Princeton, Princeton University Press, 1979).

72. Su Wenming (ed.), *Economic Readjustment and Reform* (Beijing, Beijing Review Publishers, 1982), pp. 27–40.

73. This point was initially developed by Peter Ekeh, "Colonialism and the Two Publics in Africa: A Theoretical Statement," *Comparative Studies in Society and History*, Vol. 17, No. 1 (1975), pp. 91–112.

74. Gellar, op. cit., pp. 35–39.

75. Kenneth King, *The African Artisan: A Study of Training, Technology and the Informal Sector in Kenya* (New York, Columbia Teachers College Press, 1975).

76. Cf., e.g., publications listed in note 62.

77. Cf., e.g., Caldwell, "African Rural-Urban Migration," op. cit.

78. Michael Lipton, *Why Poor People Stay Poor: Urban Bias in World Development* (Cambridge, Mass., Harvard University Press, 1977).

79. Richard Rhoda, "Rural Development and Urban Migration: Can we Keep them Down on the Farm?," *International Migration Review*, Vol. 17, No. 1 (Spring 1983), pp. 34–64.

80. Economic Commission for Africa, op. cit., p. 26.

81. Alex Inkeles and David H. Smith, *Becoming Modern: Individual Change in Six Developing Countries* (Cambridge, Mass., Harvard University Press, 1974).

82. Johannes F. Linn, "The Costs of Urbanization in Developing Countries," *Economic Development and Cultural Change*, Vol. 30, No. 3 (April 1982), pp. 625–648.

CHAPTER 9

# African Relations
# with the Major Powers

*Crawford Young*

In 1979, Anatoly Gromyko, director of the Soviet Africa Institute, told a visiting group of Western scholars that Soviet policy toward Africa over the past two decades had remained essentially unchanged; "Only opportunities have changed," he asserted. In 1983, African-American Institute director, and former Assistant Secretary of State for African Affairs (1973–74), Donald Easum told another academic audience that changes over time of American African policy had been more of style than substance. Echoing this perception of essential stability were the private comments of ranking African diplomats who attended the African-American Institute conference in Harare in January 1983; the basic foundations of American policy in Africa remained unchanged from one administration to another, a bedrock fact they viewed with dismay and disappointment.

And yet, amid the sound and fury of daily events, major shifts do seem to occur. The decisive Soviet actions in the Angolan and Ethiopian crises of 1975 and 1977 appeared to mark a rupture with the caution of the past, leading to widely voiced Western allegations of "adventurism." Detente, growled then–National Security Adviser Zbigniew Brzezinski, "is buried in the sands of the Ogaden." The controversial NSSC memorandum 39, in 1969, appeared to engage the United States in a crucial shift toward reliance upon the "white redoubts" of southern Africa.[1] In 1981, Assistant Secretary of State for African Affairs Chester Crocker launched a new policy ideology for Southern Africa, under the label of "constructive engagement"; to its friends and foes, this appeared to betoken a major new direction, whether viewed as inspirational or demonic.[2] Is it conceivable that, beneath the well-roiled surfaces, the deeper currents of policy continued to flow along the same channels?

This essay will explore the themes of continuity and change in the relations of the major powers and Africa. The focus will be upon the two global superpowers, the Soviet Union and the United States, with only peripheral consideration of other important extra-African national actors that have been active in African international relations: China, Cuba, East Germany, France, Britain, and Israel. While these important but less potent external forces, to varying degrees, have been of great significance, economy of exposition compels a more narrow focus. Primary attention will be visited upon the superpowers; however, one must not, by subliminal analytical process, cast African states in the role of mere passive objects of superpower action. The universe of African states, and the fifty-one sovereign entities which compose it, is much more than a simple arena. Their actions, perceptions, and choices play an autonomous part in the unfolding drama, however asymmetrical the relationships may be.[3]

Continuities may certainly be discovered in the overarching sets of premises and assumptions with which Africa and the great powers view each other. On the African side, a half-dozen central themes stand out. At the top of the list is the central priority accorded to completion of the task of liberation of the continent from foreign or white minority rule. It is above all on this principle that African states succeed in acting in concert, and which serves as the primary cement for their vehicle for continental collaboration, the sometimes creaking Organization of African Unity (OAU). Partly derivative from this master principle are some others which relate to liberation and autonomy: nonalignment in world affairs, however wide the variations in interpretation of this doctrine, and the security of African states. In the economic realm, the pursuit of economic independence and development, however elusive, is central. The political aim of nonalignment is sought within the broader frame of a vocation of African unity, whose minimalist contemporary incarnation is the state-based concert of African nations and preservation of their existing borders and internal unity. Economically, the Third World "New International Economic Order" claims define the agenda, however remote their achievement may be.[4] Finally, African dignity and racial justice round out the set of basic commitments.

These orienting principles are lodged within a set of standing perceptions of the global political arena. These may be distilled from the corpus of African nationalist thought, particularly in its mainstream variants. The central historical fact governing the African integration into a world system of states is that it occurred, politically, through imperial conquest (and its ancestral forerunners, such as the Atlantic slave trade). In intimate symbiosis with this enduring political fact is the accompanying economic incorporation as a subsidiary part of the complex of Western economic institutions and relationships collectively labeled as capitalism. The structural flaws of the African state system—its fragmentation, illogical boundaries, high cultural pluralism, and inherently problematic state-civil society ties—derive from this fundamental historical determinant. In the economic realm, the vulnerabilities of African states as well originate in the externally imposed structure of trade and production.

The second great disability facing Africa arises from patterns of global international relationships rooted in the character of interstate relations as they emerged in Europe in the sixteenth century. An "anarchic society" took form, based upon the competitive aggrandizement of the most powerful states at any given point in time.[5] At the much later date when African states joined this system of states, its dominant rivalry was the global struggle between the United States and the Soviet Union. The two megapowers looked upon the entire world as an arena for their mutual hostilities. The "great game" had goals African states found irrelevant, was governed by a logic which they rejected, had rules of conduct they repudiated, yet they could not resist the extension of the playing field to include the nominally independent African continent. Add to this the many-stranded fabric of relationships to secondary players in the great game, the former West European colonial powers, and the compelling logic as well as the impossible obstacles to nonalignment become clear.

These central premises found eloquent statement by President Julius Nyerere, in a 1978 denunciation of a stillborn scheme for a Western-sponsored "African peace force." "There is only one reason why the idea . . . does not meet with immediate and worldwide amazement and consternation," he declared.

> It is the continuing assumption that Africa is, and must always remain, part of the West European sphere of influence. This assumption is hardly being questioned yet. Even some African states take it for granted. . . . Nor will the whole of Africa acquiesce in being used in the East-West confrontation. We are weak, but weak countries have before now caused a great deal of embarrassment and some difficulty for big powers. If the West wants to prove, either to the Russians or to their own people, that they are not soft on communism they should direct their attention to where the Soviet tanks are. . . . They should not invent an excuse to bring the East-West conflict into Africa.[6]

The African state system is thus placed at continuing risk by the polarizing effects of recurrent great-power crises. The competitive recruitment of friends and allies, and the continuing impact of their global competition upon American and Soviet approaches to Africa, exacerbate some tensions within Africa (the Horn) and artificially introduce others (the "linkage" imbroglio in Namibia). Moreover, the aim of continental unity encounters enduring obstacles in some instances in the persisting privileged relationships with former colonizers, above all among those states formerly under French rule. Symbolic of this phenomenon was the dispiriting fact that, in 1982, more African states attended the Franco-African summit in Kinshasa than were on hand for either of the abortive OAU summits in Tripoli.[7]

Joining the principles to the premises, we may identify several specific persistent African diplomatic interests. However daunting the task, Africa should insulate itself from the East-West rivalry: thus the urgency of finding machinery within Africa to mediate inter-African conflict. All possible avenues for African interstate cooperation—not only in the OAU, but also at the United Nations and other international forums and at regional levels (ECOWAS, SADCC)—merit exploration. African states ask for higher aid levels, debt relief, primary commodity price stabilization programs. They also stress self-reliance and internally directed priorities, central themes in the most important synthesis of African development thought, the 1980 Lagos Plan of Action. The campaign for southern African liberation is not only a moral imperative, but—for the nearby states—a matter of survival, as South Africa in the 1980s has moved into a new phase of aggressive punitive action and preemptive strikes against its neighbors.[8]

Pursuing the same analysis for American policy, one may identify a few salient principles whose persistence through time contributes to the image of continuity. They appear in all the major declarations of American policy, from Mennan Williams to Chester Crocker. A desire to minimize Soviet influence is a bedrock postulate. Henry Kissinger, with his singular penchant for the lapidary formulation, states this axiom simply: "To foreclose Soviet opportunities is . . . the essence of the West's responsibilities."[9] Maintenance of the comity of the NATO alliance is an evident corollary, imposing a deference to the interests and concerns of the withdrawing colonizers. A controlled, non-violent transition to African rule is supported; support for guerrilla national liberation movements, however, is precluded.[10] Apartheid is verbally condemned, but peaceful means are prescribed for its dismantlement. "Moderate" regimes are preferred to aggressively radical and populist ones. African development merits modest amounts of American aid, but is most effectively pursued through the application of market economy principles and the promotion of a propitious climate for foreign capital.[11]

The permanent premises of American African policy have been few and simple. The most central has been the low significance of Africa in the hierarchy of United States external priorities. Speaking of South Africa but with equal application to the entire continent, Foltz argued that Africa "must be seen, thus, as an area of peripheral concern for the American people and for most decision-makers concerned with the overall shape of American foreign policy."[12] In general, stability and crisis aversion favors low-cost preemption of Soviet influence. So also does tacit support to other Western powers inclined to maintain spheres of influence, in particular France, even at the cost of conceding "chasse gardée" prerogatives; the August 1983 Reagan press conference reference to Chad as a French sphere of influence, while crudely phrased, was profoundly revealing of a deeply rooted assumption in the official mind.

African states are presumed to be weak and fragile; thus the preference for stability occurs in a setting where elements of instability are to be expected. The combination of inherent weakness of African states and episodic political crises, though their origins may be local and their initial determinants African, contains a fatal dialectic which will necessarily take on an East-West dimension.[13] There tends to be a zero-sum assumption concerning Soviet relationships in Africa: a Soviet gain is an American loss, and vice versa. The global nature of the Soviet-American competition and the elemental obligations incumbent upon a superpower require an American diplomatic presence everywhere. The diplomacy of presence requires in turn at least a minimal aid program as widely distributed as possible, even if only in the form of tantalizing hints of assistance that might in future materialize.

Since the 1950s, there has been a general assumption that colonial and white minority regimes could not persist indefinitely. While it was not the function of the United States to accelerate inevitable historical processes, American global interests did require that the transitions be brokered and managed in such a way as to avert Soviet gains. If at all possible, this was to be done in cooperation with the colonial powers, to ensure controlled change.

The weakness and poverty of most African states made democratic institutions seem unlikely, and little sustained effort was made to promote them. "Democracy" as an issue in African-American relationships had much less saliency than in Latin America, however inconsistently this commitment was applied in the latter region. This is illustrated in the generally autocratic institutions that obtained even in those African states with which the United States had the most sustained tutelary relationship: Liberia, Ethiopia until 1974, Zaire.[14] Only extreme forms of tyranny, as in the later phases of the Idi Amin and Francisco Macias Nguema regimes in Uganda and Equatorial Guinea respectively, exceeded the bounds of toleration.

Development is viewed as a useful antedote to weakness and instability, as well as an inevitable postulate of industrial world–less developed country relationships. The capitalist pathway was clearly preferred as the most efficacious means to this end. However, African ideological projects of socialist content, while certainly not encouraged, were not taken altogether seriously for the most part. Chase Manhattan President David Rockefeller expressed the dominant view of the policy community in suggesting, after a 1982 African swing, that "Africans mean something special by socialism." The first wave of socialist declarations in the early 1960s did bring some momentary tremors of anxiety, and the second wave of "Marxist-Leninist" statements in the mid-1970s brought apprehension to Secretary of State Henry Kissinger. But the dominant view most of the time was that ideological claims of most regimes, even "scientific socialism," were neither irrevocable nor incompatible with "pragmatic" policy reason in the context of specific issues. Much more important in the informal classification of regimes into "friendlies" and "hostiles" was the perceived degree of Soviet influence, above all in the military and security sphere.[15]

From these principles and premises flow some more concrete interests, observable over time.[16] Political factors have predominated. The powerful concern with Soviet preemption leads to a permanent commitment to a supportive or even protective relationship for regimes willing to perform valued services relating to broader global interests of the United States: Egypt since 1972, Sudan since the mid-1970s, Morocco, Zaire. The more tutelary linkage with Liberia, when threatened by the unexpected coup of Sergeant Samuel Doe in 1980, dictated an immediate shift from the long-standing backing for the True Whig Americo-Liberian autocracy to smothering with aid and friendship any disposition of the uncertain new rulers to seek alternative patrons. Demands for security assistance from African states asserting Western-leaning forms of nonalignment far exceed what any administration is disposed to give; nonetheless, pleas from such leaders as Senegalese President Leopold Senghor find receptive ears within the policy community:

> The Americans . . . want Africa to resist the East's offensive but will not help it to do so. . . . They refuse to supply us with the modern weapons we need to defend ourselves. . . . We are asking our Western friends . . . simply to help us in the same way the Marxist-Leninist states are helped by their friends.[17]

In strategic terms as well, Africa has not weighed heavily in policy calculus. With the exception of Egypt and South Africa, African military forces do not figure in what Soviet analysts term the "correlation of forces." In the geopolitical thought of global strategists, Africa entered the picture mainly because of its juxtaposition to, or location en route to, other areas deemed more critical. The Horn was important because of its contiguity to the Middle Eastern oil fields. Kenya, Somalia, and Egypt took on new significance in 1979 when forward basing for a rapid development force became incorporated into strategic thought, replacing earlier interest in air and communication bases in Morocco, Libya, and Ethiopia. For the lonely band of neo-Mahanian thinkers who fancied that the Cape sea lanes were crucial, these were viewed as a "choke point" for oil shipping from the Gulf to Western Europe.

The raw material issue lies at the intersection of strategic and economic concerns. Access to African raw materials, especially the relatively scarce minerals concentrated in southern Africa, always figured on listings of American interests in Africa, but until the first oil crisis in 1973 and the running debate concerning the Byrd amendment permitting Rhodesian chrome imports in 1971–1977 the question was purely abstract. Its saliency was briefly reinforced in 1978, when the second invasion of Shaba by Angola-based insurgents temporarily closed the major Zaire cobalt mines. A rash of alarmist speculation about potential vulnerability of Western economies was epitomized by the 1980 Santini Report;[18] more sober analysis discounting the probability of prolonged interruptions under any plausible political scenarios and the surprisingly quick technological adjustments to the two oil crises and the cobalt scare returned the raw material issue to a more subdued place on the roster of policy interests.[19]

The American economic engagement in Africa, while forming a part of United States policy interests, has generally been subordinated to political concerns. It figures most prominently in South Africa, where approximately $4 billion of American equity is committed in mines and manufactures (and by some estimates substantially more). These sums are significant, and become more so when lending by the major American banks is added. Nonetheless, this is a very small part of global commitments by American capital, whether considered as a whole or at the level of the individual firm.[20] In the rest of the continent, oil is by far the most important investment stake. The petroleum majors have generally fended for themselves, without requiring active foreign policy support, as is demonstrated by the excellent relationships between Gulf Oil and Angola, despite the absence of diplomatic ties, or the 59.1 percent profit rate of American oil companies in Libya in 1976, when that state was well on its way to earning the 1981 Haig characterization as a "cancer."[21] The real deterioration in American-Libyan relations began primarily following large-scale Libyan arms purchases from the Soviet Union and not-so-covert aid to causes and movements deemed "terrorist" in nature by American diplomacy (Irish Republican Army, Moro National Liberation Front, Basques, Corsicans, Palestinians, among others), and not with the partial oil nationalizations affecting American corporations in 1972–73.[22]

On the Soviet side, several salient policy principles may be deduced. As a great power, which views itself as endowed with a special historical mission as the pioneer of socialism and prides itself on having built the military strength to project its power on a global scale, the Soviet Union has a natural desire to maintain a diplomatic presence wherever possible. This status, as Albright states, must be "self-asserted, self-achieved, and self-sustained."[23] African states entered the era of sovereignty still shackled by many residual bonds of subordination to the world of imperialism; as well, they were subject to the solicitations of the American head of the imperialist camp to acquire new links of political clientage. Therefore, the Soviet Union encourages whenever opportunity arises the reduction (though not severance) of ties to the Western world. National liberation movements, particularly those committed to an anti-imperial perspective, deserve support and encouragement. Their potential for weakening capitalism is particularly important in that subimperial bastion South Africa. Another major hostile force, perceived as objectively serving the cause of imperialism because of its anti-Soviet animus, is China. Soviet policy accordingly actively combats Chinese influence in Africa.

In the economic realm, African development, perceived as being at an early stage, merits some limited assistance from the Soviet Union, so designed as to enlarge the possibilities for a noncapitalist pattern of development. The Soviets, however, are not in a position to assume central responsibility for the organization and financing of the development of any particular African states, even those which officially adopt a Marxist-Leninist ideology. Particularly for states seeking a socialist pathway, military and security assistance could play a more vital role, to put them in a position to maintain themselves in power.[24]

Related to these policy principles are several important premises. In terms of the Soviet theory of history, African states are characterized by "backwardness," which has important implications for the kinds of options open to them. As one analyst put it, "It is impossible to build a socialist society in countries with age-old backwardness in the shortest period of time."[25] Because of the early stage of their development, the socal classes which might form a support base for "scientific socialism"—in particular the proletariat—are relatively weak.[26] South Africa is a major exception to this general rule.

There are possibilities, however, for exploiting "noncapitalist" models of development, in spite of the limitations of social structure. These must necessarily rest upon the leadership of elements of the intelligentsia and petty bourgeoisie. The latter, despite its ideologically ambiguous position, might play an important transitional role. As one leading Soviet analyst wrote in 1974, the petty bourgeoisie "has grown, as a rule, faster than the ranks of the proletariat. In its majority it lacks the basic sources of accumulating capital, it is patriotically minded and it is a motive force of the anti-imperialist struggle. Together with the peasantry and the semi-proletariat, this section is the main force from which revolutionary democracy springs and by which it is supported."[27]

The important concept of "national democracy" offers ideological justification for laying the foundations for socialist transition even without the requisite social formations. The national democratic state, taking advantage of the weakness of capitalist as well as socialist classes, through reliance on "the state sector in industry, a state system of banking and finance and a cooperative sector in agriculture and light industry, . . . can consistently restrict the exploiting classes and promote the economic and political prerequisites for the movement along the way of socialist orientation."[28] In such states, ". . . the specific structure of society, the absence in most of these countries of clear-cut class differentiation gives relative independence to the state, which has an extensive area for economic maneuvre."[29] The noncapitalist pathway, despite its intrinsic weaknesses, is thought to have a real possibility of viability because it can draw upon the "rich experience" of the Soviet Union and the growing economic and military strength of the "socialist camp." In particular, the Soviet Union and its junior partners (East Germany and Cuba) can help ensure the perennity of these constructions by concentrating their aid on the consolidation of the "Leninist core" of the national democracy state: its security apparatus; its political control organs, especially a Leninist party; and its communications capabilities.[30]

The corpus of potential "revolutionary democrats" has a somewhat surprising military wing in the officer corps. The military in Africa is not necessarily tied to capitalism, either in the social origins or petty-bourgeois class position of its leadership, or through institutional ties. Further, in the turbulence of "transitional" conditions and social "backwardness," the military is a relatively stable institution, as argued by one Soviet commentary a decade ago:

> The advantage of the army as against political parties is obvious if one compares the sources for financing the parties, which are limited and not always reliable, with the resources allocated to maintaining the army. . . . The army is a state organization, which receives the funds for its support entirely from the state budget. It does not need to worry about the business situation in the country, nor about the financial power of the bourgeoisie. . . . In other words, as distinct from political parties, the army . . . is an institution paid for not by any one or other class grouping, but by the whole nation. . . . It also differs from plain civilian institutions in that the character of its hierarchy and of its discipline is incomparably more rigorous. This has meant that a politically active officer corps has been able with great success to use the army for its own politcial aims.[31]

Efforts at socialist construction in Africa, however, occur in a climate of high risks and uncertainties. The affirmation of Marxist-Leninist aspiration by particular regimes is welcomed, but not entirely taken at face value; as Gromyko put it, in "countries such as Angola, Mozambique, Benin, Congo, and Ethiopia, despite numerous difficulties, revolutionary democracy is coming closer and closer to the ideology of Marxism-Leninism";[32] otherwise put, they are not yet in the promised land. As yet, most such regimes are not to be sharply distinguished from others of "socialist orientation" such as Tanzania, Algeria, or even Libya.

Kosukhin clarifies the problematic aspects of revolutionary democracy:

> . . . inside the revolutionary-democratic movement there is a trend whose repre-
> sentatives (owing to petty-bourgeois, religious-nationalist and othr deep-rooted be-
> liefs, to imperialist pressure and other factors), show inconsistency, vacillations in
> regard to scientific socialism, to worldwide experience in socialist construction.
> Some factions of revolutionary democracy do not go beyond the framework of
> petty-bourgeois relations in their socio-economic reforms.
>
> . . . the wavering of some revolutionary-democrat leaders leads to their slipping
> into Right nationalist and even chauvinist positions. In such cases we see a politi-
> cal degeneration of revolutionary democrats who have actually become bourgeois
> nationalists and no longer express the interests of the radical petty bourgeoisie and
> the working masses.[33]

These important flaws lead to a crucial assumption in Soviet policy thought concerning Africa: the pursuit of socialist orientation by given regimes is not necessarily irreversible. This realization emerged after the surprising series of coups which eliminated the first of national democracies: the overthrow of Kwame Nkrumah in Ghana, Ben Bella in Algeria, and Modibo Keita in Mali. The conviction was reinforced by the loss of ideological rectitude, without benefit of coup, by important quondam architects of noncapitalist development such as Anwar Sadat of Egypt, Siad Barre of Somalia, and Sékou Touré of Guinea. The inevitable conclusion is drawn by authoritative East German commentators:

> Because of the weaker social base, the inconsistencies . . . in the thinking and
> behavior of predominantly petty-bourgeois–peasant forces of leadership, the lack
> of experience and cadres, and not least of all on account of the strong economic
> positions and the ideological influence over which imperialism continues to dis-
> pose in these countries, the development of the countries with a socialist orienta-
> tion is by no means irreversible. Changes—conceivably of a precipitous nature—
> are possible.[34]

In strategic and military terms, the Soviets generally share the perceptions of American policy that Africa is a secondary zone. Until recently, placing Africa in a broader global perspective, there was a zero-sum view of "counter-imperial" action; virtually any weakening of "imperial" (American and Western) positions in the Third World was advantageous to the socialist camp. The anti-imperial component of African nationalist thought created natural affinities with Soviet views. The diverse national liberation struggles were seen as positive developments, as they automatically led to a weakening of imperialist positions in Africa; they thus merited moral and (more cautiously) material support, although constrained by the simultaneous post-Stalin commitment to "peaceful coexistence" and, in the 1970s, "detente," and also by the powerful anti-Chinese impulses in Soviet policy thought, where given movements were drawing doctrinal inspiration or military support from the Maoist heresy. All of this dictated a posture of prudent, if not "constructive," engagement.

Translating these principles and premises into specific interests, we may discern limited but significant ongoing Soviet concerns. In the political sphere, there is a marked interest in preserving those regimes of socialist orientation, although not all are of equal value or affinity. There is very little Soviet involvement in the security core of, say, Algeria or Tanzania, while this is crucial in the cases of Angola and Ethiopia. This interest takes account of the essential instability of the African environment and the possibility of "precipitous" changes; Egypt and Somalia were "lost" despite the gossamer bonds of a Treaty of Friendship and Cooperation and extensive linkages with the respective security forces.[35] The Brezhnev doctrine of the "limited sovereignty" of socialist states does not appear to apply, at least as yet, to Africa.

In military terms, Africa has some value in Soviet global strategy. This interest has three components. The expanding horizons of Soviet naval strategy and its extension in the 1970s into the Indian Ocean require some coastal base points for refueling and supply. Secondly, the security need for monitoring movements and location of American nuclear submarines makes valuable airbase rights in coastal locations on both the Atlantic and Indian Ocean sides. Finally, the need for leverage and credibility gives value to standing overflight rights and staging points in the event that sudden and unexpected opportunities arise for military involvement by the Soviet Union or its associates (for example, Pointe Noire in Brazzaville was a crucial staging point for Soviet and Cuban logistical and military support for the MPLA in Angola in 1975–1976).

Economically, the Soviet stake is very small. The Soviet Union has no need for or interest in most African primary commodities, nor has it been successful in selling its products in African markets (except for armaments). There are some exceptions, and there may be more in the future; the most obvious, up to the present, have been phosphates and fish. In the former case, a $2 billion Soviet commitment to Morocco occurred simultaneously with the spectacular Moroccan rule as Western gendarme in Zaire in 1977 and 1978, to help rout the "Katanga gendarme" insurgents who invaded from Angola.

Fish meal is an important element in both human and animal diets in the Soviet Union, and the vast fleet of Soviet fish factory ships is deployed across the globe. Fishing accords have been negotiated with most African littoral states, and have been a source of considerable friction in many instances, as

African governments have suspected their Soviet counterparts of overfishing, exceeding agreed catch limits, concealing their true value, and failing to fulfill pledges for the development of African commercial fishing capabilities. The growing severity of economic constraints affecting Soviet policy, in particular the regular shortfalls of grain harvests, increases the importance of fish meal as animal feed and doubtless places pressures upon the Soviet fishing fleets to maximize their catches irrespective of vexations this may produce in their po- litical relations with coastal African states.

Another major Soviet natural resource development project occurred in Guinea in 1973, with the initiation of a joint bauxite-mining scheme. Mercan- tile calculations rather than ideological affinities appear to have conditioned this transaction, with Guineans subsequently objecting that their Soviet part- ners were valuing the bauxite ore at one-third its world market value (on the grounds of its purported "poor quality") and that their proceeds from the ven- ture were entirely devoted to repayment of the Soviet loan.

In addition to weakening the political positions in Africa of their Western adversaries, the Soviet Union has evinced an economic interest in undermin- ing or offering alternatives to international capitalist structures. Soviet eco- nomic aid—though at very modest levels—has aimed at the construction of a state industrial sector as a buttress for the possible "noncapitalist" pathway. Also, the Soviets have pursued their countercapitalist interest in the natural- resource field by offering aid in mineral surveys and assisting public-sector resource development, most notably in the petroleum field (especially in Al- geria and Libya).[36]

Thus, there are broad, powerful continuities in the principles, premises, and interests which Africa, the United States, and the Soviet Union bring to their triangular relationship. The perception of essential continuity is by no means false. It is, however, incomplete. To round out our analysis, attention must be directed to factors which have led to significant variations over time in this set of relationships. Focus is placed upon three factors of change: political balances and the policy machinery; landmark, realigning events; and long- term processes of change.

In all three poles of the triangle, there have been important alterations in the political balance. In Africa, of the fifty-one currently independent states, some nineteen have experienced important shifts in foreign-policy align- ments, as measured by their relative proximity to one or the other of the super- powers.[37] The first polarization of African states bore the label, at the begin- ning of the 1960s, of the "Casablanca" and "Brazzaville" groups; each descriptor has changed ideological hue. The "precipitous" changes are an ongoing part of the African political scene; each year brings its harvest of volte-faces, in 1983 Upper Volta and Mauritius. These changes are not always sudden and dramatic; they may be slow and gradual, as with the thaw in animosity between America and Congo-Brazzaville or Mozambique or the gradual warming of Libyan-Soviet relationships during the course of the 1970s. The concept of nonalignment, while it may be a single doctrine, in diplomatic practice resolves itself into a rather wide spectrum along which particular countries may be located at any given time. These divergencies are periodically subjected to polarizing pressures by dramatic events, such as the Angolan civil war in 1975, the abortive Libya summit of the OAU in 1982, or the ongoing struggle over the Western Sahara, where East-West dimensions are usually detectable.

Another source of fluctuation in political balance within Africa has been the presence, throughout this period, of one or two maverick states which did not accept the existing state system. Egypt in the early Nasser era, particularly from the 1956 Suez crisis until the breakup of the United Arab Republic in 1961, nurtured the dream of Cairo-centered Arab unification. A more Islamic-tinctured vision of this goal was then resurrected by Mu'ammar Qadafy of Libya in the 1970s. Somalia, from the moment of its 1960 independence, has pursued Somali-unification aims, leading to wars with Ethiopia in 1963 and 1977 and shaping its foreign policy and internal political dynamics throughout.[38] Ghana in the Nkrumah years subordinated its external relations to the pan-African aspiration, investing heavily in the abortive Ghana-Guinea-Mali (and, almost, Lumumba's Congo) Union and backing radical opponents of neighboring regimes which resisted Nkrumah's aspirations.[39]

Neither the United States nor the Soviet Union found intrinsic value in the pan-Arab, pan-Somali, or pan-African challenges to the African state system bequeathed by the colonial partition, and both were threatened by a new Islamic-defined international order. However, the opportunities and threats posed by the disturbances within the African concert of nations resulting at various times from these antisystem drives attracted their involvement. The maverick state required extracontinental military supply to support its claims and to protect itself against those threatened by its ambitions. Neighboring states which stood in the immediate path of these projects for redefining the state system (Ethiopia, Kenya, Sudan, Tunisia, Ivory Coast, Niger, Chad, for example) solicited external protection. The globalist reason of state of the superpowers supplied motivations quite unrelated to the immediate goals of the mavericks or their opponents to accommodate these requests; the shifting patterns of external intervention in the Horn of Africa or Chad are excellent examples of this dialectic.

In the American case, one may, with some oversimplification, identify two broad policy factions, to which the labels "globalist" and "regionalist" came to be attached at the time of the Angolan civil war. The globalist, as Weberian ideal-type, sees Africa essentially as one of a number of arenas in which the broader, and decisive, East-West struggle is conducted. Their categories of policy thought are rooted in geopolitical strategy, woven into what Henry Kissinger was fond of calling a "conceptual framework." The regionalist vision, on the other hand, perceived African conflicts and crises as originating within the political dialectic of the continent and appropriately analyzed in these terms; East-West concerns are distracting intrusions, which falsify the premises of policy choice.

Thus defined, the globalist and regionalist are evident caricatures of the real actors on the policy scene; almost nobody fully conforms to either of these poles. However, they do locate themselves at different points on a spectrum joining the two poles, and there have been significant differences in where the overall center of policy gravity is located over time. The initial Kennedy "new frontiersfolk" took office with the policy perspectives tinctured with regionalism, only to be sharply pushed back toward globalism by the Congo crisis and the spillover impact of crises in Cuba, Berlin, and Indochina. After the Johnson years, when Africa was completely eclipsed by the Vietnam war, there was a policy drift in the Nixon-Kissinger years in a globalist direction, whose most concrete indicator was the line of reasoning embodied in the 1969 NSSM 39. Above all, in the Kissinger years, until the Angolan civil war captured his attention, Africa was utterly inconsequential, a source of the "Idi Amin" jokes which used to regale his staff meetings. In the 2,700 pages of the first two volumes of his memoirs, as prominent a figure as President Mobutu Sese Seko of Zaire merits but a single passing reference. The drift was halted by the policy fiasco in Angola; Kissinger in his April 1976 Lusaka speech indicated a perspective incorporating regionalist elements.

The Carter administration, in its early months, assembled within the African policy apparatus a number of figures of regionalist tendencies: U.N. Ambassador Andrew Young and Assistant Secretary of State for African Affairs Richard Moose among others, with academician Ruth Schachter Morgenthau playing an important role in the campaign and transition. A package of policy initiatives, particularly focused upon the Southern African situation, was assembled, largely based on a regionalist perspective (and building upon the Lusaka speech). The magnitude of the shift which seemed in prospect was blunted by major events (the first Shaba episode in March 1977, the Soviet-Cuban intervention in Ethiopia) which strengthened the hand of identifiable globalists, such as National Security Adviser Brzezinski. Nonetheless the center of gravity remained somewhat different than in the early 1970s.

The advent of the Reagan administration brought another significant shift. The policy design crafted by Assistant Secretary of State for African Affairs

Chester Crocker was not in itself a globalist project; it would be more accurately described as a careful balance between the two. Indeed, as a "conceptual framework" it is perhaps the most meticulously constructed policy blueprint that has ever existed for American African policy. It was, however, subjected to strong globalist pressures from the Reagan entourage (Clark, for example), from strong-willed incumbents in the Department of Defense (Casper Weinberger), and from the U.N. Ambassador (Jeane Kirkpatrick). As well, the ideological right, represented most effectively by North Carolina Senator Jesse Helms, mustered its forces to block what it saw as excessive regionalist weaknesses.

The globalist-regionalist polarity does not precisely correspond to political party or domestic ideological spectrum, although there is some evident overlap. Representatives of both tendencies are found in both political parties and all administrations. Southern African issues have been the most important single catalyst for precipitating this division.

Shifts along the spectrum have not simply been the result, however, of changes of administration. The movement away from the globalist tilt of the early 1970s may be dated from the Kissinger Lusaka speech in April 1976: policy reached its regionalist peak in 1977 and by 1980 had already receded well back toward globalism, before Reagan took office.

"Bureaucratic politics" have some impact on policy oscillations. Various agencies develop their own fragment of the "official mind" in addressing African issues. Within the Department of State, the Bureau of African Affairs is naturally more prone to a regionalist orientation than are those offices concerned with Europe, the Middle East, or Soviet relations. In the Central Intelligence Agency, there is an ongoing division between the analysis and operations wings. The latter is more propelled by a Cold War logic of direct and ongoing combat with the Soviet adversary than are the intelligence analysts. During the Carter years, following the Church and Rockefeller Commission investigations into assassination plots and other unsavory ventures of the operations branch, it was in relative disrepute. The Reagan years have witnessed its resurrection.

The Department of Defense, by the nature of its mission, will address policy issues in relation to military and strategic concerns. For the most part, these are of low intensity in Africa, and the Pentagon pays little heed to African questions. Crisis episodes, such as the Angolan civil war, may draw Defense into the policy debate. So also will changing strategic requirements, such as the spread of Soviet-American military competition to the Indian Ocean or the decision to create a "rapid development force" targeted on the Middle Eastern oil fields, requiring logistical facilities in Africa.

Other sporadic players include the Department of Commerce, whose concerns revolve around American investments and trade, and the Treasury, with similar concerns. These agencies do not have sustained interest in African policy or significant specialized staffs to assemble independent information. But they can have an impact when American economic interests come into play. For example, in early 1977 an interagency study group, examining Carter administration proposals for a graduated series of economic measures aimed at bringing pressure against South Africa, encountered powerful and effective opposition from the Commerce representatives, who advanced an arsenal of legal and economic arguments challenging the practicality, constitutionality, and financial value of the proposals—which indeed, for the most part, vanished into the bureaucratic sands.[40]

Congress also plays a part, perhaps of growing significance.[41] Here as well as is a fragmented arena, with the most visible action occurring within the Africa Subcommittees of the House Foreign Affairs Committee and Senate Foreign Relations Committee. Congress acquired real importance on African issues in the 1970s, beginning with the initially lonely work by Representative Charles Diggs of Detroit as Chairman of the House Africa Subcommittee.[42] When Diggs was driven from Congress by issues of personal peculation, the Subcommittee came under the leadership of Representative Stephen Solarz of Brooklyn, who continued the pattern of aggressive use of the hearing process initiated by Diggs to make the Subcommittee an effective policy instrument. In 1981, Solarz chose to move to Asian affairs, and Representative Howard Wolpe of Kalamazoo, a former academic specialist in African affairs, succeeded to its helm.

With the support of the slowly expanding Congressional Black Caucus, twenty-one members by 1983, and a small but active core of liberal Congressmen, the impact of this regionalist voice has slowly increased. Its primary strength is in the lower chamber, where it probably now has sufficient strength and resources to block any legislation offensive to its perspective (comparable, for example, to the 1971 Byrd amendment); the Reagan administration, for example, was unable to repeal the 1975 Clark amendment, banning covert action in Angola. The Black Caucus can as well force itself into a dialogue on some of the specifics of aid legislation and through these debates introduce some constraints on broader policy orientations. On South Africa, the Black Caucus and the Africa Subcommittee begin to have some offensive capabilities; in October 1983, amendments were pushed through, by substantial voice votes, forbidding new American investment in South Africa, making the Sullivan Code mandatory, banning Kruggerrand sales in the United States, and mandating American representatives to oppose International Monetary Fund advances to South Africa. According to Wolpe, even a few months earlier these votes would have been impossible to achieve.[43]

On the Senate side, the regionalist perspective has much less weight. For a brief period in the mid-1970s, Senator Richard Clark of Iowa made the Africa Subcommittee an active base, of pivotal importance during the Angolan civil war. The Africanist interest was probably a liability in his reelection campaign in 1978, partly because it apparently attracted South African money into the coffers of his successor, Senator Roger Jepsen. The partisan division has differed in the Senate in recent years from that of the House, there is no Black Caucus, and the Senate Africa Subcommittee, in its staffing and leadership, is not disposed to play the role that it briefly did in the Clark years.

The nature of the congressional role has thus significantly changed over the years. In the 1960s, its role was small and unpredictable, susceptible to the random interventions of the venal but influential curmudgeon Representative Otto Passman of Louisiana, especially in aid policy. In retrospect, the swift and stealthy passage of the 1971 Byrd Amendment[44] marked the end of an epoch.

At the same time, it is important to recognize the limits to these changes. The South Africa amendments in 1983 passed on a voice vote; there would have been less backing on a recorded vote. Further, a number of members voted favorably secure in the expectation that the amendments would not pass the Senate. More broadly, even with vigorous use of the hearing and oversight levers, the House Subcommittee on Africa has limited legislative vehicles for imposing its will. The major annual pieces of legislation which serve as oversight focus are the aid authorization and appropriations bills. While these provide the opportunity for hearings to force the administration to defend itself, in the final analysis congressional effectiveness is diluted by the inability of Congress to pass aid bills. In recent years, only in 1977 and 1981—presidential honeymoon years—have aid appropriations actually passed. On all other occasions, aid is renewed by continuing resolution, reinstating the current appropriations.

Congress now offers, through the House, a point of access for Afrophile constituencies. Of these, the most important is Transafrica, founded in 1978 by the Congressional Black Caucus for Afro-American constituency-building purposes. It enjoys intimate access not only to the Black Caucus, but also to the House Subcommittee on Africa, through members and staff. While some have been critical of Transafrica for dividing the Afrophile constituency on racial lines and others have found its positions too implacable,[45] it clearly has more impact than the church-supported Washington Office on Africa and especially the American Committee on Africa.

All such activist organizations face a profound dilemma in mediating the positions demanded by their own membership base, generally far beyond the range of acceptability within the policy apparatus. If they lose their base, they have no standing; by speaking for the progressive end of their membership they lose the capacity, as Kitchen puts it, to engage in the "social and political stroking" that marks such highly effective lobbies as that of Israel.[46] The important 1981 "Statement on United States Foreign Policy" by the then eighteen members of the Congressional Black Caucus gave clear formulation to its regionalist orientation:

> We find the assumption that the Soviet Union and Cuba are all-controlling forces in the Third World misses the major thrust of a positive Third World policy and is extremely dangerous. . . . The Congressional Black Caucus believes that the most realistic perspective for a global policy during the latter half of the 20th century is one that recognizes a North-South as well as an East-West dimension on foreign policy issues.[47]

Through the vehicle of Congress, this perspective may have marginally increased weight.

On the Soviet side, there have been substantial policy oscillations over time, although it is more difficult to discern the extent to which these may reflect alterations in the policy machinery or sustained factional divergences. A real Soviet African policy became possible only after the frozen ideological positions and personal tyranny of the Stalin years had been dismantled. Doubtless there have been some differences between the professional party apparatus, the security machinery (KGB and armed forces), the economic agencies, and the specialized research institutes.

Some overall Soviet-American trends may serve to alter the relative balance: the Cuban missile crisis, by its dramatic revelation of Soviet strategic weakness and the sustained buildup which this triggered;[48] the more aggressive Reagan administration policy of military challenge to the "evil empire," and the disintegration of detente that this reflected and accelerated.[49] These events doubtless increased the leverage of the security agencies over Soviet policy, with their own versions of globalism. The Soviet research institute personnel play an ambiguous role, in some respects—*mutatis mutandi*—analogous to the regionalists on the American scene. Specialists on Soviet policy generally believe their real policy influence to be as marginal as that of American academic Africanists. Yet those who study Soviet African policy rely heavily on their writings, which are far more extensive and accessible than authoritative statements within the party apparatus or security organs.

Whatever the nature of internal policy formulation, important changes in Soviet interpretations of the African situation have occurred. Within the framework of "peaceful coexistence" and "detente," varying degrees of interest have been exhibited for radical African political experiments. In the final Khrushchev years, partly inspired by the Cuban developments, high hopes were held for the national-democracy formula. The 1965–66 wave of coups for a time seemed to discredit this theory with relation to Africa; also, apparently charges that Khrushchev had recklessly overcommitted the Soviet Union in Egypt was one element in his downfall. A period of disillusionment with Africa seemed to follow, in intriguing parallel with a similar phase in the United States.

The major Soviet African policy initiative of the late 1960s was its strong engagement in suport of the (capitalist) Federal Military Government of Nigeria through arms supply and the pledge of major aid support for an iron and steel complex (finally opened, after innumerable delays, in 1983).[50] This reflected a state-centered concept of Soviet interests in Africa, far removed from the national-democracy theories; whatever his merits, General Yakubu Gowon was in no sense a revolutionary democrat. Indeed, this commitment required a nimble reweaving of ethnosocial analysis, to transform Ibo from a progressive community into reactionaries and the erstwhile embodiments of feudalism and mercantile capitalism, the Hausa-Fulani and Yoruba, into worthy partners for progress.

The appearance of the Afro-Marxist state, in eight installments from 1969 to 1977, rekindled the interest in national democracies. While these states were viewed with some caution, they represented a very welcome trend. Since 1977, the process seems arrested, and indeed in one instance official Marxism-Leninism has been so strongly anesthetized, without formal renunciation, that one may doubt whether the doctrine can be reawakened (Somalia).[51] As well, the new wave of experiments in socialist orientation have in several cases experienced severe economic difficulties (especially Mozambique and Angola, partly but not wholly because of South African pressure and drought), and none but oil producers (Libya, Congo, Algeria) have had much developmental success. These facts have produced privately expressed doubts about the pedagogical value, in an immediate sense, of Soviet developmental experience.

The prickliness of some regimes where the Soviet involvement is most extensive (for example, Ethiopia) have also produced cautionary thoughts of the possible frustrations of overcommitment and the difficulties of finding adequate leverage even over such dependent clients as Mengistu Haile Meriam.[52] Mengistu has resisted repeated Soviet solicitations to fully launch the Leninist party the Soviets believe to be indispensable to the construction of a Leninist state core and, with equal persistence, has engaged them in one military fiasco after another in Eritrea, where Soviet military personnel have provided logistical support, while the Cubans have stood conspicuously aside.[53]

However, desite these frustrations, Soviet analysis has given increasing importance to the three African Marxist-Leninist states which, along with

South Yemen, constitute the "left wing" of national democracy, Angola, Ethiopia, and Mozambique. These are now seen in the words of an Algerian analyst, as states of "confirmed socialist orientation," whose ideological commitment to scientific socialism and advance along the noncapitalist pathway significantly beyond those of other Afro-Marxist states, and perhaps even those of such low-credibility members of the socialist camp as Afghanistan and Cambodia.[54] Of these three key states, Mozambique is doubtless the most important ideologically, though not strategically. It most closely approximates the structural requisites of scientific socialism, and its ruling party has conducted a sustained theoretical dialogue in the adaption of Marxism-Leninism to African conditions. It is no accident that Mozambique alone took the step of applying for admission to the Soviet-led economic community COMECON in 1981. The application (along with that of Laos) was rejected for the moment, apparently because of the lack of large-scale economic links with the Soviet bloc, Soviet reluctance to take on the economic aid obligations implicit in Mozambique COMECON membership, and apprehensions over the possible reversibility of the Mozambique ideological commitment. The special standing of the confirmed socialist orientation states is also demonstrated by the massive security commitments of the Soviet Union and its Cuban and East German allies in Angola and Ethiopia and the $2 billion aid pledge made to Angola in 1982 for infrastructure projects mainly in the Luanda hinterland within the political realm of the ruling MPLA.[55] The essential task, wrote one Soviet commentator, "is to ceaselessly consolidate, to render ever more stable and sure the situation of countries of socialist orientation."[56]

In the realm of strategic and military thought, some important developments deserve note. New types of warfare have become recognized, which greatly complicate the older classifications which recognized only (in addition to world wars) civil wars pitting the proletariat and its allies against classes tied to capitalism, wars between imperialist powers, and wars of national liberation. New kinds of Third World wars have emerged, lacking clearly defined class content: the Nigerian civil war and the Tanzanian invasion of Uganda, for example (and elsewhere, such imbroglios as India-Pakistan, or Iraq-Iran). As well, wars pitting states of socialist orientation against internal insurgents which cannot be classified as bourgeois elements have become important (Ethiopia, Angola, Mozambique). While the United States and subimperial powers such as South Africa (or China) can be blamed for these conflicts, they add a troublesome new dimension to Soviet analysis. The capacity of Soviet military support to contain such challenges is also viewed with less confidence.[57] Now, broadly, they appear to lead to a more complex analysis of overall African (and Third World) trends, which moves away from the earlier zero-sum assumptions that an American "loss" is automatically a Soviet "gain," and more explicitly recognizes that the logic of North-South developments operates somewhat differently than suggested by classical ideological versions of the struggle between capitalism and socialism, and inevitable historical progressions.

Clearly a major element in disturbing long-term policy equilibria lies in the realm of events. Dramatic, unforeseen episodes force sudden policy responses on all sides. In the African case, these would include the 1960 "Congo crisis"; the wave of 1965–66 coups; the Nigerian civil war of 1967–70; the coups in Portugal and Ethiopia in 1974, and the 1979 Iranian revolution. The final dramatic episode of the Congo crisis, the Lumumba assassination in January 1961, substantially aborted the regionalist project of the Kennedy administration before it really got underway. The 1965–66 coups affected both camps; in the United States, it contributed significantly to an emergent cynicism concerning African events, which removed the residual regionalist impulses in favor of the implicit globalism in the premise that African states were hopelessly weak and unstable and could only be realistically seen as subsidiary to the global struggle. On the Soviet side, the demise of several populist leaders in the coup epidemic (and the simultaneous fall of Sukarno in Indonesia) discredited for a time the national-democracy school of analysis.

The Nigerian civil war could not be fitted by either the United States or the Soviet Union into existing policy assumptions and alignments. African states as well were torn by this conflict, with four (Zambia, Tanzania, Gabon, Ivory Coast) actually recognizing the sessionist republic of Biafra, in flagrant contravention of extant African state values endorsing the sanctity of the colonial partition boundaries.[58] In the United States, the proficient Biafran information agencies brought deep fissures in the normally regionalist African affairs constituency, and reverberated within the policy community itself. The result was a hesitant and ambiguous support for the Federal Government, which—in its sharp contrast with Soviet backing—complicated relations with Nigeria for some years.

The Portuguese coup provoked a major reevaluation of American Southern African policy before the advent of the Carter administration; on the Soviet side, it produced a risky but highly successful intervention on the winning side in Angola. The Ethiopian revolutionary regime created a dramatic reversal of military partnerships in which each side had heavy investments; the Soviets had, from the early 1960s through 1977, provided training to 2,395 Somali officers, a higher figure than for any other African state except Egypt (Algeria, 2,195; Libya, 1,300, for example).[59] The United States had invested more in developing the Ethiopian military, from about 1952, than in any other

African state, and, up to that point, had cumulatively committed more in economic assistance to Ethiopia than to any other country in Africa.

The Islamic revolution in Iran was a dramatic episode which not only transformed the geopolitics of the Middle East, but also accelerated trends toward greater saliency of Islamic ideology in African politics. In its international implications, this process can be traced back to about 1961, when Saudi Arabia quietly began to counter the secular pan-Arab nationalist threat to its more theological polity by financing Islamic cultural and religious institutions in Africa. The 1967 and 1973 Arab-Israeli wars both had important spillover effects on the structure of African international relations, through imposing a choice between what Mobutu Sese Seko of Zaire in 1973 called the "brother" (Egypt) versus the "friend" (Israel). The 1973 and 1979 oil price surges placed vastly escalated resources in the hands of states whose international perspectives were shaped by Islamic orientations (in addition to Saudi Arabia, increasingly Libya). The fusion of radical anti-imperialism and militant Islam embodied in the Khomeini revolution gave a powerful impetus to this trend, linking Islamic ideology to state doctrine in new ways in states such as Sudan, Guinea, Morocco, and Algeria and bringing new issues to the fore in such secular states as Nigeria. The multiple reverberations of Islam, its powerful mass appeal, its quintessentially African and Arab roots, and its disjuncture with the ideological weapons of the superpowers (liberal capitalism and state socialism) create a potent and unpredictable new vector to African relations with the major powers.

Events not only force alteration of standing policy assumptions, but may alter the structure of forces within the policy community. This is most visible in the American case, where major crises, once they take on an East-West dimension, draw into the debate the security agencies which are, by organizational mentality and routine, wedded to geopolitical reason. They also force the debate into the White House, where a calculus of political cost and benefit on the domestic front not normally present in African policy formulation may enter the picture. As well, there will be a powerful tendency for globalist logic to dominate the discussions; a National Security Adviser to the President is role-cast as a globalist.

Beyond immediate events, several long-term processes may be identified which have an impact upon the Africa-America-Soviet triangle. The growing economic crisis in Africa is one evident trend, which became apparent in and out of Africa by the late 1970s. This was reflected in an economic report prepared for the 1979 Monrovia OAU meeting, which concluded, "Africa . . . is unable to point to any significant growth rate or satisfactory index of general well-being" after two decades of independence. This led both to the Lagos

Plan of Action and to the Berg Report for the World Bank.[60] Crises over food, debts, droughts, refugees, and generally mediocre economic performance have placed most African states in an extraordinarily precarious situation. On the one hand, this leads to some spectacularly mendacious behavior: Sierra Leone's sale of its attendance at the failed OAU summit in Tripoli to Libya;[61] Sudanese support of the Camp David settlement, followed by an increase of American aid from $6 to $90 million; Zairian resumption of relations with Israel in 1982, to cite but a few examples. These dependency-escalating trends tend to push Africa, in economic relations, toward the United States and its Western allies. The economic crisis has vitally muted African criticism of American African policy; one hears no more of the Nigerian "oil weapon." The Soviet Union, burdened by some very costly low-performance economies in its own immediate orbit (Cuba, Vietnam, Afghanistan, Poland), has neither the inclination nor the resources to make significant economic aid commitments in most of Africa, whose economic ills, in Soviet eyes, are in any event the fault and responsibility of "international capitalism." As Foreign Minister Andrei Gromyko recently put the matter, with his characteristic penchant for understatement, "The Soviet Union's potential for rendering economic assistance is not infinite."[62]

Even the most moderate African states, such as Ivory Coast, consider the Western response to the African economic crisis to be lacking in compassion, understanding, and especially scale; even the most radical, such as Mozambique, have multiplied their overtures toward private and public Western sources of help. Indeed, American aid to Africa, Egypt excepted, has long been constrained by the political limits on total aid levels and the political priorities which commit much of it to other crisis areas: Indochina in the 1960s and the Middle East since the Yom Kippur War and the exorbitantly expensive shuttle diplomacy by Secretary of State Kissinger, which followed it. In recent years, Israel and Egypt have each received between two and three times as much aid as all of sub-Saharan Africa, with Israel, Egypt, Jordan, and Syria absorbing nearly forty percent of the total aid outlays. In 1982, Syria alone—despite its frequent stigmatization by American officials as a Soviet pawn—received more aid than any African state except Egypt, Sudan, and Kenya ($86 million). In 1982, de St. Jorre characterized the general mood of Africa as a "loss of confidence . . . in their ability to regulate their interterritorial conflicts as well as in their capacity to develop their economies and cope with growing socioeconomic problems."[63] In seeking a similar theme for 1983, Whitaker employs the grimmer term of "survival."

A second, disquieting trend is the rising levels of interstate conflict within Africa. A series of regional theaters of prolonged crisis have emerged: Southern Africa, the Horn, Western Sahara, Chad. These have brought in their train

escalating levels of arms transfers, as the competitive pursuit of an elusive
security carries its costly dialectic.[64] As the Soviet Union has been more active in arms transfers than has the United States and has been willing to provide munitions to a wider range of states (Nigeria, Idi Amin's Uganda, Zambia, for example, as well as those of clearly socialist orientation), this factor
has tended to deepen relationships with the Soviet Union, particularly because
of the dependencies created by the shallow logistical capabilities of nearly all
African armies, except Egypt and South Africa. Thus weapons supply of ar-
mored vehicles, sophisticated artillery, naval craft, and especially aircraft
comes with a logistical leash; spare part supply, maintenance services, and
sometimes operational personnel are all subject to immediate withdrawal, in
which case the equipment becomes swiftly inoperative.

Related to this trend is the growing disposition of African states (and others) to deploy their military forces in other states: Morocco in Zaire in 1977
and 1978; Libya in Chad in 1980; Tanzania in Uganda in 1979, and in the
Seychelles, Zaire in Burundi in 1972, probably Central African Republic in
1979, and Chad in 1981 and 1983; Nigeria in Chad in 1981, Senegal in Gambia 1981. These instances are by no means limited to circumstances where
they are invited by incumbent regimes: South Africa invaded Angola in 1975
and has had armed forces permanently garrisoned in that country since 1981;
brief cross-border operations have been carried out in Mozambique, Lesotho,
and Zimbabwe. Zaire invaded Angola in 1975, Tanzania invaded Uganda in
1979, and Libya invaded Chad in 1983. Beyond these events is the supply of
palace guards to other regimes; Tanzanians in Seychelles, Guineans in Sierra
Leone, Moroccans in Equatorial Guinea. Extra-African contingents such as
Cubans, Palestinians, French, and Israelis also have been conspicuous in this
role. Progressively these interventions have corroded the civility of interstate
relations and created a psychological climate where armed interventions appear an inevitable part of the landscape. We are far removed from the shock
waves created by the French-British-Israeli invasion of the Suez in 1955 or the
furor created by French bombing of a Tunisian border village at Sakhiet-sidi-
Youssef in 1958.

Two African powers have shown a particular disposition for an aggressive
and militarized diplomacy, South Africa and Libya. Both have only recently
become significant military factors. Until 1960, South Africa spent less than 1
percent of its GNP on defense; from 1972 to 1978, outlays rose from $581
million to $2.6 billion.[65] Libya, from 1976 to 1980, purchased $8.6 billion in
weapons, $5.5 billion from the Soviet Union (and $12 billion since 1974).[66]

South Africa is by far the more important. In the 1980s, building upon
ambitions developed in the 1970s to create a regional cluster of client states
and its desire to deny bases to insurgent challengers, especially the African

National Congress (ANC), South Africa moved aggressively to join economic pressures with military action to tighten the squeeze on its neighboring states. For the weakest states, such as Lesotho, the combination of the 1982 Maseru commando raid, sanctuary for armed opposition to the Leabua Jonathan regime, and economic pressures forced this hostage state into abject compliance with South African demands that all refugees suspected of ANC links be expelled.

As Singleton has argued, these measures make available some inexpensive options for Soviet diplomacy. Soviet, Cuban, and East German presence in Angola, and to a much lesser extent in Mozambique, contributes to South African paranoic security policies and has the added advantage of strengthening the hand of those policy actors in the United States, particularly in security circles, who view South Africa as a "strategic asset." Thus, as Singleton points out, "The great irony is that the Soviet Union and South Africa, because they share an overwhelming interest in moving the United States into closer association with Pretoria, are tactical allies in the restructuring of southern Africa now under way."[67]

The Libyan objectives are less clear and appear to have changed over time. Qadafy has always dreamed of a larger, Arabo-Islamic realm; early in his career, he signed a series of merger agreements, with Egypt, Sudan, and Tunisia, in which he was prepared to be the junior partner. Since the middle 1970s, his projects have postulated a leading place for Libya. His loosely defined radical anti-imperial visions have opened his well-filled purse to revolutionary and violent movements from the Philippines to Ulster. Progressive deterioration of Libyan relations with the United States, which his militant anti-imperialistic positions began to erode from 1970, soon accelerated as his swelling oil revenues made possible massive Soviet arms purchases in the middle 1970s and financing of sundry groups falling into what were regarded as the "terrorist" category. While Qadafy is evidently not subject to Soviet instruction, his conception of anti-imperialism is unlikely to run seriously counter to Soviet views, and he pays cash, in hard currency, for his weapons. By the time of the Reagan administration, American official statements describing him as a cancer would give him every reason to believe that curative measures might be taken, enhancing the value of the Soviet connection.

The real potential for military action by Libya bears no comparison with that of South Africa. Libyan logistical capabilities are modest, even rudimentary. While relatively small forces, with some Libyan involvement and complete aerial supremacy, can oust a small, weakly trained Chad unit from a desert oasis in Faya-Largeau, they can certainly not penetrate the screen provided by a couple of thousand French troops with air support. But Libya nonetheless plays a significant role in the American-Soviet competition in Africa by the very fact that its behavior tends to be viewed within the policy community as that of a Soviet client or even proxy.[68]

To return to the query which began this analysis: Is it continuity or change which dominates African relations with the major powers? In my view, it is the broad continuities of principle, premise, and interest which stand out, imposing important limits on the possible range of variation. For the great powers, the official mind, however differently it is constituted, reasons on similar lines over time, despite the constant change in role occupants.

Yet there are also changes, some of great moment. The official mind is conditioned by a shifting array of contributers, whose relative influence varies over time. Great lurches may be generated by sudden events beyond the control of any actor. Long-term processes gradually alter the shape of the African arena: a cruel set of economic trends, a rising level of conflict on the continent, increasing tendencies toward military actions of the most diverse sorts.

African relations with the United States and the Soviet Union are perhaps best seen as a triangle, whose base, the American-Soviet relationship, is critical to the other two. The intensification of antagonisms observable since 1977, and especially since 1981, has sharpened their rivalries in Africa as elsewhere. An Africa battling for its survival is likely to be the loser unless detente can be disinterred from its burial place in the Ogaden and African diplomacy can achieve a more regionally defined pattern of relationships with both superpowers.

## NOTES

1. Mohammad A. El-Khawas, *The Kissinger Study of Southern Africa* (Westport; Conn.: L. Hill, 1976). This paper was drafted while in residence at the Woodrow Wilson International Center for Scholars, whose superb hospitality and support I gratefully acknowledge.

2. The concept is articulated in Chester Crocker, "South Africa: Strategy for Change," *Foreign Affairs*, LIX, 2 (Winter 1980), pp. 323–351; "A US Policy for the 1980s," *Africa Report*, XXVI, 1 (January–February 1981), pp. 7–14. For useful discussions, see Christopher Coker, "The United States and South Africa: Can Constructive Engagement Succeed?," *Millenium*, XI, 3 (Winter 1982–83), pp. 223–241, and John de St. Jorre, "Constructive Engagement: An Assessment," *Africa Report*, XXVIII, 5 (September–October 1983), pp. 48–51.

3. For a comprehensive review of this dimension, see Timothy M. Shaw and M. Catharine Newbury, "Dependence or Interdependence: Africa in the Global Political Economy," in Mark W. DeLancey (ed.), *Aspects of International Relations in Africa* (Bloomington: African Studies Program, Indiana University, 1979), pp. 39–89.

4. Robert L. Rothstein provides a useful review of this issue: *The Weak in the World of the Strong* (New York: Columbia University press, 1977).

5. Hedley Bull, *The Anarchical Society: A Study of Order in World Politics* (New York: Columbia University Press, 1977); Martin Wight, *Systems of States* (Leicester: Leicester University Press, 1977).

6. Julius K. Nyerere, "Some Questions About Assumptions," in Helen Kitchen (ed.), "Options for U.S. Policy toward Africa," *AEI Foreign Policy and Defense Review*, I, 1 (1979), pp. 22–23.

7. John de St. Jorre, "Africa: Crisis of Confidence," *Foreign Affairs*, LXI, 3 (1983), p. 680.

8. This emergent strategy is well analyzed in the *Economist*, 16 July 1983, pp. 19–28.

9. Henry Kissinger, *The White House Years* (Boston: Little, Brown, 1979), p. 119.

10. CIA support for the FNLA, and later UNITA, during the Angolan civil war is a partial exception to this rule; this occurred only after the question of liberation was settled and the issue was which group would inherit power. There have been some efforts to resume clandestine support for UNITA in 1978 and again in 1981, but these were blocked by 1975 congressional action.

11. Among the numerous sources concerning American-African relations in addition to those already mentioned, I have found particularly useful Henry F. Jackson, *From the Congo to Soweto: U.S. Foreign Policy Toward Africa since 1960* (New York: Williams Morrow and Company, 1982); "La politique africaine des Etats-Unis," special issue, *Politique Africaine*, 12 (December 1983); Helen Kitchen, *U.S. Interests in Africa* (New York: Praeger Publishers, 1983); the forthcoming symposium volume on African-American relations sponsored by the University of California, Los Angeles; Andrew Young, "The United States and Africa: Victory for Diplomacy," *Foreign Affairs*, LIX, 3 (1981), pp. 648–666; Pauline Baker, "The Lost Continent?" *SAIS Review*, III, 1 (Winter–Spring 1983), pp. 99–114; Francis A. Kornegay, *Washington and Africa: Reagan, Congress, and an African Affairs Constituency in Transition* (Washington: African Bibliographic Center, 1982); Michael Clough, *Changing Realities in Southern Africa: Implications for American Policy* (Berkeley: Institute of International Studies, University of California, Berkeley, 1982); John de St. Jorre, "Constructive Engagement: An Assessment," *Africa Report*, XXVIII, 5, (September–October 1983), pp. 48–51; Donald Rothchild, "U.S. Policy Styles in Africa," in Kenneth Oye, Donald Rothchild, and Ronald J. Lieber (eds.), *Eagle Entangled* (New York: Longman, 1979), pp. 304–335; John J. Stremlau (ed.), *The Foreign Policy Priorities of Third World States* (Boulder: Westview Press, 1980); Kenneth L. Adelman, *African Realities* (New York: Crane, Russak & Co., 1980); Marina Ottaway, *Soviet and American Influence in the Horn of Africa* (New York: Praeger Publishers, 1982); Robert Jaster, *Southern Africa in Conflict: Implications for U.S. Policies in the 1980s* (Washington: American Enterprise Institute, 1982); Anthony Lake, *The "Tar Baby" Option* (New York: Praeger, 1969); Frederick S. Arkhurst (ed.), *U.S. Policy toward Africa* (New York: Praeger, 1975); Rupert Emerson, *Africa and United States Policy* (Englewood Cliffs, N.J.: Prentice-Hall, 1967); Jennifer S. Whitaker (ed.), *Africa and the United States: Vital Interests* (New York: New York University Press, 1978); Robert M. Price, *U.S. Foreign Policy in Sub-Saharan Africa: National Interest and Global Strategy* (Berkeley: Institute of International Studies, University of California, Berkeley, 1978); Henry Bienen, "U.S. Foreign Policy in a Changing Africa," *Political Science Quarterly*, XCII, 1 (Spring 1977), pp. 47–64; René Lemarchand (ed.), *American Policy in Southern Africa: The Stakes and the Stance* (Washington: University Press of America, 1978).

12.  William J. Foltz, "United States Policy toward South Africa: Is One Possible?," conference on African Crisis Areas and American Foreign Policy, University of California, Los Angeles, March 1983, p. 1.

13.  Thus argued Assistant Secretary Crocker at the Zimbabwe African-American Institute meetings in 1983, articulating an assumption that transcends the globalist versus regionalist debate. His predecessor, Richard Moose, in testimony before the House of Representatives Subcommittee on Africa in March 1978, argued that a sudden vacuum in Zaire would be dangerous as "those people (the Soviets) tend to get their act together more quickly" than do local forces enjoying Western support.

14.  There are some modest qualifications that might be noted. The United States has quietly encouraged Sergeant Samuel Doe to introduce some form of constitution after his 1980 coup. During the "reform" efforts in Zaire in 1977–78, although the primary thrust was economic, Mobutu was asked to temper his personal autocracy with some openings for participation and accountability (partly on the assumption that this would lead to more rational economic policies).

15.  For a more extended discussion of the impact of African ideological preference on American policy, see Crawford Young, *Ideology and Development in Africa* (New Haven: Yale University Press, 1982), pp. 253–296.

16.  For a useful summary, see Kitchen, *U.S. Interests in Africa*.

17.  Quoted in Adelman, *African Realities*, pp. 12–13.

18.  United States Congress, House of Representatives, Subcommittee on Mines and Mining, Committee on Interior and Insular Affairs, *Sub-Saharan Africa: Its Role in Critical Mineral Needs of the Western World*, 96th Congress, Second Session (July 1980).

19.  For evidence placing the raw materials issue in less alarmist perspective, see United States Congress, House of Representatives, Subcommittee on Africa, Committee on Foreign Affairs, *The Possibility of a Resource War in Southern Africa*, 97th Congress, First Session (July 1981).

20.  For recent evidence on this score, see Jaster, *Southern Africa in Conflict*, pp. 23–31. For an argument laying much more stress on American economic interests, see Jackson, *From the Congo to Soweto*, pp. 169–201.

21.  Gordon Bertolin, "U.S. Economic Interests in Africa: Investment, Trade, and Raw Materials," in Whitaker (ed.), *Africa and the United States*, p. 27. In 1976, American investments in Libya ranked second to those in South Africa.

22.  James K. Cooley, "The Libyan Menace," *Foreign Policy*, 42 (Spring 1981), pp. 74–93.

23.  David E. Albright, *The USSR and Sub-Saharan Africa in the 1980s* (New York: Praeger, 1983), p. 35.

24.  Major studies of Soviet African policy include Robert Legvold, *Soviet Policy in West Africa* (Cambridge: Harvard University Press, 1970); Warren Weinstein (ed.), *Chinese and Soviet Aid to Africa* (New York: Praeger, 1975); Christopher A. Stevens, *The Soviet Union and Black Africa* (London: Macmillan, 1976); Roger Kanet, *The Soviet Union and the Developing Nations* (Baltimore: Johns Hopkins University Press, 1974); David Albright (ed.), *Communism in Africa* (Bloomington: Indiana University Press, 1980); Henry Bienen, "Soviet Political Relations with Africa," *International Security*, VI, 4 (Spring 1982), pp. 153–173; Marina Ottaway, *Soviet and American Influence in the Horn of Africa* (New York: Praeger, 1982); Milene Charles, *The Soviet Union and Africa* (Washington: University Press of America, 1980); Oye Ogunbadejo, "Soviet Policies in Africa," *African Affairs*, LXXIX, 316 (July 1980), pp. 297–325.

25. L. Ratham and H. Schilling, "The Non-Capitalist Development in Asia and Africa—Balance, Problems, Prospects," in Research Center for Africa and Asia, Bulgarian Academy of Sciences, *Developing Countries and the Non-Capitalist Road* (Sofia: 1974), p. 23, cited in Marina Ottaway, "Soviet Marxism and Socialism," *Journal of Modern African Studies*, XVI, 3 (September 1978), p. 480.

26. However, this point is diversely interpreted. At a colloquium of Soviet and American Africanists at Berkeley in November 1982, heated debate broke out among the Soviet participants on this issue, obviously central to Marxist-Leninist analysis.

27. R. Ulianovsky, *Socialism and the Newly-Independent Nations* (Moscow: Progress Publishers, 1974), p. 21.

28. V. F. Stanis, G. B. Khromushin, and V. P. Mozolin, *The Role of the State in Socio-Economic Reforms in Developing Countries* (Moscow: Progress Publishers, 1976), p. 9. The national democracy theory, in its present form, won official sanction at the 1961 summit conference of communist parties in Moscow. The theory may be traced back, however, to early debates in the Comintern in the 1920s, concerning strategies for combating imperialism and defining the socialist pathway in Asia and Africa; these are ably traced in Charles, *The Soviet Union and Africa*, pp. 4–23.

29. Ibid., p. 27.

30. This notion is developed by Kenneth Jowitt, "Scientific Socialist Regimes in Africa: Political Differentiation, Avoidance, and Unawareness," in Carl Rosberg and Thomas Callaghy (eds.), *Socialism in Sub-Saharan Africa: A New Assessment* (Berkeley: University of California Institute of International Studies, 1979), pp. 151–158.

31. Quoted by David Morrison, *African Contemporary Record*, 1976–1977, p. A78. see also Mark N. Katz, *The Third World in Soviet Military Thought* (Baltimore: Johns Hopkins University Press, 1982). Not all Soviet commentators have agreed on this assessment of the military.

32. Anatoly Gromyko, "Present Stage of the Anti-Imperialist Struggle in Africa," *Social Sciences*, X, 4 (1979), p. 29.

33. Nikolai Kosukhin, "Revolutionary Democracy: Its Ideology and Policies," *Social Sciences*, X, 4 (1979), p. 51.

34. Freidel Trappen and Ulbricht Weishauft, "Aktuelle Fragen des Kamfes um Nationale and Social Befreiung in Subsaharischen Afrika," *Deutsche Aussenpolitik*, XXIV, 2 (February 1979), p. 30. I am grateful to Melvin Croan for drawing this citation to my attention.

35. Alvin Z. Rubinstein, *Red Star on the Nile* (Princeton: Princeton University Press, 1977).

36. Public-sector industrial projects and mineral surveys have been the two leading spheres of Soviet economic assistance programs; Robert S. Walters, *American & Soviet Aid: A Comparative Assessment* (Pittsburgh: University of Pittsburgh Press, 1970), p. 140. See also Arthur Jay Klinghoffer, *The Soviet Union & International Oil Politics* (New York: Columbia University Press, 1977).

37. By my classification, these include Morocco, Libya, Egypt, Sudan, Ethiopia, Somalia, Uganda, Burundi, Zaire, Congo, Equatorial Guinea, Ghana, Upper Volta, Mauritania, Guinea, Madagascar, Comoros, Mauritius, Seychelles.

38. *Ottaway, Soviet and American Influence*, demonstrates in great detail the intimate relationship between Somali unification visions and the shifting global alignments of Somalia.

39. W. Scott Thompson, *Ghana's Foreign Policy 1957–1966* (Princeton: Princeton University Press, 1969). For Nkrumah's account of his secret accord with Patrice

Lumumba in 1960 to bring Zaire (then Congo) into his union, see Kwame Nkrumah, *Challenge to the Congo* (New York: International Publishers, 1967).

40. For an excellent discussion of the bureaucratic politics dimension, see Anthony Lake, *The "Tar Baby" Option* (New York: Columbia University Press, 1976).

41. Thomas Franck and Edward Weisband, *Foreign Policy by Congress* (New York: Oxford University Press, 1979).

42. See the valuable study by Francis A. Kornegay, *Reagan, Congress, and an Affairs Constituency in Transition* (Washington: African Bibliographic Center, 1982). Excellent coverage of Afro-American efforts to influence African policy is found in Jackson, *From the Congo to Soweto,* pp. 121–168.

43. At a gathering of his supporters following these votes, 27 October 1983.

44. For a detailed case history of its adoption, see Lake, *The "Tar Baby" Option,* pp. 199–238.

45. Kitchen, *U.S. Interests in Africa,* pp. 9–11; Kornegay, *Reagan, Congress, and an African Affairs Constituency,* pp. 22–25.

46. Kitchen, *U.S. Interests in Africa,* p. 9. Lake, *The "Tar Baby" Option,* makes the same point, directing his fire particularly on the American Committee on Africa, which he charges with aiming its salvos primarily at its sole potential ally in the policy apparatus, the Bureau of African Affairs; p. 71.

47. Kitchen, *U.S. Interests in Africa,* pp. 11–12.

48. To a more limited extent, the 1960–61 Congo crisis provided a similar lesson; for the most careful study of the global diplomacy in this affair, see Madeleine Kalb, *The Congo Cables* (New York: Macmillan Publishing Company, 1982). During the Brezhnev era, Soviet military analysts were permitted to express doctrinal analysis which diverged from existing positions, though not to challenge party authority; Katz, *The Third World in Soviet Military Thought.*

49. Lawrence Caldwell and Robert Legvold, "Reagan Through Soviet Eyes," *Foreign Policy,* 52 (Fall 1983), pp. 3–21.

50. Oye Ogunbadejo, "Ideology and Pragmatism: The Soviet Role in Nigeria, 1960–1977," *Orbis,* xxi, 4 (Winter 1978), pp. 803–830; John J. Stremlau, *The International Politics of the Nigerian Civil War 1967–1970* (Princeton: Princeton University Press, 1977).

51. In the postrupture Congress of the Somali Revolutionary Socialist Party (srsp), created only in 1976 on Soviet prodding, the nominal commitment to scientific socialism was reaffirmed; Ottaway, *Soviet and American Influence,* pp. 119–122.

52. These limits are amply documented in Ibid., pp. 137–151.

53. Soviet participants in the 1982 Berkeley Soviet-American colloquium made these points in private conversation. On the Cuban role, see Carmelo Mesa-Lago and June S. Belkin (eds.), *Cuba in Africa* (Pittsburgh: Center for Latin American Studies, University of Pittsburgh, 1982).

54. See the well-documented study by Zaki Laidi, "L'URSS et l'Afrique: vers une extension du système socialiste mondiale?" *Politique Etrangere,* 4 (1983), pp. 679–699.

55. Ibid., p. 689.

56. B. Ponomarev, "La cause de la liberté et du socialisme est invincible," *Nouvelle Revue Internationale,* 1 (January 1981), p. 28, cited in Laidi, "L'URSS et L'Afrique," p. 684.

57. Mark Katz, "The Third World in Soviet Military Thought," Woodrow Wilson Center, Washington, 26 October 1983; Robert Legvold, "The Soviet View of the

Changing International Political System," Woodrow Wilson Center, 12 October 1983;
Seth Singleton, "The Shared Tactical Goals of South Africa and the Soviet Union,"
*csis Africa Notes*, 12 (26 April 1983).

58. See Crawford Young, "Comparative Claims to Political Sovereignty: Biafra,
Katanga, Eritea," in Donald Rothchild and Victor A. Olorunsola (eds.), *State Versus
Ethnic Claims: African Policy Dilemmas* (Boulder: Westview Press, 1983); Stremlau,
*The International Politics of the Nigerian Civil War*.

59. National Foreign Assessment Center, Central Intelligence Agency, *Communist
Aid Activities in Non-Communist Less Developed Countries, 1979 and 1954–79* (October 1980).

60. International Bank for Reconstruction and Development, *Accelerated Development in Sub-Saharan Africa* (Washington: 1981).

61. de St. Jorre, "Africa: Crisis of Confidence," p. 678.

62. Albright, *The USSR and Sub-Saharan Africa*, p. 36.

63. de St. Jorre, "Africa: Crisis of Confidence." The Jennifer Whitaker article is
forthcoming in the 1984 annual review issue of *Foreign Affairs*.

64. For recent data, see inter alia Ruth Leger Sivald, *World Military and Social
Expenditures 1982* (Leesburg, Virginia: World Priorities, 1982).

65. Chester A. Crocker, "Current and Projected Military Banaces in Southern Africa," in Richard E. Bissell and Chester A. Crocker (eds.), *South Africa in the 1980s*
(Boulder: Westview Press, 1979).

66. de St. Jorre, "Africa: Crisis of Confidence," p. 683.

67. Singleton, "The Shared Tactical Goals," p. 1.

68. For recent analysis, see Alex Rondos, "Why Chad?" *Africa Notes*, 18 (31 August 1983); Eric Rouleau, "Guerre et intoxication au Tchad," *Le Monde Diplomatique*, 354 (September 1983).

CHAPTER 10

# International Assistance and International Capitalism: Supportive or Counterproductive?

*S. K. B. Asante*

## I. Introduction

One of the more significant contemporary issues in African economic development which have generated extensive debate in the literature during the past twenty-five years relates to the overall impact of external resources on development. Studies like the World Bank–sponsored Pearson Commission Report (1970)[1] have presented arguments contending that external assistance, by adding to the resources available to a developing country, has had a positive impact upon development. The central theme of the Pearson Report, therefore, is the uncompromising advocacy of a large and sustained expansion of intergovernmental aid to the developing countries, to enable them to achieve self-sustaining growth by the end of the century. Quantitative studies which support this contention have also been published.[2] The Pearson Report has in recent years been given a new lease of life with the publication of the two Brandt Commission Reports (1980 and 1983)[3] and, more importantly within the special African context, the African Report of the World Bank, *An Agenda for Action* or the Berg Report.[4] This widely publicized World Bank Report, about which more later, has reinforced the main theme of the Pearson Report and strongly advocated the importance of external resources in African economic development. Its fundamental message is that "accelerated development" can only be achieved through increased external assistance.

On the other hand, some critics have argued that external assistance is no more than a new form of neocolonialism or dependency relationships designed to benefit the donor rather than the recipient countries.[5] Studies have been published indicating a negative impact of international assistance and foreign capitalism upon economic growth and well-being. Development econo-

**249**

mists like Griffin and Bauer have gone as far as to assert that "capital imports, rather than accelerating development have in some cases retarded it." It is contended that external assistance may even be inimical to greater self-reliance and to desirable structural reorganization in recipient nations, and that aid even as charity may be bad as an instrument of economic development in the recipient's country.[6]

What must be stressed is that although various forms of external assistance were extended to Africa at the time of independence "to accelerate the pace of growth and modernization," the economic development of the African countries has continued to lag, and the gap between the rich donor nations and the poor recipient African countries to widen. This failure of international resources to effect the necessary changes in economic structures and relationships since independence, coupled with the dismal developmental prospects for Africa in the 1980s and beyond, has led to two diametrically opposed responses to the current continental economic crisis. On the one hand, increasing "commitment to larger aid flows in the 1980s" is vigorously advocated in the World Bank Report and fosters more reliance on the international economic system. On the other hand, there is an emergence of a refreshing emphasis on the importance of indigenously determined national, subregional, and regional priorities and of self-reliant development strategies as strongly espoused in the Organization of African Unity's *Lagos Plan of Action*.[7] This historic document constitutes the first comprehensive continent-wide formulation and articulation of the preferred long-term economic and development objectives of African countries.

Without falling into either extreme category, this chapter attempts to do two things. First, it argues that while substantial external resources may in some cases have the potential for accelerating economic development, evidence available in Africa suggests that international capitalism's aid programs, as currently administered, are frequently counterproductive. Moreover, they have resulted in a growing debt burden on African countries, precipitating acute balance of payments problems and severe restrictions upon the conduct of domestic economic policy. The second main concern of this essay is to examine critically the extent to which African countries have responded to the disillusioning performance of their political economies. Before considering some of these issues, it would seem appropriate to set the stage with a brief review of the key concepts of this study.

## II. The Key Concepts

The literature on "international assistance" and "international capitalism" in their various forms is vast, sophisticated, and sometimes controversial. It is not intended to survey the literature on these concepts in any detail. For as Judith Hart, the ex–British Minister of the Overseas Development Ministry, has candidly admitted, much of what goes under the rubric of aid is highly questionable.[8] Commonly termed "foreign aid," international assistance was originally used to cover various activities—defense support, market expansion, foreign investment, missionary enterprise, general postwar rehabilitation, cultural extension, and multilateralism. However, since 1961 when the Foreign Assistance Act replaced the old Mutual Security Act as the legislative basis for the United States aid programs, international assistance has been focused largely on long-range assistance to promote economic and social development.[9] The only real means of promoting this goal is, in effect, through capital and technical assistance.

As an important aspect of foreign assistance, technical assistance, as Karl Mathiasen III noted in the sixties, "remains a poorly understood tool for promoting development."[10] Simply put, this type of international assistance "consists in the transmission of learning, knowledge, and techniques or material and human resources in order to help those who receive it to solve specific problems in more suitable manner in keeping with their needs."[11] It is an external contribution which assumes a very wide variety of forms, including visits of experts and technicians, exchange or dissemination of information or documents, or supply of material and equipment. Technical assistance makes up a very high proportion of the official development assistance to independent African states—roughly half of the value received in terms of grant equivalents.

Gerald Helleiner refers to technical assistance as "human capital" and considers it as the most important form of capital flow, whether public or private. In his view, the main bottleneck restricting development in Africa "is at present human" rather than physical or financial capital or foreign exchange, for the economies of Africa have a "limited absorptive capacity for further financial aid."[12] Sidney Sufrin shares this view and argues that international assistance should be focused on knowledge and information, with material and financing being of secondary importance.[13] But much of the impact of foreign assistance on Africa depends on the quality and appropriateness of experts provided under technical assistance schemes.

An important form of international assistance which has played a dominant role in the development of African economy is international capitalism or direct foreign investment characterized by the activities of Transnational Corporations (TNCs). Broadly defined, a TNC is a large firm which undertakes direct foreign investment in two or more countries; that is, it owns productive assets in a number of countries.[14] TNCs are responsible for the bulk of direct foreign investment to Africa, but they must be distinguished analytically from foreign investment as they also contribute other factors—skills, technology, etc.—along with the capital that they invest.[15] The former Secretary of State Henry Kissinger once suggested that the TNCs are "one of the most effective engines of development."[16]

Thus the two operative concepts of this chapter—international assistance and international capitalism—are closely related to the issue of development, or more specifically economic development in Africa, which has been the primary objective of African states since attaining independence. Within the context of this essay, then, "international resources" or "foreign aid" in its various forms and "economic development" have come to be so closely linked as to be almost interchangeable. Since much empirical knowledge already has been accumulated on economic development, it is not necessary to dwell here on well-known facts, or to start defining already well-known concepts. Suffice it to say that modern theories of economic development investigate the process by which a poor, stagnant economy like that of Africa "can be transformed into one whose normal condition is sustained growth."

There is general agreement on the principal changes that characterize this transformation: an increase in human skills, a rise in the level of investment and saving, the adoption of more productive technology, a substantial change in the composition of output and employment, the development of new institutions.[17] The question that poses itself, therefore, is this: To what extent have foreign assistance and external capitalism encouraged or hindered such changes in Africa? Put differently, how far have external resources eased the constraints on economic development in Africa?

### III. Development Constraints and the White Man's Burden

In attempting to review the postindependence development policies and constraints of the sub-Saharan African countries, an analyst is immediately confronted by the enormous variety of policy choices and diversity of problems. To do justice to this richness of experience would require a separate study of over fifty odd countries. What is done here, therefore, is to highlight the common development strategies and constraints upon development.

Since coming into power, the new African leaders had been absorbed in the immediate task of governing and in the urgent drive for economic progress. The ultimate objective was to bring about the reality of the "nation" in their respective countries by creating independent states out of the colonial territories. These leaders were acutely aware that the new political units which had resulted from the breakup of the Western colonial empires were as yet "by no means always 'nations'; rather they represent the shells of territorial independence in which the kernel of national identity has been planted by the independence movements."[18] It therefore became the major task of the new African governments to provide the soil in which "the seed can grow." The most urgent feature of this task was to promote national unity and especially economic development. In the latter case governments pledged themselves to programs of modernization and development of the economy designed to bring to their people the benefits of the higher living standards that industrial and technological skills have brought to other parts of the world. This was held to be a logical sequence to the attainment of political independence.

During the early years of independence, each of the African governments took some steps to promote industrial development as a means of bringing about a much greater rate of economic growth than was achieved in the past under colonial rule. The rationale behind the thrust to industrialize was manifold. The rapid transformation of the Soviet Union into an industrialized power, achieved with the help of comprehensive national planning, had a definite influence on the newly independent governments of many African countries. Besides, expansion of industry was thought to have considerable external effects on development "in the form of learning processes, modernization of attitudes, and promotion of managerial skills." With this in mind, many African governments commissioned special studies, prepared development programs, created development agencies, and appropriated funds. These programs sought to bring about more fundamental changes in the economic structure inherited at independence. But it soon became appallingly apparent that, mostly as a consequence of their colonial heritage and subsequent integration into the world system, there were formidable bottlenecks to development. Progress in a majority of African countries was effectively constrained by the insufficient availability of some crucial resource.

One of these crucial constraints was the acute scarcity of trained indigenous manpower: technical, managerial, and administrative cadres. More serious perhaps, the available skills were not particularly well geared to the development effort. Thus at a time when most African governments were poised to embark on bold new development programs, the higher-level skills that existed within the boundaries of these new nations were, especially in the case of Zaire, Zambia, Tanzania, and Kenya, sadly almost unavailable. Because of their poverty, many of these countries found it hard to afford adequate training for a sufficient number of nationals to supply the skills required in the development effort.

The two other resource bottlenecks were domestic capital formation and foreign exchange, both of which might also be explained in terms of the colonial heritage. In the case of the latter, for example, the heavy concentration on primary commodity exports, along with the undiversified structure of the economy, were to a great extent a result of colonial status and constituted a strong tie between the colony and the mother country. As Radetzki notes, this one-sidedness of the structure of the domestic economy, coupled with the absence of capital goods production, "necessitated a very high import content in the development expenditure." [19] Particularly was this the case when it is realized that the modern technologies of the industries that had been set up were not only capital and skill intensive, but also import intensive.

Since success of the transformation of the economy required a simultaneous increase in skills, domestic savings, and export earnings which were extremely limited and, in some cases nonexistent, African governments had to rely on external resources which could make possible fuller use of domestic resources and hence accelerate growth. Some of the potential bottlenecks—of skills, savings, and foreign exchange—could then be temporarily relaxed by adding external resources for which current payment was not required. It was generally argued that capital assistance plus technical assistance to improve use of both domestic and external capital would enable the creation of conditions for self-sustaining economic growth. Besides, international capitalism or direct foreign investment would also have a positive impact on economic development. Such investment would fill important resource gaps in African countries and improve the quality of factors of production. It would provide capital which might not otherwise be available because of a low level of domestic saving and because access to bonds and other portfolio finance from developed countries was very limited. More importantly, direct foreign investment would bring with it a complementary package of inputs, notably managerial and marketing expertise, knowledge of technical processes not easily obtainable by other means, and scarce labor skills. There seemed to be no strong reason to doubt that well-thought-out external resources could promote development in Africa. Not surprisingly, since independence African countries have negotiated loans, entered into bilateral and multilateral aid agreements, and offered various incentives or inducements to investors.

Both the World Bank Report and development economists like Gerald Helleiner are agreed that sub-Saharan Africa has been a particularly favored beneficiary of concessional external assistance. [20] As a share of imports and of GNP, official development assistance, Helleiner has noted, "looms larger in most tropical African countries than the rest of the Third World." [21] Thus an essential component of Africa's economic development has been the continuing import of capital from abroad. The World Bank Report has shown that a net Official Development Assistance (ODA) per capita in 1980 was $13.70 for Africa compared with $9.60 for all developing countries. [22] Table 1 below sets forth details of net disbursements of ODA by Development Assistance Committee (DAC) countries combined to individual receipts for the period 1976 to 1982.

Also to be noted is technical assistance, which makes up a very high proportion of the official development assistance to independent African states—"roughly half of the value received in terms of grant-equivalents." In the late 1970s, about 25 percent of ODA was in the form of technical assistance grants.[23] These large external resources in their various forms have been transferred not only to individual African countries but also to African regional groupings. What has been the impact of this massive flow of external resources on the economic development of Africa?

Despite the massive transfer of resources to ease the constraints on development, the reality of today is that the economic transformation of the continent that was expected to follow closely on the heels of political independence still remains only a hope. There has been no marked improvement in many African economies since 1960. Zulu and Nsouli of the International Monetary Fund (IMF) in a recent study have analyzed the manifestations of sluggish economic growth, rising inflation rates, and widening deficits on the aggregate current account of the balance of payments in African countries during the 1970s. Real per capita income declined while "the rate of inflation approximately doubled, reaching an average annual rate of over 20 percent during 1977–1979." The combined current account deficit of the balance of payments "rose from about $4 billion in 1974 to close to $10 billion annually in 1978–79."[24] This continental condition has been well-described by Adebayo Adedeji, the Executive Secretary of the Economic Commission for Africa (ECA):

> The African economy today is still basically underdeveloped: low per capita income, a very high proportion of the population engaged in agriculture, low levels of productivity, a circumscribed and fractured industrial base, a high dependence on a vulnerably narrow spectrum of primary export commodities, a transport network geared largely to the export sector . . . a high degree of illiteracy, low levels of life expectancy. . . .[25]

Thus, if Africa's inheritance from colonialism in 1960, when external resources began to be injected into the economy, was "inauspicious," to borrow Timothy Shaw's description, by 1980 it has become even less promising. For while the post–Bretton Woods global inflation and recession in the mid-1970s might have intensified the African crisis, it was certainly not the fundamental cause of the present condition. Given Africa's incorporation in, and dependence on, the world system, a phenomenon which has greatly been accentuated by its almost absolute reliance on foreign assistance and external forces, the continent had less resources and resilience than any other region to withstand the global shocks of the mid-seventies.

TABLE 1

Net Disbursements of Official Development Assistance by DAC Countries
Combined to Individual Receipts

|  | 1976 | 1977 | 1978 | 1979 | 1980 | 1981 | 1982 |
|---|---|---|---|---|---|---|---|
| NORTH OF SAHARA |  |  |  |  |  |  |  |
| Algeria | 128.8 | 112.7 | 118.8 | 97.6 | 117.6 | 146.1 | 248.6 |
| Egypt | 428.1 | 617.0 | 860.2 | 1,011.6 | 1,187.0 | 1,105.4 | 1,236.8 |
| Libya | 6.4 | 5.3 | 4.0 | 1.9 | 9.9 | 2.0 | 2.4 |
| Morocco | 147.4 | 158.7 | 180.4 | 168.8 | 187.8 | 208.9 | 229.5 |
| Tunisia | 150.5 | 164.2 | 252.7 | 151.1 | 157.7 | 161.6 | 150.1 |
| North of Sahara |  |  |  |  |  |  |  |
| Unallocated | 6.2 | 6.2 | 8.2 | 14.9 | 3.0 | 0.7 | 11.2 |
| TOTAL | 867.4 | 1,064.1 | 1,424.3 | 1,445.9 | 1,663.0 | 1,624.7 | 1,878.4 |
| SOUTH OF SAHARA |  |  |  |  |  |  |  |
| Angola | 10.6 | 7.9 | 28.9 | 29.4 | 35.8 | 39.4 | 40.0 |
| Benin | 27.5 | 26.6 | 30.3 | 48.6 | 35.7 | 45.0 | 40.9 |
| Botswana | 40.6 | 38.1 | 55.1 | 73.6 | 83.5 | 75.9 | 83.2 |
| Burundi | 25.9 | 28.8 | 38.6 | 44.1 | 59.7 | 64.9 | 75.2 |
| Cameroon | 88.0 | 122.5 | 117.2 | 183.8 | 171.4 | 134.2 | 155.3 |
| Cape Verde | 6.8 | 15.8 | 25.0 | 27.2 | 39.0 | 36.3 | 42.6 |
| Central African |  |  |  |  |  |  |  |
| Republic | 25.7 | 30.2 | 29.7 | 51.2 | 75.1 | 72.8 | 68.8 |
| Chad | 43.2 | 49.6 | 70.9 | 49.4 | 20.2 | 31.3 | 35.3 |
| Comoros | 8.4 | 1.8 | 1.8 | 6.3 | 13.4 | 17.8 | 14.2 |
| Congo | 46.0 | 32.7 | 44.7 | 50.1 | 55.4 | 42.7 | 59.5 |
| Djibouti | 28.1 | 32.7 | 29.3 | 19.0 | 32.0 | 36.3 | 44.4 |
| Equatorial Guinea | – | – | – | 0.1 | 1.2 | 4.3 | 5.1 |
| Ethiopia | 72.8 | 59.0 | 56.0 | 70.5 | 91.4 | 76.2 | 76.9 |
| Gabon | 30.3 | 23.6 | 36.9 | 26.8 | 49.1 | 35.9 | 58.0 |
| Gambia | 5.4 | 12.6 | 14.8 | 13.2 | 16.5 | 19.2 | 23.6 |
| Ghana | 34.0 | 52.0 | 57.2 | 88.6 | 107.1 | 87.4 | 65.5 |
| Guinea | 4.4 | 5.1 | 9.9 | 14.2 | 32.5 | 31.2 | 26.8 |
| Guinea-Bissau | 11.8 | 26.1 | 36.8 | 33.9 | 34.4 | 41.4 | 33.7 |
| Ivory Coast | 75.6 | 75.2 | 85.7 | 138.6 | 151.9 | 91.2 | 102.2 |
| Kenya | 137.0 | 121.2 | 186.7 | 283.8 | 276.6 | 362.9 | 333.4 |
| Lesotho | 18.0 | 20.7 | 29.1 | 43.7 | 59.6 | 59.2 | 53.4 |
| Liberia | 21.2 | 21.7 | 22.0 | 30.4 | 60.0 | 86.4 | 85.2 |
| Madagascar | 29.2 | 32.6 | 39.6 | 73.5 | 90.8 | 93.4 | 159.2 |
| Malawi | 46.2 | 54.1 | 56.4 | 92.0 | 75.6 | 82.1 | 65.2 |
| Mali | 53.3 | 60.9 | 93.0 | 93.9 | 131.4 | 133.0 | 96.3 |
| Mauritania | 17.8 | 24.8 | 39.6 | 35.4 | 53.5 | 66.7 | 61.8 |
| Mauritius | 10.7 | 12.5 | 18.1 | 24.3 | 25.2 | 47.7 | 30.8 |
| Mayotte | – | 6.9 | 12.9 | 18.2 | 22.7 | 14.7 | 12.7 |

TABLE 1 (continued)

|  | 1976 | 1977 | 1978 | 1979 | 1980 | 1981 | 1982 |
|---|---|---|---|---|---|---|---|
| SOUTH OF SAHARA |  |  |  |  |  |  |  |
| Mozambique | 34.3 | 65.9 | 75.3 | 114.3 | 114.8 | 110.0 | 160.6 |
| Niger | 80.1 | 59.4 | 77.7 | 116.7 | 105.0 | 122.5 | 123.6 |
| Nigeria | 46.3 | 28.7 | 23.7 | 10.6 | 17.3 | 16.7 | 16.6 |
| Reunion | 301.0 | 317.0 | 371.4 | 391.8 | 486.7 | 633.6 | 397.3 |
| Rwanda | 56.6 | 61.4 | 78.9 | 88.4 | 96.6 | 102.6 | 99.0 |
| St. Helena | 2.8 | 4.2 | 7.1 | 8.4 | 8.8 | 8.2 | 10.2 |
| Sao Tome and Principe | 0.8 | 1.6 | 1.8 | 1.4 | 1.2 | 1.8 | 3.8 |
| Senegal | 81.6 | 89.3 | 121.6 | 148.8 | 181.9 | 214.6 | 189.0 |
| Seychelles | 6.9 | 10.2 | 15.8 | 22.0 | 18.3 | 13.7 | 14.7 |
| Sierra Leone | 7.5 | 12.0 | 13.5 | 28.2 | 56.8 | 34.0 | 55.7 |
| Somalia | 20.1 | 25.2 | 46.8 | 49.8 | 139.4 | 139.8 | 141.6 |
| Sudan | 54.4 | 55.8 | 113.0 | 149.3 | 271.6 | 294.8 | 357.3 |
| Swaziland | 9.0 | 21.6 | 33.1 | 31.8 | 32.5 | 23.6 | 18.7 |
| Tanzania | 212.0 | 257.3 | 332.3 | 457.4 | 523.1 | 484.7 | 483.7 |
| Togo | 20.5 | 42.4 | 66.5 | 68.9 | 52.1 | 36.9 | 50.4 |
| Uganda | 9.6 | 3.8 | 7.5 | 16.1 | 42.3 | 78.7 | 52.8 |
| Upper Volta | 60.1 | 71.7 | 96.6 | 132.0 | 151.1 | 158.0 | 147.0 |
| Zaire | 148.7 | 170.9 | 204.0 | 288.7 | 316.8 | 277.1 | 250.8 |
| Zambia | 55.6 | 95.5 | 164.5 | 211.9 | 233.8 | 178.5 | 188.5 |
| Zimbabwe | 6.2 | 6.7 | 8.5 | 12.4 | 110.4 | 136.9 | 141.9 |
| East African Community | 19.2 | 6.7 | 12.5 | 3.4 | 5.5 | 5.0 | 4.2 |
| DOM/TOM Unallocated | 0.8 | 24.9 | – | – | – | – | – |
| EAMA Unallocated | 4.6 | 85.7 | 123.4 | 130.1 | 94.7 | 2.1 | 4.6 |
| TOTAL | 2,228.5 | 2,548.3 | 3,315.4 | 4,198.0 | 5,009.9 | 5,103.9 | 5,097.8 |
|  |  |  |  |  |  |  |  |
| Africa Unspecified | 42.0 | 71.1 | 95.5 | 114.4 | 141.5 | 128.7 | 132.6 |
| AFRICA TOTAL | 3,137.8 | 3,683.5 | 4,835.2 | 5,758.4 | 6,814.4 | 6,857.2 | 7,108.8 |

Source: OECD, Geographical Distribution of Financial Flows to Developing Countries (Paris: 1984)

This appalling condition has placed a considerable doubt about the effectiveness of external resources as a crucial prerequisite for growth in Africa. Thus the decade of the 1980s has reopened the old debate about the actual benefits of international resources and their various manifestations: foreign capital, foreign technology, foreign expertise, foreign theories of development and economic growth, and all other foreign stimuli. This has given rise in recent years to a series of such crucial questions as the following: Is foreign assistance really directed toward relieving the recipient African country's resource constraints? Is it provided in a form which will help in overcoming these constraints? And, in any case, when one government lends to another at less-than-commercial interest rates so that the borrower can buy capital goods from the lending government's country, how much of the loan is aid, how much of it is an export subsidy, and how much of it is just a straight business deal? Are the aid resources efficiently used and suitably combined with domestic inputs in bringing about the specific objectives pursued? What is the quality and relevance of the knowledge and experience transferred with the aid personnel? Does aid contribute to a more smoothly functioning system for resource allocation, or does it reinforce market and price distortions existing in the recipient African country? How well conceived are the technologies, policies, and institutions introduced and promoted by the aid effort for the circumstances prevailing in the recipient African country? Are they creating economic and social enclaves, or do they help in the integration of the country's political, social, and economic structure? And, finally, what role do the African governments play in the administration of external resources? How far have they pursued policies which support economic growth and the general well-being of the mass of the people? And to what extent are they committed to the issue of development in their countries?

These questions cannot be conclusively answered here a priori. To throw light on some of them, two case studies have been adopted—first, the experience of an African country with foreign resources and, second, foreign aid to an African regional grouping—to illustrate the impact of external assistance on economic development.

## IV. Foreign Resources: Help or Hindrance?

### THE CASE OF SOMALIA

The experience of the Democratic Republic of Somalia with diversity of foreign resources illustrates a unique case of a typically poor African country which depended almost entirely on foreign assistance for development on attaining independence in July 1960.[26] One of the poorest countries of the world, with an estimated income per capita of about $50, Somalia was unquestionably one of the largest recipients of foreign aid during 1964–69, with an annual average of about $15 per head of its then 3 million population. This rate of aid is more than "three times the figure of $4.5 per capita," which, according to the Pearson Report, represents the average annual aid to other developing countries during 1964–67.[27] Of considerable significance is the fact that about 85 percent of Somalia's total development expenditure up to the end of 1969 was externally financed, whereas in other developing countries "typically foreign resources account for only about 10 percent of total investment expenditure." [28] This is a rare case of dependence on foreign financing among developing countries. Thus Somalia's development in the 1960s presents not only a unique example of development with foreign resources; it also presents a unique opportunity for a case study of the effectiveness of foreign assistance to a country at an early stage of development.

Unable to undertake any significant scale of economic development by itself, given its meagre domestic resources and other crucial constraints on development, Somalia relied almost entirely on loans and grants from abroad to finance its First Five-Year Plan, 1963–1967, which was estimated at a total of 1,400 million Somali shillings or about $200 million. This was followed in 1968 by a two-year Short-Term Development Program launched to consolidate the work of the first plan. Similarly, there was almost complete reliance on foreign economic assistance in financing development projects detailed in the program. Aid, both bilateral and multilateral (in order of magnitude), poured in from the USSR, the USA, the European Economic Community (EEC) under the Yauonde regime, the World Bank, the United Nations, the Federal Republic of Germany, Italy, China, Saudi Arabia, and others.[29] This took a diversity of forms: "tied aid," technical assistance, "soft" or concessional loans, commercial loans at relatively low rates of interest but for short to medium terms, and, finally, food aid.

Although aid inflows were substantial on a per capita basis, the first decade in the life of independent Somalia "closed with little demonstrable progress" toward the objectives spelt out in the development programs. The great hopes and the ambitious attempt at social and economic development remained merely a dream. According to a special report by a German Planning and Economic Advisor Group, evidence "suggests that living standards, on average, were lower at the close of the decade than at its beginning." [30] What, then, had gone wrong? What useful role did foreign resources play in the development programs of Somalia? What sort of contribution did foreign assistance make toward the economic development of Somalia? Did aid fail because of improper policies pursued by the Somalia government? It would be highly revealing to analyze some of the principal reasons for the ineffectiveness of aid to Somalia in order to gain an insight into the contribution of foreign resources to economic development in Africa.

WHO IS AIDING WHOM?

As elsewhere in Africa, bilateral aid to Somalia was both project-tied and country-tied. Under the project-tied aid, Somalia was provided with a number of low-priority projects, including, for example, a large and modern technical school in a country without industry; a national theater in the capital of Mogadiscio, even though there were already several theaters; and a university equipped to produce social science graduates only. By diverting scarce development funds into low-priority schemes, project-tied aid made a smaller contribution to the economic development of Somalia than if it had been utilized in higher-priority projects such as land development or highway construction.[31]

Almost everywhere in Africa, aid tends to be concentrated in the modern, more efficient sector of society or prestigious and easily identifiable projects rather than on those which serve the real development interests of the country concerned. On the whole, the external resources are more commonly used to support large, modern industries than to augment cottage-industry production. In the transport sector, for example, there has been higher external aid involvement in developing trunk lines and expanding truck freight than in opening up the back country with the help of feeder roads or investment ox-carts. Similarly in agriculture, the tendency is to assist the market rather than the subsistence part of production. The showpiece projects have not only had low or negative returns, but also the maintenance of the capital and services associated with them has been a major burden on the budgets of the African recipient countries. A characteristic case in point is the huge Akosombo Volta Dam in Ghana which is becoming increasingly not only something of a white elephant, but also a significant drain on the country's already scarce foreign exchange earnings for maintenance and repairs.

Again, as elsewhere in Africa, bilateral aid to Somalia was not only tied to specific projects; it was also tied to purchases of goods from the donor countries only.[32] This type of external assistance to Africa tends to diminish not only the spirit of beneficence in giving aid but also the effectiveness of the aid itself as an agent of development. It results in the necessity to buy more expensive and less efficient products and services than could be obtained from sources other than the donor. The borrower African government is not permitted to search for the cheapest equipment, or materials, or advisers, but is forced to accept those which the lending country provides. The purchases of very expensive equipment and the construction of plants of less than optimum scale may well result. The African country is thus, from the beginning, encumbered with a costly operation. According to United Nations studies conducted in a number of developing countries, tied aid makes the cost of goods and services some 15 to 25 percent more expensive.[33]

With very few exceptions, external resources to Africa over the years would seem to have taken the form of commercial transactions, the main difference being that the tag on them reads "aid" and is more expensive. It would be naive indeed to hope for the speedy growth of African countries while they have to pay "one out of every eight dollars" of the export earnings on the payment of interest and loan installments. As George Woods, former president of the World Bank, was forced to admit, "to the extent that foreign aid is tied, it represents help for the exporters in the donor country. . . . Some countries have made it clear that they see development finance as nothing more than a disguised subsidy for their exporters."[34]

In this regard, it is the developing African countries, indeed the developing countries as a whole, which are assisting the industrial countries more than the latter helping the former. Through the process of tied aid, the developing African countries help the advanced countries to expand exports and maintain full employment.[35] This is the import of the statement by Reg Prentice, British Minister of Overseas Development from August 1967 to October 1969:

> Our aid programme can be seen as an investment in our own overseas markets. This applies to all donor countries. . . . We provide at the moment about 7½ percent of the global flow of aid, but we get about 12 percent of the orders for goods imported by the developing countries from the developed countries. Our aid programme, being a part of an international aid flow, is almost certainly a help to our balance of payments. . . . Taking into account the indirect effects ('trade follows aid'), and the orders we get from other countries' aid programmes, the total result is in our favour. . . . So are many of the other donors, to a greater or lesser extent.[36]

Thus, although aid flows to African countries have been substantial, their effectiveness is open to question.

HOW HELPFUL IS THE EEC AID?

Observers of EEC relations with African, Caribbean, and Pacific (ACP) countries are divided on whether EEC's official development assistance—either through the conventional project aid or the trade/aid hybrid of Stabex (Stabilization of Export Earnings)—has contributed to the economic development of the African countries. While it is almost always agreed that Stabex does not contribute to development, questions have been raised regarding the impact of the EEC conventional project aid on the objectives and priorities of the African states, or on the advancement of the goals of the Lomé scheme. How, for example, does EEC aid, as applied, compare with other forms of aid? Restated, is aid directed via the EEC superior to that which is directed through other channels, such as the bilateral programs of member states? Does the EEC aid represent better value to African states than it would if it were channeled, say, bilaterally?

An evaluation of Lomé aid hinges largely, therefore, upon its comparative development effectiveness. This seems to be a difficult area, both because the comparison is with a range of donors with different performance standards and because of the normative nature of the concept of "aid effectiveness," as Adrian Hewitt and Christopher Stevens of the Overseas Development Institute in London have noted.[37] Both Hewitt and Stevens have argued that a comparative study of the EEC aid and that of other donors does not tend to show that the former is more effective; on the contrary, what available evidence does exist suggests that EEC aid "may be less effective than some of the alternative channels for the aid" provided by the EEC members.[38] On the other hand, Cecil Rajana of the Guyana Ministry of Economic Planning and Finance has in a recent extensive evaluation of EEC economic assistance to the ACP states concluded that, on balance, the EEC aid under the Lomé scheme has "contributed to a measure of development in the ACP states," which arguably, would not have occurred in the absence of the EEC aid, or would have been of a lesser order had this come from member states as either bilateral or multilateral development assistance.[39]

Evidence tends to suggest that Rajana's contention is somewhat overstated. Although the overriding aim of the Lomé aid program is to "correct the structural imbalances in the various sectors" of the African (ACP) economies by financing "projects and programmes" which contribute essentially to economic and social development in accordance with the priorities and objectives laid down by the African (ACP) states (Article 40 of Lomé 1), in practice, the contrary is the case. The sectoral distribution of aid has been concentrated heavily on relatively capital-intensive industrial activities, with a small proportion of resources allocated to meeting basic needs through the provision of health, water supply, housing, etc. Where industrial projects have been favored, these have been overwhelmingly to increase energy supplies, and very little attention is paid to the importance of local industrial development linked to agricultural development. As a recent study of European Development Fund (EDF) aid to Cameroon has concluded, "Judged against the current criteria for aid effectiveness—sustained economic development, increases in local administrative competence, and improvement in the lot of the poor—the EDF's aid allocation mechanism seems to have missed the mark. . . ."[40] Hence, the EEC aid has not resulted in any dramatic upsurge in the development of African countries.

Even the aid from the Stabex scheme, one of the most notable innovations in the Lomé regime, which is designed to compensate ACP states for loss of export earnings due to fluctuations in certain eligible commodity prices, has proved of questionable importance for the African states so far as their economic development is concerned. A point worth stressing here is that only unprocessed commodities on the Stabex list qualify for financial transfer. Thus the scheme is biased against the development of processing for exports, since it applies to raw materials only. And, because processed raw materials are not included in the overall calculations, related domestic industry is not encouraged, nor is domestic consumption. There is thus a large measure of truth in Lynn Mytelka's contention that Stabex is at one and the same time "an incentive to maintain the present levels of production" in the specified commodities listed under the scheme and "a disincentive" to diversify commercial agricultural production, process raw materials locally, or develop domestic food production.[41] Hence Stabex looks like stabilizing poverty. It is not intended to contribute to the economic development of the African countries.

IS EXTERNAL AID AIDING? THE CASE OF REGIONAL INTEGRATION

In the area of promoting regional economic integration among African countries as part of a new development strategy capable of generating rapid growth where older strategies had failed, external resources have also not proved to be beneficial, as the experience of the East African Community (EAC) and the Customs and Economic Union of Central Africa (UDEAC) has demonstrated. In some cases, external resources from international capitalism have turned out to be counterdevelopmental.

To facilitate the process of consolidation and acquisition of legitimacy, both UDEAC and EAC believed it desirable, indeed essential, to mobilize external resources. Each sought to cultivate relationships with a whole host of extraregional actors, most notably with Western Europe, the United States, the Soviet Union, the World Bank, and the United Nations system of organizations.[42] It was hoped that external resources could significantly affect integration of member states by increasing the total resources available to integrative systems, thereby lowering the cost of integration and making possible a more equitable distribution of integration's benefits, as well as encouraging the development of regional projects.[43] Besides, through technical assistance combined with training, donor agencies were to do as much as possible to strengthen the capacities of the integration secretariats to manage their own affairs better.

Although to some extent external resources did contribute to the integration process in the early years of both the UDEAC and EAC by enhancing their sense of self-worth and providing much-needed technical assistance in the form of planners and technicians, on balance the capacity of donors to affect collectively the integration process in ways deemed desirable in the area of development remained very much circumscribed. The availability of external resources in various forms did not demonstrably affect the nature of goal setting within the integration scheme of either the UDEAC or EAC. Rather, they tended to reinforce dependence, exacerbate problems of nationalism, and maintain economic disparities. In both the UDEAC and EAC, these resources were not used to reduce asymmetries within the integration scheme. Instead, they contributed to widening the development gap and increasing the frustrations of the relatively less-developed partner states in their attempt to gain an equitable share of the benefits of integration. Foreign assistance in fact tended to favor the relatively wealthy states like Kenya in the EAC and Cameroon in the UDEAC to the detriment of their less-developed partners—Tanzania in the former and Chad in the latter.

Again, foreign resources extended in the form of direct investment manifested in the operations of TNCs have also been one of the most powerful impediments to development in Africa, about which much has been written in recent years[44] and therefore does not require repetition. Studies have focused on TNC's impacts upon African countries' balance of payments, export-import structures, employment, income distribution, and political sovereignty as well as other economic and political aspects. Suffice it to highlight briefly a particular case of TNC impact on development of local enterprises and capital formation in Africa.

Growth ultimately depends less on expanding development finance than on developing a vigorous, local, private, and public entrepreneurial group. The experience in Africa tends to confirm that capital imports, particularly direct private foreign investment, hinder the development of local entrepreneurship. This is because the foreign private firms preempt the best investment opportunities, because they borrow on the local capital market and divert funds away from domestic firms, or because they take over going domestic concerns. Besides, the practice of the TNCs to send back their huge profits to their home offices has (1) impeded domestic capital formation in Africa and (2) resulted in a net outflow of capital from the African economies to the developed capitalist economies. Moreover, this repatriation of profits and remittances to the metropolitan countries "requires that the African countries give up for this purpose the foreign exchange earned from the sale of their exports and needed for the purchase of their essential imports."[45] Thus not only does international capitalism prevent the development of local entrepreneurship in Africa or domestic capital formation in most of the African countries, it also results in a drain on their valuable foreign exchange earnings.

Within the contest of African regional economic cooperation, too, the dominant importance of TNCs and their interlocking activities have greatly influenced the structure of trade, specialization and industrial development, equitable distribution of integration costs, and benefits and consequently affected the sovereignty of member states over the key sectors of the regional economy.[46] The analysis of Steven Langdon and Lynn Mytelka[47] of the Customs and Economic Union of Central Africa and that of Peter Robson[48] of the

West African Economic Community (CEAO) provide excellent case studies of the way in which TNCs have not only derived benefits from African regional integration to the disadvantage of partner states; they have also rendered African countries unable to take full advantage of the economic cooperation institutions to introduce changes in production and industrial structures as a means of encouraging intra-African trade and thereby reducing their dependence on external forces. A recent ECA special report[49] has indicated how TNCs have thwarted UDEAC's efforts at regional industrial planning.

### FROM AID TO RECOLONIZATION?

The two case studies we have examined have thrown considerable light on the role of external resources in African economic development. Summing up the experience of African countries both at the national and at the regional levels it is no exaggeration to suggest that, on balance, foreign assistance, especially foreign capitalism, has been somewhat deleterious to African development. It must be admitted, however, that the pattern of development is complex and the effect upon it of foreign assistance is still not clearly determined. But the limited evidence available suggests that the forms in which foreign resources have been extended to Africa over the past twenty-five years, in so far as they are concerned with economic development, are, to a great extent, counterproductive. For when actual aid is examined in practice, as noted in the two case studies, it is fairly clear that aid programs have not been administered in a way as to provide dynamizing development input. A large proportion of publicly sponsored foreign assistance is channeled into activities which either are not directly productive or have long gestation periods. By tying a major share of foreign resources provided to specific projects, aid and foreign capital help in overcoming resource scarcities for establishing modern ventures, but usually leave to the African country itself the increasing problem of obtaining enough foreign exchange to run them at full capacity. Moreover, the aid process is so heavily laden with motives of self-interest on the part of the donor countries that it is not clear "who is helping whom." The situation is not in the least improved by technical assistance schemes. Doubts have been raised about the quality and appropriateness of experts provided to Africa and other developing countries under technical assistance schemes. It is generally agreed that technical assistance "has been . . . probably the least efficient segment of all foreign aid" and that Africa seems to have done "less well with it than anybody else."[50] All too often the "experts" are men of second-rate ability, especially those on longer assignments.

Generally, also, international assistance has been hindering institutional reforms. A lending country may not accept the wisdom of such changes. Hence foreign assistance tends to strengthen the status quo; it enables African leaders to evade and avoid fundamental reforms; it does little more than patch plaster on the deteriorating social edifice. Even the all-important food aid, as the Report of the Presidential Commission on World Hunger concluded, has in some cases undermined "the efforts of recipient nations to develop a more self-reliant base of their own" and enabled some recipient governments to postpone essential agricultural reforms and to maintain a pricing system which gives farmers inadequate incentives to increase local production required for greater self-reliance in basic foodstuffs.[51]

Above all, the growing debt burden of the African countries, the consequent acute balance of payments difficulties, and the severe constraint this imposes on growth is a major problem of contemporary aid programs which stems directly from the concentration on loans rather than grants. Between 1970 and 1979 external indebtedness of sub-Saharan Africa rose from $6 billion to $32 billion, and debt service (for the oil-importing countries) increased from 6 to 12 percent of export earnings in the same period.[52] By 1982 debt service ratios for Africa had risen from 6.5 percent in 1970 to 28.3 percent.[53] And as repayments grow, they become more of a burden to the indebted African country. In several African countries like Ghana, where the debts have increased beyond the ability of the country to liquidate them, this has led to a move in the game of default, namely "rephrasing." Is aid, then, leading to recolonization?

But Africans would be less than honest if we were to put the entire responsibility for our failure to achieve a breakthrough in development at the doors of donor countries. Indeed the primary responsibility for development rests on the African countries themselves; aid can be best used only as a supplement to the full mobilization of domestic resources. Thus international assistance should be guided by the priorities laid down by the recipient country. In the case of Somalia, for example, the ambitious First Five-Year Plan gave relatively low priorities to such essential engines of development as education, health, and water supplies. The relatively low priority that was assigned to education, community development, and other social infrastructure would seem to have retarded further the rate of social transformation, so necessary for realizing higher living standards through economic growth. Besides, like many other countries in Africa, foreign resources were not properly utilized by the Somali Government. The Short-Term Development Program, for example, "admits unproductive and wasteful utilization of aid proceeds." There were popular charges of widespread corruption and maladministration of development funds and foreign-aid proceeds by government.[54]

Part of the trouble stems from the "nature of the post-colonial state" in Africa and, more especially, the relationship that has been established between foreign capital and major aid-giving bodies and the local power elite.

This relationship has often led to projects and actions which have not seemed to be in the best interests of development in its broader sense. In order to enhance their electoral appeal, the local elite have sometimes tended to support the channeling of foreign assistance into prestige projects, which in many cases is acceptable to the donors, who wish to have something to show for their money. But often, as noted already, the showpiece projects have had low or negative returns, and the maintenance of the capital and services associated with them has been a major burden to the budgets of African countries. Thus, while foreign resources have not in any way proved to be supportive to the cause of African economic development, the role of African local political elites in this whole process of development constitutes a vital area requiring special mention.[55]

Africa's economic performance over the past two and a half decades has been extremely disappointing and the outlook for the eighties is dim. Instead of development, the deterioration in the economic situation of African countries, which characterized the 1970s, has continued into the 1980s. This has created a continental crisis. Confronted with this implacable reality, African leaders have been forced into a sobering reassessment of what their options are, or what really is the correct path toward economic development. Given the imminence of catastrophe and collapse innovative responses are an imperative. For if the deterioration in economic performance is to be halted and then reversed, new directions of policy are required. Africa's hope then lies in a fundamental redirection of national and regional development strategies. Thus by the close of the 1970s, Africa was faced with a choice between (1) continuing to support an inherited structure of dependence involving massive flow of external resources, and therefore subordination of its own development to special interests of the international capitalist system, or (2) beginning to break away from this structure to determine its own fate.

## V. Which Way Africa? Dependent Development or Self-Reliant Development

The 1980s has opened with a great debate in Africa about two contrasting development strategies and prescriptions in response to the current African crisis—the *Lagos Plan of Action* (LPA) and the World Bank Report, *Agenda for Action*, to both of which reference has already been made. The fundamental objective of the collective indigenous response to the crisis, as indicated in the *Lagos Plan of Action*, is the establishment of self-sustaining development and economic growth, based on the principles of collective self-reliance: "Africa. . . . must map out its own strategy for development and must vigorously pursue its implementation. . . . Africa must cultivate the virtue of self-reliance."[56] Thus the global approach based on national and collective self-reliance has been adopted by African countries. In the *Lagos Plan of Action*, African governments have collectively committed themselves to cooperate for the establishment and strengthening of joint-sub-regional and regional institutions which will concentrate on the key sectors of the African economy.

But whereas the historic Lagos document advocates a departure from "orthodox assumptions and prescriptions," the *Agenda* is essentially a "revisionist developmentalist perspective within the modernization *genre*," charting no new path for Africa, breaking no new ground, and offering no new perspectives. Rather, it accepts the validity of the existing approach to African development and therefore appeals for further capitalist penetration of African economies through, inter alia, foreign capitalism and increased external assistance: "Additional aid commitments will have to be made *now* if disbursements are to reach required levels by the mid-1980s."[57] The recently published *Progress Report* of the World Bank has reinforced this approach to African development by advocating that "external assistance must not only be remarkably increased but also sustained over many years."[58]

To be sure, the *Lagos Plan of Action*'s concept of self-reliance does not mean autarchy; rather it is an assertion of "Africa first" in economic as well as in diplomatic matters. It recognizes the important contribution that external assistance can make toward Africa's socioeconomic development, but argues that as long as external aid is beyond the control of beneficiaries, its long-term benefits would be limited. Hence the plan states: "outside contributions should only supplement our own efforts; they should not be the mainstay of our development."[59] Psychologically, this is the only way that Africa can develop the necessary self-confidence that would enable it to pull its economy "out of the shadows of backwardness and underdevelopment."

Africa's stand on the issue of external resources is supported by the fact that "not one of today's developed countries" developed by depending excessively on external sources for the supply of the strategic inputs into their processes of generating and sustaining development and economic growth.[60]

But while advocating increase in external aid, the *Agenda* does not recognize that a greater part of the external aid must be paid in foreign exchange and that the cost of such repayment increases year by year, leading to debt accumulation, as already noted in this essay. Neither does the *Agenda* address itself to the "problems of tied aid," nor the effects which the recommended increases in external assistance will have no debt accumulation. Thus in brief, the development strategy of the *Agenda* may be described as "outward looking" or "externally oriented," or "export-led" in contrast with the *Lagos Plan of Action*'s "inward oriented," or self-reliant, approach.[61]

Based on the twin principles of national and collective self-reliance and

self-reliant and self-sustaining development, the *Lagos Plan of Action* is designed to restructure the economy of Africa. This restructuring implies the
increasing dependence of economic growth and development on internal demand stimuli and the gradual substitution of domestic for imported factor inputs. Hence it constitutes an alternative type of development in Africa implying
(1) a full mobilization of Africa's domestic capabilities and resources; (2) reduction and alteration of traditional trade and investment relationships;
(3) comprehensive limitations on the amount of foreign investment and expatriate manpower; and (4) the reorientation of development efforts in order
to meet the basic social needs of the people of Africa. The underlying premise
is the desire by African states to determine their own economic policies based
on their national aspirations, national resources, and political ideologies outside the influence of external forces.

## VI. Is the Self-Reliant Strategy Being Implemented?

Although self-reliant development as a strategy designed to redefine the
role of international assistance and international capitalism and all other external linkages in Africa's development process has been formally adopted at
the African continental level, its implementation has not yet advanced beyond
the stage of theoretical discussions. Specifically, the *Lagos Plan of Action*
concepts are not yet reflected in country as well as regional development
plans, as was made evident in a recent ECA report.[62] Given the entrenchment
of neocolonialism in Africa and the extent of diversification of markets and
sources of investment and technology among different metropolitan countries, the prospects for significant restructuring of Africa's economy from the
short-term point of view are very limited. To illustrate, the *Lagos Plan of
Action* states that the first call on Africa's natural resources should be Africa
itself, with exports limited to whatever surplus production remains after Africa's needs are met. As a long-range plan this is a welcome proposition, but
for Africa to develop the capability to utilize its raw materials will require
years, if not decades, "and with Africa currently drowning in balance of payments deficits, exports will remain a major and vital African concern for the
foreseeable future."[63] In other words, transformation of Africa's raw materials
output into consumer and capital goods in accordance with the concepts of the
*Lagos Plan* is a task of massive proportions.

In a long-term perspective, however, the self-reliant strategy of development of the *Lagos Plan* is a splendid option, indeed one which would lead
Africa to overcome its excessive dependence on external resources, raise the
living conditions of its people, and assert its position as a major economic
unit within the global economy. But as an immediate strategy option a self-

reliant strategy of development involving "delinkage" or restructuring of Africa's economy does not seem to be a feasible proposition. Thus it is not likely that there will be any major changes in Africa's present strategy during most of the 1980s.

The *Lagos Plan* recognizes this aspect of the implementation of its programs. Aware of the fact that all development problems, like all human problems, require time to solve, the *Plan* makes recommendations for short-, medium-, and long-term action. Hence it advocates a systematic or progressive reduction of Africa's external links until the establishment of a genuine interdependence of equals. This partly explains the *Plan's* "extensive exhortation" on training and skill acquisition of all sorts, on adapting technology to African capabilities, and on research and exchange of information. Thus, the major challenge in the implementation of the strategy of self-reliant development envisaged under the *Lagos Plan* implies planned development of local capacities, domestic resource-based industries, local technologies and financial institutions as a basis for (1) negotiations with foreign-owned TNCs and external assistance agencies; (2) accurate interpretation of the legal, social, economic, and political implications of international assistance and internationl capitalism, and (3) restructuring of the domestic production and distribution through a definite shift in the patterns of ownership and distribution of the major means of production. The *Plan* recognises that self-reliant development cannot be achieved in a vacuum and neither can technology be acquired or accumulated if there is no local expertise to receive it.

## VII. Conclusion

The conclusion toward which this study tends is that the prescriptions for Africa's development in the form of international assistance and international capitalism over the past twenty-five years are hardly appropriate or successful. International assistance programs, as currently administered, tend to promote continued Africa's dependence rather than Africa's development; provide resources of the wrong kind in the wrong ways, and in the wrong quantities. Specifically, many of the resources have often been channeled into projects unconnected with agricultural or rural development—the sphere best able to improve the lot of the majority—and have further separated the twin sectors of African economies and sharpened the social and geographical dualism as well. Added to this, the assumption that international capitalism or direct foreign investment or TNCs are an "engine" of development in that they contribute resources not otherwise available or only available in insufficient quantities has proved to be mistaken in the case of Africa.

It is, however, important to stress that external resources without internal reform will not be in the best interest of sub-Saharan Africa. And to think that the way for a spontaneous development of the economy is open when "external difficulties" are overcome is dangerous self-deception. There is therefore the need for a general commitment by the sub-Saharan African countries to introduce relevant, practical, and effective measures to accelerate the pace of growth and development. In this regard, the adoption of the self-reliant and self-sustaining strategy of development is a step in the right direction. After all, development is "endogenous"; it springs from the heart of each society, which relies first on its own strength and resources and "defines in sovereignty the vision of its future," cooperating with societies sharing its problems and aspirations. Thus the economic prosperity of African countries in the 1980s and beyond will depend, to a considerable extent, on their ability to transform the concepts of the *Lagos Plan* from political slogans into a framework for policy and action. As the distinguished African historian Ade Ajayi recently observed in a "mood of cautious optimism":

> The vision of a new society in Africa will need to be developed *in* Africa, born out of the African historical experience and the sense of continuity of African history. The African is not yet master of his own fate, but neither is he completely at the mercy of fate.[64]

NOTES

1. See *Report of the Commission on International Development: Partners in Development*, L. B. Pearson (Chairman), (New York: Praeger, 1970).
2. H. B. Chenery and N. G. Carter, "Foreign Assistance and Development Performance, 1960–1970," *American Economic Review* 63 (2), May 1973, pp. 259–268.
3. *North-South: a programme for survival. Report of the Independent Commission on International Development Issues* (Brandt Commission), (London: Pan, 1980), pp. 221–227; *Common Crisis, North-South: Co-operation for World Recovery* (London: Pan, 1983), pp. 74–86.
4. IBRD, *Accelerated Development in Sub-Saharan Africa: An Agenda for Action* (Washington, D.C., 1981).
5. For an example of this position, see A. G. Frank, "The Development of Underdevelopment," *Monthly Review*, XVIII (4), September 1967, pp. 17–31.
6. P. T. Bauer, *Dissent on Development* (London: Weidenfeld and Nicolson, 1971), Ch. 2; K. B. Griffin, "Foreign Capital, Domestic Savings and Economic Development," *Bulletin of Oxford Institute of Economics and Statistics*, 32 (2), 1970, p. 100.
7. Organization of African Unity, *Lagos Plan of Action for the Economic Development of Africa 1980–2000* (Geneva: International Institute for Labour Studies, 1981).
8. Judith Hart, *Aid and Liberation* (London: 1973), p. 16.
9. Samuel P. Huntington, "Foreign Aid for What and for Whom," *Foreign Policy*, 1 (Winter 1970–71), pp. 161–189; and 2 (Spring 1971), pp. 115–134.

10. Karl Mathiasen III, "Multilateral Technical Assistance," *International Organization*, 22 (2), Winter 1968, p. 204.

11. *Technical Assistance in Public Administration: Lessons of Experience and Possible Improvement* (Vienna: International Institute of Administrative Sciences [Twelfth International Congress], July 1962), p. 12, quoted in Sidney L. Sufrin, *Technical Assistance—Theory and Guidelines* (Syracuse, N.Y.: Syracuse University Press, December 1966), p. 44.

12. G. K. Helleiner, "New Forms of Foreign Investment in Africa," *The Journal of Modern Africa Studies*, 6 (1), May 1968, p. 18; also, by the same author, "Aid and Dependence in Africa: Issues for Recipients," in Timothy M. Shaw and Kenneth A. Heard (eds.), *The Politics of Africa: Dependence and Development* (New York: Africana Publishing Company, 1979), pp. 238–239.

13. Sufrin, p. 45.

14. For full details about transnational corporations see United Nations Centre on Transnational Corporations, *Transnational Corporations in World Development: Third Survey* (New York: United Nations, 1983).

15. For the basic African perception of TNCs see *The Proposed International Code of Conduct on Transnational Corporations: The African Perspective*, Doc. E/ECA/ UNCTNC/20, 10 January 1983.

16. Address by Henry R. Kissinger on "*Global Consensus and Economic Development*," delivered by Daniel P. Moynihan, U.S. Representative to the United Nations, Seventh Special Session of the U.N. General Assembly, 1 September 1975.

17. Hollis B. Chenery and Alan M. Strout, "Foreign Assistance and Economic Development," *The American Economic Review*, LVI (4) Part 1, September 1966, p. 679.

18. L. Gray Cowan, *The Dilemma of African Independence* (New York: Columbia University, 1965), p. IX.

19. Marian Radetski, *Aid and Development: A Handbook for Small Donors* (New York: Praeger, 1973), pp. 60–61.

20. See IBRD, Accelerated Development, pp. 7, 121–124; Helleiner, "Aid and Development," p. 228.

21. Helleiner, "Aid and Development," p. 228.

22. IBRD, *Accelerated Development*, p. 121.

23. Ibid., p. 131.

24. Justin B. Zulu and Saleh M. Nsouli, "Adjustment Programs in Africa," *Finance and Development*, 21 (1), March 1984, p. 5.

25. Adebayo Adedeji, "Development and Economic Growth in Africa to the Year 2000: Alternative Projections and Policies," in Timothy M. Shaw (ed.), *Alternative Futures for Africa* (Boulder, Colo.: Westview Press, 1982), p. 280.

26. I have relied to some extent on the information provided in Oxay Mehmet, "Effectiveness of Foreign Aid: the Case of Somalia," *Journal of Modern African Studies*, 9 (1), May 1971, pp. 31–47.

27. Pearson, *Partners in Development*, Table 27, p. 392.

28. Mehmet, "Effectiveness of Foreign Aid," p. 31.

29. For details of aid provided see ibid., p. 37.

30. German Planning and Economic Advisory Group, *Report on the Progress of Development Projects in the Somali Democratic Republic* (Mogadicio and Frankfurt: 1969, mimeo). Cited in Mehmet, p. 36.

31. Mehmet, p. 42.

32. For an extended discussion of tying of aid, see J. Bhagwati, "The Tying of Aid," UNCTAD Secretariat: *Progress Report*, TD (7) Supp. 4, U.N., 1967.

33. See UNCTAD Secretariat: *Progress Report*, TD (7), Supp. 8, U.N., 1967.

34. *The Guardian* (Manchester), 1 August 1967.

35. See Mostafa Elm, "Who Is Helping Whom in the Mirage of Foreign Aid?" *Columbia Journal of World Business*, iii (4), July–August 1968, p. 15.

36. Reg Prentice, "More Priority for Overseas Aid," *International Affairs*, 46 (1), January 1970, pp. 5–6.

37. Adrian Hewitt and Christopher Stevens, "The Second Lomé Convention," in Christopher Stevens (ed.), EEC *and The Third World: A Survey* (London et al.: Hodder & Stoughton, 1981), p. 40.

38. Ibid., p. 41.

39. Cecil Rajana, "The Lomé Convention: an Evaluation of EEC Economic Assistance to the ACP States," *The Journal of Modern African Studies*, 20 (2), 1982, p. 215.

40. A. Hewitt, "The European Development Fund as a Development Agent: some result of EDF aid to Cameroon," *ODI Review*, No. 2-1979 (London), p. 55.

41. Lynn K. Mytelka, "The Lomé Convention and a New International Division of Labour," *Journal of European Integration* 1 (1), September 1977, p. 24. See also S. K. B. Asante, "The Lomé Convention: Toward Perpetuation of Dependence or Promotion of Interdependence," *Third World Quarterly*, 3 (4), October 1981, pp. 658–672.

42. For UDEAC see Lynn K. Mytelka, "Foreign Aid and Regional Integration: The UDEAC Case," *Journal of Common Market Studies*, XII (2), December 1973, pp. 138–158; and for the East African Community see, Thomas S. Cox, "Northern Actors in a South-South Setting: External Aid and East African Integration," *Journal of Common Market Studies*, XXI (3) March 1983, pp. 283–312.

43. U.N. Department of Economic and Social Affairs, *Report of the East African Team, Cooperation for Economic Development of Eastern Africa, Part Three: Development Implications of Cooperation* (New York: U.N., 1971), Doc. No. ST/ECA/140/ Part III.

44. See, for example, *Transnational Corporations in Africa: Some Major Issues* (A Note by ECA Secretariat), E/ECA/UNCTC/21, 13 January 1983.

45. Richard Harris, "The Political Economy of Africa: Underdevelopment or Revolution," in Richard Harris (ed.), *The Political Economy of Africa* (New York et al.: John Wiley & Sons, 1975), p. 15.

46. See, for example, *The Proposed International Code of Conduct on Transnational Corporations: The African Perspectives; Report of the Second African Regional Meeting on a Code of Conduct on Transnational Corporations* (Addis Ababa: 18 February 1983), Doc. E/ECA/UNCTC/26.

47. Steven Langdon and Lynn K. Mytelka, "Africa in the Changing World Economy" in Colin Legum et al. (eds.), *Africa in the 1980s: A Continent in Crisis* (New York: McGraw-Hill Book Co., 1979), p. 179.

48. Peter Robson, *Integration, Development and Equity: Economic Integration in West Africa* (London: George Allen & Unwin, 1983), p. 41.

49. UN ECA, *Report of the ECA Mission on the Evaluation of UDEAC* (Libreville [Gabon]: 1981). For the impact of TNCs on the East African Community see Mahmood Mamdani, "The Breakup of the East African Community: Some Lessons." Paper presented at the fifth biannual conference of African Association of Political Science, Dakar (Senegal), June 1983.

50. Philip M. Allen, "The Technical Assistance Industry in Africa: a case for nationalization," *International Development Review*, 3 (1970), p. 8.

51. Report of the Presidential Commission on World Hunger, *Overcoming World Hunger: The Challenge Ahead*, (Washington, D.C., 1980), p. 140.

52. IBRD, *Accelerated Development*, p. 3.

53. *World Development Report 1983* (Oxford University Press, 1983), p. 21.

54. For details of economic development in Somalia in recent years see Nur Calika, "Somalia's adjustment experience, 1981–83," *Finance and Development*, 21 (1), March 1984, p. 8. See also *The Economist*, 25 February, 1984, p. 63.

55. For further details see David Wheeler, "Sources of Stagnation in Sub-Saharan Africa," *World Development*, 12(1), 1984, pp. 1–23.

56. OAU, *Lagos Plan*, para. 14.

57. IBRD, *Accelerated Development*, p. 7.

58. IBRD, *Sub-Saharan Africa: Progress Report on Development Prospects and Programs* (Washington, D.C., 1983), p. iii.

59. OAU, *Lagos Plan*, para. 14.

60. For an extended discussion of this see the "Response of the OAU/ECA/ADB (African Development Bank) to the Berg Report" in Robert S. Browne and Robert J. Commings, *The Lagos Plan of Action vs The Berg Report* (Lawrenceville: Brunswick Publishing Co., 1984), p. 153.

61. Ibid., p. 25.

62. ECA, *Critical Analysis of the Country Presentations of African Least Developed Countries in the Light of the Lagos Plan of Action and the Final Act of Lagos*, doc. no. ST/ECA/PSD.2/31, Addis Ababa, 1982.

63. Browne and Communings, *The Lagos Plan of Action*, p. 49.

64. J. F. Ade Ajayi, "Expectations of Independence," *Daedalus*, 3(2), Spring 1982, p. 8.

CHAPTER 11

# Africa between Ideology and Technology: Two Frustrated Forces of Change

*Ali A. Mazrui*

Kwame Nkrumah once said: "Socialism without science is void."[1] He was laying the foundation stone of what he thought would become the Ghana of the nuclear age. He initiated a program of nuclear research, but today Nkrumah's nuclear reactor has still not materialized. If anything, Ghana is even further behind technologically than it was when Nkrumah dreamt his atomic dreams. The question arises: Why?

By linking socialism with science Nkrumah was also linking ideology with technology. The advancement and maturation of both ideology and technology occur when economic conditions are right, the political situation is receptive, and the cultural context is congenial. Was Nkrumah trying to force the technological pace of Ghana for purely ideological reasons? Was Ghana's ideology too far ahead of its technology?

In the past African cultures produced their own ideologies and technologies. But the spread of Western skills and values to other countries in the last two centuries has posed dilemmas in African countries. One persistent question has been whether technological modernization is possible without cultural and ideological westernization.

Japan after the Meiji Restoration in 1868 decided that it was indeed possible to industrialize and modernize without capitulating to Western culture. Hence the slogan of Meiji industrialism, "Western Technique, Japanese Spirit." Japan had politically opted for a strategy of selective transformation.

Turkey under Mustapha Kemal Ataturk in the interwar years this century took a different position. Post-Ottoman Turkey decided that it was *not* possible to modernize economically without Westernizing culturally. So a strategy of comprehensive Westernization was adopted—the Arabic alphabet was

275

replaced by the Roman one, the Turkish fez was replaced by the Western hat, Arabic loan words were sometimes replaced by words from European languages, and the secular state replaced the Islamic political structures. In order to modernize technically, Turkey had politically opted for a strategy of comprehensive cultural Westernization. Ataturk's political will sought to mobilize Western culture in pursuit of broad societal transformation.

One major worry concerning Africa is whether the continent is culturally Westernizing without economically modernizing. The African configuration is neither the same as Japan (minimum cultural Westernization in pursuit of rapid modernization) nor the same as that of Ataturk's Turkey (maximum cultural Westernization in pursuit of rapid modernization). The African predicament betrays minimum modernization in pursuit of rapid cultural Westernization. Ends and means are switched around. Instead of using Western culture as a means to technological transformation, there is evidence of minimum technological change in order to cater for newly acquired Western tastes.

The pursuit of these Western tastes is undertaken with greater vigor than the pursuit of Western skills. What is more, many of the skills are pursued precisely for the sake of those alien tastes.

And even when some genuine skill transfer does take place, other social distortions often occur. Particularly ominous is the marginalization of women in the wake of even modest modernization. Uneducated African women in the countryside are often at the core of agricultural production. In some African societies women are even more productive than men. They till the soil while men supervise. But with Western education women move from the productive sector to the service sector. They learn a European language and other verbal and literary skills—only to leave the soil in favor of the office. Western education turns African women into clerks and secretaries instead of cultivators. This is a case of functional marginalization.

But even when Western techniques are made relevant for cultivation, the marginalization of women takes new forms. For example, the mechanization of agriculture tends to push back the woman cultivator and bring forward the male. When rural agriculture is based on the hoe, women are often at the center of production. But when the tractor replaces the hoe, the driver behind the wheel is a man. On the whole, mechanization in Africa tends to peripheralize the role of women.

The third process which harms the economic role of women in Africa is the internationalization of African economies. As African economies have strengthened their linkages with the world economy and transnational corporations have opened up managerial positions to Africans, the economic roles of men have become more diverse and even global, while the economic roles of women have remained parochial. Internationalized African economies are more male dominated than tribal economies. There are no internationalized equivalents of the vigorous and aggressive market women of West Africa. The Boards of Directors of the import-export sectors of African economies are overwhelmingly male in composition.

The impact of the West upon Africa may have raised the legal status of women, but it has narrowed the economic functions of women. Women's rights are better protected in the postcolonial era, but the role of women in the economy is becoming less fundamental for society than it was before. In short, the African woman is confronted with expanding rights and a shrinking role in the postcolonial state.

But when all is said and done, Africa as a whole is relegated to the periphery of the global system. Both men and women in Africa have been marginalized by the relentless dialectic of the world economy. It is against the ominous shadow of this relentless dialectic that desperate voices have been heard—voices crying for a New International Economic Order (NIEO). Are they mouthpieces of middle-of-the-road *ideologies*? Or are they champions of New International *Technological* Order?

How *new* is the New International Economic Order? If it is indeed to be really new and innovative, can it be achieved without the following apparent preconditions?

1. Fundamental political change in the northern hemisphere
2. Ideological radicalization of the Organization of Petroleum Exporting Countries (OPEC)
3. Wider fundamental economic changes in the southern hemisphere as a whole
4. Creation of a New International *Technological* Order

It is very unlikely that the Western world would get drastically radicalized and socialized this side of the year 2000. Such radicalization would be one route toward a genuinely transformed world economy.

A more realistic alternative is to pray for one monumental coincidence—the coincidence of major Western democracies voting their left-wing parties into power at approximately the same time.

At the moment France has moved to the left at precisely the time when Britain and the United States are under the control of the right. NIEO would stand a better chance if Tony Benn or even Michael Foot was in power in England, Mitterrand in power in France, Teddy Kennedy in power in the United States, and the equivalent of Willy Brandt in power in the Federal Republic of Germany.

There are alternative political changes in the North which would help the NIEO cause. One would be changes in the balance of domestic lobbies in the North below the governmental level.

For example, an increased importance of the black lobby in the U.S.A. could be a major asset to the Third World. Black America is the most important enclave of people of Third World extraction lodged in the northern hemisphere. There are twice as many black Americans as there are Jews in the whole world added together. If black Americans became *half* as influential in shaping American policy toward the Third World as American Jews are in shaping American policy toward the Middle East, the North-South equation could indeed be tranformed.

In the absence of either a monumental electoral coincidence which makes the Western governments extra-liberal at the same time or the coincidence of such new powerful lobbies as potential black leverage on the American Congress, the Third World has to postulate transformation within itself. The ideological radicalization of OPEC could create greater OPEC readiness to put pressure on the industrialized world to make concessions to the South.

Some people argue that the North would only agree to make concessions when northern economies are *internally strong*. In reality the North would only make concessions when northern economies are externally vulnerable. A radicalized OPEC—including a radicalized Saudi Arabia—would help to make the North recognize its vulnerability.

But over and above issues of ideology and electoral successes are the more *fundamental* issues of comparative *technological* development. The international class structure is not really based on rich and poor; it is based on developed and underdeveloped. The new international stratification is based less on who *owns* what than on who *knows* what. Kuwait is richer than France in terms of per capita income, but less developed than France.

And so the real economic transformation of a Third World country is not to be sought in the income derived from such resources as oil; it is to be sought in hard technological skills.

But how near are we to a New International Technological Order?

## Technology: Between Culture and History

One factor to bear in mind is that in parts of Africa primordial or ancient technology coexists with advanced modern technology, prehistoric rudimentary skills coexist with the emergence of highly trained modern scientific know-how. A look at Africa can in fact capture the entire span of the history of technology.

Historians of the evolution of technology have sometimes traced a progression from hunting and gathering to hoe agriculture, and then onwards to plough agriculture. Hoe agriculture is sometimes combined with keeping cattle. Hunting societies and societies which are cattle keepers tend to have a way of life where the male is economically dominant. Killing wild animals and controlling large numbers of domestic animals is the kind of work which gives the man in the family a central economic role. But with the coming of the hoe and settled agriculture the primacy of the male in the economy could no longer be taken for granted. On the contrary many hoe societies have been known to develop a central economic role for the woman. Wives take to the shambas and become quite often economically more important than their husbands.

But with the coming of the plough, pulled by an animal, men in the history of Europe and Asia became once again the main providers of food. The control of the animal pulling the plough was deemed to be a man's job—more so than the use of the hoe to cultivate a little plot of land. This itself had a variety of other social and cultural consequences. In the Middle East patrilinealism began to reassert itself among the ploughing peoples. Even religion began to respond to these changes. Male deities and male priests, characterizing the new social organization of the Fertile Crescent, may also have been connected with the new masculine role in agriculture.

In parts of East Africa the stabilization of the ox plough as the central aspect of agriculture could also affect such social arrangements as the division of labor between men and women in the economy. Labor migration in East Africa, with men going to the towns and the mines while women tend the farms, could be significantly modified if not arrested. If the man is now needed at home to control the ox that pulls the plough and it is no longer easy to leave domestic agriculture in the rural areas to women alone, an extra incentive will have come into being to keep the African male tied to his soil—and thus discourage the male drift to the cities and the mines. The men would thus be kept busy in the rural areas, tending the oxen and sharpening the plough blades.

President Julius Nyerere of Tanzania did grasp fairly early that even a move from the hoe to the plough could be a major technological change. Indeed, although Nyerere believes in an ideological revolution, he also believes in technological gradualism. In matters concerned with the relations between man and man, Nyerere is a revolutionary. But in matters concerned with relations between man and machines, Nyerere is a gradualist. He is in favor of rapid elimination of class divisions as a basis of relationship between man and man. But he is against pushing technological change so fast that village life is prematurely disrupted and dependence on outside powers increased. Rapid mechanization and industrialization increases dependence on technologically more advanced countries. But a slower pace of technological change could both preserve village life from premature bewilderment and contribute toward genuine self-reliance. As Julius Nyerere said to his people:

> Instead of aiming at large farms using tractors and other modern equipment and employing agricultural labourers we should be aiming at having ox-ploughs all over the country. The *jembe* (hoe) will have to be eliminated by the ox plough before the latter can be eliminated by the tractor. We cannot hope to eliminate the *jembe* by the tractor.[2]

Nyerere emphasized other aspects of technological gradualism as a method of ensuring that the nation developed from its own roots and preserved that which was valuable in its own traditional past. As Nyerere put it:

> Instead of thinking about providing each farmer with his own lorry, we should consider the usefulness of oxen drawn carts, which could be made within the country and which are appropriate both to our roads and to the loads which each farmer is likely to have. Instead of the aerial spraying of crops with insecticide, we should use hand-operated pumps and so on. In other words, we have to think in terms of what is available, or can be made available, at comparatively small cost, and which can be operated by the people. By moving into the future along this path, we can avoid massive social disruption and human suffering.[3]

Uganda from time to time has also tried a new emphasis on rural development and agricultural training. The policy proclaimed in 1971 of introducing agriculture in as many schools in the country as possible was certainly in the direction of helping the nation to grow from its own roots and avoid too big a cleavage between those who worked on the farms and those who entered other areas of national endeavor. Until now, education in Africa as a whole has been a process of deruralization—a method of severing the ties with rural life. The introduction of agricultural training in schools should help to reduce this role of education as a process of depopulating the countryside.

Nor must we forget the political implications of changes in military technology in East Africa. There are still parts of Africa where military skills are assessed in terms of prowess in handling spears and in the use of the bow and arrow. If our weapons were still spears and bows and arrows it would have been difficult to create a nation-state even on the relatively small size of Uganda. Building states requires the centralization of power and consolidation of authority and a monopolization of violence as far as possible. It has been well said that the bow and arrow is essentially a democratic weapon. As Dr. Jack Goody of the University of Cambridge said of this weapon, "Every man knows how to construct one; the materials are readily available, the techniques uncomplicated, the missiles easy to replace (though more difficult with the introduction of iron that affected even hunting people like the Hadze of Tanzania and the Bushmen of the Kalahari). With the technologies of the bow and stone tipped arrow every kind of centralization of power is almost impossible. But with the introduction of metals, kingdoms and states are on the cards."[4]

With the coming of the rifle in colonial Africa and the tank in independent Africa, there emerged specialization in military techniques. The old days of military democracy, when everyone passed through the warrior stage and the weapons were the simple ones capable of being manufactured by the warrior himself, were now replaced by the era of military professional specialists, with weapons requiring high technological skill to manufacture and some specialized training to use. In the totality of concentrated technological power of destruction, the armed forces in an African country are now in a position to assert periodically special rights of political primacy and power.

Yet how real is technological power based almost entirely upon imported hardware? Is Africa a "technological power" at all in modern terms?

The total industrial output of the developing countries generally has been estimated at about 7 percent of the total industrial output of the world. Half of the Third World's industrial production occurs in Latin America. Africa's share of the world industrial output accounts for less than 1 percent of the total. One consequence for the Third World as a whole is acute technological dependency.

> Owing to relatively small output of machinery and input commodities, highly insignificant industrial research and development, and a relative dearth of skilled personnel, the majority of developing countries are completely dependent for their industrialization upon companies in the developed countries. They have to buy a technology developed by and for the big international corporations. An estimated 5 per cent of the export revenues of the developing countries are used to pay for imported technology (licences, royalties).[5]

But does this amount to effective technology transfer? Is the dependence temporary?

*Technology transfer* is a comprehensive term which encompasses both short-term and long-term technological movements, from computers on lease to African countries to the establishment of local Institutes of Technology. What fits and what does not fit is subsumed under *technology transfer*.

In contrast, *technology transplant* borrows a metaphor from biology to imply the need for receptivity in the host body. Some compatibility is needed between the thing "transplanted" (be it a heart or a seed) and the recipient.

Our first proposition in this assessment is that there has been a considerable amount of technology transfer to the Third World in the last thirty

years—but very little technology transplant. Especially in Africa very little of
what has been transferred has in fact been successfully transplanted. Very
little has taken root. The question is: *Why*?

## Technology: Good Climate, Bad Soil

We propose to argue (with special reference to Africa) that while the normative climate is favorable to technology transplant, the structural and sociological soil is still relatively barren. While indeed there is interest in, and
enthusiasm for, a technological culture, the actual sociological soil still tends
to reject what is being transplanted. Let us look at these two parts of the argument more closely.

The climate of opinion in much of the Third World favors moves toward
"modernization," "industrialization," more efficient "rural development,"
and faster modes of travel. Apart from a few poets and philosophers, there
are no major agrarian movements opposed to industrialism and technology
change. Even in revolutionary Iran the passions are directed more against cultural Westernization than against industrial modernization.

India loves and reveres the late Mahatma Gandhi, but even those contemporary Indians who favor cottage industries often tend to see them more as an
additional developmental strategy than as an alternative to the Tatas and the
steel industries. The more militant economic Gandhians (urging a return to
economic simplicity) have so far had little impact on policy or indeed on organized mass opinion.

Africa and the West Indies have also produced from time to time dedicated
economic primitivists. The whole Négritude school in Africa and the West
Indies has at times included nostalgia for the economic simplicity of the African past. As the poet and politician Aimé Cesaire of Martinique once bril-
liantly put it:

> Hooray for those who never invented anything
> Who never explored anything
> Hooray for joy,
> Hooray for Love,
> Hooray for the pain of incarnate tears.
> . . . . . . . . . . . . . . . . . . . . . . . . . . . . . . . . . .
> My Negritude is no Tower and No Cathedral
> It delves into the deep, red flesh of the soil.[6]

Cesaire reveled in the nontechnicalness of original African cultures.

Africa's most distinguished champion of Négritude is Léopold Senghor.
But although Senghor was president of Senegal for more than twenty years, he

did not embark on a program of revived simplicity. On the contrary, official policy in Senegal under Senghor was in the direction of expanding the industrial and monetary sectors.

What all this means is that the religion of industrialism is not in danger in the Third World. Even countries like Burma and the People's Republic of China—which turned their backs for a while on the lure of Western technology—have more recently shown signs of renewed fascination with that technology.

It is because of these considerations that the normative climate for technology transplant appears—at least on first estimate—favorable in most of the Third World. Parents are eager to send their children to Western-type schools: governments are eager to formulate five-year plans; there are technical experts galore temporarily imported from outside. With such a favorable climate, why is not the plant of technology taking root? Yes, why?

This is what brings us back to the metaphor of a barren soil. We see the soil in terms of the sociology of the society in relation to its structural links with the outside world. This soil is not congenial. A series of contradictions are part of the explanation.

Firstly, are parts of the Third World experiencing cultural Westernization without economic modernization? Is there a transmission of Western *consumption* patterns without a transmission of Western *production* techniques? Is there a craze for Western technological gadgets without a program of how to produce them locally?

Consumption patterns are a reflection of values, either new or old. Production techniques would have been a reflection of skills. The West has been more successful in popularizing its values and tastes than in transplanting its skills. This imbalance has often been deliberate. Creating a taste for Western goods without a local capability for producing them was often more profitable for the West than exporting both tastes and techniques.

Even in exporting capitalism as a system the West has been more effective in exporting the profit motive than the entrepreneurial skills. The profit motive is a desire for profit. It is not necessarily a skill in obtaining it. To be motivated for profit is not necessarily to be skilled in securing it.

African businessmen in places like Nigeria, the Ivory Coast, and Kenya are eager enough to maximize their returns. But many are more comfortable sitting on Boards of Directors than trying out new trading techniques. Risk-taking as an aspect of creative entrepreneurship is often underdeveloped in the Third World. Easy money and safe investment are preferred.

Even the Western puritanical principle of "Make money—but do not spend it," is honored in the breach. Money is made—but promptly spent ostentatiously. Reinvestment in better equipment or more effective techniques is seldom elevated to a priority. When new equipment is bought, it is the wrong equipment.

As for the Protestant principle of "industriousness" (or the work ethic) as a moral principle, this is often more characteristic of African peasants than of the African bourgeoisie. The latter have indeed been converted to the profit motive in many parts of Africa; but even when they are religiously Protestants, they have not necessarily been converted to the "Protestant ethic" in the classical economic sense that Max Weber reminded us about in his study *The Protestant Ethic and the Spirit of Capitalism*. The profit motive is strong in much of Africa, but entrepreneurship is still weak. This is part of the barrenness of the sociological soil for effective transplantation of relevant technology.

Even the educational systems in Africa are better in transmitting Western values and tastes than Western skills and techniques. The schools bequeathed by colonialism are instruments of cultural reorientation and not instruments of economic transformation. In the classroom there is acculturation rather than training, the cultivation of the arts of conversation rather than the transfer of techniques of production.

African universities are, on the whole, designed to produce communicators rather than creators, masters of verbal and literary "skills" rather than practitioners of the craft of innovation. Colonialism preferred imitative communicators to innovative creators. Colonial schools were designed accordingly.

Scientism rather than the scientific spirit emerged out of colonial educational structures. The *ideology* of "modern scientism" rather than the principle of genuine scientificity held sway on graduation day and beyond. Africans were trained to be awed by science rather than to master it, to be impressed by Western scientific achievements rather than to cultivate their own scientific self-confidence. The ideology of scientism made Africans not only awed by Western science but helplessly dependent upon it psychologically. The stage was set for long-term African technological dependency as well.

These are some of the contradictions which have gone toward making the postcolonial soil so inhospitable for effective technology transplantation. The climate of opinion is still in favour of technological development, but fundamental changes are needed sociologically and structurally.

To carry the metaphor of the soil a stage further, fertilizers are needed to help enrich the soil and enable the plant of new technology to take root. It is not enough to complain about North-South abuses and the genuine excesses of transnational corporations. It is not enough to focus on limitations of copyright and patent or excesses of exploitation, real as these problems are. Sooner or later we have to confront the deficiencies of the host soil, those caused by colonial distortions and those caused by indigenous cultural divergencies.

What may be at stake are factors which range from motivation patterns to educational systems, from a distorted Protestant ethic to the imbalances of the world economy.

But it is not just Western technology which is having trouble taking root in Africa. It is also certain *aspects* of Western ideology *in practice*. To profess an ideology is of course different from practicing it. African emotional responses are often positive toward both science and socialism. Yet Africa's sociological realities often militate against *both* science and socialism. Africans have often found it easier to *applaud* socialism than to *apply* it. They are more comfortable with genuine socialist *belief* than with genuine socialist *behavior*. Is this a case of hypocrisy? Or are we dealing with a special dialectic between aspiration and achievement, between emotion and practice? Let us look more closely at the fate of socialism in Africa in a historical perspective.

One distinctive factor about the decade of the 1960s in Black Africa was that it was a decade of laissez-faire socialism. One African leader after another proclaimed himself a socialist, but then let economic forces and class formation take their own courses. Black African leaders who claimed the label of socialist ranged in the ideological spectrum from Sékou Touré in Guinea to Léopold Senghor of Senegal, from Tom Mboya in Kenya to Kwame Nkrumah in Ghana.

There was also a wide range of theorizing. Some of the works by Nkrumah and the speeches of Sékou Touré are in the Marxist tradition, while Mboya, Senghor, and Julius Nyerere sometimes romanticized about *African* socialism. In the decade of the 1960s socialism in Africa was therefore very rhetorical and very diverse.

If the 1960s constituted the decade of laissez-faire socialism in Africa, the 1970s witnessed both the rise of Marxism among African intellectuals and the establishment of significant Marxist and neo-Marxist regimes in Southern Africa and the Horn. The overthrow of Emperor Haile Selassie in Ethiopia in 1974, the triumph of the Popular Movement for the Liberation of Angola in 1975–76, and the liberation of Mozambique in 1975 were all major steps in the apparent penetration of Marxism into important parts of Black Africa.

One question which arises for the 1980s is whether even Marxism in Africa (let alone African socialism) will quickly become "laissez-faire Marxism." Are African economies so weak that they automatically tend to drift? Are conditions in Africa still uncongenial for the establishment of vigorous socialist economies? Is the proximity of the Republic of South Africa to Mozambique forcing FRELIMO to move to the right as evidenced by the Nkòmati Accord? Is the social fabric in Ethiopia so disrupted by the overthrow of the imperial system of Haile Selassie that Marxism does not stand a chance of being truly consolidated? And is the continuing challenge of the United Front for the Total Liberation of Angola (UNITA) posing a major question mark on the future of Marxist structures in Angola? Is the new liberalization of the government of Guinea (Conakry) the beginning of a move to the right in that previously Stalinist country as well?

But behind these particular questions lie even broader questions. If in the 1960s there was so much lip-service paid to socialism without adequate socialist performance, and if in the 1980s the possibility of African Marxism going "laissez-faire" is real, is this due to a lack of seriousness in African leadership? Are we to say about Africa what Hamlet said of woman: "Frailty, thy name is Africa!"? Or should we say about Africa what Virgil said of woman: "*Varium et mutabile semper Femina*" ("Woman is always fickle and changing")?

Such a judgment is as unjust when applied to Africa as it has been when applied to woman. The truth of the matter is that there are factors in the African condition which make socialism appear attractive as a solution to African problems, while at the same time there are other factors which militate against the realization of socialism in practice. Africa's interest in socialism has outstripped Africa's capacity for realizing it.

The two most fundamental questions concerning Africa's love-hate relationship with socialism are these: First, what are the elements in the African condition which seem favorable to the pursuit of socialist goals? Second, what are the elements which militate against the realization of those goals?

But for someone also interested in Marxism as a system of thought there is another pair of questions worthy of attention. First, to what extent does the African condition vindicate Marxist interpretations of reality? Second, to what extent do African realities contradict Marxist theory?

The fifth question before us concerns how those two pairs of questions mentioned earlier relate to each other. The questions concerning factors which favor socialism or militate against it and the questions about whether African realities are evidence for or against Marxist theories have in turn to be examined in relationship to each other.

## The Lure of Socialism

There is a sense in which we might say that Africa's infatuation with socialism is partly a case of "courtship on the rebound." Sometimes Africans are attracted toward socialism as a way of rebelling against the West. A deep-seated love-hate relationship also lies in Africa's attitude to Western culture and civilization. African experimentation with radical socialism can at times be a method of making the West jealous, a strategy of ambivalent dependency.

But more important are the underlying alignments of historical and social forces. Africans know for a fact that Western imperialism and Western capitalism came together into the African continent. Originally Africans were opposed to Western imperialism, the external domination of their own societies by Western powers. Africans were relatively neutral in attitudes to capitalism. Yet, as the basic historical alliance between capitalism and imperialism became clearer to many African leaders and thinkers, there was a predisposition to distrust capitalism almost as much as imperalism deserved to be distrusted. The forces of anti-imperialism began to merge with the forces of anticapitalism.

To change the metaphor, there is another side to this coin. If on one side is the design of fused opposition to both imperialism and capitalism, there is on the other side the shape of an alliance between nationalism and socialism. From an African perspective, the strongest enemy of imperialism is the nationalism of the colonized peoples. The strongest enemies of capitalism are the forces of socialism and class solidarity. If capitalism and imperialism in their historical role in Africa had been aligned so closely, did it not now make sense that their enemies (nationalism and socialism) should similarly fuse into each other?

Yet another predisposing condition in favor of socialism in Africa is the frustrations of independence. Standards of living have improved in many African societies, but not enough to narrow the gap of expectations adequately. A number of African countries which used to export food before independence are now net importers of food, with severe shortages of basic products. Corruption in the majority of African countries is rampant, and political institutions remain fragile and vulnerable to either perversion or subversion or total collapse.

In the midst of the agonies of these frustrations many Africans are scanning the horizon for possible models of development and change. How can African societies save themselves from the overwhelming insecurities and failures of independence?

Inevitably, among the major contenders as models of social transformation is the socialist paradigm. Can it be translated into practice? Could things under socialism really be worse than under the prevailing conditions of laissez-faire ideologies since independence?

The fourth predisposing condition in Africa favorable to socialism is an element of cultural continuity. In many parts of Africa individualism, which is such a great value in liberal capitalism, is culturally alien to indigenous communities. This distrust of individualism becomes extended to a negative attitude toward capitalism. Capitalism acquires the image of an ideology predicated on the selfishness of man and the rugged pursuit of profit.

The other side of this coin is the "tribal" collectivism which formed the core of many African cultures. In this sense socialism and "tribalism" have one bond linking them normatively: they are both collectivist cultures.

Thus Kenya's Tom Mboya could argue in the euphoric days of the first decade of independence:

> In Africa the belief that 'we are all sons and daughters of the soil' has always exercised a tremendous influence on our social, economic and political relationships. From this belief springs the logic and the practise of equality, and the acceptance of communal ownership of the vital means of life—the land. . . . The acquisitive instinct, which is largely responsible for the vicious excesses and exploitation under the capitalist system, was tempered by a sense of togetherness and a rejection of graft and meanness. There was loyalty to the society, and the society gave its members much in return: a sense of security and universal hospitality.[7]

Given this premise, it made sense for Julius Nyerere across the border from Mboya to reaffirm as follows:

> We, in Africa, have no more need of being 'converted' to socialism than we have of being 'taught' democracy. Both are rooted in our past—in the traditional society which produced us.[8]

What African leaders like Mboya and Nyerere were asserting was that traditional societies in their own countries were based on a kind of socialist way of life within each "tribe." The question which arose on attainment of independence was whether twenty welfare tribes added together in Kenya or Tanzania could ever produce one welfare state. This seemed to be the ultimate test for this idea of a cultural continuity from African collectivism to modern socialism.

The sixth predisposing factor favorable to socialism in Africa is, in contrast, a cultural contradiction. The most important source of Marxist ideas in Africa is Western culture itself. Indeed, it is a sociolinguistic impossibility for an African to be a sophisticated Marxist without being at the same time substantially Westernized. This is because access to Marxism is overwhelmingly through works written in European languages. To become a sophisticated Marxist requires substantial access first to the primary literature by the founding fathers of Marxism (Marx and Engels) and subsequent innovators such as Lenin, Trotsky, and Mao Tse-tung, and secondly to the secondary literature on Marxism consisting of commentaries across the generations. Very little of either the primary Marxist literature or the secondary is as yet available in such African languages as Yoruba, Amharic, Hausa, or Kiswahili—let alone such smaller African languages as Kidigo and Lunyoro-Lutoro. For Africans to enter the universe of Marxism a substantial command of a European language is therefore indispensable.

And how do Africans normally acquire their first European language? Not simply by learning a new medium of communication, as would happen if an American was learning Japanese or Kiswahili. The acquisition of the first European language by an African is in fact a whole process of socialization and acculturation. Africans in anglophone countries go to schools which are modeled on British or American systems of education. Africans in French-speaking countries pass through the acculturation process based on the culture of France or francophone Belgium. Such institutions gallicize (or anglicize as the case may be) Africans before they begin to have direct access to the works of Karl Marx and his successors.

It is of course possible for some Africans to learn their Marxism after going to a university in Peking or Moscow. But neither Peking nor Moscow recruits its African students directly from the villages of Africa without the mediating role of Western European languages. African students selected for universities in Eastern Europe or the People's Republic of China are drawn from a pool of young Africans already partly or substantially Westernized.

It is because of this that we have advanced the proposition that for the time being it is a sociolinguistic impossibility for an African to be strikingly sophisticated in Marxist theory without at the same time being substantially Westernized. This is a major part of the contradictions of culture and their effect on Africa's predisposition toward socialism. This is particularly so if we remember that Marxism is a child of the West in rebellion against the West.

But this is not the only cultural contradiction that has tended to favor socialism in parts of Africa. There is also the strange phenomenon of African feudalism as a breeding ground for African radicalism. The most striking illustration is of course Ethiopia. Until the 1970s Ethiopia was an elaborate African feudal system. In some ways it was reminiscent of the Russia of the Czars.

Classical Marxist theory would not have expected a Marxist revolution in Africa to occur in such a backward and feudal society. Yet it was precisely in Ethiopia, and through the mediation of soldiers rather than workers, that a radical revolution got under way in 1974. Extreme backwardness had resulted in rapid radicalization.

A form of radicalization through soldiers also occurred in Libya. The regime of King Idris was swept aside in 1969, resulting in an ideology which kept on struggling to fuse Islamic fundamentalism with socialist fervor.

Further south earlier in the 1960s the Sultanate of Zanzibar had also illustrated how a neofeudal system could rapidly give way to angry radicalism. It has been argued that the revolution in Zanzibar in 1964 was itself a contributory factor toward the radicalization of the mainland of Tanzania and the emergence of Julius Nyerere as a relatively radical innovator.

Theorists of African socialism had assumed that what made Africa an ideal laboratory for socialism were the egalitarian and collectivist values of those African societies which were decentralized and often stateless. Many of these were in an important sense classless. African thinkers in the 1960s therefore sometimes sounded like romantic Russian socialists of the second half of the nineteenth century. In 1874 Peter Tkachoff wrote and published an "Open Letter to Mr. Friedrich Engels in Zurich." Tkachoff disputed some statement which Engels had once made about the chances of a social revolution in Russia. Tkachoff said:

> Our people are permeated in the large majority . . . with the principle of communal property; they are, if I may say so, instinctively, traditionally communist. . . . From this it follows that our people, despite their ignorance, are much nearer to a socialist society than the peoples of western Europe with their higher education.[9]

Engels dismissed this as a "childish conception"—emphasizing:

> Communal ownership of land is a form of property which was predominant among the Germans, Celts, Indians—in short in all Indo-Germanic peoples—it still exists in India. . . . In fact it is an institution common to all peoples at a certain stage of development. . . . In some primitive and pre-literate societies class distinctions are frequently absent, and every people has gone through such a stage of development. To re-establish this phase cannot be our aim. . . ."[10]

African Marxists more recently have had similar reservations about romantic schools of African socialism which aspire to build modern socialism on the collectivist values of traditional Africa. Julius Nyerere's own principle of *ujamaa* (an African word meaning "familyhood") is itself in the tradition of Tkachoff. Nyerere, like Tkachoff, used to argue that Africans did not need to be "converted" to socialism or "taught" democracy.

And yet the examples of Zanzibar in Nyerere's own country, and later on the example of Ethiopia, revealed that it is not necessarily those African societies which were indeed egalitarian which become socialist. It could quite often be the elaborate feudalism of Ethiopia or Libya which provides the breeding ground of rapid radicalization.

The seventh predisposing aspect of the African condition which is favorable to socialism concerns the role of the Soviet Union and to a much lesser extent other external socialist countries. The Soviet Union has been an imperialist force in Europe and a liberating force in Africa and has had a mixed record in Asia.

In Europe the Soviet Union has been an imperialist force because it permitted itself to be heir to both the Czarist empire and the Nazi empire. What the Czars annexed the communist regime after 1917 retained and sometimes augmented. On the other hand, what the Nazis occupied in the 1930s and 1940s and Soviet troops ostensibly liberated the Soviet Union maintained hegemony over. There is therefore very little doubt that within the European continent the role of the Soviet Union has on balance been that of an imperialist power.

In contrast, the impact of the Soviet Union on Africa's fortunes has been liberating. This is because the Soviet Union provided a challenge to the preexistent Western hegemony. Even the West's inclination to give independence to African countries was at times a response to the Soviet challege. And in Southern Africa the West moved rapidly toward liberalizing the racial situation there only when the Soviet threat became particularly acute after the collapse of the Portuguese empire and the arrival of Soviet-backed Cuban troops in support of the Marxists of Angola.

Then there is Soviet military aid to liberation movements in Southern Africa. It seems rather unlikely that Western sources could possibly have provided the level of military hardware that found its way into the liberation armies of Robert Mugabe and Joshua Nkomo in the struggle for Zimbabwe. It seems quite likely that if the Soviet Union had not existed in the world, the liberation of Southern Africa would have been delayed by at least a generation.

The motives of the Soviet Union are quite often cynical. As a superpower the rivalry between the Soviet Union and the United States is in fact a rivalry for hegemony. On this issue the People's Republic of China is quite right. The superpowers always think in terms of "a power vacuum" and tend to regard themselves as the proper "vacuum fillers."

But regardless of the actual motives of the Soviet role in Africa, its actual effect on the continent has indeed been emancipatory. This diplomatic and political alignment between African liberation and Soviet foreign policy has itself been an additional predisposing factor in Africa favorable to socialism. After all, the largest socialist country in the world in terms of power (the Soviet Union) and the largest socialist country in terms of population (China) have often demonstrated a basic posture against colonialism and racism even when they themselves are at odds with each other.

The final factor which has made socialism attractive to Africans concerns the presumed centralizing and mobilizing efficacy of the ideology. Many African societies are deeply fragmented and the political fabric is often fragile. One school of thought in Africa has emphasized the need for an ideology capable of involving the masses and giving them a sense of political engagement and participation. The ideology also needs to be, from this point of view, centralizing. Socialism has appeared as a strong candidate for this kind of role, especially when it is interpreted as an ideology of state intervention in the economy and of mass mobilization in politics.

### Elusive Socialism

In spite of these formidable factors which, especially in the first decade of independence, seemed to predispose so much of the African continent in favor of socialism, the ideology has in fact found it rather hard to take political root in Africa. Many African voices that used to sing socialist songs have now gone silent. Many African leaders that attempted a socialist path of development are relegated to the limbo of history. Is the African soil inhospitable to the seeds of socialism in spite of the initial appearance of favorable climatic conditions?

There are in fact a number of factors which tend to militate against the successful introduction of socialism to Africa. Some of those factors also militate against other forms of social, economic, and political organization, since Africa's problems are sometimes due more to general conditions of instability than merely to lack of congeniality to particular ideologies. Nevertheless, some ideologies do stand a better chance than others. And socialism is one of the most difficult to transplant to Africa. The question therefore arises: Why?

One reason concerns historical continuities between the imperial past and the postcolonial period. Links between some African countries and the former colonial powers and links between African economies and international capitalism have at times turned out to be too strong to be severed abruptly. Those African countries that have attempted to do so precipitately have sometimes found themselves in the agonies of serious economic hemorrhage.

The links may sometimes be with a country other than the former colonial power as such. This is particularly true of Mozambique with its own historical connections with the Republic of South Africa. Mozambique still hires out thousands of workers to the Republic of South Africa in exchange for gold and related contributions to Mozambique's foreign exchange reserves. Other economic links between the Marxist regime in Maputo and the racist regime in Pretoria, which were temporarily severed on attainment of Mozambique's independence, may in fact be restored and strengthened. The policy of encouraging South African investment in Mozambique and certainly the probability of increasing trade with South Africa are all part of the picture of historical continuities in Mozambique's predicament.

Then there is the problem that African countries encounter when they assume that to go socialist domestically is a way of disengaging from the international capitalist system. Many soon discover that they are as heavily dependent on international capitalism as ever—in spite of adopting socialist or neosocialist policies in their own countries.

One reason is simply the fact that global capitalism is much more obstinate and resilient than its critics assume. Even the largest of the communist countries—the Soviet Union and the People's Republic of China—are sensing a growing dependency on the world market, which in turn is dominated by capitalism and its methods. International trade is substantially born out of the rules of capitalist interaction. The major currencies of world exchange are currencies of capitalist powers. The major centers of the technology of production are disproportionately capitalist. The nerves of the world economy are at the same time nerves of world capitalism. Small countries in Africa that decide to go socialist domestically may find that they are still prisoners of the international monetary system, of the international market for copper and cocoa, of the international rules of credit, and of the international fluctuations of supply and demand. Going socialist in Nkrumah's Ghana or Nyerere's Tanzania is not an exit visa from world capitalism. Because African economies are particularly fragile, this global background of capitalism makes even domestic socialism shaky. That is one major reason why there has not been a single really successful socialist experiment in Africa—not even the equivalent of the success story of either Kenya or the Ivory Coast as a *capitalist* model.

A related difficulty which confronts socialism in Africa is the prior distinction between dependent capitalism and indigenous capitalism in Africa. This is a matter of degree rather than a sharp dichotomy. Dependent capitalism is of the kind in which, even locally within a society like the Ivory Coast, there is a disproportionate role for foreign capital, personnel, and expertise. Thus the French role in the Ivory Coast economically is much greater than seems necessary to most impartial observers. Therefore capitalism in the Ivory Coast is more dependent than capitalism in, say, Nigeria.

Kenya lies somewhere in between. Radical African analysts of the Kenyan economy in the past tended to draw no distinction between it and the model of the Ivory Coast. But there has been a growing realization that the local entrepreneurial class in Kenya is more assertive, aggressive, and autonomous than its equivalent in the Ivory Coast. From the point of view of the prospects for socialism, the question has arisen as to which one is the surer road to radicalization.

A major British political economist, Colin Leys, wrote an influential book about "neocolonialism" in Kenya some years ago.[11] The main thrust of the book at the time was that Kenyan capitalism was of the "compradore" variety. But less than three or four years later Leys was busy reexamining his original thesis, and was coming to the conclusion that capitalism in Kenya was less dependent and more autonomous than he had at first assumed.

One classical debate among Africanist Marxists is whether endogenous capitalism of the Kenyan variety or of the Nigerian model is a more effective prelude to socialism than dependent capitalism of the Ivorian variety. Western history would seem to teach us that when capitalism reaches a certain level of maturity it becomes difficult to dislodge. Marxists have been expecting a socialist revolution in places like Great Britain since the nineteenth century, but Marxists are still waiting.

On the other hand, situations where capitalism has only just begun and is still very dependent have turned out historically to be precisely the appropriate breeding grounds for effective radicalism. The history of countries as diverse as the Soviet Union and North Korea, Cuba and South Yemen, would seem to imply that *dependent* capitalism is a surer way toward socialism than indigenized (and more deeply entrenched) capitalism.

But history is one thing and doctrine is another. Marxist theory in its classical formulation did assume that a bourgeois stage of development was a necessary and inevitable precondition for a socialist revolution. As Engels put it in 1873:

> A bourgeoisie is . . . as necessary a pre-condition of the socialist revolution as the proletariat itself. A person who says that this revolution can be carried out easier in a country which has no proletariat or bourgeoisie proves by his statement that he has still to learn the ABC of socialism.[12]

By this argument, Kenya must surely be closer to socialism than Tanzania is since Kenya has more of a bourgeoisie and more of a proletariat than Tanzania has evolved so far. Similarly the Republic of South Africa is closer to a genuine socialist revolution than Mozambique is since South Africa is at a higher stage of capitalist development and has evolved a much bigger African proletariat class proportionately as well as absolutely than Mozambique can claim to have done.

Although framed differently, such debates have been known to shake the political climate of such ideologically active campuses as the University of Dar es Salaam. Are there autonomous processes of class formation taking place in Africa or are these mere reflections of the wider forces of imperialism? The Left at the University of Dar es Salaam has sometimes been torn asunder by such doctrinal considerations. The campus itself is on the whole to the left of Julius Nyerere and his government. Criticisms of the government on campus tended to be attacks from the left.

Until recently, one remarkable factor about ideological fervor on the Dar es Salaam campus was the disproportionate degree to which it was led by non-Tanzanians. The most eloquent voices of the extreme left were quite often white expatriate radicals or Africans from other countries. There were occasions when these ideological leaders were themselves disaffected Westerners—such as John Saul from Canada and Lionel Cliffe from the United Kingdom. The late Walter Rodney, from Guyana, was also a very visible and eloquent leader of the left when he was at the University of Dar es Salaam. In the 1970s some Ugandans in exile from Idi Amin also loomed large on the ideological scene. Especially prominent were Dan Nabudere, who became a Minister in Uganda after Amin's fall, and Yash Tandon, who became a member of Parliament in Kampala when Amin fell (the interim parliament called the National Consultative Council).

One theory concerning the prominence of non-Tanzanians linked up with the sociological theory of marginality. The same considerations which made Jews visible in certain areas of Western life had made non-Tanzanians ideologically conspicuous on the campus of the University of Dar es Salaam.

But it was not merely marginality defined in terms of citizenship which seemed to operate in Dar es Salaam, but also marginality defined in terms of race. The most extensively discussed theoretical works in the late 1960s and much of the 1970s on campus in Dar es Salaam were not the works of Julius K. Nyerere but the essays of Isa Shivji. Like Nyerere, Shivji was a Tanzanian. But unlike Nyerere, Shivji was of Indian extraction. His thesis that there was a silent class struggle going on in Tanzania, that it had a dynamism of its own, and that it included a dialectic between the bureaucratic and the commercial bourgeoisie provoked considerable debate and controversy, much of which was genuinely sophisticated and intellectually exciting.

Another marginal but eloquent figure at the University of Dar es Salaam was Mahmood Mamdani, another East African of Indian extraction, who was forced by circumstances to become a British citizen. Mamdani—who got a distinction in his Harvard Ph.D. defense—was also a superb orator and eloquent theoretician.

By the middle of the 1970s the battle lines were basically drawn between anti-imperialists like Nabudere and Tandon, on one side, and anticapitalists, like Shivji and Mamdani, on the other. The anti-imperialists defined the enemy as being basically external, the penetration of world capitalism into Africa; the anticapitalists allowed the African continent the dignity of producing its own indigenous capitalist devils, without necessarily reflecting the machinations of external imperialist forces.

The class struggle in Tanzania may or may not be silent. What is certain is that the ideological struggle in Tanzania, especially at its national university, has tended to be loud and clear.[13]

## The Vanguard of the African Revolutions

While there has been a good deal of sophisticated debate in Africa as to who are the main carriers of capitalism into Africa, there has been relatively limited discussion about the main carriers of revolution. Who in fact are the great instruments of change in Africa at this radical level? One line of analysis has compared the revolutionary credentials of the peasants to those of the urban workers. This is a debate that has been quite important in the history of Marxism, and has at times led to heated theoretical controversies in Russia before and after the October Revolution and in China before and after the revolution of 1949. Inevitably the debate had to rear its head on the African radical scene as well. Shivji in Tanzania has a good deal to say about the labor aristocracy of Africa—the urban workers who are, as compared with the rural masses, themselves privileged in some sense. A bigger radical theorist than Shivji, Franz Fanon, had entered the debating arena even earlier, putting not only the peasantry before the proletariat as instruments of revolution but also the lumpen proletariat before the proletariat. Those newly arrived and bewildered lumpen elements in the ghettos of African cities could be, according to Fanon, solid recruiting material for revolutionary armies.[14]

But the least explored area in African radical debate is the role of the Westernized intelligentsia. We mentioned earlier that it was impossible for an African to be a sophisticated Marxist without first being substantially Westernized. A Marxist revolutionary in African sociological conditions is therefore inevitably a Westernized revolutionary.

Every revolution has ultimately two sides, the destruction of the old order and the inauguration of the new. The workers and the peasants, when they have suffered enough and will no longer tolerate the status quo, can rise and pull down the old order in one massive outburst of revolutionary fury. But can the workers and the peasants then proceed to design a new alternative order? Can the peasants of Ethiopia or Angola shape on their own a sufficiently revolutionary alternative design?

In the light of these questions, it might turn out to be that the most revolutionary of all social classes is neither the proletariat nor the peasantry but the bourgeoisie itself. A segment of the bourgeoisie is often at odds with the system as a whole. V. I. Lenin was sensitive to this issue. To use Lenin's own words:

> The theory of socialism . . . grew out of the philosophic, historical, and economic theories elaborated by educated representatives of the property classes, by intellectuals. By their social status, the founders of modern scientific socialism, Marx and Engels, themselves belonged to the bourgeois intelligentsia.[15]

The Shivjis and Nyereres of Africa, the Nkrumahs, Tourés, and Fanons, belong to the African equivalent of bourgeois intelligentsia. At any rate the architects and designers of revolutions in Africa are not drawn from the toiling masses in the countryside but from the more privileged sectors of African societies.

But the revolutionary intelligentsia in Black Africa is disproportionately Westernized. A combination of two forces has produced the sophisticated African Marxists or revolutionaries—domestic class formation and cultural imperialism. The domestic class formation has given birth to a black bourgeoisie and petty bourgeoisie. Cultural imperialism has assimilated a large segment of this bourgeoisie into Western culture. They are the people that read *Das Kapital*, debate silent class struggle in Tanzania, advise bewildered soldiers like Mengistu Haile Mariam, ideologically tutor the rulers of Angola and Mozambique, and are represented by such gifted translators of Shakespeare as Julius K. Nyerere.

Who then are the ultimate carriers of revolution in the modern world? Karl Marx expected them to be the most exploited class in the most advanced societies, the Western proletariat. In fact Africa's experience demonstrates that it is the most privileged class in the least advanced societies that are closer to that historic revolutionary role. It is the Westernized bourgeois intelligentsia of the Third World (most privileged groups of least advanced societies) rather than the workers of Birmingham, Detroit, and Marseilles (the least privileged groups in the most advanced countries) that have been carrying the torch of radicalism in the last third of the twentieth century.

Once again Africa's experience poses major dilemmas to radical theoreticians both in Africa itself and in the wider world where revolution and reflection touch, recoil, and reconcile.

### Conclusion

A major thesis of this essay is that Africa has a favorable climate for both science and socialism but an infertile soil. The favorable climate is intellectual and normative. Many Africans who are politically conscious find both socialist doctrines and scientific solutions intellectually satisfying. On the other hand, the infertile soil is sociological and economic. The actual material conditions in Africa do not seem to be hospitable to successful scientific or socialist experiments. While the continent has indeed witnessed such relatively impressive capitalist experiments as the Ivory Coast and Kenya, the continent has not as yet been able to display a strikingly successful socialist model. But technologically even Kenya and the Ivory Coast only work when they are dependent on outsiders.

The favorable climate for socialism in Africa is part of contemporary African political culture; the unfavorable and infertile soil for socialism is part of Africa's contemporary structure. The political culture of anti-imperialism has often evolved into intellectual anticapitalism. African nationalism has interacted at times with socialist fervor.

On the other hand, the structural realities of Africa continue to bind it to the world capitalist system. Those same structural realities domestically reveal patterns of class formation which are not yet ready to sustain a socialist structure.

The cultural climate of Africa also includes a traditional distrust of individualism and generations of experience in collectivist behavior. This is part of Africa's cultural predisposition toward socialism.

On the other hand, the disturbing impact of Western culture and the effects of capitalism have released new forms of self-interest, new patterns of self-fulfillment, new manifestations of personal greed. Profit is often at its most naked among those who are newly converted to the profit motive.

It is because of this configuration of factors that the cultural climate of Africa appears cool and wet for both science and socialism, but the soil is still too rocky and sandy to enable socialism to take roots. The normative orientation seems right; the material conditions are wrong. Socialist conversion seems to have disastrously preceded class consciousness; the ideology of scientism is ahead of the skills of science.

But in addition to demonstrating the gap between political culture and structural realities, this essay has also related those issues to some of the wider theoretical concerns posed by Marxism and African radicalism. These have included the classical dilemma of whether a shortcut to either technological development or socialism is feasible without undergoing the agonies of capitalism. Since much of Black Africa has produced neither a large proletariat nor a large bourgeoisie, the problem is posed at its most dramatic in African conditions.

Then there is the equally basic question of radicalism concerning revolutionary credentials of different social groups. Do we look for agents of transformation among urban workers, among peasants, among the lumpen proletariat, or in the ultimate analysis among the bourgeoisie? The African experience once again shows a disproportionate revolutionary role by the bourgeois intelligentsia—cast in the role, if not of destroying the old order, then at least of attempting to design a new one. We have reminded ourselves that Marx and Engels thought it was the least privileged of the most advanced societies that would stage a revolution. Africa's experience seems to indicate that it is the most privileged of the least developed societies that sometimes produce leaders in revolutionary transformation. Here we have as a vanguard not the workers of the United States but a section of the middle class of South Yemen and Cuba in charge of societal transformation.

In addition, there is in Africa the pervasive presence of Western culture and its dialectical implications for both class consciousness and ideological radicalism. We have sought to demonstrate in this essay that for the time being it is a sociolinguistic impossibility for an African to be a sophisticated Marxist without being at the same time substantially Westernized. The interplay between consciousness and culture is at its most dramatic within this particular dialectic. Bourgeois Africans become socialist not because class consciousness has at last arisen but because class consciousness has been negated. Bourgeois Africans identify with the proletariat and the peasantry in a fit of class amnesia. The culture of the imperial power becomes both a factor in individual psychology and a factor in class behavior in the new realities of the African continent.

Finally, we have sought to demonstrate in this essay that while the 1960s were a decade of socialist rhetoric all over the continent and the 1970s a decade of Marxist models in parts of Africa and capitalist paradigms in others, the 1980s and 1990s are likely to reveal more fully the basic tensions between cultural myths and technological realities in an Africa caught up in the bewilderment of change.

The corridors of Ghana's modest nuclear research center today still reverberate with Nkrumah's words "Socialism without science is void." But in Ghana both socialism and science have been in a void for a long time—a sociological void. The type of socialism and the kind of science attempted in postcolonial Ghana have been inattentive to Ghanaian realities, insensitive to the continuities of its history, and deaf to the whispers of its culture.

Science without culture is dead; socialism without ancestors is still-born.

## NOTES

1. See *Ghana Today*, vol. VIII, no. 21 (16 December 1964), p. 1.
2. Julius K. Nyerere, "The Purpose Is Man," in his *Freedom and Socialism* (London: Oxford University Press, 1968), p. 320.
3. Ibid.
4. Jack Goody, *Technology, Tradition and State in Africa* (London: Oxford University Press, 1971), pp. 43–46.
5. F. Stewart, *Technology and Development* (London: Macmillan, 1977).
6. Aimé Cesaire, *Return to My Native Land* (Paris: Présence Africaine, 1939).
7. Tom Mboya, *Freedom and After* (London: André Deutsch, 1963), p. 163.
8. Julius K. Nyerere, "Ujamaa" Speech at TANU Conference on Socialism, Dar es Salaam, April 1962. See *Africa Report* (U.S.A.), May 1963.
9. Friedrich Engels quotes Tkachëv in "Russia and the Social Revolution," an article first published on 21 April 1875 in the *Leipzig Volksstaat*, organ of the German Social Democratic Workers Party.
10. Engels, "Russia and the Social Revolution Reconsidered," an essay written in 1894 and translated in Karl Marx and Friedrich Engels, *The Russian Menace to Europe*, a collection of articles, speeches, letters, and news dispatches selected and

edited by Paul W. Blackstook and Bert F. Hoselitz (Glencoe, Ill.: The Free Press, 1952), pp. 229–241.

11. Colin Leys, *Underdevelopment in Kenya: The Political Economy of Neo-Colonialism* (London: Heinemann Educational Books, 1975). I had discussions with Colin Leys in Nairobi on a subsequent research trip of his when he was reexamining his original thesis.

12. Engels, "Russia and the Social Revolution," loc. cit., p. 205.

13. Consult Isa Shivji, *Class Struggle in Tanzania* (London: Heinemann Educational Press, 1976) and Mahmood Mamdani, *Politics and Class Formation in Uganda* (London: Heinemann Educational Press, 1976).

14. Franz Fanon, *The Wretched of the Earth* (New York: Grove Press, 1963).

15. V. I. Lenin, "What Is To Be Done?" *Selected Works* (Moscow: Foreign Languages Press, 1960), vol. 1, p. 149.

CHAPTER 12

# Ideology in Africa:
# Decomposition and Recomposition

*John S. Saul*

The terms of comparison between the two very different "moments"
which mark the beginning and the end of the first quarter century of African
postcolonial independence have become almost clichéd: high hopes versus
grim reality, in the manner of a recent *Time* magazine cover story ("Africa's
Woes: Coups, Conflict and Corruption"). Not surprisingly, ideological currents on the continent have reflected this trajectory, though not in an entirely
straightforward manner. In fact, as the superficial unity of ideological expression which characterized the initial moment of independence has been as-
sailed by reality, it has been refracted in not one, but two main directions.

In one direction has lain a far more overt embracing of capitalist rationali-
zations for policy choices than would have seemed possible in the atmosphere
which prevailed twenty-five years ago. However, as we shall see, this capitalist
discourse makes relatively little claim to occupy the realm of "high ideology."
Generally it is cast in far more narrow and calculating, even cynical, terms
than the capitalist discourses—liberalism most prominent among them—
which accompanied the self-confident rise of the Western bourgeoisie to
prominence. A second main direction is even more novel in the manner of its
thrusting itself upon the scene. Thus Marxism, very much held in the wings in
the late 1950s, is now sufficiently center stage on the continent to have attracted great attention, spawning a range of writings—on "Afro-Marxism,"
"Afro-communism," and the like—in recent years. Moreover, at its best, this
Afro-Marxism has been markedly innovative, albeit in ways that most commentators on the phenomenon have had difficulty in grasping clearly. For this
latter reason, in particular, we shall have a great deal to say about it in this
paper. It scarcely needs adding that Afro-Marxism—rather like Afro-capitalism
in this respect, as it happens—has found the realities of deep-seated African

underdevelopment sufficiently daunting that very little of its promise has been
realized up to now. Yet promise there undoubtedly is, a promise which more
Africans may wish to seize hold of as the second quarter century of independence begins.

## I. The Ideology of Independence

Let us look more closely at the "moment of independence" in terms of its
characteristic ideological expression. The components of independence ideology were the following: populism (with this, in turn, grounding a flurry of
discourse around the theme of "African socialism") and nationalism, plus just
a *soupçon* of liberalism (although such liberalism as was present in the mix
was of an even more tactical variety than the other components!). We shall
look at each of these elements briefly.

### POPULISM

As I had occasion to write some fifteen years ago, populism—its theory
and practice premised on the notion that "legitimacy resides in the people's
will"—is an obvious term by means of which to characterize much of the
ideological discourse that accompanied anticolonial movements to power in
Africa.[1] There can be no doubt that the more sophisticated of the colonialists
saw, by the 1950s, that shepherding the nationalist leadership into power was a
way to stem any further radicalization of the challenge to colonial hegemony.
Not all those who, on the African side, rode the crest of anticolonial nationalism to power were so cynical. As with other rising classes and leadership cadres in history, their own ambitions dovetailed neatly with more generalized demands for liberation, and the radical democratic phraseology that
came so easily to their lips certainly had some life and substance beyond mere
manipulative rationalization.

Still, as Ernesto Laclau has emphasized, "popular-democratic ideologies
never present themselves separated from, but (instead are) articulated with,
class ideological discourses."[2] African populism had a relatively open-ended
quality to it because the class primarily responsible for its formulation—the
African petty bourgeoisie—was somewhat amorphous, still very much in formation. However, more often than not this class-in-the-making did consolidate itself qua class in entrepreneurial and bureaucratic roles, and, as it did
so, its populism became more and more manipulative, a fact increasingly evident not only to this class itself but also to those populaces whom it had come
to rule. Unwilling to deepen its populism along radically democratic-cum-
revolutionary socialist lines on the one hand, the "new class" was also inca-

pable of institutionalizing and domesticating it, on the terrain of peripheral capitalism, in liberal-democratic structures on the other. In consequence, those in power increasingly allowed cynicism and self-interest to replace whatever more elevated resonance the populist impulse might once have had for it.

### "AFRICAN SOCIALISM"

It was not a very great step beyond the political premises of populism—those of radical democratization—to a critical stance regarding the socioeconomic structures inherited from colonialism. Many students of populist ideologies have emphasized the manner in which they also come to "uphold . . . resistance against the spreading of capitalist relations";[3] such was the apparent logic of the African socialism which was so much heralded in the early years of independence. Often the invocation of this theme was a completely cynical maneuver, of course; one thinks here of Kenya's notorious "Sessional Paper #10" as an example.* But sometimes, as in Tanzania, this impulse represented, at least momentarily, the establishment of a rather more positive dialectic between petty-bourgeois leadership and the mass of the population.

Unfortunately, even in its most positive expressions this African socialism encapsulated a characteristic ambiguity of populism: looking backwards to a rather romantically conceived (classless) past as some kind of guarantee against the inequalities and depredations of capitalism rather than forwards to the imperatives of struggle—class struggle—for a modern alternative to actually existing peripheral capitalism. Although any kind of socialist project faces real obstacles in Africa, it was to become painfully apparent that African socialists lacked the tools for the kind of class analysis which alone could premise the class struggle necessary to progress. Moreover, as the petty bourgeoisie proceeded to *make itself*, thus developing into a more self-consciously "dominant class" throughout Africa, it became equally apparent that it had little taste for making democratization real and thus empowering the popular classes to shift African socialism onto the terrain of genuine socialist transformation. Of course, there may have been some progressive legacy from this African socialist moment on the continent. Crawford Young has suggested that in such countries as Tanzania, Algeria, and Guinea-Bissau the "earnest effort visible in both theory and practice to retain the egalitarian vision of socialism" makes a positive difference in their texture and quality of life.[4] Nonetheless, it is the weaknesses, "in both theory and practice," of the African socialism project which seems to have been the most prominent thing about it—even where it had some substance as a developmental initiative.

---

*Houphuët-Boigny was one of the few to dispense vigorously with this fig leaf of respectability right from the outset and openly to embrace African capitalism.

NATIONALISM

Self-evidently, nationalism, anticolonial nationalism, was a prominent component of the populist brew that premised the independence struggle. "The common object—with minor variations—of these [national] movements [was] the creation of self-governing States in which political power will rest, effectively, with Africans."[5] The national claim was often tenuous enough historically, needless to say, qualified by the arbitrariness of the lines of nationality on the map and by the strength of various subnational identifications. But these facts did not make such claims any the less important or, in comparison with the colonial presence, any the less legitimate. Equally clearly (as we have seen to be true of populism more broadly conceived) nationalism has, in Laclau's phrase, no "necessary class belonging." "Is it feudal, bourgeois or proletarian ideology? Considered in itself it has no class connotation."[6] Its content, in the postcolonial period, would be shaped in substantial measure by the process of class formation and by "ideological class struggle." Yet those who set the pace ideologically were increasingly assuming their "historic mission" as, in Fanon's words, a "national middle class" who serve as "intermediary," as a "transmission line between the nation and a capitalism, rampant though camouflaged, which today puts on the masque of neo-colonialism."[7] Under such circumstances their nationalism was not likely to deepen into a more fully articulated anti-imperialist perspective and practice. Instead, nationalism became an increasingly rhetorical bottom line both of legitimation of those in power and of defense against the disintegration of deeply divided countries.*

LIBERALISM

What of the discourses of liberal democracy? The last days of colonialism saw a grotesque shadow dance around this theme. The colonialists, authoritarian and racist in their dealings with Africans from the first days of imperialist aggression on the continent to (very near) the last suddenly became liberals and democrats, as it served their interests to so present themselves. The "new elites of Tropical Africa" conformed to the prevailing rules of the game, of course, and became sunshine liberal democrats in turn. Yet it is the case that even during the decolonization process they appeared much more comfortable with the discourses of populism and of anticolonial nationalism. Moreover, even those leaders who embraced most aggressively a capitalist option right from the outset of the independence period (like Houphuët-Boigny, for example) made little

---

*This latter manipulation of nationalist themes has been rendered particularly ironic by the fact that it was the political in-fighting of an increasingly opportunistic petty bourgeoisie which, simultaneously, breathed into ethnic divisions much of the political life which they have come to have!

attempt to embrace either the liberal-democratic practices or the liberal-democratic discourses attendant upon some capitalist systems elsewhere in the world. As we shall argue in the next section, there was in fact little socio-economic basis for liberal democracy in independent Africa, a fact which also helped to define the nature of African capitalist ideology as it came much more forcefully to the fore in the wake of the decomposition of "independence ideology."

## II. African Capitalism

It is no longer easy for classes linked to capitalist practices to rationalize their activities in quasi-socialist terms. Most such classes do not have the inclination to do so in any case. The Africa of the 1980s is a much more hard-boiled and worldly wise place than it was in the 1950s, and dominant elements increasingly accept the logic of capital, world-wide and local, as being merely the common sense of the matter. Moreover, they do so not just as the "intermediaries" for foreign capital which Fanon presented them as being. They have that role, but capitalist classes—active both in the marketplace and within the state apparatus—have also found more room for independent maneuver than dependency theorists have sometimes granted. This may even give some novel class basis for a reinvigorated nationalism, for example—a nationalism which is more than merely manipulative although also one very different from the independence version which had been ambiguous and uncertain as to its class content. For it can now come to provide ideological reinforcement for the struggles of indigenous capitalist classes either to better, at the margins, the terms of their bargain with neocolonialism or to strike down indigenous rivals (African nationalism as racism vis-à-vis Asians in Kenya and Uganda, for example). Nonetheless, in such guises (and so rooted in the much firmer consolidation of the postcolonial class structure) the invocation of nationalism has become a far more calculated and circumscribed exercise than previously.

There is, in short, the occasional shuffling of the deck of old ideological themes. Yet how bloodless an exercise this is in so many countries when compared with the populist heyday of the rising tide of anticolonial nationalism. Much more apparent with the decomposition of independence ideology has been a kind of "de-ideologization" of politics, a virtual reduction of politics and of political-cum-ideological discourses to the mean level of interests and of aggressive individualism. This is a situation in which some form of dependent capitalism shapes economic life, and the political power structure tends to rest on a byzantine web of crosscutting deals and bargains. Not that traces of formal "ideologizing" disappear altogether. Indeed it is almost a truism to say that even the stance of "pragmatism" and "anti-ideology" adopted by African capitalists implies, in and of itself, the taking of a profoundly ideological position. It was with this in mind, and despite the fact that "the capitalist pathway in Africa has numerous followers but few partisans," that Crawford Young has sought to draw out and to systematize the various themes which he sees as comprising the ideology of African capitalism.[8]

In so doing he suggests that familiar notions regarding the centrality of the market, of capital, of an "open economy," of equality of economic opportunity as keys to economic progress comprise "an inter-related set of premises that collectively represent a paradigm and are derived from neo-classical economics as modified by the Western school of development economics." Even such premises are often more implicit than explicit, of course, and the preferences they evidence tend to be primarily the stuff of elite opinion. Young himself hastens to admit that "the political acceptability of the African capitalist path rests not upon widespread philosophical preference among the populace for the liberal market economy as is the case for a number of Western countries." Moreover, these premises are remarkably economistic in their purview. And, as Young also notes, they are closely linked in ruling circles to a preference for "the bureaucratic-authoritarian state"! This is of interest. As with the significance to Sherlock Holmes's enlightened understanding of the dog's *not* barking in the night, there is much to be learned by examining instructive *silences* in the ideological realm. For Afro-capitalism such a silence lies, as we shall see, in the absence of any very developed discourse around the theme of liberal democracy.

First, however, we must follow up on Young's professed scepticism regarding the weight even his "inter-related set of premises" has as popular ideology; instead of a "philosophical preference" there is a "more contingent consent grounded in the effectiveness of the regime's performance." True in part perhaps, but there is also a great deal of *force* at play in the interest of regime stability in Africa; more important for our present purposes is the fact that there is a great deal more to ruling-class ideological hegemony in capitalist Africa as well. To understand this we must expand our terms of reference somewhat. So far this paper has tended to steer clear of some of the more tortuous theoretical questions regarding the status and meaning of the very concept of "ideology," favoring a rather commonsensical notion of the phenomenon. It should be borne in mind, however, that in much of the Marxist tradition "ideology" is a synonym for mystification, the very opposite of science and true knowledge. In fully established capitalist systems, for example, it is the superficial manifestations of the system (commodity fetishism, etc.) which premise both popular understanding and something so apparently sophisticated as "bourgeois" economics. The more important mechanisms of the system (viz., exploitation) tend to slip by unnoticed, blocked off both from popular comprehension and from possible illumination by any very effective science of society.

The workings of peripheral capitalism in Africa which we have briefly epitimized above tend to produce an ideological veil of their own. This is not merely a result of commodity fetishism, although, as and when Africans are drawn more tightly into the market, the latter does help reduce the likelihood of their gaining any real sense of possible class or collective purpose in their society. Yet the undermining of their potential sense of collectivity is facilitated in other ways as well, most notably by the extreme fragmentation of the sociopolitical realm that the politics of interest, discussed earlier, facilitates. The political infrastructure of ethnic and regional bargaining and patron-client concerns which are so central to the system of African peripheral capitalism spins off an image, as far as it goes, of the broader sociopolitical realm as being merely a zero-sum game of competing interests. In consequence, for the vast majority of Africans the satisfactions of collectivity are to be sought not in looking toward the broader social realm but in retreating from it, hiving off a realm of familial or quasi-traditional sociality for that purpose. Of course, this "retreat" of the peasantry has economic roots as well, the relative weakness of capitalist development often having the effect of merely *marginalizing* the peasantry. But the result is clear. Many of the "existential" and "historical" aspects of human subjectivity that a less economistic, more philosophically rich ideology might be expected to speak to are thus merely fragmented, decentralized, and, in the end, depoliticized. The narrowness of overt "capitalist ideology" in Africa thus appears as being a far from arbitrary phenomenon.

Capitalist ideology elsewhere has also operated to fragment consciousness and thus preempt the possibility of social vision. Yet there is a difference: in more advanced capitalist settings it has succeeded in speaking less economistically to other aspects of social existence and collective meaning as well. For, as we have noted several times, what is most noticeably absent is anything like a fully rounded liberal-democratic discourse, that ideological icing on the cake of more self-confident capitalisms elsewhere. Clearly, the surfacing of such a liberal-democratic discourse has had a historical integrity and resonance of its own, a "relative autonomy" from the production process which has been rooted in intellectual and political practices. Nonetheless, there can be little doubt that it was grounded in the rise of capitalism, both in the assertions of a rising bourgeoisie vis-à-vis a decaying feudal order and in the tactical adjustments on the part of that bourgeoisie which were necessary to contain the demands of popular classes which capitalist development also stimulated. And though this liberal tradition does have some life of its own it has also proved to be all too easy to jettison when capitalist contradictions have escaped the stable control of the major beneficiaries of the system.

Historically, liberal democracy represents the outcome of two phases of capitalist development that Africa has not experienced:

1. a confrontation between a relatively strong bourgeoisie and a relatively strong movement of the popular classes (especially of a large proletariat) which falls short of revolution but which nonetheless forces the striking of a liberal-democratic bargain between the classes

2. a subsequent stabilization of that bargain by means of a sufficiently high level of economic performance (and, generally, some measure of redistribution) and a sufficiently well-entrenched apparatus of "socialization" to guarantee (bourgeois) "hegemony," in the Gramscian sense

Liberalism represents, in short, the guaranteeing of various freedoms, some formal, some more real, within a framework of stable bourgeois hegemony. Small wonder that the main protagonists of African liberalism have been expatriate Africans in Western universities, for so to argue is to risk an idealism, to imagine that the realm of liberal discourse is far more autonomous than it is likely to be.

This is not to deny that practices linked to liberal-democratic discourse do occasionally evidence themselves in Africa. There has been some pull in this direction in Nigeria certainly, where formal democratic institutions have also had appeal, from time to time, as possibly providing a "neutral" arena for registering "objectively," and thereby (it might be hoped) defusing, regional and ethnic tensions. Various attempts to ventilate one-party systems with quasi-competitive elections and reduced central control over the media can also be important in this respect; so, perhaps, was the somewhat bizarre initiative taken by the state in Senegal to create, out of whole cloth, a range of opposition parties to spread across the ideological spectrum, an opening-up which more recently seems even to have deepened beyond this ultra-manipulative starting point. Indeed, it would be wrong to sneer at the least manipulative of these developments. Some degree of achieved liberalism—elements of the "rule of law," for example, or some measure of parliamentary vitality—is clearly better than no freedom at all. Nonetheless, when all is said and done, "coups, conflict and corruption" and the "bureaucratic-authoritarian state" are far more symptomatic of the current political situation in capitalist Africa than are such examples (not least in Nigeria, as the most recent developments there attest). Such is the level of capitalist development in Africa and of the class struggle that the situation does not call forth, very powerfully, liberal-democratic bargains, the risks and irrelevance of liberal-democracy still far outweighing its potential benefits to the dominant classes which are emerging.

Understood in this light, the absence of a broader, more philosophical reso-nance which characterizes African capitalist ideology is likely to continue for some time to come.

### III. "Afro-Marxism"

As stated at the very outset of this paper, there has been an alternative kind of "recomposition" of African ideology, and it is one which, for better or worse, does cast its project in much more heroic terms. The reference is to Afro-communism or Afro-Marxism. Less than a decade ago, with more than fifteen years of Africa's first quarter century elapsed, Marxism remained pro-fane knowledge on much of the continent, confined to college campuses and to micromovements. Then—it seemed almost overnight—"nearly 20 percent of African states had adopted such a self-definition," a self-definition as (the phrase, however, belongs to Young) an "Afro-Marxist state," with every possi-bility that the number may grow. "This new species of polity is, accordingly, of considerable interest," concludes Young[9]—and of special interest to the stu-dent of ideology in Africa. What we seem to be witnessing is a shift to the left, which promises, on the terrain of left practice and left discourse on the continent, a considerable deepening of the populist-cum-African socialist project. More specifically, drawing on the Marxist tradition might be expected to permit a deepening of conventional nationalism into a more coherently anti-imperialist perspective and the deepening of populism and African so-cialism into a more consistent and coherent orientation toward class struggle and a clearer comprehension of the imperatives of socialist reconstruction.

INTERPRETATIONS

Has Afro-Marxism in fact represented advances in these spheres? This is a question to which we will return. First it may be useful to clear the scholarly ground of some impediments to our understanding of what is really afoot here. For there has been a flowering of scholarly and quasi-scholarly writing on the subject. Unfortunately some of this writing is very misleading while, even at its best, it has not been sufficiently sensitive either to the creative ten-sions which exist within the Marxist tradition or to the extent to which Af-rican regimes can make innovative and creative advances on the very terrain of Marxism itself. Reviewing some of its literature may be a useful starting point for our analysis here. Moreover, taken cumulatively, this literature can tell us something about the intensity of the "ideological class struggle" which is currently being waged on the scholarly front over the very interpretation of ideology in Africa!

The Cold War optic is, of course, a familiar one, epitomized with passing crudity by Thomas Henriksen in a volume he edited in 1981 for the Hoover Institution entitled *Communist Powers and Sub-Saharan Africa*.[10] Consider the proposition that "realizing the importance of Africa to its long-term goals, the Kremlin strove successfully to give wide-spread currency to the communist idea of neo-colonialism. African leaders and intellectuals . . . adopted the concept." As if it were not precisely an awareness of the palpable realities of capitalist "neo-colonialism" that carried many Africans toward Marxism. Or consider: "Moscow took advantage of anti-white feelings in the former Portuguese colonies, Zimbabwe and South Africa, which led proponents of African majority rule to turn to radical solutions at home and closer identification with the Communist world." As if it were not precisely because many Africans saw the severe limitations of "anti-white feelings" for the grounding of their own revolutionary processes that facilitated their finding a Marxist-based class analysis a more adequate tool for understanding and acting upon their situation. Or consider, on a slightly different tack and more specifically, Henriksen's trivializing of struggles—cast by him in terms of ethnic and personality conflicts and the cynical jockeying for position of manipulative elites—within Mozambique's FRELIMO during the liberation struggle in such a way as to completely obscure that movement's ability to sustain the concept and practice of class struggle into the phase of an attempted transition to socialism. Yet, as we shall see, the latter has been a process of fundamental significance.

Or take another book, one similarly preoccupied with Soviet expansionism at the expense of benighted Africans, Peter Wiles's *The New Communist Third World*.[11] Although Wiles grants a Mozambique some room for maneuver, that room—as with other like-minded African regimes as well—is very limited, the "irreversibility" of the absorption of such regimes into the Soviet orbit being a virtual axiom of his approach. Even more than with Henriksen, this version of "Soviet manipulation" theory crosses the thin line which separates it from racism: "Africans are simply not educated enough, nor have they a long and impressive enough tradition, to find a viable native form of Marxism, or indeed any other all-embracing ideology." (No problem. As he hastens to add, "Marxist-Leninist ideology is of course excellent for semi-educated people"!) He continues, "Those who believe that an independent non-Soviet ideology or policy will emerge among the African countries we have selected do Africa too much honour. They must specify exactly what its present beginnings are: exactly which African traditions, country by country, are in conflict with exactly which Soviet traditions; and how these particular countries will get out of the trap they seem to be in." As it happens, the independence, both potential and realized, of Afro-Marxism is not so difficult to demonstrate, although this is less because of the saliency of "African traditions" than because of different interpretations, on the Marxist terrain, of theoretical and practical imperatives.

We shall demonstrate this shortly. However, we might also note that much the same tone as that of Henriksen and Wiles infects the somewhat more sophisticated account by Kenneth Jowitt in his essay "Scientific Socialist Regimes in Africa: Political Differentiation, Avoidance and Unawareness" to be found in the Rosberg/Callaghy volume *Socialism in Sub-Saharan Africa: A New Assessment*.[12] Jowitt presents a more elaborate, if equally cynical, version of that part of the Henriksen argument mentioned above which reduced Marxism in Africa to a mere bargaining counter used by manipulative elites in their jockeying for power, nationally and internationally—all this in the interests of "political differentiation, avoidance, and unawareness" (as his arcane and singularly misleading lexicon would have it). The same racist tone? Consider his argument that "appropriation of a free good like Marxism-Leninism may in a fundamental respect have *quasi-magical meanings*—e.g., it may to some extent be seen as a 'guarantee' of development and as a 'political amulet' capable of offsetting the neo-colonial threat to a recently acquired and fragile political autonomy. . . . Situations of great constraint generate a climate of elite desperation with a consequent tendency to adopt quasi-magical solutions to overwhelming problems." Small wonder that we find "the recent adoption of Marxist-Leninist facades in Ethiopia, Angola and Mozambique."

Facades? Facades because of the manipulative politics Marxism-Leninism merely screens, because of the quasi-magical resonance it has, and because, too, Africans who adopt Marxism-Leninism refuse to bite the bullet of the "hard choices" which, for Jowitt, Marxism-Leninism necessarily connotes:

> The defining feature of self-designation by an African elite as either 'scientific socialist' or 'Marxist-Leninist' appears to be an effort to establish an intermediate domestic and international political position—to avoid hard (i.e. mutually exclusive) choices of international alignments and domestic political organization.

One may read this as saying that adoption of Marxism-Leninism as a defining ideology implies uncritical absorption into the Soviet camp in the international sphere and a tough authoritarian (in Jowitt's terminology, "Leninist") solution to the problem of power domestically. For Jowitt, African regimes can only temporarily (and confusedly) sojourn in the dream world of not going hard in this direction—or in quite another (non-Marxist) one.

This is pretty silly stuff. Of course, we must be alert to the use of Marxism as a "facade"—though not for the reasons Jowitt advances and certainly not in all of those countries which he specifically mentions. What is one to make, for example, of Kenneth Kaunda's recent dabbling with Marxism! There is a tendency, without doubt, for some African leaders to seek a more credible grounding for their progressive image at home and abroad in something beyond the largely discredited nostrums of African Socialism. A rather manipulative bow in the direction of Afro-Marxism might seem to hold promise in this regard. Discussing a somewhat different case, Edmund Keller[13] has recently advanced the argument that Marxism-Leninism in Ethiopia has come primarily to rationalize and legitimate the assertions of an aggressive new "state-class"—Afro-Marxism as a kind of "super-populism," in effect. Ideologic class struggle rather than juju is what is at stake here, of course. But, this said, we have far from exhausted all relevant discussion about Marxism in Africa.

What is most dubious in Jowitt's case are his fiats about what scientific socialism *must*, by definition, connote for Africans. Moreover, this particular distortion in his argument is especially noteworthy since it anticipates a problem in comprehending the specificity of Marxism in Africa which is shared by far more intelligent commentators on the phenomenon such as Crawford Young and David and Marina Ottaway.[14] These latter authors know perfectly well that Marxism in Africa is first and foremost an *African* phenomenon, but even they have a tendency to present much too rigid and univocal a conception of Marxism and/or Marxism-Leninism upon which to premise the analysis of the African regimes they seek to discuss. In fact, it is the creative tensions within Marxism, the flexibility and subtlety which these produce, that African Marxists at their best have seized hold of (despite the fact that they also have not always avoided the temptation to absorb the rigidities inherent in some interpretations of Marxism). Moreover, they have availed themselves of the fact that the Marxist tradition is a *contested* one, where the answers are still in hot debate. Indeed, far from offering "quasi-magical solutions," to "semi-educated people" Marxism is seen as offering *the best questions*, the most urgent that those who seek to construct socialist solutions to the problem of underdevelopment must canvass if they are to advance.

Certainly Marxism has served to bring the socialist development challenge more clearly into focus in Mozambique, the one Afro-Marxist regime about which the present author can speak from firm first-hand experience, experience which ranges from editorial work with FRELIMO's Department of Information in the 1960s and a visit to the liberated areas with FRELIMO guerillas to a recent year spent teaching in the FRELIMO Party School and working both with the party's Department of Ideological Work (DTI) and in the Faculty of Marxism-Leninism at the University of Eduardo Mondlane. It is the Mozambique case which I shall focus upon in the following section in order to elaborate and concretize my argument.

THE MOZAMBICAN CASE

Fortunately there are other good reasons for paying special attention to the Mozambican case beyond the fact of my own experience there! Thus Crawford Young has argued that

> the Mozambique regime has become a bellweather for the future of socialism in Africa. . . . An ultimate verdict on the Afro-Marxist pathway will probably hinge on the political evolution and economic performance of Mozambique in the 1980s. . . . Only in Mozambique are all the elements of the exemplary experience assembled: a sophisticated and united leadership; a relatively clear-cut ideological identity; a coherent political underpinning in FRELIMO. The 1980s will be a critical decade for this interesting experiment in political economy.[15]

Of course, as Young goes on to admit, "in the real world . . . clear-cut historical verdicts are the exception." This is perhaps even more the case for Mozambique than elsewhere, given the state of extreme socioeconomic backwardness in which the country was trapped by a Portuguese colonialism which was itself backward in the extreme, given the catastrophic pattern of flood and drought which has haunted it since independence and given the extremely high costs of the brutal war of destruction and intimidation being waged against it by South Africa and its proxy guerillas. Such stark variables simply cannot be "held constant" in order to evaluate with great confidence the precise "effectiveness" of Mozambique's Marxist ideology in overcoming underdevelopment. Nonetheless, we can say something intelligible about the way in which it has helped or hindered the mounting of the attempted "transition to socialism" which is on the agenda in that country. What we will see, *pace* Wiles, is real *creativity* on the ideological plane, an interesting attempt not only to advance socialist practice in Mozambique but also to illuminate certain gray areas of the Marxist tradition itself. *Ex Africa sempre aliquid novi*, as the saying goes.

Would it be taking Henriksen, Wiles, and Jowitt more seriously than they deserve to devote much attention to the origins of Marxism in Mozambique? For what is immediately evident to all serious students of Mozambique is the fact that FRELIMO's formally opting for Marxism-Leninism at its Third Congress in 1977 was the end product of a firmly indigenous process, the choice being shaped, more specifically, by the very dynamics of the armed struggle itself. Obviously, there was an awareness of the theory and practice of people, parties, and regimes who called themselves Marxist elsewhere in the world. And there were certain prominent individuals within the movement who brought a prior Marxist culture to the liberation struggle. What was most striking, however, was the kind of "elective affinity" which manifested itself between the movement's own evolving practice *and* the Marxist tradition.

Thus FRELIMO, especially that wing of its leadership which had become most deeply linked with popular aspirations and which sought further to consolidate that linkage, increasingly found in the insights of Marxism an analytical framework which could help better to comprehend the realities and the choices which confronted it.

Here, for example, FRELIMO began to find the tools for an effective class analysis when class-based right-wing assertions—N'Kavandame's private-sector aggrandizement in Cabo Delgado and Gwenjere's petty-bourgeois elitism within the structures established by the movement—surfaced in the late sixties. Here too (as noted earlier) were precisely some of the tools of cutting through the limitations of an exclusively racial categorization of the enemy, a categorization which merely played into the hands of neocolonially-minded elements. It helped reinforce the commitment to active mass involvement in the struggle by exemplifying, even breaking down, vague populist categories in order to focus more clearly on the class actors involved ("peasant," "worker," "petty bourgeoisie"). It helped further to concretize, in the war context, a growing comprehension of the nature of colonialism into an even firmer conceptualization of the imperial network which, beyond Portugal, had to be confronted. Marxism "worked" on these many fronts and, as a result, the movement became increasingly Marxist. In the words of Oscar Monteiro, presently a member of FRELIMO's Political Bureau, "It is our experience which led us towards Marxism-Leninism. We have spontaneously demonstrated its universal character. We have, on the basis of our practice, drawn theoretical lessons."[16] Thus, as early as 1969 and just shortly before his death, Eduardo Mondlane, FRELIMO's first president, anticipated clearly the direction of ideological development in Mozambique:

> I am now convinced that FRELIMO has a clearer political line than ever before. . . . The common basis which we all had when we formed FRELIMO was hatred of colonialism and the belief in the necessity to destroy the colonial structure and to establish a new social structure. But what type of social structure, what type of organization we would have, no-one knew. No, some did know, some did have ideas, but even they had rather theoretical notions which were themselves transformed by the struggle. Now, however, there is a qualitative transformation in thinking which has emerged during the past six years which permits me to conclude that at present FRELIMO is much more socialist, revolutionary and progressive than ever and that the line, the tendency, is now more and more in the direction of socialism of the Marxist-Leninist variety. Why? Because the conditions of life in Mozambique, the type of enemy which we have, does not give us any other alternative. I do think that, without compromising FRELIMO which still has not made an official announcement declaring itself Marxist-Leninist, I can say that FRELIMO is inclining itself more and more in this direction because the conditions in which we struggle and work demand it.[17]

The move to Marxism was thus self-conscious—and self-confident. Certainly the break with the nostrums of African Socialism was forthright:

> We refuse the idea of "African socialism" because then there would have to be a european socialism, an asian socialism, an american socialism. How many socialisms would there have to be? Socialism is a science . . . the result of hard work and the development of that science by the workers. And that's where we have the key, where we find the spinal column of struggle in the world—in the class struggle. If we want to launch a serious combat, if we want to develop our country in a balanced, clear, organized way, only science will serve. And science is in the hands of the workers. . . . Our strategy for struggle is very simple: to define correctly our enemy and to define correctly our objectives. And it is for this reason that we use the term "scientific socialist" analysis.[18]

At the same time, Samora Machel did not apologize for the fact that this Marxist perspective was to be concretized with clear reference to local realities—not a Mozambican Marxism (nor even an Afro-Marxism!) but certainly a Marxism cast firmly by Mozambicans in Mozambique's own terms. Machel has made this point with great force on a number of occasions, not least when he asserted that

> the historical experience of our people, of our party, constitutes a novel experience within the international communist movement which must be evaluated accordingly. . . . Marxism-Leninism sprang up among us as a product of our struggle and of the debates over ideas within FRELIMO itself. To underestimate this fact is to deprive Marxism-Leninism of the vital force which it possesses in Mozambique, it is to reduce it to clichés and abstract stereotypes, to pale copies of realities beyond our borders. "Historical materialism" must be studied with reference to the realities of Mozambican society and to the specific circumstances of its historical evolution. . . . [Such studies] are not to be made in an abstract manner, independently of Mozambican reality, or by treating Mozambican reality with merely passing references.[19]

But it is a recurring theme of his: "Africans must use Marxism, but Marxism cannot be allowed to use Africans" is the way he once put the point in my presence. It should be noted that this is an emphasis which Western commentators seem to have difficulty in understanding. Thus Young writes of a related case that Somalia's Siad Barre "joins the Soviet analysts in castigating the concept of 'African socialism'—there is only universal 'scientific socialism'. In the same breath he denies the universality: 'A Soviet socialist cannot tell me about Somali problems, which must be put in an African context.'"[20] Barre might have made the case more felicitously, and his own credentials as Afro-Marxist are quite suspect. But there is no fundamental inconsistency. Lenin himself once presented the relevant argument quite clearly: "We do not regard

Marx's theory as something complete and inviolable: on the contrary we are convinced that it has only laid the foundation stone of the science which socialists *must* develop in all directions if they wish to keep pace with life. We think that an *independent* elaboration of Marx's theory is especially essential for Russian [read "Mozambican"] socialists; for this theory provides only general *guiding* principles which, in particular, are applied in England differently than in France, in France differently than in Germany and in Germany differently than in Russia." This FRELIMO has grasped and it is one important vaccination against a dead, abstract, and ultimately counterproductive form of Marxism.

Moreover, there are growing signs that an even more profound point is being made by Mozambicans. There is a sense that not only must Marxist theory, to be useful, be applied creatively to the concrete realities of Africa but that, as anticipated above, it is itself a *contested theory*. Though here too, as we shall see, Western commentators have difficulty in comprehending the point, Mozambicans obviously feel that they have a creative role to play in further developing scientific socialism as a science! To be sure, this has not been equally true of Mozambique at every point in the development of its socialist project. Nor is it even now equally true in every sector. Building on its liberation experience FRELIMO did move further to systematize its own practice ever more self-consciously in Marxist terms at its Third Congress in 1977:

> If it is to be a real vanguard force of the labouring classes, our party must be armed with a revolutionary theory which enables its members to understand exactly the laws of social development and of the Revolution. Without this ideological and theoretical basis, the Party is not in the position to direct and lead the struggle of the labouring masses. This ideological and theoretical basis is Marxism-Leninism or Scientific Socialism. . . . Applied and developed creatively in the process of our struggle, it is a powerful beacon which lights the way that the labouring classes must follow in the process of constructing the new society. Scientific Socialism is not a static doctrine; it is a science that is continually enriched by the daily experiences of mass struggle.[21]

However, it must be admitted that one particular definition of what is at the theoretical core of Marxism-Leninism, the orthodox Soviet version, did initially have a very strong impact upon this new, now more formalized, ideological synthesis. The costs of this impact were high—and the reasons for it numerous. The Eastern European countries and the Soviet Union had played a very positive role in supporting the armed struggle and were already trusted allies. They were Marxists to boot. With so few trained and politically tested people within its ranks (and given the range of jobs that had to be done at independence) FRELIMO was tempted to cede part of the task of filling in the blanks of its more systematic statement of Marxism to Eastern European "experts." This occurred most notably throughout the education system where the need to systematize the logic of FRELIMO's practice as a more coherent pedagogy and a method of work which would be accessible to Mozambicans who had not had the direct experience of the guerilla war was particularly evident.

There was a second reason of at least equal importance for what might appear to some to have been the undue prominence of Soviet Marxism in Mozambique. Some of the negative aspects of Soviet Marxism actually fit the Mozambican situation all too neatly—thus *sanctioning* certain negative tendencies within Mozambique's attempted transition to socialism which had other, ore structural foundations, beyond the ideological. To elaborate this point we must underscore the fact that, as a model of socialist construction, the Soviet Union leaves a great deal to be desired. Moreover, the weaknesses of its socialist practice are entirely congruent with weaknesses in its ideological formulations. Its Marxism has come to serve far more as rationalization and legitimation of a bureaucratic, technocratic, and authoritarian status quo than as an intellectual tool of emancipation. But in Mozambique, too, there have been strong pressures toward an excessive degree of centralization (the apparent imperatives of mobilization for a seemingly unending war, of economic planning, and the like), pressures which, at the extreme, have threatened to freeze up the vibrant links between mass action and progressive leadership which had lain at the heart of successful armed struggle. Obviously the mechanic and unproblematic definitions of "vanguard" and "dictatorship of the proletariat" central to a certain kind of Marxism could serve merely to lock such a negative tendency comfortably into place.

Take another example. There is an almost universal temptation for Third World countries to look to shortcuts in order to bridge the economic development gap, shortcuts which tend to be conceived in terms of "high-tech" and "large-scale" solutions. FRELIMO experienced this temptation, with the delicate balance between the claims of such "modernization" on the one hand and mass involvement in the development process on the other sometimes being lost in the shuffle. Here, too, a "neo-Stalinist" version of Marxism-Leninism can come to sanction a one-sided undialectical tendency—by economistically privileging changes in the forces of production as being more basic than any simultaneous changes in the relations of production. Perhaps these are the kinds of oppositions that Jowitt would identify as defining "hard" and unavoidable choices. Yet is it precisely here that FRELIMO has shown the resiliency of its revolutionary process—and of its Marxism. For it has backed away from choices cast in such stark terms—whether so cast by Jowitt or by some equally shrill Soviet "ideologue." In doing so, the movement is also demonstrating the openness and complexity of the Marxist tradition itself, and the extent to which Africans can be expected to make novel contributions to it.

### DEVELOPING MARXISM IN AFRICA

Let us examine, in this section, some crucial areas where creativity has begun to manifest itself on the terrain of "Marxism in Africa," once again drawing primarily on the Mozambican case.[22]

#### Class Struggle

The question of ongoing class struggle within the transition to socialism itself is a case in point. Far from adopting an approach which sees this transition as unproblematic in class terms, the FRELIMO leadership came, in the postindependence period, slowly but surely to zero in on the process of class formation, both in the private sector and, especially, in the state/party realm itself. As regards the former, it is primarily the black marketeers who have been identified as undermining the attempt to establish more collective institutions—much as N'Kavandame had done in the liberated areas years before. As for the state/party sphere the focus was upon the process of *bureaucratization*. This danger, too, carried with it echoes from the days of armed struggle:

> Some Mozambicans conceived of independence as a simple change of personnel within the same colonial structure: having expelled the Portuguese Mozambicans would take their places, keeping intact the colonial political-administrative machinery. Exploitation and all the other negative aspects of the colonial system would then simply remain in place, run now by Mozambicans. Such an attitude was personified at the time by Lazaro N'Kavandame, allied with other elements within the organization who did not at first dare expose themselves so openly. Various notions linked to this . . . revealed themselves with the passage of time; for example, the elitism represented by Mateus Gwenjere who defended the creation of a group of intellectuals who would be spared the necessity to participate in the armed struggle and granted privileged status and who, with the coming of independence, would move in as the leaders of Mozambique.[23]

Now this kind of perception was brought to bear upon the postindependence social structure. Yet it is scarcely a theme to be found within the Soviet version of Marxism-Leninism (even if it is not entirely absent from the contribution of Mao Tse-tung to the Marxist tradition!).

Perhaps the Soviet silence on this question is what leads even so sympathetic a pair of observers as the Ottaways so far astray on this question. "Class conflict," they write, "is a very artificial concept in both Mozambique and Angola; only in Ethiopia does it possess a reality. This has forced the government to become a motor of change, substituting an artificially induced sense of class conflict for a real one."[24] Not true. Indeed only an extremely stereotyped version of what Marxism has to offer to socialist revolutionaries could permit such a conclusion. Given the track record of many attempted transitions to socialism elsewhere in the world—their involution into extremely authoritarian systems, for example—it is also a very dangerous conclusion. Fortunately, Mozambicans have not been inhibited by prejudgments about what Marxism *must* have to say about the process of class formation, but instead have sought to apply that tradition as a creative instrument for analyzing their own class structure and acting upon it. In the Political and Organizational Offensive launched in 1980 one saw a serious attempt to deal with a real problem—the crystallization of privilege, the possibility of corruption and abuse of authority—in class terms: "We placed those who studied in charge to use their knowledge for your [the people's] good," Samora Machel told a gathering at the time, "but some of them are using it against you"! This was also a note struck firmly in the central document prepared for FRELIMO's Fourth Congress in April 1983, the need for class struggle becoming a major and very concrete focus of discussion in the Congress itself.

> Our country has a social stratum that enjoys levels of consumption unavailable to the overwhelming majority of the people. From the social point of view, it consists chiefly of citizens originating from the social strata that were already privileged in the colonial period. Politically, this social stratum is opportunistic, elitist, unscientific and hopeful of transforming itself into an authentic bourgeoisie. All it admires in the bourgeoisie is its corrupt consumerist nature.
>
> From the cultural standpoint, aspirants to the bourgeoisie are alienated and estranged. They are unaware, or pretend to be unaware, of the value of Mozambican culture and they spurn the people's wisdom and knowledge. These individuals are slaves to everything that comes from Europe, particularly from the West. *For this reason, they try to distort the class character of our revolution by transforming it into a technocratic process through which they can control power.*
>
> This social stratum actively opposes any measures that aim at simplifying organization and methods, democratizing leadership or increasing the workers' share in planning and controlling production. Because of their book-learning, aspirants to the bourgeosie despise solutions from the people. They are unable to learn from the people. So they reject the experience of the liberated areas. They reject the small-scale projects that require the intelligence, sensitivity and understanding of the people and prefer the projects that come ready made from abroad.[25]

Note, in particular, the manner in which this formulation establishes a link between class formation and distortions in the policy sphere; the kind of one-sided emphasis on "high tech–big project" solutions is now seen as being

very far from an accidental phenomenon. This is a critical perspective of particularly great promise.

### Democratization

Not surprisingly, in light of FRELIMO's history, a crucial counterweight to
such tendencies was seen to be the revitalization of popular control over the
revolutionary process, an imperative which had preoccupied FRELIMO during
the period of armed struggle. Moreover, at that time Marcelino dos Santos, a
senior FRELIMO leader, had even anticipated the current moment; asked what
would guarantee the advances made during the period of armed struggle in the
postindependence period, he said that "the main defense must be to popu-
larize the revolutionary aims and to create such a situation that if for one reason or another at some future time some people start trying to change these
aims, they will meet with resistance from the people." Mozambicans were
quite prepared to carry such preoccupations onto the terrain of Marxism, and
there these preoccupations find real resonance. Thus, on any number of occasions both Marx and Lenin had insisted quite specifically that they were not
Jacobins, not Blanquists; the dominated classes must make their own revolution. Nor is an understanding of Marxist and/or Marxist-Leninist approaches
to the tension between the simultaneous imperatives of mass action and leadership to be exhausted by a reading of Lenin's *What is to be Done*, although
this is in fact what often passes for an adequate understanding of Leninism
among many Western observers.

We could, of course, scan the debate between Lenin and Rosa Luxemburg
to get some feel for the richness of the Marxist tradition on these matters,
recalling such passages from Luxemburg as the following:

> Without general elections, without unrestricted freedom of press and assembly,
> without a free struggle of opinion, life dies out in every public institution, be-
> comes a mere semblance of life, in which only the bureaucracy remains as an ac-
> tive element. Public life gradually falls asleep, a few dozen party leaders of inex-
> haustible energy and boundless experience direct and rule. Among them, only a
> dozen outstanding heads do the leading and an elite of the working class is invited
> from time to time to meetings where they are to applaud the speeches of the lead-
> ers and to approve proposed resolutions unanimously—at bottom, then, a clique
> affair—a dictatorship to be sure, not the dictatorship of the proletariat, however,
> but only the dictatorship of a handful of politicians, that is the dictatorship in the
> bourgeois sense, in the sense of the rule of the Jacobins.[26]

But one does not even have to leave the terrain of Lenin's own thought—a
simple juxtaposition of Lenin's *What is to be Done* and his *The State and Revolution* would be instructive enough in this respect—to get a sense of the real

tensions between the legitimate claims of leadership on the one hand and mass action on the other which he was prepared to acknowledge and to struggle to reconcile. To ignore this aspect of Leninism is to construct "an absurd Leninist dogmatism in which Lenin usually is seen through Stalin's eyes," as Antonio Carlo has phrased the point in a particularly subtle and sensitive article on "Lenin and the Party." [27] Not that Lenin ever resolved this tension, either in theory or in practice, entirely effectively, a point Carlo stresses. But serious questions were posed. Now Mozambicans, too, are living such tensions and living them in ways that demand their continuing creativity.

It is when seen in this light that the situation presents itself as being far more complicated than Jowitt's "hard choice" for Leninism (as "seen through Stalin's eyes," I hasten to add) would suggest. More complicated, too, than the Ottaways' own version of the "hard choice," articulated at the point when they chide "radicals" for "naiveté" in their critique of tendencies towards "statism, centralization and bureaucracy" in Afro-communist regimes. "What makes the radical untenable is not a rejection of such tendencies and advocacy of participatory democracy and workers' control. Rather, it is the assumption that such democracy and control are reconcilable with the dictatorship of the proletariat, the rule of the vanguard party, and centralized economic planning. In other words, the radicals are refusing to recognize the dilemmas built into Marxism-Leninism and to make a choice." [28] Yet no such "choice" need be made, at least not in such stark terms as this—not if the transition to socialism is to remain alive. Rather the contradiction between the twin imperatives of leadership and mass action must be accepted, lived with, worked upon. For the "dilemmas" so structured cannot be wished away. *They define the politics of the transition to socialism*—the experience of the Soviet Union to the contrary notwithstanding—and must therefore be resolved anew every day. We have noted that Mozambicans are struggling to so resolve such dilemmas, harking back, in particular, to their tradition of mass action in the liberation struggle and attempting to carry over that emphasis into their contemporary Marxist-Leninist formulations. What bears emphasizing here is that this is no arbitrary smuggling of an earlier "populism" into the Marxist tradition. It is the reviving of certain aspects of that tradition which are essential to it.

This is not to argue that Mozambicans are resolving all these dilemmas as creatively as they might. For good reasons and bad, they still have a formidably centralized system, perhaps one that is dangerously so in terms of participation and information flows. But popular participation in selecting party cadres has occurred, popular assemblies have some significance, and some genuine workers' participation in management has been facilitated. Most recently, in the run-up to last year's Fourth Congress, there was effective participation in a country-wide debate on economic and other priorities, a debate which had a very profound impact on policymaking at the Congress itself. Indeed, it helped to shift economic priorities (as we shall see), challenging precisely the logic of big-project/high-technology development mentioned above. Moreover, the recuperation of the popular term in FRELIMO's political equation has had an impact on FRELIMO's military calculation as well. Decentralized regional commands and active popular militias are now much more central to strategy, along lines first developed in the liberated areas and now very much to the advantage of Mozambique in its struggle against the South African–sponsored MNR.

### Economic Strategy

The flexibility of the Marxist tradition as regards the question of economic development has also facilitated Mozambican creativity contrary to what one might expect from the Ottaways' almost exclusive emphasis upon the presumed imperatives of centralized economic planning to Marxist-based practice and Young's unqualified equation of the core of Marxist economics with "the dream of a command socialist economy." [29] For here, too, the range of possible solutions which can be developed within the Marxist tradition is much broader than the Ottaways and Young can grant. Certainly one such "solution," the Stalinist solution, has involved extreme centralization, an emphasis upon "primitive socialist accumulation" at the expense of the peasantry and in the interest of heavy industry (Preobrazhensky's program as expropriated by Stalin), the priority given to large-scale state farms in the rural sector. It has been a proposed solution tempting to Mozambicans as well, but not the only one and probably not the best—a point Mozambicans themselves have come to understand. Thus, at the Fourth Congress, Mozambique's disastrous economic performance was confronted head-on. Much of the explanation for it was seen, correctly, to lie in factors beyond the movement's immediate control—the continuing drag of the past, flood, drought, the war. But there was also a sharp critique of big project-itis, of the fixation with technology and with hypercentralization, of any too one-sided an emphasis upon heavy industry, of a lack of understanding of the importance of the peasant sector.

Instead the emphasis was on, among other things, smaller projects and on decentralization of decision making which would be geared to the technical capacities of Mozambicans and to the requirement that people have more direct control over their own development decisions. Equally crucial was further qualification of the "primitive socialist accumulation" model of socialist development. Although an important party educational document had, only a year or so earlier, placed much emphasis upon "sacrifice" for accumulation as a key to progress, it was another model altogether which was closer to the core of the economic analysis of the Fourth Congress. Now the emphasis would be much more strongly upon the centrality of urban-rural, industrial-agricultural exchanges to drive the economy forward. Something of the wisdom of the Soviet Union's own New Economic Policy in its original formulation—before the false polarizations of the Industrialization Debate and the brutal resolution of that debate by Stalin—was to be found in the relevant formulations. Far from socialist accumulation being a zero-sum game Congress documents suggested that accumulation can be carried forward precisely by finding outlets for its production in meeting the growing requirements, the needs, of the mass of the population. An effective industrialization strategy would thus base its "expanded reproduction" on the exchanges suggested above, with food and raw materials moving to the cities, with consumer goods *and* producer goods (defined to include centrally such modest items as scythes, iron ploughs, hoes, axes, fertilizers, and the like) moving to the countryside. Collective saving geared to investment can then be seen as being drawn essentially, if not exclusively, from an expanding economic pool.[30]

This socialism of expanded reproduction thus makes the betterment of the people's lot a short-term rather than a long-term prospect. It promises, in this way, a much sounder basis for an effective, rather than merely rhetorical, alliance of workers and peasants and for a democratic road to revolutionary socialism. It does so in part by taking the peasants seriously (something Stalinoid Marxism has had grave difficulties in doing). It is aware that the "sacrifice model" may merely drive the peasant further back into the world of subsistence agriculture and quasi-traditional sociality. Much of the emphasis at the aforementioned Congress was therefore placed upon reviving the "family sector," even if, in the first instance, along petty-capitalist lines. Of course, the long-term program of cooperativization of the peasant sector was now to be rescued from the underfunding and understaffing from which it had suffered in comparison with the state-farm sector. But such cooperativization was to be viewed less romantically, cast in terms much closer to the spirit of Lenin than Stalin, to Lenin's sense that the virtues of cooperativization would have to prove themselves on the terrain of the NEP: "We must win the competition against the ordinary shop assistant, the ordinary capitalist, the merchant who will go to the peasant without arguing about communism. . . . Either we pass this test in competition with private capital or we fail completely."[31] Interestingly, the same spirit can be found in Marx:

Either the peasantry hinders every workers' revolution and causes it to fail, as it has done in France up to now; or the proletariat (for the landowning peasantry does not belong to the proletariat and even when his own position causes him to belong to it, he does not *think* he belongs to it) must as a government inaugurate measures which directly improve the situation and win him for the revolution; measures which in essence facilitate the transition from private to collective property in land so that the peasant himself is converted for economic reasons. . . .[32]

Can it be so very difficult to see the considerable creativity inherent in the Fourth Congress emphases upon the "economics of expanded socialist reproduction" and upon a more nuanced definition of the passage to collectivization.

### The International Front

On the international plane Mozambique has attempted to make "mutually exclusive" choices—and not to apologize for doing so. As seen, Mozambique has made no secret of its Marxist predilections, and its affinity for "the socialist countries." But it has also professed, and sought to practice, a policy of nonalignment. More than that, it has felt confident enought of its own sense of direction to deal with "imperialist countries" in ways which it feels can be beneficial to it. Especially this has been the case in the past few years as Mozambique has sought to establish economic arrangements (in terms of investment, technology, and personnel) with Western firms and governments. Mozambique does not do this from a position of great strength, needless to say. In part it seeks to present a conciliatory image in order to help lift the great weight of Western hostility from its back (and from the side of South Africa); in part it seeks what it considers to be key economic inputs for its battered economy, inputs which the Eastern bloc cannot readily provide. As experience elsewhere suggests, this is a bow in the direction of global capitalist economic and military might that can be very damaging to the socialist thrust of the country undertaking it. But from the Mozambican point of view these are carefully considered tactical adjustments, representing, on the one hand, an acknowledgment of the "historical backwardness" and vulnerability of Mozambican society and, on the other, an affirmation of the vitality and strength of its long-term commitment to socialist transformation. It would be too great an oversimplification, FRELIMO seems to be saying, to suggest that it has no room for maneuver on this front.

Mozambique feels no more inclined to make overly schematized choices within the socialist camp itself, having kept the door firmly open to diverse linkages and influences—and to the imperatives of its own experience. "This is our socialism which is different from that of the Soviet, the Chinese or the Cuban." In reporting this statement from a recent interview which he had with Samora Machel, the Portuguese journalist concerned went on to paraphrase some further comments by the President in the following terms:

Cooperation with China had experienced some difficulties owing to the introduction of certain themes alien to FRELIMO's philosophy. Thus with independence there began to appear pro-Soviet and pro-Chinese lines, introducing into Mozambique a conflict which opposed the USSR and China. . . . Samora Machel had to intervene on various occasions. He explained to us that this kind of thinking came from outside, especially from intellectuals returning from Portugal. It represented a kind of rootless intellectualism.[33]

To analyze ideological intentions is not to analyze all the factors that go into either the shaping of a state's policy or the outcomes of that policy, of course. Nonetheless, as a strong statement of ideological independence this is one more clear indication of what has been a consistent and deeply felt Mozambican position.

### Ideological Elaboration

But what of Mozambique's "ideological practice"? Much that is relevant to this topic had already been said, both as to the *independence* of Mozambique's Marxism and as to the *creative* manner in which it is attempting to develop an independent elaboration of Marxist theory and practice. Once again, however, progress has been made in fits and starts. We hinted earlier at one problem: in the kind of Marxism presented formally in party schools, the university, and the school system a gap did exist between the "practical Marxism" which characterized FRELIMO's own developing ideology and the more theorized framework taken over (sometimes somewhat uncritically) from Eastern European textbooks and teachers in the postindependence period. The uneasiness of the mix was soon manifest in the pedagogical programs themselves, in their formidable abstractness and the mechanical and lifeless (undialectical!) manner in which they sought to explain social interconnections.

The main complaint was that the resultant theory did not facilitate real comprehension of Mozambican realities and therefore did not provide an adequate guide to action. In the formal school system the result tended to be demobilization rather than the reverse; at the University students even took to calling the Department of Dialectical and Historical Materialism, charged with providing political-cum-social science background courses to all faculties, the Department of Diabolical and Hysterical Materialism! Within the party itself, where students were more spontaneously accepting of officially sponsored courses, there were criticisms nonetheless, criticisms which centered around the fact that those who took courses in Marxism-Leninism were given little in the way of analytical tools with which they could grapple with *concrete* realities in the field. In 1981–82 I myself participated in a number of attempts to develop new curricula for the party schools and the Faculty of Marxism-Leninism (the renamed Department of Dialectical and Historical Materialism), involving syllabi which it was hoped would overcome these limitations. These efforts have continued. Indeed, in early 1983, in a dramatic move, it was decided to close the Faculty and all party schools for a period. They were to reopen only when stronger curricula, more firmly rooted in a Mozambique-relevant Marxism, were available to premise their activity.

Not surprisingly, the need to develop a Marxism more sensitive to Mozambican realities was also underscored at the Fourth Congress. Moreover, there were clear signs that the critique was going beyond this first level of commentary (the unrootedness of existing Marxism in Mozambican realities) to wrestle more forthrightly with some of the first principles around which different conceptualizations of Marxism turn. This development bears the promise of, in effect, systematizing some of the imaginative emphases of FRELIMO's Marxist practice, as discussed above, into a distinctive theoretical problematic. There is certainly a link between bureaucratization (with its attendant preoccupation with hypercentralization and technocratic solutions) and an abstract Marxism which undialectically privileges the determinacy of the productive forces. It was clear to me in discussions I had with FRELIMO leaders at the time of the Fourth Congress that such linkages are beginning to be made, even if some of the theoretical innovation this would seem to imply on the terrain of Marxism in Mozambique is still more implicit than fully realized. With reference to the task of ideological elaboration, as in so many other spheres, shortfalls in trained-person power are painfully apparent and progress slow. Moreover, there are probably some differences of emphasis on such questions within the FRELIMO leadership itself. Ideological class struggle continues, but at least it may be obvious by now that the Marxist tradition is very much alive in African hands, in Mozambique as elsewhere—this despite the absence Professor Wiles thinks he sees of "a long and impressive enough tradition"; or perhaps, if the staleness of political discourse in the northern world, both East and West, is anything to go by, precisely because of that fact!

## IV. Conclusion

Perhaps the preceding section's extended case study of Mozambique will be felt to have introduced an imbalance into the present paper. Yet it has served to underscore the point made at the very outset: that as the first twenty-five years of African independence draw to a close Marxism has become rooted in Africa in a way unforeseeable in the late 1950s.[34] Of course, Mozambique is atypical. But so too are all African states: transcontinental generalization is a very tricky, probably unduly heroic, business indeed. In fact, perhaps the most that can be said about Mozambique in transcontinental perspective is that it marks quite clearly one end of the spectrum in the greater polarization of ideological positions on the continent which has followed from the decomposition of "independence ideology." But independence ideology had the ultimate effect of muffling and blurring the real choices which confronted and continue to confront Africa. Polarization, therefore, must be considered an advance because the terms of those choices are likely to be better clarified by this kind of overtly contested "recomposition" of the African ideological terrain.

Arbitrating the competing claims of Afro-Capitalist and Afro-Marxist ideologies is another matter. Such judgments will be primarily the business of real classes engaged in real struggles in any case—not of debates in seminar rooms. Nonetheless, the latter debates will continue; and they will be difficult, if not impossible, to resolve. Perhaps this is the only thing demonstrated clearly by Crawford Young's noble attempt to measure "how effective" various African ideologies are in the final chapter of this useful book *Ideology and Development in Africa*. Given the diverse goals and diverse constituencies of the differing ideologies the exercise becomes a little like comparing apples with oranges. Then, too, there is a problem mentioned earlier, that of holding other variables sufficiently "constant" to zero in on ideology per se. Mozambique, for example, has certainly failed as yet to find the key to economic progress, even if it has begun to ask a range of crucial questions about its failures. Consider as well its most recent attempt to compromise, the better to control its difficult environments: the negotiations with a South Africa which has spent the past several years attempting, precisely, to bludgeon Mozambique into submission. If not quite the strategic retreat the Western press would picture them as being, such negotiations, culminating in the Nkomati Accords of March 1984, appear to be even less a tactic premised on strength than those earlier openings toward Western capitalist countries referred to earlier. Yet in what excruciatingly difficult circumstances has Mozambique been forced to test the effectiveness of its project in the first place. Meanwhile, at the other pole, and even judging by means of the grossest economic indicators, it would be difficult to argue that the Ivory Coasts and the Kenyas—to say nothing of the Zaires—have escaped altogether the contemporary continental malaise. Still, if much too little has been accomplished, a great deal has been learned in the first quarter century. The high level of ideological discourse in Mozambique which we have attempted to bring to light in the latter part of this paper should be proof enough of that. Moreover, insights generated in Mozambique as elsewhere are part of a continental learning experience: no small matter, even if insight alone is not sufficient.

## NOTES

1. See my "On African Populism" in Giovanni Arrighi and John S. Saul, *Essays on the Political Economy of Africa* (New York: Monthly Review Press, 1973). The definitional phrase is actually that of Aidan Southall.

2. Ernesto Laclau, *Politics and Ideology in Marxist Theory* (London: New Left Books, 1977), p. 108.

3. Giovanni Arrighi as quoted in "On African Populism," op. cit.

4. Crawford Young, *Ideology and Development in Africa* (New Haven: Yale University Press, 1982), p. 182.

5. Thomas Hodgkin, *Nationalism in Colonial Africa* (New York: New York University Press, 1957), p. 187.

6. Laclau, op. cit., p. 160.

7. Frantz Fanon, *The Wretched of the Earth* (Harmondsworth: Penguin, 1967), p. 122.

8. Young, op. cit., p. 183.

9. Ibid., p. 23.

10. Thomas Henricksen (ed.), *Communist Powers and Sub-Saharan Africa* (Stanford: Hoover Institution Press, 1981).

11. Peter Wiles (ed.), *The New Communist Third World* (New York, St. Martin's Press, 1982).

12. Kenneth Jowitt, "Scientific Socialist Regimes in Africa: Political Differentiation, Avoidance and Unawareness," in Carl G. Rosberg and Thomas M. Callaghy, eds., *Socialism in Sub-Saharan Africa: A New Assessment* (Berkeley: Institute of International Studies, 1979).

13. Edmond J. Keller, "State, Party and Revolution in Ethiopia," unpublished manuscript (Santa Barbara, Calif., February 1984).

14. Young, op. cit., and David and Marina Ottaway, *Afrocommunism* (New York: Africana Publishing House, 1981).

15. Young, op. cit., pp. 89, 96.

16. Quoted in Augusta Conchiglia, "Frelimo: un róle capital," in *Afrique-Asie*, 217 (7–20 July 1980), p. xiii (Spécial: *Mozambique: une décennie pour vaincre le sous-développement*).

17. I have transcribed and translated this statement by Eduardo Mondlane from a tape in the possession of Aquino da Bragança, who conducted the interview and was kind enough to lend me the tape; portions of this interview have been reproduced on the phonograph record "Liberdade e Revoluçao," Ngoma 0118 (Maputo, Mozambique, n.d.).

18. Interview with Samora Machel, *Tempo*, #325 (Maputo, 26 December 1976, my translation).

19. Samora Machel, "Dominar A Ciencia e Artes Militares Para Defender Conquistas da Revoluçao," speech in Nampula on the opening of the Military School printed in *25 de Septembro*, #88 (Maputo, December 1979, my translation).

20. Young, op. cit., p. 63.

21. Central Committee of FRELIMO, *Report to the Third Congress of FRELIMO* (London: Mozambique, Angola and Guiné Information Centre, n.d., original in Portuguese, 1977).

22. For further discussion of many of these points see John S. Saul (ed.), *A Difficult Road: The Transition to Socialism in Mozambique* (New York: Monthly Review Press, 1984).

23. Samora Machel, cited in Cedimo, *Documento Informativo* (Maputo, 1978), p. 20.

24. Ottaway, op. cit., p. 199.

25. Central Committee of FRELIMO, *Out of Underdevelopment to Socialism: Report to the Fourth Congress of FRELIMO* (Maputo, 1983), pp. 71–72.

26. Rosa Luxemburg, "The Russian Revolution," reprinted in Mary-Alice Waters (ed.), *Rosa Luxemburg Speaks* (New York: Pathfinder, 1970).

27. Antonio Carlo, "Lenin on the Party," in *Telos*, 17 (Fall 1973), pp. 2–40.

28. Ottaway, op. cit., p. 207.

29. Young, op. cit., p. 30.

30. See John S. Saul (ed.), op. cit., esp. chs. 1 and 3.

31. As quoted in Charles Bettelheim, *Class Struggles in the USSR/1923–30* (New York: Monthly Review Press, 1978), p. 35.

32. Karl Marx, "Marx on Bakunin," as quoted in David McLellan, *The Thought of Karl Marx* (London: Macmillan, 1972), p. 210.

33. Quoted in Augusto de Carvalho, "Samora Machel: histórias para un retrato" in *Expresso* (Lisboa), 8 October 1983, p. v.

34. Other evidence of the renewed vitality of Marxism might have been presented if this paper had been cast more widely in order to include consideration of Marxist oppositional currents in Afro-capitalist settings. At Wingspread, for example, Goran Hyden noted that prior to the wholesale repression of recent years there had emerged in Kenya a very vibrant and creative Marxist intellectual practice. More might have been said as well about the rich South African experience of inquiry and action rooted in varying intrepretations of the Marxist tradition. On quite a different front I should note, albeit in passing, my sensitivity to the criticism, made at Wingspread, by Sheldon Gellar and John Paden in particular, that this paper does not confront the reality of ideological discourses—located from left to right on the more conventional ideological spectrum—linked to differing readings of the Islamic tradition. Yet this is an increasingly prominent phenomenon in certain parts of Africa.

CHAPTER 13

# Africa and the World System: How Much Change since Independence?

*Immanuel Wallerstein*

There is little argument among either Africans or Africa scholars about the position of Africa in the world system as of circa 1945. With the exception of Egypt, Ethiopia, Liberia, and South Africa—all founding members of the United Nations—the entire continent was composed of colonial territories, in which formal sovereignty lay in the hands of five European states—Great Britain, France, Belgium, Portugal, and Spain.[1] It seemed unlikely in 1945 to most people that any of these areas would be sovereign states in any near future. If one reads the most militant African statement issued in 1945, the declaration of the Pan-African Congress in Manchester, one finds imperialism denounced and all kinds of freedom demanded, but even there the word *independence* is skirted.[2]

The year 1957 is generally considered a key date in modern African political history. It is the year of Ghana's independence, that of the first African state south of the Sahara—in 1957 this distinction was still commonly made (and the Sudan was somehow considered "north" of the Sahara)—to be proclaimed independent. The road to Ghana's independence may be traced, in constitutional terms, to the Report of the Committee on Constitutional Reform in 1949 (known as the Coussey Commission). They recommended the form of local self-government under which the CPP and Kwame Nkrumah were to come to power in 1951. If one looks at this report, one finds in it an Appendix which contains an "extract from an article circulated at the request of a member of the Committee." The article is by Felix S. Cohen and is called "Colonialism: A Realistic Approach."[3] It is a very "balanced" appraisal. On the one hand, Cohen notes the suspiciousness with which one should approach the good intentions of the colonial power.

**330**

Colonial status is commonly justified to-day as a temporary institution designed to give way, in the long run, either to independence or to assimilation. The only difficulty with this theory is that, as John Maynard Keynes has observed, in the long run we are all dead. Certainly the process of terminating a colonial status in an orderly non-violent manner is one of the most difficult of political operations. . . .

Returning to our principle of political realism, we may observe that not only in determining the existence or abandonment of colonial status but also in actually carrying out a pledge of freedom, the power of government is a corrupting force. . . .

From this one may deduce that the carrying-out of a decision to relinquish power cannot safely be left to the wielder of such power.

On the other hand, Cohen expresses his doubts about the leadership of the "aborigines."

Cynicism, however, must not be one-sided. The diseases of colonalism are not limited to those who govern. Those who are governed develop equally stubborn and serious maladies. Chief among these maladies are: (1) native toadyism, in which the native politician secures crumbs of power by adopting the usual habits of lickspittles, sycophants, and courtesans; (2) blablaism, in which natives aspiring to posts of leadership among their people, having no opportunity to demonstrate capacities for nonvocal behaviour, are appraised, selected, and bred solely on the basis of the noises that come from their mouths; and (3) noitis, in which the patient, deprived of the opportunity of action, is reduced to a position of continuous objection to the course of administration.

A combination of the last two maladies generally produces a situation in which a depressed group will choose its leadership from those who most eloquently express the common distrust of the power that governs. To expect such a leadership to accept with joy promises of self-government, or of better conditions in the future, is childish. Apparently, however, Sir Stafford Cripps expected that Indian leaders who had attained their positions of leadership by warning their people not to trust the British, these warnings have been frequently substantiated by the course of events, could turn around to their followers and say, "The promises which the British now make are to be believed." In all probability the only rational approach to this type of situation is the immediate transfer of new realms of responsibility to native control. Such a solution not only does away with the need for trust in promises but also inevitably modifies the character of the native leadership by instilling the habits, tests, and responsibilities of actual administration and thus replacing leaders-in-discourse with leaders-in-action.

Our realism, finally, if it is to result in a balanced judgment, must extend to the alternatives to colonialism. Do the "Banana Republics" of Central America present a fitting ideal towards which peoples now held in colonial subjection are to aspire? Why is it that force of reaction in domestic politics (Edmund Burke and W. R. Hearst, to take two notable examples) often throw their support to independence movements of subject peoples? The answer to both questions is to be found, I think, in a recognition of the fact that economic imperialism is not necessarily dependent upon, and is sometimes even hindered by, political imperialism. Where such hindrances arise it will be to the interest of the economic imperialists to eliminate the political phase of colonialism.

Having intruded this theme of neocolonialism a decade before Kwame Nkrumah was to make it a fundamental stalking-horse of postindependence politics, Cohen concludes thus:

> Political independence, then, is not an adequate answer to all colonial problems. Recognising the distinction between economic and political dominance, we can formulate our basic problem in this way: How can we minimise the evils of political overlordship without increasing the evils of private economic exploitation?

Writing in the 1980s, I think it is easy to see that Cohen was on to the key issues, however paternalist his formulation.

Today, with a very few exceptions, all of Africa is constituted of sovereign states, members of the United Nations (and of the Organization of African Unity). As such, it is difficult to contest the assertion that relatively more African political autonomy exists now than in 1945. That is to say, it is to be sure true that in this world system, all political actors are to some extent constrained by the structural pressures of the interstate system (expressed through the power of the multiple states, but also through the power of powerful economic aggregations and of political movements). Nonetheless, it is surely the case that the power of Africans vis-à-vis others in the world system has moved along the continuum from an extremely low point to a point somewhat higher. But how much higher, that is the question.

At the same time that Nkrumah began to talk of neocolonialism,[4] Julius Nyerere proclaimed that Africa was "entering a new phase, the phase of the Second Scramble for Africa and, I believe, for Asia." He concluded this early talk with what has become quite classical North-South "dependency" language:

> Internationally, however, the picture is very different. Even between socialist countries the class divisions are getting greater. There are now not only rich capitalist countries and poor capitalist countries. There are also rich socialist countries and poor socialist countries. Further, I believe that the socialist countries themselves, considered as 'individuals' in the larger society of nations, are now committing the same crime as was committed by the capitalists before. On the international level they are now beginning to use wealth for capitalist purposes, that is, for the acquisition of power and prestige.
>
> Yet whatever the internal policies may be, the use of national wealth for any

purposes other than the banishment of poverty wherever it is found can have only one result. The class struggle will be transferred from a national to an international plane. Karl Marx's doctrine that there is an inevitable clash between the rich and the poor is just as applicable internationally as it is within nation states.

This is the coming division of the world—a class, not an ideological division. And unless we begin to act now in accordance with our declared socialist convictions, we shall find that it is a division with capitalist and socialist countries on both sides of the conflict.[5]

What can we say about the years of independence in terms of the world class struggle? Is Africa better or worse off than in 1945? Let us not jump hastily to either the one answer or the other. It is a more complicated question to answer than it may actually seem.

The complications of assessing "improvement in situation" of a geographical area revolve around (1) the measurements one uses, (2) the other areas with which the comparison is made, (3) the time-span one analyzes, and (4) the historical trajectories one projects. Let me address these questions.

Whom and what does one measure? The whom is not an easy question to answer. The traditional measurements of developmentalist social science are of characteristics of a state: GDP or GDP per capita, foreign trade structure, population. If one looks at some of these figures, Africa does not look too good. Among low-income countries, Africa's growth rate of GDP, exports, or imports in the period 1965–1977 is below that of Asia. Among middle-income countries, "sub-Saharan" Africa has the lowest growth rates in that same period. If one takes GDP per capita for 1960–1990 (as projected), it is again lower than all other developing countries, the industrialized countries, and the centrally planned economies.[6]

But one can wonder if these are relevant statistics. In fact, they could hide important internal maldistributions. The improvement might be, for example, largely that of the top tenth of the population. The problem is that no one is collecting the relevant data for us to get real measures of this phenomenon. We might want, for example, comparative total household income figures (from all sources and in all forms) to measure absolute and relative rates of growth of the income of the "working strata."[7] Or we might want comparative data on real work hours per week or per year of these same working strata. Since we don't have such data, we can only use very indirect indicators of the comparative state of well-being of these strata. One such indirect measure is the degree of famine and undernourishment.

It is clear that the famines which struck primarily the Sahelian-Ethiopian band of countries in 1968–74 and then a more southerly band of countries in Africa in the last few years have been severe. There were perhaps similarly severe famines in the Indian subcontinent, in Central America, and else-

where. But there were none such in the North. And while no one has sat down
and quantified the comparison in minute detail, it is quite obvious that such
unequally distributed famines must widen the gap of real incomes and real
life-styles of the working strata, North and South.

The wide literature devoted to the Sahelian famine seems to be in accord,
despite distinct differences in emphasis, on the socioeconomic element in
transforming drought into famine. There is agreement that, in Lofchie's formulation, "independent Africa's recent agricultural record has been one of
consistent failure in food production, . . . [but] one of booming success in the
cultivation of export crops." For Lofchie, this is a "paradox."[8] For others, the
expansion of export crops is quite directly linked to the decline in food-crop
production.[9]

As for time-span, the further one goes back in history, the less is the gap in
real income and real life-style between the peoples who today are located in
the core of the capitalist world economy and those who today find themselves
in the periphery. If the secularly widening gap did not narrow during the extraordinary world economic boom of 1945–67, it is hard to believe that it is
doing anything but accentuating itself in the present long phase of economic
stagnation.

The question is, has independence in any way slowed down the widening
of the gap? It was of course a hope that it would in the sense that one of the
main motifs of African nationalism was that if they could control the "political kingdom" (in Nkrumah's image), then economic betterment would follow.
In one sense it is too early to tell. The dates of African independence hover
around the year 1960. Perhaps we would do better to assess this in 2010 or
even 2060. But the initial results have been sufficiently discouraging that one
is tempted to infer that one of the reasons why "decolonization" was in many
ways an easier process than anyone anticipated in 1945—and I do not here
deny the crucial and difficult role of African political mobilization and warfare to attain this goal—may be that far-sighted policymakers in the core
thought that the process of the "commodification of everything" (and therefore the process of polarization in the world economy) would proceed faster
rather than more slowly under "indigenous" governments. If so, this would fit
what has been the historical trajectory of the capitalist world economy since
its inception.[10]

Worse yet, might it not be argued that "indigenization" is a mode of deepening and encrusting the internal formation of the standard class structure of
the world capitalist system, and a way of expanding gaps internally as well as
world-wide? Indeed, it might be so argued, as this seems to be what everyone
knows has happened everywhere. The "waBenzi," as they are called in Tanzania, are nowhere seriously challenged, yet.

Was then the struggle for African independence a gigantic case of self-deception? No, not at all, but to see this, we must turn away from the dismal economic picture I have just been discussing and look at the *political* implications *world-wide* of the political struggles in Africa.

The nationalist upsurge in Africa (and its transformation more recently into the creation of national liberation movements) was of course part of a far wider scene. At one level, it was part of the reaction of the non-Western world to its conquest (or in a few cases its quasi-colonization) by Europe which culminated in the late nineteenth century. The rollback of "Europe," if you will, is a central cultural theme of the twentieth-century world. But it would be a mistake to see this in such limited terms. The fact is that there has been *organized* antisystemic activity within the capitalist world economy since the nineteenth century, in which one must include the rise of the social movement in Europe, the multiple Internationals, and the Russian Revolution. That all these antisystemic movements have been ambiguously antisystemic (but so, of course, has been African natioanlism) does not take away from the fact that a world-wide political "force" has been in creation which has affected concretely the history of the world system and all its local units or zones in quite precise ways.

We can in some sense "measure" the overall strength of antisystemic activity in the world system as whole over time. I would argue the curve has been steadily upward for 150 or so years *for the world system as a whole*, if less sharply upward than many had hoped or claim. Vis-à-vis this world-wide movement, the fact that the "revolution" or the mobilization in a given country or area does not have spectacular results in terms of economic distribution or human life-style may not necessarily detract from its contribution to a cumulative *political* effect. In this sense, there is no doubt that the wave of independence movements in Africa, and the creation and maintenance of the OAU against many obstacles, must be credited with affecting the world political *rapport de forces* in a way that has weakened, if only to a small extent, the stability of the existing world system.

At this point, however, we must intrude what might be called the "ratchet" effect. No social action goes unambiguously in a single direction. Contradiction is built into all complex structures, and an antisystemic movement is a very complex structure. For one thing it inevitably brings together in a single social organization persons with a range of social backgrounds, a range of social objectives, and a diversity of degree of commitment. Secondly, creating an organization as a tool of social change is by definition double-edged, since its virtue (efficacity) also involves its vice (the tool becoming for the staff the end).

What does this mean? It means that, for all antisystemic movements, the achievement of an "interim" objective, state power, *both* undermines *and* reinforces the existing world system. This reinforcement exists even in those cases (such as China, Vietnam, Mozambique, Algeria) when there was extraordinary mass mobilization. It is a fortiori true of the numerous situations in Africa where "decolonization" came more or less as a side effect of a struggle somewhere else.

The issue is not to make a pseudo-quantitative calculation: more undermining than reinforcing, or vice versa, in case x or y? As I said before, my clear sense is that, world-wide, there has been more undermining than reinforcing, though I would hesitate to say this was true of the African zone taken in isolation. The issue is quite otherwise. Social transformation is a cumulative process. The 150 years or so of organized antisystemic activity have collectively an impact on the social psychology of current actors.

There are three such impacts.

1. Success breeds success. If today SWAPO militants persist against great odds, it is in part because their reading of recent African history leads them to expect that persistence will pay off, that sooner or later the South African regime will have to yield.
2. Success breeds disillusionment. This occurs primarily in countries which "feel" they have had their "revolution." The reality of the postrevolutionary situation is in so many ways far from the prior expectations that the "believers" grow few and the cynics abound (the cynics who profit and the cynics who withdraw into personal worlds).
3. Success breeds fear among the world upper strata. As a general social process, those on top of social hierarchies normally react to opposition in three successive ways. First, they repress. When repression no longer works, they make concessions hoping to co-opt. And when this no longer works, they adapt the old slogan: if you can't lick 'em, join 'em. Specifically, they attempt to maintain their hierarchical advantage by a total transformation of form which, however, still leaves the same consequence of a stratified structure.

All three consequences point to the fact that the crucial political battleground of the next twenty-five–fifty years is not interstate rivalry, or the classical forms of class struggle (private bourgeois entrepreneurs versus proletarian industrial workers), but within the antisystemic movements and the family of antisystemic movements themselves.

This is very clear in most parts of Africa, even more so than in those countries which have had more dramatic and long-drawn-out popular mobilizations. The relative political lull of Africa's postindependence governments (punctuated by politically irrelevant coups d'etat) may not last too much longer. The question is, what is the new form that serious antisystemic struggle will take in Africa. Will it for example still give priority to the acquisition of state power by still newer organizations? I do not have the answer. But this is not an African problem alone. Against the de facto "social-democratization"/welfare states of the core, we have seen the rise of a so-called New Left, which is far from having resolved its rationale or its strategy. Against the regimes of the socialist camp, we have seen multiple attempts to find alternative forms of struggle, of which Solidarność is the most salient, but is far from the definitive form. And in the peripheral areas, which are still completing the "phase" of national liberation movements coming to power, the serious question is, what next?

Let us be clear about the stakes. The alternative is not the existing capitalist world economy or a Utopian future. The existing capitalist world economy has been crumbling for some time, the result of contradictions bred by its "successes." The real question is, what comes after. The choice is between a hierarchical historical system, different from the present but still hierarchical, and a relatively nonhierarchical one. That question, it seems to me, will be determined in large part by the organizational struggles of the next twenty-five years. Africa is in many ways a key zone. For various historical reasons, Africa is less subjugated intellectually to the "universalizing" ideology of the Enlightenment which has done so much to sustain the present system.[11] It is therefore quite possible that some of the most creative organizational rethinking and reassessment will take place there. At least one can hope so.

## NOTES

1. In addition, South Africa had a mandate in Southwest Africa, and the legal status of the erstwhile Italian colonies was about to be decided as part of the postwar settlement.

2. The nearest thing is in the Declaration of the Colonial Peoples: "The peoples of the colonies must have the right to elect their own Governments, without restrictions from foreign Powers." Appendix in Colin Legum, *Pan-Africanism: A Short Political Guide* (New York: Praeger, 1962), p. 137.

3. United Kingdom, Colonial Office, Gold Coast: *Report to His Excellency the Governor by the Committee on Constitutional Reform, 1949*, Colonial No. 250, London: HMSO, 1949, Appendix XIV, 100–104.

4. Kwame Nkrumah, *Neo-Colonialism: The Last Stage of Imperialism* (Edinburgh: Thomas Nelson, 1965).

5. Julius K. Nyerere, *Freedom and Unity* (London: Oxford University Press, 1967), 205, 208. This is a talk first given to a world youth conference in 1962 and repeated in expanded form to the Afro-Asian Solidarity Conference in Moshi on 4 February 1963.

6. See Tables 11 and 13 in The World Bank, *World Development Report, 1979* (New York: Oxford University Press, 1979), pp. 11 and 13.

7. For a discussion of the theoretical problems of measuring this, with some data from the United States and southern Africa, see Immanuel Wallerstein, William G. Martin, and Torry Dickinson, "Household Structures and Production Processes: Preliminary Theses and Findings," *Review*, v, 3, Winter 1982, 437–458.

8. Michael F. Lofchie, "Political and Economic Origins of African Hunger," *Journal of Modern African Studies*, xiii, 4 December 1975, 554.

9. See Nicole Ball, "Understanding the Causes of African Famine," *Journal of Modern African Studies*, xiv, 3 September 1976, 517–522; R. W. Franke and B. H. Chasin, *Seeds of Famine: Ecological Destruction and the Development Dilemma in the West African Sahel* (Montclair, N.J.: Allanheld, Osmun & Co., 1980); Comité d'Information Sahel, *Qui se nourrit de la famine en Afrique?* (Paris: Maspéro, 1975).

10. See chapter 1 of my *Historical Capitalism* (London: New Left Books, 1983).

11. See chapter 3 of ibid.

CHAPTER 14

# Bibliographic Essay:
# A Twenty-Five-Year Perspective

*Hans Panofsky*

The historical moment which occasioned the conference at Wingspread on Africa in 1984, and set the parameters for this bibliography, was the
observance of the anniversary of the first twenty-five years of African independence from colonial rule and the concomitant desire on the part of many
scholars to explore the impact of African independence on the continent of
Africa, on the outside world, and on the writings of Africanist scholars.
Within such a framework, the bibliographic appendix to the conference does
not pretend to be an evaluation of Africanist scholarship of the last twenty-five
years, nor is it the result of a careful, objective, and exhaustive scrutiny of the
vast output. It is simply a personal review of those works whose significance
seems to have improved with time and which have persistently seemed to offer
the students of Africa in their respective fields a solid ground from which they
could continue to build in the direction of new knowledge. There is no doubt
that even such a task cannot adequately be carried out by one individual in a
generalized way. The most striking development of Africanist scholarship, in
fact, has been the progressive disappearance of the general, all-encompassing
monographs dealing with wide-ranging problems affecting a large area. The
trend has been instead toward a higher degree of specialization within a much
narrower geographic and disciplinary scope. One could say that the macro
perspective has given way to the micro approach which seems to have temporarily halted the kind of synthetic surveys that were still possible thirty years
ago. Another development has been the sheer quantity of the material produced
all over the world, amounting to thousands of publications yearly.

Additional drawbacks to the present bibliography are its limitation to
sources in the English language and its exclusion of journal articles. It is also
limited by a strong disciplinary bias which has privileged the Social Sciences—Political Science in particular—at the expense not only of the sci-

ences but also of the humanities and literature, of which only the most noteworthy examples are cited.

The disciplinary imbalance is partly due to the character of the conference
and to the fact that African collections tend to gravitate around Social Science
programs while the purely scientific literature tends to remain a speciality
within the science departments. The literary works and literary criticism so
far have been more the domain of English, French, and African languages
departments maintaining so far a disciplinary insulation which has only
slightly affected the practice of the Social Sciences.

The items in the bibliography fall into three main sections: a list of un-
usually significant bibliographies; a list of general works arranged chronologi-
cally; and a section with entries arranged by regions and individual countries.
The selections of the last section will show the general direction of the prevalent scholarly interests generally tied to the availability of funds, receptivity of
the host countries, research trends, and the presence or absence of strife in the
research areas, as well as a host of other reasons. The results have been, for
instance, a higher concentration on anglophonic countries and, within the anglophonic countries, a higher concentration on West Africa than on East Africa due, no doubt, to the greater distance from the United States and to the
fact that East African countries have been more strife torn.

The time limits have been interpreted loosely. For the most part only one
work by one author has been included.

Thanks are given to the conference participants and to many others for
their help.

Apologies for obvious omissions and superfluous entries are humbly submitted. The hope is expressed for an opportunity to remedy these matters in a
future edition.

### BIBLIOGRAPHIES

Besterman, Theodore. *A World Bibliography of African Bibliographies*. Revised and brought up to date by J. D. Pearson. Totowa, NJ: Rowman and
Littlefield, 1975.

International African Institute. *Cumulative Bibliography of African Studies*.
Boston: G. K. Hall, 1973. 5 vols.

Pearson, J. D., ed. *International African Bibliography, 1973–1978*. London:
Mansell, 1982.

Scheven, Yvette, comp. *Bibliographies for African Studies*. Waltham, MA:
African Studies Association, Crossroads Press, 1970–75 publ. 1977; 1976–
79 publ. 1980; Munich: Zell/Saur, 1980–83 publ. 1984.

Melville J. Herskovits Library of African Studies. *The Africana Conference
Paper Index*. Boston: G. K. Hall, 1982. 2 vols.

Duignan, Peter, and L. H. Gann. *A Bibliographical Guide to Colonialism in sub-Saharan Africa*. London: Cambridge University Press, 1973. (Colonialism in Africa 1870–1960, vol. 5).

Panofsky, Hans E. *A Bibliography of Africana*. Westport, CT: Greenwood, 1975.

Britz, Daniel A., and Hans E. Panofsky. "African Bibliographies." In Smith, Margo L., and Yvonne M. Damien, eds. *Anthropological Bibliographies, A Selected Guide*. South Salem, NY: Redgrave, 1981. 3–54.

McGowan, Patrick J. *African Politics, a Guide to Research Resources, Methods and Literature*. Syracuse, NY: Syracuse University, Program of Eastern African Studies, 1970. (Occasional Paper no. 55.)

Siegel, Eric. *Bibliography of African Politics*. vol. 3. Los Angeles: Crossroads Press, African Studies Association, 1984.

Witherell, Julian W. *The United States and Africa: Guide to U.S. Official Documents and Government-sponsored Publications on Africa, 1785–1975*. Washington, DC: U.S. Superintendent of Documents, 1978. Supplement in press.

Zell, Hans M., Carol Bundy, and Virginia Coulon. *A New Reader's Guide to African Literature*. 2nd completely rev. and expanded ed. New York: Africana Publishing Co., 1983.

Wiley, David. *Africa on Film and Videotape, 1960–1981*. East Lansing, MI: African Studies Center, Michigan State University, 1982.

GENERAL

Hodgkin, Thomas. *Nationalism in Colonial Africa*. London: Muller, 1956.

International African Institute. *Social Implications of Industrialization and Urbanization in Africa South of the Sahara*. Prepared under the auspices of UNESCO. Westport, CT: Greenwood Press, 1973, c.1956.

Padmore, George. *Pan-Africanism or Communism? The Coming Struggle for Africa*. London: Dobson, 1956. Introd. by Azinna Nwafor. Garden City, NY: Doubleday, 1971.

Hailey, William Malcolm, Baron. *An African Survey*. Revised 1956. A study of problems arising in Africa south of the Sahara. London: Oxford University Press, 1957.

Bascom, William H., and Melville J. Herskovits, eds. *Continuity and Change in African Cultures*. Chicago: The University of Chicago Press, 1958.

International Labour Office. *African Labour Survey*. Geneva: ILO, 1958. (Studies and reports, new series no. 48.)

Murdock, George Peter. *Africa: its Peoples and Their Cultures*. New York: McGraw-Hill, 1959.

Emerson, Rupert. *From Empire to Nation; the Rise to Self-assertion of Asian and African Peoples*. Cambridge: Harvard University Press, 1960.

Kimble, George Herbert Tinley. *Tropical Africa*. New York: Twentieth Century Fund, 1960. 2 vols.

Ottenberg, Simon and Phoebe, eds. *Cultures and Societies of Africa*. New York: Random House, 1960.

Davidson, Basil. *Black Mother; the Years of the African Slave Trade*. Boston: Little, Brown, 1961. Revised ed. 1970.

Hodgkin, Thomas. *African Political Parties*. Harmondsworth, Middlesex: Penguin, 1961.

Jahn, Janheinz. *Muntu: an Outline of Neo-African Culture*. Tr. by Marjorie Greene. New York: Grove, 1961.

Vansina, Jan. Oral Tradition; a Study of Historical Methodology. Trans. by H. M. Wright. Chicago: Aldine, 1961.

Wallerstein, Immanuel. *Africa, the Politics of Independence*. New York: Vantage Books, 1961.

American Society of African Culture. *Pan-Africanism Reconsidered*. Berkeley: University of California Press, 1962.

Bohannan, Paul, and George Dalton, eds. *Markets in Africa*. Evanston, IL: Northwestern University Press, 1962. Abbreviated ed. New York: Doubleday, 1965.

Herskovits, Melville J. *The Human Factor in Changing Africa*. New York: Knopf, 1962.

Legum, Colin. *Pan-Africanism, A Short Political Guide*. New York: Praeger, 1962.

Goldschmidt, Walter, ed. *The United States and Africa*. Revised ed. New York: Praeger, published for the American Assembly, Columbia University, 1963.

Greenberg, Joseph A. *The Languages of Africa*. Bloomington, IN: 1963. (International Journal of American Linguistics, vol. 29, no. 1, pt. 2, January 1963).

Hausman, Warren H., ed. *Managing Economic Development in Africa*. Cambridge, MA: The M.I.T. Press, 1963.

Bown, Lalage, and Michael Crowder, eds. *The Proceedings of the First International Congress of Africanists, Accra, 11–18 December 1961*. Evanston, IL: Northwestern University Press, 1964.

Coleman, James Smoot and Carl Gustav Rosberg, eds. *Political Parties and National Integration in Tropical Africa*. Berkeley: University of California Press, 1964.

Herskovits, Melville J., and Mitchell Harwitz, eds. *Economic Transition in Africa*. Evanston, IL: Northwestern University Press, 1964.

Robinson, E. A. G., ed. *Economic Development for Africa South of the Sahara*. London: Macmillan, 1964.

Gibbs, James L., ed. *Peoples of Africa*. New York: Holt, Rinehart and Winston, 1965.

Gluckman, Max. *Politics, Law and Ritual in Tribal Society*. Chicago: Aldine, 1965.

Lystad, Robert A., ed. for the African Studies Association. *The African World, a Survey of Social Research*. New York: Praeger, 1965.

Lewis, I. M., ed. *Islam in Tropical Africa*. London: Oxford University Press for International African Institute, 1966.

Lloyd, P. C., ed. *The New Elites of Tropical Africa*. London: Oxford University Press for International African Institute, 1966.

Meynaud, Jean, and Anisse Salah Bey. *Trade Unionism in Africa, A Study of its Growth and Orientation*. Tr. by Angela Brench. London: Methuen, 1967.

Green, Reginald H., and Ann Seidman. *Unity or Poverty? The Economics of Pan-Africanism*. Harmondsworth, Middlesex: Penguin, 1968.

Carter, Gwendolen M., and Ann Paden, eds. *Expanding Horizons*. Proceedings of the Twentieth Anniversary Conference, 1968. Evanston, IL: Northwestern University Press, 1969.

Hill, Adelaide Cromwell, and Martin Kilson, comps. and eds. *Apropos of Africa: Sentiments of Negro-American Leaders on Africa from the 1800s to the 1950s*. London: Cass, 1969.

Kuper, Leo, and M. G. Smith, eds. *Pluralism in Africa*. Berkeley: University of California Press, 1969.

Cohen, Ronald, and John Middleton, eds. *From Tribe to Nation in Africa*. Scranton, PA: Chandler, 1970.

Rotberg, Robert I., and Ali A. Mazrui, eds. *Protest and Power in Black Africa*. New York: Oxford University Press, 1970.

Berry, Jack, and Joseph H. Greenberg, associate eds. *Linguistics in Sub-Saharan Africa*. The Hague: Mouton, 1971. (Current Trends in Linguistics, vol. 7).

Bohannan, Paul, and Philip Curtin. *Africa and the Africans*. Revised edition. Garden City, NY: Natural History Press, 1971.

*The Horizon History of Africa*. New York: American Heritage Publishing Co., 1971. Thirteen contributors.

Lofchie, Michael F., ed. *The State of the Nations: Constraints on Development in Independent Africa*. Berkeley: University of California Press, 1971.

Rich, Evelyn Jones, and Immanuel Wallerstein. *Africa: Tradition and Change*. New York: Random House, c.1972.

O'Barr, William M., David A. Spain, and Mark A. Tessler, eds. *Survey Re-*

*search in Africa, Its Applications and Limits.* Evanston, IL: Northwestern University Press, 1973.

Tessler, Mark A., William O'Barr, and David H. Spain. *Tradition and Identity in a Changing Africa.* New York: Harper and Row, 1973.

Mair, Lucy. *African Societies.* London: Cambridge University Press, 1974.

Oliver, Roland, and J. D. Fage. *A Short History of Africa.* 3rd ed. London: Collings, 1974.

Rodney, Walter. *How Europe Underdeveloped Africa.* Washington, DC: Howard University Press, 1974.

Fortes, Meyer, and Sheila Patterson, eds. *Studies in African Social Anthropology.* London: Academic Press, 1975. Essays presented to Professor Isaac Schapera.

Abu-Lughod, Ibrahim, ed. *African Themes.* Northwestern University Studies in honor of Gwendolen M. Carter. Evanston, IL: Northwestern University, Program of African Studies, 1975.

Harris, Richard, ed. *Political Economy of Africa.* Cambridge, MA: Schenkman, 1975.

Mbiti, John S. *Introduction to African Religion.* London: Heinemann Educational, 1975.

Sandbrook, Richard, and Robin Cohen, eds. *The Development of an African Working Class: Studies in Class Formation and Action.* Toronto: University of Toronto Press, 1975.

Haley, Alex. *Roots.* Garden City, NY: Doubleday, 1976.

Knight, C. Gregory, and James L. Newman, eds. *Contemporary Africa: Geography and Change.* Englewood Cliffs, NJ: Prentice-Hall, 1976.

Mazrui, Ali A. *A World Federation of Cultures: An African Perspective.* New York: Free Press, 1976.

Young, Crawford. *The Politics of Cultural Pluralism.* Madison: University of Wisconsin Press, 1976.

Gutkind, Peter C. W., and Peter Waterman, eds. *African Social Studies, A Radical Reader.* New York: Monthly Review Press, 1977. "Radical Themes in African Social Studies, A Bibliographical Guide." Comp. Christopher Allen. 424–462.

Kuper, Leo. *The Pity of It All: Polarisation of Racial and Ethnic Relations.* Minneapolis: University of Minnesota Press, 1977.

Markovitz, Irving Leonard. *Power and Class in Africa. An Introduction to Change and Conflict in African Politics.* Englewood Cliffs, NJ: Prentice-Hall, 1977.

Martin, Phyllis M., and Patrick O'Meara, eds. *Africa.* Bloomington: Indiana University Press, 1977. Note particularly: Jean E. Meeh Gosebrink, "Bibliography and Sources for African Studies." 415–466. A new edition is expected.

Curtin, Philip, Steven Feierman, Leonard Thompson, and Jan Vansina. *African History*. Boston: Little, Brown, 1978.

Gutkind, Peter C. W., Robin Cohen, and Jean Copans, eds. *African Labor History*. Beverly Hills, CA: Sage, 1978. (Sage series on African Modernization and Development, vol. 2.)

Whitaker, Jennifer Seymour, ed. *Africa and the United States: Vital Interests*. New York: New York University Press for Council on Foreign Relations, 1978.

Arnold, Guy. *Aid in Africa*. New York: Nichols, 1979.

Damachi, Ukandi, G., H. Dieter Seibel, and Lester Trachtman, eds. *Industrial Relations in Africa*. New York: St. Martin's, 1979.

Tevoedjre, Albert. *Poverty, Wealth of Mankind*. Oxford; New York: Pergamon, 1979.

July, Robert William. *A History of the African People*. 3rd ed. New York: Scribner, c.1980.

Paden, John N., ed. *Values, Identities and National Integration; Empirical Research in Africa*. Evanston, IL: Northwestern University Press, 1980.

*Accelerated Development in sub-Saharan Africa: An Agenda for Action*. Washington, DC: World Bank, c.1981. Report prepared by Elliot Berg.

Heyer, Judith, Pepe Roberts, and Gavin Williams, eds. *Rural Development in Tropical Africa*. New York: St. Martin's Press, 1981.

Oliver, Roland, and Michael Crowder, eds. *The Cambridge Encyclopedia of Africa*. Cambridge University Press, 1981.

Alpers, Edward A., and Pierre-Michel Fontaine, eds. *Walter Rodney, Revolutionary and Scholar: a Tribute*. Los Angeles: Center for Afro-American Studies and African Studies Center, University of California, 1982.

*Black Africa: A Generation after Independence*. Cambridge, MA: Proceedings of the American Academy of Arts and Sciences, *Daedalus*, vol. III, no. 2. Spring 1982.

Gifford, Prosser, and Wm. Roger Louis, eds. *The Transfer of Power in Africa, Decolonization 1940–1960*. New Haven: Yale University Press, 1982. Bibliographical essays by David E. Gardinier, 515–566, and A. H. M. Kirk-Greene, 567–635.

Jackson, Robert H., and Carl G. Rosberg. *Personal Rule in Black Africa: Prince, Autocrat, Prophet, Tyrant*. Berkeley: University of California Press, c.1982.

Young, Crawford. *Ideology and Development in Africa*. New Haven: Yale University Press, 1982.

Ghai, Dharam, and Samir Radwan, eds. *Agrarian Policies and Rural Poverty in Africa*. Geneva: International Labour Office, 1983.

Hyden, Goran. *No Shortcuts to Progress: African Development in Perspective*. Berkeley: University of California Press, 1983.

Michell, Robert Cameron, Donald George Morrison, and John Naber Paden. *Social Change and Nation Building: A Guide to the Study of Independent Black Africa*. New York: Irvington Press, c.1983.

Robinson, Pearl T., and Elliott P. Skinner, eds. *Transformation and Resiliency in Africa as Seen by Afro-American Scholars*. Washington, DC: Howard University Press, 1983.

Rothchild, Donald and Victor A. Olorunsola, eds. *State versus Ethnic Claims: African Policy Dilemmas*. Boulder, CO: Westview Press, 1983.

Browne, Robert S., and Robert J. Cummings. *The Lagos Plan of Action vs. the Berg Report: Contemporary Issues in African Economic Development*. Lawrenceville, VA: Brunswick, c.1984.

Welch, Claude E., Jr., and Ronald I. Meltzer, eds. *Human Rights and Development in Africa, Tradition, Conflict and Leadership*. Albany, NY: State University of New York Press, 1984.

### MUSIC AND THE ARTS

Nketia, J. H. Kwabena. *The Music of Africa*. New York: Norton, 1974.

Owomoyela, Oyekan. *African Literatures: An Introduction*. Los Angeles: UCLA, African Studies Assocation, Crossroads Press, 1979.

Willett, Frank. *African Art, An Introduction*. New York: Praeger, 1971.

Newman, Thelma R. *Contemporary African Arts and Crafts: On-site Working With Art Forms and Processes*. New York: Crown Publishers, 1974.

Wahlman, Maude. *Contemporary African Arts*. Chicago: Field Museum of Natural History, 1974.

### NORTH AFRICA

*General*

Gallagher, Charles. *The United States and North Africa*. Cambridge: Harvard University Press, 1963.

Hermassi, Elbaki. *Leadership and National Development in North Africa*. Berkeley: University of California Press, 1972.

Gellner, Ernest. *Muslim Society*. New York: Cambridge University Press, 1981.

Zartman, I. William, Mark A. Tessler, and others. *Political Elites in Arab North Africa: Morocco, Algeria, Tunisia, Libya and Egypt*. London: Longman, 1981.

*Algeria*
Fanon, Frantz. *The Wretched of the Earth*. Preface by Jean-Paul Sartre. Tr. by Constance Farrington. New York: Grove Press, c.1963.
Quandt, William B. *Revolution and Political Leadership: Algeria, 1954– 1968*. Cambridge, MA: M.I.T. Press, 1969.
Ottaway, David and Marina. *Algeria: The Politics of the Socialist Revolution*. Berkeley: University of California Press, 1970.

*Egypt*
Abu-Lughod, Janet L. *Cairo: 1001 Years of the City Victorious*. Princeton, NJ: Princeton University Press, 1971.
Cooper, Mark Neal. *The Transformation of Egypt*. London: Croom Helm, c.1982.

*Libya*
First, Ruth. *Libya: The Elusive Revolution*. Harmondsworth: Penguin, 1974.
el Fathaly, Omar I., and Monte Palmer. *Political Development and Social Change in Libya*. Lexington, MA: Lexington Books, 1980

*Morocco*
Maxwell, Gavin. *Lords of the Atlas, the Rise and Fall of the House of Glaoua, 1893–1956*. New York: Dutton, 1966.
Waterbury, John. *The Commander of the Faithful: Moroccan Political Elite— A Study in Segmented Politics*. New York: Columbia University Press, 1970.
Gellner, Ernest. *Saints of the Atlas*. Chicago: The University of Chicago Press, 1969.
Eickelman, Dale F. *Moroccan Islam: Tradition and Society in a Pilgrimage Center*. Austin: University of Texas Press, 1976.

*Tunisia*
Micaud, Charles A., Clement Henry Moore, and Leon Carl Brown. *Tunisia: the Politics of Modernization*. New York: Praeger, 1964.
Moore, Clement Henry. *Tunisia Since Independence*. Berkeley: University of California Press, 1965.
Rudebeck, Lars. *Party and People: A Study of Political Change in Tunisia*. New York: Praeger, 1969.
Stone, Russell A., and John Simmons, eds. *Change in Tunisia*. Albany, NY: State of New York Press, 1976.

### Ethiopia
Levine, Donald N. *Wax and Gold, Tradition and Innovation in Ethiopian Culture*. Chicago: The Univerity of Chicago Press, 1965.
Pankhurst, Richard. *Economic History of Ethiopia, 1800–1935*. Addis Ababa: Haile Selassie I. University Press, 1968.
Legesse, Asmarom. *Gada: Three Approaches to the Study of African Society*. New York: Free Press, 1973.
Spencer, John H. *Ethiopia at Bay, A Personal Account of the Haile Selassie Years*. Algonac, MI: Reference Publications, 1984.

### Sudan
Deng, Francis Mading. *Tradition and Modernization; A Challenge for Law Among the Dinka of the Sudan*. New Haven: Yale University Press, 1971.
Warburg, Gabriel. *Islam, Nationalism and Trade Unionism in a Traditional Society: The Case of Sudan*. London: Frank Cass, 1978.
Lewis, I. M. *A Pastoral Democracy*. New York: Holmes and Meier, 1981. (First published 1961.)

### WEST AFRICA

### General
Abrahams, Peter. *A Wreath for Udomo*. London: Faber, 1956.
Curtin, Philip D. *The Image of Africa, British Ideas and Action, 1780–1850*. Madison: The University of Wisconsin Press, 1964.
Kuper, Hilda, ed. *Urbanization and Migration in West Africa*. Berkeley: University of California Press, 1965.
Lewis, W. Arthur. *Politics in West Africa*. London: Allen and Unwin, 1965.
Zolberg, Aristide R. *Creating Political Order, the Party-States of West Africa*. Chicago: Rand McNally, 1966.
Meillassoux, Claude, ed. *The Development of Indigenous Trade and Markets in West Africa*. London: Oxford University Press for International African Institute, 1971.
Mabogunje, Akin L. *Regional Mobility and Resource Development in West Africa*. Montreal: McGill University, Centre for Developing Area Studies, 1972.
Ajayi, J. F., and Michael Crowder, eds. *History of West Africa*. New York: Columbia University Press, 2 vols. Vol. 1, 2nd ed., 1976; vol. 2, 1974.

### French-speaking West Africa
Morgenthau, Ruth Schachter. *Political Parties in French-speaking West Africa*. Oxford: Clarendon Press, 1964.

Foltz, William J. *From French West Africa to the Mali Federation.* New Haven: Yale University Press, 1965.

Person, Yves. *Samori; Une Revolution Dyula.* Dakar: IFAN, 1968–75, 3 vols. (Memoires de l'Institut Fondamental d'Afrique Noire, no. 80, 89).

Amin, Samir. *Neo-Colonialism in West Africa.* Tr. from the French by Francis McDonagh. Baltimore, MD: Penguin, 1973.

Kaba, Lansine. *The Wahhabiyya; Islamic Reform and Politics in French West Africa.* Evanston, IL: Northwestern University Press, 1974.

Zolberg, Aristide. *One-Party Government in the Ivory Cosat.* New ed. Princeton, NJ: Princeton University Press, 1969.

Ouologuem, Yambo. *Bound to Violence.* Tr. by Ralph Manheim. New York: Harcourt, 1971.

Stewart, Charles Cameron. *Islam and Social Order in Mauritania; A Case Study from the Nineteenth Century.* Oxford: Clarendon Press, 1973.

Senghor, Leopold Sedar. *On African Socialism.* Tr. by Mercer Cook. New York: Praeger, 1964.

Skinner, Elliott P. *African Urban Life, the Transformation of Ouagadougou.* Princeton, NJ: Princeton University Press, 1974.


### Ghana

Nkrumah, Kwame. *Ghana; the Autobiography of Kwame Nkrumah.* New York: Nelson, c.1957.

Apter, David E. *Ghana in Transition.* Rev. New York: Atheneum, 1963.

Hill, Polly. *The Migrant Cocoa-farmers of the Southern Ghana: A Study in Rural Capitalism.* Cambridge: University Press, 1963.

Brokensha, David. *Social Change at Larteh, Ghana.* Oxford: Clarendon Press, 1966.

Awoonor, Kofi. *This Earth My Brother: An Allegorical Tale of Africa.* New York: Doubleday, 1971.

Peil, Margaret. *The Ghanaian Factory Worker: Industrial Man in Africa.* London: Cambridge University Press, 1972.

Wilks, Ivor. *Asante in the Nineteenth Century: the Structure and Evolution of a Political Order.* London: Cambridge University Press, 1975.


### Liberia

Liebenow, J. Gus. *Liberia, The Evolution of Privilege.* Ithaca, NY: Cornell University Press, 1969.

Sundiata, Ibrahim K. *Black Scandal, America and the Liberian Labor Crisis, 1929–1936.* Philadelphia, PA: Institute for the Study of Human Issues (ISHI), 1980.

*Gambia*

Gailey, Harry A. *A History of the Gambia*. London: Routledge and Kegan Paul, 1964.


*Nigeria*

Dike, Kenneth Onwuka. *Trade and Politics in the Niger Delta, 1830–1885*; An Introduction to the Economic and Political History of Nigeria. Oxford: Clarendon Press, 1956.

Bohannan, Paul. *Justice and Judgment Among the Tiv*. London: Oxford University Press for the International African Institute, 1957.

Coleman, James S. *Nigeria, Background to Nationalism*. Berkeley: University of California Press, 1958.

Achebe, Chinua. *Things Fall Apart*. New York: Aster Honor, c.1959.

———. *A Man of the People*. Garden City, New York: Anchor Books, 1967.

———. *Arrow of God*. New York: John Day, c.1964.

———. *No Longer At Ease*. London: Heinemann Educational Books, 1975, c.1960.

Smythe, Hugh H., and Mabel M. Smythe. *The New Nigerian Elite*. Stanford, CA: Stanford University Press, 1960.

Sklar, Richard L. *Nigerian Political Parties: Power in an Emergent African Nation*. Princeton, NJ: Princeton University Press, 1963.

Soyinka, Wole. *The Interpreters*. With introduction and notes by Eldred Jones. London: Heinemann, 1970.

Whitaker, C. S. *The Politics of Traditional Continuity and Change in Northern Nigeria, 1946–1966*. Princeton, NJ: Princeton University Press, 1970.

Paden, John N. *Religion and Political Culture in Kano*. Berkeley: University of California Press, 1973.

Baker, Pauline H. *Urbanization and Political Change: the Politics of Lagos, 1917–1967*. Berkeley: University of California Press, 1974.

Wolpe, Howard. *Urban Politics in Nigeria: A Study of Port Harcourt*. Berkeley: University of California Press, 1974.

Thompson, Robert Farris. *Black Gods and Kings: Yoruba Art at UCLA*. Bloomington: Indiana University Press, 1976, c.1971.

Soyinka, Wole. *Ake: The Years of Childhood*. London: Collings, 1981.

Dudley, B. J. *An Introduction to Nigerian Government*. Bloomington: Indiana University Press, 1982.

Shaw, Timothy M., and Olajide Aluko, eds. *Nigerian Foreign Poilcy*. New York: St. Martin's Press, 1983.


*Sierra Leone*

Banton, Michael. *West African City, A Study of Tribal Life in Freetown*. London: Oxford University Press for the International African Institute, 1957.

Kilson, Martin. *Political Change in a West African State: Study of the Modernization Process in Sierra Leone*. Cambridge, MA; Harvard University Press, 1966.

Jackson, Michael. *Allegories of the Wilderness: Ethics and Ambiguity in Kuranko Narratives*. Bloomington: Indiana University Press, c.1982.

*Former French Equatorial Africa*

Balandier, Georges. *The Sociology of Black Africa; Social Dynamics in Central Africa*. Tr. by Douglas Garman. New York: Praeger, 1970.

Clignet, Remi. *The Africanization of the Labor Market: Educational and Occupational Segmentation in the Cameroons*. Berkeley: University of California Press, 1976.

Warmington, W. A. *A West African Trade Union, A Case Study of the Cameroons Development Corporation Workers' Union and its Relation with the Employers*. London: Oxford University Press published for the Nigeria Institute of Social and Economic Research, 1960.

Johnson, Willard R. *The Cameroon Federation. Political Integration in a Fragmentary Society*. Princeton, NJ: Princeton University Press, 1969.

Kalck, Pierre. *The Central African Republic, A Failure in Decolonization*. Tr. by Barbara Thomson. New York: Praeger, 1971.

Thompson, Virginia, and Richard Adloff. *Conflict in Chad*. Berkeley: Institute of International Studies, 1981.

Weinstein, Brian. *Gabon: Nation Building on the Ogooue*. Cambridge, MA: M.I.T. Press, 1966.

Fernandez, James W. *Bwiti—An Ethnography of the Religious Imagination in Africa*. Princeton, NJ: Princeton University Press, 1982.

*Zaire, Rwanda, Burundi*

Young, Crawford. *Politics in the Congo: Decolonization and Independence*. Princeton, NJ: Princeton University Press, 1965.

Douglas, Mary Tew. *The Lele of the Kasai*. New ed. London: International African Institute, 1977.

Lemarchand, Rene. *Rwanda and Burundi*. New York: Praeger, 1970.

Maquet, Jacques J. *The Premise of Inequality in Rwanda: A Study of Political Relations in a Central African Kingdom*. Reprinted (1st ed. 1961) London: Oxford University Press for International African Institute, 1970.

EAST AFRICA

*Kenya*

Kariuki, Josiah Mwangi. *'Mau Mau' Detainee, the Account by a Kenya African of his Experiences in Detention Camps, 1953–1960*. London: Oxford University Press, 1963.

Mboya, Tom. *Freedom and After*. Boston: Little, Brown, 1963.

Rosberg, Carl Gustav, and John Nottingham. *The Myth of "Mau Mau"; Nationalism in Kenya*. Stanford, CA: Published for the Hoover Institution on War, Revolution and Peace by Praeger, New York, 1966.

Kenyatta, Jomo. *Suffering Without Bitterness: The Founding of the Kenyan Nation*. Nairobi: East African Publishing House, 1968.

Leys, Colin. *Underdevelopment in Kenya: The Political Economy of Neocolonialism, 1964–1971*. Berkeley: University of California Press, 1975.

Ngugi wa Thion'go. *Petals of Blood*. New York: Dutton, c.1977.

Strobel, Margaret. *Muslim Women in Mombasa, 1890–1975*. New Haven: Yale University Press, 1979.

### Tanzania

Nyerere, Julius K. *Freedom and Unity; Uhuru na umoja, A Selection from Writings and Speeches, 1952–1965*. London: Oxford University Press, 1969.

McHenry, Dean E. *Tanzania's Ujamaa Villages: The Implementation of a Rural Development Strategy*. Berkeley: University of California Institute of International Studies, 1979.

### Uganda

Elkan, Walter. *Migration and Proletarians, Urban Labour in the Economic Development of Uganda*. London: Oxford University Press published on behalf of the East African Institute of Social Research, 1960.

Fallers, Lloyd A. *Bantu Bureaucracy*. Chicago: The University of Chicago Press, 1965.

Richards, Audrey Isabel, ed. *Economic Development and Tribal Change: A Study of Immigrant Labour in Buganda*. Rev. ed. Nairobi: Oxford University Press, 1975.

### Lusophonic Africa

Duffy, James. *Portuguese Africa*. Cambridge, MA: Harvard University Press, 1959.

Cabral, Amilcar. *Revolution in Guinea*. New York: Monthly Press, 1970.

Marcum, John. *The Angolan Revolution*. 2 vols. Cambridge, MA: M.I.T., 1969, 1978.

Neto, Agostinho. *Sacred Hope*. Tr. by Margo Holness. Dar es Salaam: Tanzania Publishing House, 1974.

Bender, Gerald J. *Angola Under the Portuguese; The Myth and the Reality*. Berkeley: University of California Press, 1978.

Stockwell, John. *In Search of Enemies. A CIA Story*. New York: Norton, 1978.

First, Ruth. *Black Gold. The Mozambican Miner, Proletarian and Peasant.* Brighton, Sussex: Harvester, 1983.

Isaacman, Allen F., and Barbara Isaacman. *Mozambique: From Colonialism to Revolution, 1900–1982.* Boulder, CO: Westview Press, 1983.

Mondlane, Eduardo. *The Struggle for Mozambique.* Introduction by John Saul; biographical sketch by Herbert Shore. London: Zed, 1983. (First published in 1969.)

SOUTHERN AFRICA

*Zambia*

Epstein, Arnold Leonard. *Politics in an Urban African Community.* Manchester: published on behalf of the Rhodes-Livingstone Institute by Manchester University Press, 1968, c.1958.

Colson, Elizabeth. *Social Organization of the Gwembe Tonga.* Manchester: published on behalf of the Rhodes-Livingstone Institute by Manchester University Press, 1960.

Kaunda, Kenneth. *Zambia Shall Be Free: An Autobiography.* New York: Praeger, 1963.

Kapferer, Bruce. *Strategy and Transaction in an African Factory, African Workers and Indian Management in a Zambian Town.* New York: Humanities Press, 1972.

Bostock, Mark, and Charles Harvey, eds. *Economic Independence and Zambian Copper, A Case Study of Foreign Investment.* New York: Praeger, 1972.

Sklar, Richard L. *Corporate Power in an African State: The Political Impact of Multinational Mining Companies in Zambia.* Berkeley: University of California Press, 1975.

Turner, Victor. *Revelation and Divination in Ndembu Ritual.* Ithaca, NY: Cornell University Press, 1975.

Bates, Robert H. *Rural Responses to Industrialization: A Study of Village Zambia.* New Haven: Yale University Press, 1976.

Prins, Gwyn. *The Hidden Hippopotomus: Or Reappraisal in African History: The Early Colonial Experience in Western Zambia.* New York: Cambridge University Press, 1980.

*Zimbabwe*

O'Meara, Patrick. *Rhodesia: Racial Conflict or Coexistence.* Ithaca, NY: Cornell University Press, 1975.

Lake, Anthony. *The "Tar Baby" Option: American Policy Toward Southern Rhodesia.* New York: Columbia University Press, 1976.

Caute, David. *Under the Skin, the Death of White Rhodesia*. Evanston, IL: Northwestern University Press, 1983.

### South Africa

Carter, Gwendolen M. *The Politics of Inequality, South Africa Since 1948*. New York: Praeger, 1958.

Kuper, Hilda. *The Swazi: A South African Kingdom*. New York: Holt, Rinehart and Winston, 1965.

Horwitz, Ralph. *The Political Economy of South Africa*. New York: Praeger, 1967.

Wilson, Monica, and Leonard Thompson, eds. *The Oxford History of South Africa*. Oxford: Clarendon Press, 1969–71. 2 vols.

Wilson, Francis. *Labour in the South African Gold Mines, 1911–1969*. New York: Cambridge University Press, 1972.

Brutus, Dennis. *A Simple Lust, Selected Poems including Sirens, Knuckles Boots, Letters to Martha, Poems from Algiers and Thoughts Abroad*. New York: Hill and Wang, 1973.

Western Massachusetts Association of Concerned Africa Scholars. *U.S. Military Involvement in Southern Africa*. Boston: South End Press, 1978.

Davies, Robert H. *Capital, State and White Labour in South Africa, 1900–1960*. Atlantic Highlands, NJ: Humanities, 1979.

Fredrickson, George M. *White Supremacy, A Comparative Study in American and South African History*. New York: Oxford University Press, 1981.

Study Commission on U.S. Policy toward Southern Africa. *South Africa: Time Running Out*. Berkeley: University of California Press, 1981.

Carter, Gwendolen M., and Patrick O'Meara, eds. *South Africa: The Continuing Crisis*. 2nd ed. Bloomington: Indiana University Press, 1982.

Clough, Michael, ed. *Changing Realities in Southern Africa*. Berkeley: University of California, Institute of International Studies, 1981. (Research series no. 47.)

Plumpp, Sterling. *Somehow We Survive, An Anthology of South African Writing*. New York: Thunder's Mouth Press, 1982.

Callaghy, Thomas M., ed. *South Africa in Southern Africa, The Intensifying Vortex of Violence*. New York: Praeger, 1983.

Nkosi, Lewis. *Home and Exile and Other Stories*. London and New York: Longeman, 1983. (First published 1965.)

# CONTRIBUTORS

S. K. B. Asante, University of Ghana; Visiting Professor, University of Florida, Gainesville

Kenneth W. Grundy, Case Western Reserve University

Goran Hyden, The Ford Foundation

Robert H. Jackson, University of British Columbia

J. Gus Liebenow, Indiana University

Michael F. Lofchie, University of California, Los Angeles

Donald F. McHenry, Georgetown University

Ali A. Mazrui, University of Michigan; Research Professor, University of Jos, Nigeria

Hans Panofsky, Northwestern University

Carl G. Rosberg, University of California, Berkeley

Donald Rothchild, University of California, Davis

John S. Saul, York University, Toronto

Richard L. Sklar, University of California, Los Angeles

Immanuel Wallerstein, State University of New York, Binghampton

Crawford Young, University of Wisconsin, Madison


GWENDOLEN M. CARTER is the dean of African scholars in the United States and the author or editor of numerous books, including *Southern Africa: The Continuing Crisis* (with Patrick O'Meara).

PATRICK O'MEARA is Professor of Political Science, Professor in the School of Public and Environmental Affairs, and Director of the African Studies Program at Indiana University.

# INDEX